Daily Guideposts, 1998

A
JANET
THOMA
BOOK

THOMAS NELSON PUBLISHERS
Nashville • Atlanta • London • Vancouver

Published in Nashville, Tennessee, by Thomas Nelson, Inc., and distributed in Canada by Word Communications, Ltd., Richmond, British Columbia, and in the United Kingdom by Word (UK), Ltd., Milton Keynes, England.

ACKNOWLEDGMENTS

All Scripture quotations, unless otherwise noted, are from *The King James Version of the Bible.*

Scripture quotations marked (NIV) are from the *Holy Bible, New International Version.* Copyright © 1973, 1978, 1984 International Bible Society. Used by permission of Zondervan Bible Publishers.

Scripture quotations marked (RSV) are from the *Revised Standard Version of the Bible.* Copyright © 1946, 1952, 1971 by the Division of Christian Education of the National Council of Churches of Christ in the U.S.A. and are used by permission.

Scripture quotations marked (NAS) are from the *New American Standard Bible,* © 1960, 1962, 1963, 1968, 1971, 1972, 1973, 1975, 1977 by The Lockman Foundation. Used by permission.

Scripture quotations marked (TLB) are from *The Living Bible,* © 1971. Used by permission of Tyndale House Publishers, Inc., Wheaton, IL 60189. All rights reserved.

Scripture quotations marked (NKJV) are from *The New King James Version of the Bible.* Copyright © 1979, 1980, 1982 by Thomas Nelson, Inc., Nashville, TN 37214.

Scripture quotations marked (GNB) are from *The Good News Bible, the Bible in Today's English Version.* Copyright © American Bible Society, 1966, 1971, 1976.

"The Touch of the Healer" series, which appears at the beginning of each month, was written by Marilyn Morgan Helleberg, Carol Kuykendall, Pam Kidd, Fay Angus, Marjorie Holmes, Kenneth Chafin, Roberta Messner, Keith Miller, Arthur Gordon, Van Varner, Dolphus Weary and Mary Lou Carney.

"A Journey to Healing" series was written by Scott Harrison.

"Keeping Vigil" series was written by Rick Hamlin.

"My Mother's House" series was written by Mary Lou Carney.

"Healing the Fear of Old Age" series was written by John Sherrill.

"The Gifts of Christmas" series was written by Marion Bond West.

Designed by Holly Johnson
Artwork by Michelle Lester
Indexed by Patricia Woodruff
Jacket photo by Thomas Hallstein/Outsight Environmental Photography
Typeset by Com Com, an R.R. Donnelley & Sons Company
Printed in the United States of America

ISBN 0-7852-7559-2

1—98

Table of Contents

TABLE OF CONTENTS

Introduction

Daily Guideposts, 1998 is devoted to "God's Healing Touch." We'll share some of the ways that wonderful power is at work today in the lives of our *Daily Guideposts* family, turning brokenness into wholeness and weakness into strength. And together we'll learn to recognize God's healing touches in our own lives, through His Word, through His gift of prayer, through His glorious creation, and through the men and women who, perhaps without ever knowing it, minister His healing to our bodies, minds and spirits.

Every month we'll experience "The Touch of the Healer" in the lives of one of our *Daily Guideposts* friends. In February, Scott Harrison will share a physician's wisdom and a father's heartbreak as he takes us on "A Journey to Healing." During Holy Week, Rick Hamlin invites us to join him in "Keeping Vigil" as he experiences the healing touch of Easter in the midst of a personal and family crisis. In June, Mary Lou Carney finds healing for her grief and a lasting legacy of hope in "My Mother's House." As the leaves turn in October, John Sherrill shows us seven memories that have helped him toward "Healing the Fear of Old Age." And at Advent and Christmas, Marion Bond West writes about six unusual Christmases in her life and the gift of healing each one gave her.

Among the fifty-three contributors to *Daily Guideposts, 1998* are many other dear friends whom we've grown close to over the years, including Ruth Stafford Peale, Van Varner, Elizabeth Sherrill, Arthur Gordon, Marjorie Holmes, Oscar Greene, Marilyn Morgan Helleberg, Daniel Schantz and Fred Bauer. Rejoining our family circle this year are Eleanor Sass, Linda Ching Sledge and Marjorie Parker. And adding their own unique colors to our tapestry of praise are our newest family members, Rhoda Blecker, a novelist from Reseda, California, Bill Peel, a minister and father of three from Nashville, Tennessee, and Kathy Peel, Bill's wife and a columnist for *Family Circle* magazine.

Here, then, is *Daily Guideposts, 1998.* We hope that it will bring you comfort and strength, help your eyes to see more clearly the work of God in your life, and move your spirit to a richer prayer life. May He use these stories of His healing touch to touch your heart with the grace that makes us whole.

—*The Editors*

JANUARY

S	M	T	W	T	F	S
				1	2	3
4	5	6	7	8	9	10
11	12	13	14	15	16	17
18	19	20	21	22	23	24
25	26	27	28	29	30	31

*He healeth the broken in heart,
and bindeth up their
wounds.*

—PSALM 147:3

THU

1

I withheld not my heart from any joy; for my heart rejoiced in all my labor. . . . —ECCLESIASTES 2:10

Celebrate every day of life. The words have a festive, optimistic ring as this year stretches before us, full of opportunities. When Norman and I were first starting out our life together, I was fortunate to learn that there is a technique you can use to help make every day a celebration.

When I was going to school, I didn't think much about "daily life," because so much was done for me. I didn't cook meals, clean the house or pay bills, but when I married a minister, oh my! I didn't let on to Norman, of course, that the daily routines and responsibilities weighed heavily on me. Then one evening, after supper, he was helping me with the dishes. He held up a lovely silver serving spoon. "Who gave us this?" he asked. When I told him, he said, "What a generous gift! Let's pray for them right now, and thank God we have them as friends."

We did, and when we finished, I had a completely new outlook on my busy, task-filled life. If I was polishing a piece of furniture, I would make a point of remembering how it came to me. Usually, there would be a nice story attached, and that would cheer me. When I tired of cooking breakfast for Norman and our young family, I pretended it was for Jesus and the disciples, and, lo and behold, breakfast became a celebration. Paying bills a chore? Imagine only the best things that the people you pay could do with your money. And be thankful you have the means to pay them.

This year bring your imagination to every daily task and join me in the adventure of celebrating every single day of the year.

Dear Lord, today is a day to celebrate—help me to find all the ways I can.
                                                    —*Ruth Stafford Peale*

FRI

2

Refrain from anger and turn from wrath; do not fret—it leads only to evil. —PSALM 37:8 (NIV)

Two friends of mine had the following conversation:

She: I have one thing to say to you. Sweeping your hair over that bald spot isn't working anymore.

He: I have one *word* to say to you. Liposuction!

They didn't speak to each other for days. Ten years of marriage, and *this* is the level of discourse? But then I, too, can successfully nurse a small sore into a big, festering wound. It's a challenge, but I can do it.

This is my public apology for untold misunderstandings, unrequited anger, unspoken pain. I have been given vast gifts in the form of a wife, children, family, friends, co-workers—but, like a spoiled child at Christmas, I've chosen instead to complain about the color of the gift wrap or notice only the price tag that's been left there by accident.

No more. This is a kinder, gentler Mark speaking to you, a New Year's resolute Mark. No more exploding with the swiftness of a hair-trigger grenade, sending young children scattering to their rooms ahead of verbal shrapnel. No more chasing drivers three miles on the highway, just to yell at them for cutting me off at the previous zip code.

My resolutions may sound ambitious, but I'm not planning for the whole year, just one day at a time.

Right now, Lord, give me a forbearing heart.   —*Mark Collins*

SAT
3

Therefore when thou doest thine alms, do not sound a trumpet before thee. . . .   —*MATTHEW 6:2*

Some people look upon me as a little eccentric. It's because of something I call my "Found Fund." I keep an eye out for money that's lying around, for it's there, if you care to pick it up, around phone booths and bus stops, in taxis where it has slipped out of pockets or in plain view on the street. Generally it's a penny (there are plenty of those), but also nickels, dimes, quarters (I don't remember ever having found a half-dollar), plus bus and subway tokens (they convert into a buck and a half!). All are cheerfully slipped into my left rear pocket for later depositing in the container I have at home.

Don't get me wrong, I don't go out of my way to find my money, though there are always exceptions. Maybe I've lingered a mite until a woman has finished her telephone call so I could pick up the penny at her feet. And I remember the long period of staring as I tried to figure out if that was a dime or chewing gum behind a subway passenger's shoes (it was a dime and I rescued it when the man got up!). But mostly it's just keeping your eyes open when walking the city streets.

Every New Year's Day I open my bank. This year's haul was pretty good: forty-one dollars and thirty-six cents. What do I do with it? I wait until I see a likely recipient, just someone who moves me, a young violinist in the subway who has a hungry look or a woman giving out leaflets on a street corner in the freezing cold. This year it was a hard-working busboy in a lunchroom that I happened into. I don't speak, I merely present my found money and hurry away. Not that the money is a fortune, but I can think of certain things that I would do with forty-one dollars and thirty-six cents.

So I don't mind being thought of as a little bit eccentric. Actually, I like it.

Father, may the little I give carry a big message of appreciation—and hope.
                                                          —Van Varner

This year, we've asked twelve of our Daily Guideposts *friends to share the ways in which they've felt God's healing touch in their own lives and in the lives of those around them. Throughout the year, they'll help us to become more aware of the signs of God's healing presence that surround us every day. Use the diary pages at the end of each month to record your own "Healing Journey."*
                                                        —THE EDITORS

SUN	THE TOUCH OF THE HEALER

4   **Healing Our Darkness**
Jesus answered. . . . I am the light of the world.
                                                        —JOHN 9:3, 5

My loss of vision came on gradually, until one day I picked up a book I'd been reading just the day before and found that, no matter how close I held it, I couldn't read it! An eye exam showed that glasses would no longer correct the problem; I needed an operation. Yet there was also a slight risk that I could lose my sight in the surgery.

"Oh, God," I prayed, "don't let me fall into darkness!" Then I thought about Jesus healing the man born blind, and I was startled to see something in this miracle I hadn't seen before. The spittle and the clay and the washing in the pool were only for the sake of the

Pharisees. These were not the real healing tools. The blind man was healed because Christ gave him His own inexhaustible light!

I carried this new awareness into the operating room with me. Awake during the surgery, with one eye covered and the other anesthetized, I could see only light and shadows. Recalling Jesus' words before the blind man's healing, I focused on the blurred light above the table while silently repeating the name of Jesus. As these two things steadied my pounding heart, I became clearly aware of a healing presence in the room—a bright and shining presence that would not let me fall into darkness.

My eye surgery is over, and I can *see* again. Thanks be to God! I'm enjoying so much the *beauty* of clean, clear colors. Pages of books are brighter, my daughter Karen's outfit today was a lovely shade of blue instead of the muddy green I'd thought, and my walls are transformed from a dullish yellow to a soft, clear white. Best of all, I can *read* again!

Though scalpel and stitches and other surgical tools were used, I believe they were only for the sake of the Pharisee in me. Whether the need is for healing of physical, mental or spiritual blindness, our task is simple: Focus on the light of Christ, trusting that He will not let us fall into darkness.

Ever-shining Christ, may I bring all my darknesses to You for healing so that I may truly say, "One thing I know, that, whereas I was blind, now I see" (John 9:25).
—Marilyn Morgan Helleberg

MON

5   *By God's will I may come to you with joy and together with you be refreshed.* —ROMANS 15:32 (NIV)

It was winter on the Canadian prairies, and I was suffering from a severe case of cabin fever. I was depressed by the lack of freedom that winter imposes. I felt isolated, alone, cut off.

I was glad when my friend Eleanor invited me to her apartment across town. Her new bird, a Gloucester canary named Captain, welcomed me with trills and warbles. Captain sported a feathery hairdo with a fringe just above his eyes. I promptly nicknamed him Ringo, and that afternoon he proved to be the star of the show. "He always sings more when I have company," Eleanor explained. "Cheering people up seems to be his mission in life."

That little bird's example put me to shame. Instead of silently brooding about being confined during the long winter, I decided to do more entertaining. I made a favorite meal for our daughter Gae and invited her over. I asked a lonely neighbor in for coffee; I baked homemade bread for my friend Helen. As the aroma of the fresh, hot loaves wafted through my kitchen, I forgot all about the frigid winter weather.

You know what else I discovered? I always sing more when I have company.

Lord, You Bless me most when You use me to bless others.
—*Alma Barkman*

TUE

6 *Come, behold the works of the Lord. . . .*
—*PSALM 46:8*

Epiphany is a Greek word meaning a disclosure or unveiling, and in the history of the Christian church, it has been used to refer to those occasions when the incarnate Lord Jesus was revealed to various groups of people—at His birth, His baptism, and at the wedding at Cana. For centuries, the feast of the Epiphany on January 6 commemorated the arrival of the Wise Men at the stable in Bethlehem, when Baby Jesus was revealed to them as the gift of God's presence.

Over the last several years, I've given my own personal tweak to this celebration. I sit down with a paper and pencil and think about the times that something about Jesus was revealed to me in the last year. Usually, I start with memorable events, and then ask myself what I learned about Jesus in each one. I plot them on a timeline graph, showing both the highs and lows. At each "event" place on my graph, I draw a small footprint. When I finish, I have my "Footprints of Faith" for the past year, which I fold and then tuck in the front of my Bible. On those down days when I need a visual aid to remind me of God's faithful presence, I reach for my "Footprints of Faith."

When I sit down today, I'll record events such as the joy and struggle of meeting a work deadline (and discovering that Jesus does provide strength for the tasks He gives); a special Fourth of July reunion with old friends at a mountain cabin (and realizing how Jesus blesses our efforts to maintain relationships); and our long car trip to deliver our youngest daughter Kendall back to college (experiencing the bittersweet challenge of loving and letting go). I plan to celebrate January 6 by remembering some of the times and places that Jesus was revealed to me in the last year . . . or the last twenty-four hours . . . or the last twenty-four seconds.

Today, on Epiphany, Lord, reveal Your presence to me.
                                                    —Carol Kuykendall

---

WED

7   *For I am the Lord, I change not. . . .   —MALACHI 3:6*

Statistics say there were 2,204,820 persons born in the United States back in 1898. My mother was one of them.

William McKinley was president then and Garrett Hobart, vice president. Mailing a letter still cost two cents, and a loaf of bread—if store-bought instead of homemade—was a nickel.

When Mom's birth became imminent on that frigid January night, with no phone at their Kansas farm, her oldest sibling harnessed the horse and galloped eight miles for the horse-and-buggy doctor.

The first Ford arrived five years after Mom was born. "Neighbors began buying horseless carriages," Mom recalled, "but Papa waited until 1910, when he thought they could never be improved on. Mama was afraid to sit in the front seat with the gas tank beneath."

About airplanes: "The first flying machine I ever saw had two wings and the pilot sat in an open, dangling seat between them. It attracted the biggest crowd of horses and buggies there'd ever been in Newton. The pilot flew one little circle not far above ground."

Shortly before her death two years ago at nearly ninety-eight, Mom said, "I've had an exciting life, from seeing the first cars and airplanes to seeing men walking on the moon."

"You've coped with change," I told her. "My grandchildren discuss cyberspace and the Internet and voice mail and lots of other things I don't really understand. I wish the world weren't going so fast. Nothing stays the same. Everything changes."

Mom gave me a reminding, knowing look. "Not *everything!*"

Thank You, Lord, that You remain "the same yesterday, and today, and for ever" (Hebrews 13:8). And so do Your promises.
                                                    —Isabel Wolseley

"My heart is changed within me. . . ."
—HOSEA 11:8 (NIV)

My very first out-of-the-U.S. vacation was a week-long trip to Montreal with my friend Allison during my first year in college. After only one day, I decided I didn't like it. I knew Canada was supposed to have a French flavor, but from shops to restaurants to our hotel desk, people *bonjour-ed* us, and I feared they'd laugh at my phrase-book French. Sodas were served without ice, but there was ice everywhere else. What the natives shrugged off as a "mild snow flurry" was to me a mammoth ice storm. "Why don't we go somewhere else?" I sulked to Allison after we were shoved down a street by the fierce wind.

Red-faced from the cold, she fumbled in her purse and pulled out a travel book. "Read this!" she commanded. Obviously, she was discontented, too, and had found us a place we could venture on to.

But what her finger pointed to—in a book by travel writer Rick Steves—was this: "When you travel, expect places to be different. And if things are not to your liking—change your liking!"

"We could have sunny weather, ice in sodas and people who speak English three hundred and sixty-five days of the year back at home," Allison pointed out. "Don't you want something more exotic on vacation? Besides, look at us. We're different ages, different majors— you English, me phys ed."

"I guess if we were the same, we might as well be friends with a mirror," I admitted.

Newly determined to "change my liking," I enjoyed a warm soda in the coffee shop, where I discovered that the employees who said *bonjour* were bilingual—and kind about interpreting my fractured Franglais.

"I'll ask where we can buy one of the big woolly hats everyone wears," I told Allison. "We can go for a walk in the snow—and make like natives!"

God, as I travel through life, help me to celebrate—not criticize—differences, and when necessary, "change my liking."
—Linda Neukrug

FRI

9 *But be doers of the word, and not hearers only, deceiving yourselves.*   *—JAMES 1:22 (RSV)*

On trips to New York City during the winter, I always take time to watch the skaters in Rockefeller Plaza. With other onlookers lining the brass railing, I look down at the sunken rink brooded over by the golden statue of Prometheus.

The skaters on any given day range from wobbly beginners to flawlessly gliding experts. While most circle the periphery of the ice in a slow, counterclockwise wheel, two or three figure skaters will be practicing their loops and spins in the center, often drawing cheers from the spectators above.

One January day I kept my eye expectantly on a young blonde woman in a flared red skirt and matching jacket trimmed in white fur. I watched eagerly as she poised one white skate at a right angle to the other and lifted her arms above her head. Lowering her arms, she repositioned the skates and placed her hands on her hips. There were several more seeming overtures to action, but in the fifteen minutes I watched, she never began to skate.

On my next trip to the city, there in center rink was the same young blonde, this time in a striking white outfit. Once more she struck a series of poses. Once more, nothing followed.

The darling costumes, the skater's gestures—suddenly I found myself asking if I, too, put more emphasis on appearances than performance. At work. In my relationships. As a Christian. How often do I put on a kind of dress-up act of following Jesus: going to church; mouthing the prayers; failing to live the reality.

Father, help me today to love You in deed and not in pose.
    —Elizabeth Sherrill

SAT

10 *A gift is as a precious stone in the eyes of him that hath it. . . .*   *—PROVERBS 17:8*

In the midnight silence, the golden nib flashes in the soft glow of the desk lamp. More than ten years ago, a friend, Ron Cox, gave this pen to me. It wasn't Christmas or my birthday. The gift wasn't wrapped with ribbon. Ron just handed me a small white box and said, "Here. I write with one of these. I thought you'd like one, too."

There was a practiced nonchalance in Ron's voice, the matter-of-fact way American men talk to hide the emotion they feel. Ron was giving me a gift to symbolize a special friendship. He knew it, and I knew it, too. And ever since, I have taken pains not to lose this fountain pen.

Since that day, I have written all my sermons with this pen. Occasionally, even poetry has struggled to find birth in my illegible handwriting. I would never trade my writing partner for another, not even a flashy computer.

Shortly after I received Ron's gift, my wife Beth and I moved to another state. Though I've tried to stay in touch with Ron, our conversations have been sporadic, at best. But every day when I take pen in hand, I think of Ron, say a prayer for him and know the friendship is still there.

In a hurting world, the gifts of friendship help heal the soul. They bridge the miles and fill the silence with memories.

Father, may I find the right gift for a special friend today.
—*Scott Walker*

SUN

11
Be ye all of one mind, having compassion one of another. . . .
—*I PETER 3:8*

My husband Whitney and I had just found out our twenty-year-old daughter Sanna was addicted to drugs and alcohol. I felt so alone in our grieving, and I was floundering for help. Yet the thought of facing people, especially strangers in our new church, was wrenching; my way of dealing with pain has always been to withdraw. Worst of all, I couldn't hear or feel anything from God. "Maybe He's telling you to come with me to the missionary dinner tonight," Whitney said gently. Reluctantly, I went.

Why did I come? I thought, pushing my back against the wall. We were standing in the crowded fellowship hall. Laughter and food smells filled the air. *Such perfect-looking families. What if someone asks about our children?*

Whitney nudged me. There was a couple about our age coming our way. "Hi, my name's Paul. This is my wife Kathleen."

We talked about this and that while the pain rolled in me like a thunderstorm. Suddenly, I snapped to attention. "One of our biggest struggles now is with our son. We had to hospitalize him for an obsessive/compulsive disorder. Yet I know God is working," Paul said. His sharing cracked open my wall of loneliness.

"We've just found out our daughter . . ." Whitney's arm stole around me. Paul and Kathleen nodded, listening while I talked, their empathy salving the doubt, guilt and fear.

Before we left, Kathleen gave me her phone number. "Call me. I know of other mothers struggling with problems like ours. We need to stick together."

As we drove home, I marveled at the "coincidence" of our new friends who'd given what I could never have received alone in my room: the flesh-and-blood comfort of people who'd walked in my shoes. I felt that we'd been planted on a road paved by the feet of many, each helping the other. From there we could make it. And we have.

Lord, when life's journey gets rough, give me the courage to reach out to fellow travelers for help.　　　*—Shari Smyth*

MON

12

Be careful for nothing; but in every thing by prayer and supplication with thanksgiving let your requests be made known unto God.　—PHILIPPIANS 4:6

A few weeks after finding out that I was pregnant with our second child—long before I could feel the baby move—I found myself grappling all over again with the classic worries of an expectant mother. In those early months, it was hard to comprehend that there was a real human being inside me. *Who is she? Or he? How will our family change? Do I have the patience and love it takes to be a good mommy? Do I have the faith?*

Elizabeth interrupted my thoughts with a demand for books. We were reading quietly when morning sickness suddenly hit. I rushed down the hall calling, "Honey, Mommy has to go to the bathroom. I'm going to be sick."

Elizabeth bounced happily after me. At fifteen months, the bathroom was a fascinating place for her. She giggled to find Mommy crouched in an unfamiliar position. Then, seeing that I was otherwise occupied, she seized the opportunity to play with the forbidden: the toilet lid. Crash! Down it came—hard—on my head. I forgot to be sick as I grasped my throbbing forehead. Blinking back tears of pain,

I turned to scold my little monkey, only to find that now a chubby little fist was eagerly reaching into the toilet to grab whatever Mommy had been hiding.

Surprised by her spunk, I grabbed her and laughed out loud. Elizabeth flashed me a huge, happy smile, as if to say, "This is fun, Mom!" I pulled her close for a big hug and kiss.

Later, while Elizabeth napped, my anxious thoughts about the new baby returned. I rested my head in my hands to pray. That's when I discovered the small but very sore bump on my forehead from the toilet lid. I touched it gently, thankful for how real and alive Elizabeth is. Then I recalled that I had had the same kinds of worries about the future when I was pregnant with her.

Loving Father, sometimes I need a good bump on the head to remind me that You give me more than responsibilities— You give me real people to love.   —*Julia Attaway*

TUE

13   *For he saith to the snow, Be thou on the earth. . . .*
                                        —*JOB 37:6*

By midnight, the room has become light enough to wake me. I get up, go to the window and peep out through the edge of the shade. What I see brings back the breathless wonder of being seven and finding a bride doll suspended in a cloud of white tulle under the Christmas tree. Snow is falling outside.

Tennessee snow is scarce, so back in the warmth of a down comforter, I decide the snow is too good to miss. Quietly I get up again. I bundle up in my winter sweats, rummage through the hall closet for gloves and boots, tug on my coat. The minute I open the door, I'm glad I've chosen the cold. The night air is alive. A few stars twinkle, and the snow, several inches deep, sparkles like a field of mica.

For weeks I've been steeped in that dreaded after-Christmas letdown. Now, everything is suddenly simple and new as I walk through the snow trying not to disturb the whiteness. *God, I feel You here in the stillness of night. It's almost as though You were waiting out here for me, hoping I would come.*

A perfect peace falls on the quiet night. Then, as more snow begins to fall, I follow my tracks back until, ahead, I see home. The kitchen light is on. And from the outside looking in, I know life's good.

This warmth of knowing will stay with me through the winter. Undressing for bed, I realize it wasn't chance that woke me up. God made the snow fall, sent the light—and then waited.

In the morning, we'll watch school closings on TV, sip old-fashioned cocoa with marshmallows, probably eat "snow cream" for lunch. And in the days following, I will remember to watch for God's subtle reminders, sent softly like the snow, to tell me that His gift of life is good.

Open my eyes, Father, and make me willing to see the goodness You lay before me this very day.   —Pam Kidd

---

WED

14 *And the Lord shall make you the head and not the tail. . . .*   —DEUTERONOMY 28:13 (NAS)

Minnie is the ultimate " 'fraidy cat." Everything that moves scares her. She's the most cautious, suspicious creature I've ever known. She won't leave the house unless I'm with her, and even then, a falling leaf can send her scurrying back inside.

We knew some adjusting would be in order when we got a golden retriever/Labrador puppy for Christmas. Lovey wasn't much of a threat when she was six weeks old and lived in a back room. But we knew there would be trouble when she got older. So we moved her outside to a newly built, roomy pen.

The new arrangement seemed to be working well for all of us. Then one day Lovey escaped, and all eighty pounds of her pushed the back door open unexpectedly, looking for someone to play with. She galloped toward Minnie, who was enjoying a leisurely late breakfast. The cat got one quick glimpse of something behind her, coming hard and fast, and took off for her favorite hiding place—underneath our unusually low bed. She remained there for almost three days, refusing food or water or affection.

When Minnie finally came out, she'd developed a peculiar fear: She was now horrified of her tail! Invariably, she'd glance over her shoulder and see her tail as she'd seen Lovey. Then the tail would start jerking. She'd spit at it and hiss at it and try to claw it, only to end up running frantically to get away from it. Often when "the tail began to chase the cat," I'd scoop her up in my arms, hold her tail completely still and speak in a soothing voice. "Minnie, your silly tail is nothing to be afraid of. Anyway, I'm here to protect you. Don't run anymore. Stand still, girl."

Sometimes I let things chase me around, just like poor Minnie. Things like fear and "what ifs" often chase me into an emotional tailspin. Now I say, *Marion, don't let fear or your imagination chase you around again. Remember, your Father is your protector. Stand still, girl.*

How amazing, Father, that You can use a cat to teach me to trust You more. Amen.   —*Marion Bond West*

THU

15
We then, as workers together with him. . . .
                                    —*II CORINTHIANS 6:1*

Several years ago on Martin Luther King, Jr., Day, I visited a gift shop owned by a wonderfully talented African-American family. Three generations had worked together to convert a dilapidated old cottage into a Victorian-style setting for one-of-a-kind collage art and sculpture. We were talking about the courage it takes to communicate struggles and triumphs through art when the topic turned to Dr. King. His dream, deeply embedded in the American dream, was that his children would one day live in a nation where they would "not be judged by the color of their skin but by the content of their character."

Those words brought to mind a private pain I'd long carried in my heart. While I have not been confronted with racial prejudice, I suffer from a disorder that has often made me the target of stares and whispers. It's called neurofibromatosis, commonly associated with The Elephant Man, who became a circus sideshow attraction in England during the Victorian era. "King's dream is for everyone," the shop owner pointed out to me. "He symbolized not only the struggles between races, but the struggles of anyone who feels the discrimination of being different."

That day, I purchased a collage made of discarded buttons, old jewels, and scraps of salvaged lace. Crafted by loving hands that are a different color than mine, it is a visible reminder that America is at its greatest when we join hands and work together.

Lord Jesus, help me to treat all my brothers and sisters with respect, for despite our differences, we are all one in You.
                                    —*Roberta Messner*

Herald of Healing

Manifest in making whole
Palsied limbs and fainting soul;
Manifest in valiant fight,
Quelling all the devil's might;
Manifest in gracious will,
Ever bringing good from ill;
Anthems be to Thee addressed,
God in man made manifest.
—CHRISTOPHER WORDSWORTH

FRI
16

For when I am weak, then am I strong.
—II CORINTHIANS 12:10

I was having lunch alone in a coffee shop, not really hungry and worrying again about my mother in a nursing home in Michigan, hundreds of miles away from rainy Manhattan. Then Bob walked in. "Want some company?" he asked, shaking out his umbrella.

I was grateful to have him join me. Sometimes I slip up and say that my friend Bob beat a terrible drug and alcohol addiction. After all these years I should know better. *"I* didn't beat anything," Bob is quick to correct me. "It beat me. All I did was surrender."

I've learned a great deal from his sobriety, watching him rebuild his life into something far richer than he could have ever imagined when he was "out there." Nowadays Bob is a great success story, and he sees a spiritual solution to nearly every problem in life, big or small. He is always "letting go and letting God."

I, on the other hand, have trouble "surrendering." I don't always like to ask for help, not even from God. I'm usually trying to do it myself, to beat my problems, like my worries over my mother's Alzheimer's, even if it drives me crazy.

The subject of my mother never came up during lunch with Bob, but afterward I felt a whole lot better. I was ready to surrender.

Help me, God, to let go and let You.   —Edward Grinnan

17 *And of some have compassion, making a difference.*
                                                     —JUDE 22

My Italian grandmother had a gift. Whenever somebody in her neighborhood had an ache or pain, they went to see Angelina. She massaged their sore muscles and manipulated their aching bones and joints like an old country chiropractor.

"She was the sweetest lady, always happy," the woman who grew up next door to my dad told me when I visited St. Louis, his hometown.

"But could she really make people feel better?" I asked.

"Oh, the neighborhood people, they felt better just knowing she'd drop what she was doing, the washing or the mending, and try to help them. She was a real comfort to them."

I can picture my little grandmother's friends and neighbors leaving her house, feeling better about an aching back or stiff hands, not even realizing how she had also listened to their troubles. I can hear her jabbering with them in Italian, sharing a laugh or a hot drink on a cold day, or maybe saying a rosary with them over an aching worry. My dad has told me these were the things that filled her days. So perhaps her real gift was her willingness to set aside her life for the moment to help people who needed her.

I didn't know my grandma Angelina well. We lived nearly a thousand miles apart and spoke different languages. But I feel a kinship with her as I discover what she must have known, that being a sympathetic ear or a prayer partner has a healing effect on both people involved. Sometimes I think my merry-go-round life is moving too fast to stop the ride for a friend in need. But I've learned that taking the time for another helps me feel whole and connected in an often disjointed world.

In my grandma's simple way, I know she understood this too. She may have been old country, but she knew a few things about the healing power God has placed inside each one of us.

Help me to be an extension of Your healing hands Lord,
whenever I'm given the chance.   *—Gina Bridgeman*

18

Yea, the sparrow hath found a house. . . .
                                        —PSALM 84:3

Being made a financial consultant at the bank was a victory for me. But misgivings came pretty quickly as I took over my new territory.

Was I too young? Some of the branch managers certainly seemed to think so. Was I tough enough for this specialized area of the investment business? The average broker lasts only three years in his or her career. What if I couldn't even last that long?

My head's swimming with such apprehensions as I drive into the church parking lot. I went out of town with some friends the week before and missed last Sunday's service. Now I slip in next to my mother, in our usual pew near the back. She smiles and pats my back. I look around. Familiar smiles and friendly faces greet me from every direction. Up in the pulpit, my father makes the usual morning announcements. Still, something's wrong. I can't shake my anxiety.

The congregation stands to sing. The sound of the organ fills the sanctuary.

"God of the sparrow, God of the whale," everyone sings.

God, You say you never forget even one sparrow, I pray silently.

"God of the ages," I hear my mom's off-key voice singing next to me, "God near at hand."

Of course, I know You are here, I continue. *You've always been here, waiting.*

"How do your children say joy, how do your children say home," the choir finishes.

How do I say "home" God, I keep praying as the children parade down the middle aisle for the children's sermon. *How do I find You in this fast-moving world that seems so full of insecurity and unrest? How can I be sure I'll make it in my job? What if I fail?*

Up front, the children bow their heads as Dad says a prayer with them: "God, please go with us this week. Help us be good." The voices of tiny children blend with Dad's. And I pray:

Of course, God! How do I keep missing this? It's just a matter of doing my best one day at a time, isn't it? So go with me this week. Help me be good. And by the way, You can expect me back here again next week. It's home. *—Brock Kidd*

<u>MON</u>   *Now the Lord said . . . "Go forth from your country*
19   *. . . to the land which I will show you."*
                                    —*GENESIS 12:1 (NAS)*

My job takes me through a lot of airports and onto a lot of airplanes. Invariably, there are delays, missed connections and even, on occasion, cancellations. So I consider myself a pretty savvy traveler who knows how to search for alternatives to reach my destination.

On the homeward leg of a recent trip, I arrived at the airport a bit late. I hurried through baggage check-in and security, and jogged down to the gate. When I got there, I found the airline check-in staff calmly counting seats and checking identification. Assuming that the flight was delayed, I sat down in the waiting area.

After awhile, I became concerned and approached the desk to ask about my flight. "Oh," replied the counter agent, "didn't you hear the announcement? The gate for that flight has been changed. They're boarding right now." Fortunately, the new gate was only a short distance away, and I made the switch with a few minutes to spare.

Looking back at where I'd been sitting, it struck me that I could have sat there all evening, fuming and fussing about not getting to my destination. What I needed was someone to tell me, "You're at the wrong gate. Just go over to the right one, and you'll get where you're going."

Lord, may I listen to You today, so I get to the right starting point for where You want me to go.   —*Eric Fellman*

<u>TUE</u>   *And be not conformed to this world: but be ye trans-*
20   *formed by the renewing of your mind, that ye may*
           prove what is that good, and acceptable, and perfect,
will of God.   —*ROMANS 12:2*

Our debate was over the virtues and vices of television. As an elementary school librarian, my wife Shirley was conducting a "No TV Week," which encouraged students and their families to turn off their television sets and read or engage in other activities that parents and their children can't seem to find time enough to do. Her list included such things as talking about family histories, going to the zoo, visiting a museum, having a picnic, attending a play and working together on a jigsaw puzzle. But reading good books to children and discussing the truths and values that they highlight were at the top of the list. "Wonderful memories are created by parents who sit close to their young children and read to them," she wrote.

Though I agreed with Shirley that most of us watch too much TV (the average school-age child in this country spends more time in front of a television set than he or she does in the classroom), I pointed out that there are some outstanding educational programs on the air. "And too much sex and violence," she countered. Obviously, there are both worthwhile and worthless programs on TV. My point was that critical judgment is required to ferret out the good and bad of anything.

Our responsibility is to see both the positives and negatives in a world of contradictions—and not to lose hope. Paul told us how, I suggested to Shirley, when he said, "Be not conformed to this world: but be ye transformed by the renewing of your mind."

"And one of the best ways to renew ourselves is to watch less television and read more good books," she last-worded.

Show me, God, how to part wheat from chaff,
When to get serious and when to laugh.
                                                —*Fred Bauer*

WED
21
Blessed be the God and Father of our Lord Jesus Christ, the Father of mercies and God of all comfort, who comforts us in all our affliction. . . .
                                        —*II CORINTHIANS 1:3-4 (RSV)*

When my friend Carol was diagnosed with brain cancer, I approached two friends with an idea for making a special quilt.

"We can hand out twelve-inch squares to anyone who wants to participate," I explained, "and ask them to embroider, paint, draw or even iron on something that would be meaningful to Carol." To my amazement, within days we had so many people wanting to contribute that we had to drop the square size down to eight inches, eliminate the borders—and make the quilt double-sided!

When the finished squares started coming back in, I was astonished by the many creative expressions of love. Carol's friends had meticulously embroidered Bible verses, drawn beautiful pictures, illustrated prayers with calligraphy. The whole quilt, front and back, was a monumental offering of love to God for Carol.

The afternoon that the quilt was taken to the hospital, I got a phone call.

"Brenda, there is a gorgeous quilt in my hospital room! I can't stop looking at it," she told me. "I keep seeing new friends, new verses. Thank you."

A few weeks later the cancer went into Carol's brain stem. "Are you going to be okay?" I asked.

Carol ran a hand lovingly over the many embroidered prayers and promises on her quilt. "Yes. I haven't had to do this alone. And when I die I won't be alone, either." She looked up and smiled. "I'll simply be trading this comforter for a far greater One."

Father in heaven, truly You are the Father of mercy and God of all comfort, comforting each and every one of us in our affliction.
                                                           —*Brenda Wilbee*

THU

22 *I thank my God, making mention of thee always in my prayers.*
                                                    —*PHILEMON 1:4*

I sent an E-mail to my colleague and waited. Not that it was such an important message, but she was usually so punctual about replying, I was surprised that the letter symbol on my computer in-box hadn't flashed, indicating a return E-mail. Only the next day, when there was no response, did I remember that she was at a weeklong conference out of the state.

A sinking sensation came over me as I recalled the complicated issues that would be discussed, the stressful arguments, the never-ending meetings and the anxiety she had expressed about the conference. "Don't worry," I'd said then. "I'm sure it'll all work out." What could I do now?

I punched in her address and typed, "I don't know if you'll be reading your E-mail while you're away, but I want you to know I'm thinking of you. I pray that you express yourself with confidence, that the conflicts are speedily resolved and that the meetings don't bore you to tears." I gazed at the words on my computer screen and uttered the same prayer to God.

A few days later I received a reply from my colleague. "You're great. Thanks for remembering me. Your message gave me a terrific boost. The conference went much better than I expected, no doubt because of your prayer."

My prayer? I couldn't vouch for it. I would be quicker at crediting the gifts of my colleague. But her response made me feel glad I'd let her know she was on my mind. Some prayers are meant to be shared.

Today, God, I want to pray for my friend _____.
(WRITE IN NAME)

—Rick Hamlin

FRI
23 *The Lord hath anointed me . . . to comfort all that mourn.* —ISAIAH 61:1-2

During her entire life, our springer spaniel Sushi slept under my husband Keith's side of the bed, but the night before her final appointment at the vet—after months of fighting liver disease she climbed onto the bed on my side and slept beside me, her head on my pillow. I was certain she knew the next morning would be her last.

Keith and I were holding her at the vet's office when she received the injection and quietly ceased breathing. Blinded with tears, I went back to the front office to pay; Keith followed, also grieving, but holding back his tears until no one but I could see. As I stood at the counter, fumbling for my checkbook, I felt a light touch on my arm and looked over to see an elderly Japanese-American woman beside me.

"Did you just put your dog down?" she asked.

I nodded, not able to speak yet. She indicated the other side of the room where an elderly, stoical Japanese-American man sat holding the leash of a white-faced Irish setter. "We, too," she said, her eyes glistening. Suddenly, she and I were hugging each other, crying openly, while our men watched us, unmoving.

I never knew who she was, and I never saw her again. She was the sharing of grief I needed, at the moment I needed it, a stranger who carried comfort with her and sought it from me. I think God gives us moments like these, the gift of strangers who exactly mirror us, who touch us for a precious second and then move on, so that we will always remember we are not alone.

Dear God, thank You for the love You show us through the kindness of other people. —Rhoda Blecker

SAT *The Lord is good. When trouble comes, he is the*
24 *place to go! And he knows everyone who trusts in*
       him!   *—NAHUM 1:7 (TLB)*

One Friday while our daughter Emily was in college, I accompanied
my husband Bob on a business trip to Nashville, Tennessee. We
planned to stay over and had tickets for the Saturday-evening performance of the *Grand Ole Opry*. But by Saturday morning the temperature had dropped below freezing, with periods of snow and sleet.
Despite our disappointment at missing the *Opry*, we decided to head
for home.

"I have a strong feeling that it's the best thing to do," Bob said.

"And perhaps we can stop by the college and see Emily," I suggested.

When our car pulled up at the big frame house where Emily was
living, we saw bundled-up girls scurrying out of the open front door.
They carried suitcases, pillows, boxes and other paraphernalia. One
of them saw us and yelled, "Emily, your folks are here! And in a *station wagon!*"

Emily bounded out of the door and, in one leap, landed in her
daddy's arms.

"I knew you would come," she squealed. "I prayed you would. We
need you!"

In short, rapid sentences she told us that the furnace had broken
down; they had no heat and were trying to move into a nearly completed dormitory across campus.

"It has heat," one girl called, "and we're freezing here!"

Several students with cars were trying to help the girls move, but
the long, empty bed of our station wagon could carry more than all
the cars combined. Less than an hour later, the relocated students
were happily sorting their possessions in the entry hall of the new
building and relishing the warmth that surrounded them.

Great and powerful is Your love, Father, that directs and
guides us to those who need us. Keep our hearts attuned to
receive Your messages and quick to respond. Amen.

                                                  —Drue Duke

SUN
25

"Blessed is the man who trusts in the Lord, whose trust is the Lord. He is like a tree planted by water...."   —JEREMIAH 17:7-8 (RSV)

My mother and her friends are the kind of people who keep this world spinning. They need glasses, those who aren't showing a little snow on the rooftop are using some camouflage, and a couple of them are shorter than they used to be. Yet, in their seventies, they're filled with faith and excited about life.

Francis, for example, emigrated to the United States from Switzerland. She learned to speak English, but never learned to drive. When her husband of nearly fifty years died, she braved the Division of Motor Vehicles office, and after several attempts emerged with a new license. Never mind her twenty-mile distance restriction; she gets where she wants to go in her small, north Idaho town.

Helen is the romantic of the bunch. Though nearing eighty, she sits with stars in her eyes while she watches her favorite love story, *Random Harvest,* for the hundredth time.

Dolly is my mom's golf partner. They are first on the course several mornings a week, after Mom has indulged in her daily thirty-minute walk. Now Dolly is patiently learning to deal with her daughter's multiple sclerosis.

Dorothy, a retired college professor, once came "too close" to getting married. Instead, she keeps in close touch with her former students and always has fix-it projects going at home. She and Mom engage in lively debates from opposite sides of the political fence.

The friends have taken their knocks in life. Yet every Sunday morning they are in church singing praises to God. And the rest of the week they are out enjoying His creation and serving others in His name. They are, to me, models of those "whose trust is the Lord" and my ideal of the woman I hope to become when I "get old."

Lord, when I trust in You, I'm like a tree planted beside the water whose leaves remain green. I think I'd like to "grow old" Your way.   —Carol Knapp

MON

26

But they measuring themselves by themselves, and comparing themselves among themselves, are not wise. —II CORINTHIANS 10:12

I have discovered a surefire formula for making myself miserable: just compare myself with others.

I do it all the time. *Why do they always ask Len to speak at the special occasions and not me? Why can't I afford a car like Chuck's?*

My students do it, too. "How come I got a B and Nicci got an A when my paper was just as good as hers?" they ask. And, "You took your children's literature class to lunch, but you never treat our class to anything special."

Even my wife does it. "Why can't I have the energy of Phyllis, the good looks of Cheryl and the income of Lori?"

The trouble with making comparisons? I'm not good at it. I compare my weaknesses with others' blessings and strengths. I'm wondering if God gave us the tenth commandment "Thou shalt not covet" just to keep us from making ourselves wretched.

If I covet my neighbor's house, do I also want his mortgage payments and repair bills? If I covet my neighbor's wife, do I also want to endure her bad temper and her spendthrift habits? If I covet my neighbor's cattle, am I also willing to pay veterinary bills and get up at 4:00 A.M. to milk the cows?

So the next time I'm tempted to make comparisons, I think I'll first make a list of the ways in which I've been blessed and spend some time dwelling on them. And then I'm going to say a sincere prayer for all of those I'm tempted to envy, something like this:

Lord, thank You for blessing my friends. Teach me to be happy for them when they flourish, instead of feeling deprived. —Daniel Schantz

TUE

27

A soft answer turns away wrath, but a harsh word stirs up anger. —PROVERBS 15:1 (RSV)

My twenty-three-year-old son Tim is a tender young man in the tough business of New York finance. As a junior analyst at a mutual fund company, he works sixteen-hour days fielding hundreds of phone calls from brokers, traders and clients who are more volatile than the stock market. His new profession operates through open conflict, and he's been yelled at, harangued, threatened, hung up on. And yet, despite his quiet nature, he has prospered. He has brought in new customers, shepherded sensitive negotiations to their successful conclusions while earning the respect of seasoned and senior associates.

"How do you do it?" I recently asked him, amazed that the gentle boy of memory could go one-on-one with hard-boiled, aggressive types.

"When somebody yells, I speak more softly," he replied. "If people throw tantrums, I keep my cool. If they're rude, I'm pointedly polite. They don't know what to do with me. Eventually, they wind up listening."

Lord, let my speech always be gracious, seasoned with good sense, that I may know how to answer everyone (Colossians 4:6).   —Linda Ching Sledge

---

WED
28
Of making many books there is no end. . . .
                              —ECCLESIASTES 12:12 (RSV)

Looking through a small catalog of used books, I came across sixteen or seventeen titles that I had either edited or that were published during the years I worked for their publishers. *Was it worth it, I asked myself, to have put in all that work on those volumes, only to see them relegated to the dusty shelves of a secondhand bookstore, probably to be ignored and forgotten? Had my work made any difference?*

Some time later, I got an answer to my question. When my Christmas letter to a friend was returned with a "moved, forwarding order expired" stamp on it, I dialed information for his new number and phoned him. As we caught up on our news, he told me, "You'll never know what a difference one book you gave me has made. Fritz Kunkel's *Creation Continues* has changed my life."

His comment stuck in my mind, and came back to me when I found the used-books catalog again and saw Kunkel's name there. *Of course, I thought, even if just one person is changed by a book, isn't that worth your time and effort?*

And then I laughed. Because my life, too, had been turned around when I read and edited *Creation Continues*. Kunkel's psychological interpretation of the Gospel of Matthew had helped me open up to Jesus' transforming kingdom. And all those other books I'd edited— I'd learned from all of them. Who knows how many other people were helped, enlightened, inspired by them? And now, on the shelves of another bookstore and in a catalog, they were given a second chance. How many more people might they not touch and change? Of course, it was worth it!

Thank You, God, for all the books, new and old, that continue to enrich our lives.   —*Mary Ruth Howes*

THU
29

Be patient with each other, making allowance for each other's faults because of your love.
                              —*EPHESIANS 4:2 (TLB)*

My husband John is a quiet man. With him, "it's either right or wrong, so what's there to talk about? If it's right, do it, if it's wrong, don't!" On the other hand, I am garrulous, with a dramatic need to talk things through. So much so that he tells me, "You're so chatty you could strike up a conversation with an empty chair!"

Our different personalities often lead to misunderstandings and irritations, but at last we have a solution. In a sermon on family relationships, our pastor suggested that we offer each other a mental burlap bag. "Through the weeks, when irritations crop up, instead of sniping at each other, toss them into your imaginary bag," he said. "Then, every couple of months, empty your bags and share your grievances."

It's amazing how well this has worked in our lives. Daily I burlap-bag my irritations: dirt clods unwittingly trekked in from the garden; the sharp, impatient answer when I interrupt a ball game; the way he hovers about when I'm phoning a friend. Conversely, into his bag go the things I do that tend to drive him mad! My insistence on doing things *my* way; the habit I have of straightening out papers on this desk when he wants them left a-jumble; the fact that my feelings get so easily hurt. We have no set schedule. But somehow we know when it's time to empty out our bags. We choose the time carefully; unhurried, often under the stars on the patio in the summer or in front of a cozy fire in the winter.

It's extraordinary that so many things that seemed important when we put them into our bags have diffused into nothingness when we're ready to take them out. Our burlap bags help us focus on what really matters; then, blended together like mulled spices, our differences become much sweeter to handle.

Help me to kindle tender mercies around our flaws, dear Lord.   *—Fay Angus*

FRI

30
I meditate on your precepts and consider your ways. . . .   *—PSALM 119:15 (NIV)*

I met Bill in my second year of college, and we fell in love within a month of our first date. When we announced our engagement, Bill's fraternity brothers couldn't believe he was marrying the campus airhead. Actually, I took college life very seriously. I always got up for my eleven o'clock class. I never missed my three-hour biology lab on rainy days. On sunny days, I studied algebra by the pool. To me, a formal education was measured by how many party dresses I had in my closet.

To say the least, my lifestyle was disconcerting to my 4.0 roommate. She set me up on the blind date that proved pivotal to my intellectual and social growth: I met Bill and liked him—a lot. I decided that I wanted to spend the rest of my life with a man I could talk to. And I determined I would have something to talk about. Since Bill was on academic scholarship, he studied constantly. If I wanted to see him, I had to meet him on his turf, the library. So I did what everyone else in the library did—I studied. To my surprise, I discovered that the more I learned, the more I enjoyed learning. I became an avid reader with an unquenchable thirst for information.

Twenty-five years, many conversations and three children later, I've learned that God knows who I am and will give me every opportunity to be that person. That blind date wasn't set up by my smart roommate—it was a gift from God, a gift I'm grateful for every day.

Lord, help me to be the best I can be.   *—Kathy Peel*

SAT

31
And a little child shall lead them.   *—ISAIAH 11:6*

Eight-year-old Heather is our neighbor. To her, every day is a discovery. When she talks, there's a lilt in her voice and her blue eyes twinkle. She's on the girls' softball team and is enrolled in a judo class. At her First Communion, she read beautifully and said she wasn't nervous.

One Saturday, Heather came to visit my wife Ruby and me. As we chatted, she told us about something that happened in school. "My teacher wrote *metamorphosis* on the blackboard, and she spelled it wrong. But I didn't say anything. When I wrote it on my paper, I spelled it right." I was impressed. Heather corrected an error without calling attention to herself or embarrassing her teacher.

I can use Heather's wisdom in my own life. Here are some ways I can "spell it right": When I return books to the library for friends without cars, I can pay the fines quietly. When I hear some hurtful gossip about a friend, I can let it end with me. When I'm in Boston and I see a meter maid approaching an expired meter, I can slip in two quarters, then hurry along. When I'm in the supermarket and I see an item on the wrong shelf, I can put it back where it belongs. When a letter for a neighbor mistakenly arrives at my door, I can walk a few blocks and slip it in the correct mailbox. When I sense misunderstandings building at home, at church or in the community, I can seek out ways to dispel them.

I can spell it right!

Dear Jesus, thank You for using a little child to teach me a big lesson. —Oscar Greene

My Healing Journey

1 _____

2 _____

3 _____

4 _____

5 _____

6 _____

7 _____

8 _____

9 _____

10 _____

11 _____

12 _____

13 _____

14 _____

15 _____

16 _____

17 _____

18 _____

19 _____

20 _____

21 _____

22 _____

23 _____

24 _____

25 _____

26 _____

27 _____

28 _____

29 _____

30 _____

31 _____

FEBRUARY

S	M	T	W	T	F	S
1	2	3	4	5	6	7
8	9	10	11	12	13	14
15	16	17	18	19	20	21
22	23	24	25	26	27	28

When the cares of my heart are many,
thy consolations cheer my soul.

—PSALM 94:19 (RSV)

THE TOUCH OF THE HEALER
Healing Our Hearts

1

*When Jesus saw their faith, he said to the paralytic,
"Son, your sins are forgiven."*   —MARK 2:5 (NIV)

When I taught a kindergarten Sunday school class, the kids loved to act out Jesus' healing of the paralytic. Four children became the four eager friends of the "volunteer" paralytic whom they carried around the room in the middle of a blanket, each holding a corner. With great determination, they broke through the roof (usually a barricade of chairs) to bring their friend to Jesus, Who was surrounded by other people. When Jesus saw the faith of these devoted friends, He told the paralytic that his sins were forgiven, and the paralytic was healed.

I had always assumed that was the main message of this story—because of the faith of a few good friends, this paralytic was healed—until last year when our eighteen-year-old daughter Kendall suffered a baffling auto-immune disease that caused her to lose her hair. In her depression and discouragement, she seemed paralyzed in her faith, so her father and I began to "carry" her to Jesus in our prayers. We prayed fervently for the healing of her disease, but we seemed to hit a barrier: Her condition worsened.

That's when I found another message in this passage. It's not uncommon to pray for physical healing first, but Jesus has something greater in mind. He healed the paralytic's heart first by forgiving his sins, because when a heart is healed, a person receives the strength and trust to endure, whether physical healing occurs or not. We "acted out" this Scripture with our daughter, carrying her to Jesus with the faith that He would heal her heart. Our prayers were answered.

Now when I read this passage about the miracle of Jesus healing the paralytic, I see a greater message: Because of the faith of a few good friends (or family members), healing can happen. Especially when our prayers are for healing first in a person's heart.

Jesus, may I always remember the importance of a healed heart.   —Carol Kuykendall

A JOURNEY TO HEALING

A few years ago, Dr. Scott Harrison's life was shattered when he lost his daughter Ann in a tragic accident. This week, he invites us to follow his patient Carl—and his own grieving heart—along the path to healing.   —THE EDITORS

<table>
<tr><td>MON
2</td></tr>
</table>

Day 1: Pain and Stillness
Be still, and know that I am God. . . .   —PSALM 46:10

"Doc, how you plannin' to fix this leg?" my patient Carl asked as he lay in the emergency room. The torn pants, matted beneath the clear plastic splint, revealed bone fragments poking through the skin. "And get me out of this pain! It's killing me!"

Pain, I'll tell you about pain, I thought as I looked down at him. *I've just buried my twenty-six-year-old daughter!*

But instead, I took a deep breath and answered, "There are lots of ways. If I put a rod down the bone, we can get you up right away. If it's too dirty, I'll put pins into the bones and connect them to a device that looks like a child's erector set, so I can keep an eye on those cuts. When they heal, we can eventually put on a cast. Let's get you up to the operating room."

As I planned the surgery, I thought of all the techniques orthopedic surgeons use to fix fractures, but that's not *real* healing. I'd just experienced how close God's spiritual healing parallels what He does in the human body.

Carl had complained about pain. Loss of loved ones, broken friendships and, of course, broken bones all hurt. Pain not only signals the injury, it allows the healing process to begin by causing us to be still. It was the same when Ann died. I needed to be still, to let those around me come and do for me. It made me feel helpless, but the pain was less when friends said, "I'm sorry, let me help," or when they arrived with a steaming chicken casserole. These things stabilized the hurt.

It wasn't easy to be still. I wanted to do something, *anything,* to make the pain go away. But just as the surgery caused Carl's bone fragments to be at rest so that repair could begin, it was *stillness,* in God's presence, that began my healing.

Great Physician, it was the unfelt touch of Your presence that began my healing. Hear my whispered thanks.
—Scott Harrison

<hr>

TUE
3

Day 2: Cleaning the Wound
O Lord, heal me, for my bones are in agony.
—PSALM 6:2 (NIV)

Carl was looking earnestly at the erector set of pins and connectors that protruded from his bandaged leg. "So that's what's goin' to knit this back together, Doc?"

"Not quite," I answered. "All that does is hold the bone ends together."

The body mobilizes an impressive array of specialized cells to heal a fracture. First to arrive are the "housekeeper cells," the macrophages. They clean up the debris. They gobble up the tiny fragments of dead bone, the torn muscle and especially any bacteria that are at the fracture. Then come the "builder cells." They use the blood clot that has formed around the fracture as a scaffold and begin layering a soft scar around the bone ends. Additional cells finally come in to rearrange the new bone that forms in the scar. But it's that unseen first group that cleans up that is crucial. Without it, pus forms and no healing will occur.

"I know it doesn't feel like it, but your fracture isn't really too bad. You'll do fine."

Not like my experience in Vietnam, I thought. Those soldiers had mangled arms and legs contaminated with shreds of filthy fatigues and rice-paddy mud. Any dead tissue or fragments of shrapnel left in the wound became seeds of death.

And that's the effect Ann's death had on me . . . horrific, shattered, dismembering. To heal, I first had to cut out the contaminated parts. Self-pity. Paralyzing grief. The "Why me?" syndrome that colored all those around me in pastels of envy because they hadn't lived through what I was trying to survive.

In those first weeks after Ann's death, two sets of parents came to comfort us who carried a similar loss. But even though it had been many years since their grief had begun, their pain was as raw as mine. They remained crippled by grief. *Not everyone gets through this whole* became the recurring stimulus that prodded me in my psychological surgery.

But like all surgery, it can't be done without something to relieve the pain. A general anesthetic dose for the deep abscess of doubt, a spinal perhaps for the unremitting grief, and a local might do for self-pity. Just the right amount, administered by "the Father of compassion and the God of all comfort, who comforts us in all our troubles" as Paul describes it (II Corinthians 1:3–4, NIV). Like most patients, I was fearful that it wouldn't be enough, but. . . .

I called upon You, my Physician, and Your comfort was sufficient.   —*Scott Harrison*

WED	**Day 3: Change**
4	*The Spirit of the Lord will come upon you in power . . . and you will be changed into a different person.*
	—*I SAMUEL 10:6 (NIV)*

Carl wasn't very happy when I saw him at six weeks. He had changed from being the breadwinner, a soccer dad, weekend golfer, to an unemployed invalid who couldn't even help around the house. It was the most drastically sudden change he'd ever experienced.

But I knew how that felt. That call, in the black of early morning announcing Ann's death, changed me so completely that I looked into the mirror to see if my face showed the changes that I felt. Sure, new lines etched my eyes, now set deep in darkened sockets. And my mouth was a thin line of lament. But inside, I was so broken that these changes hardly hinted at who I had become.

What is God's next step in healing? *God transforms!* He changes the cells that are in the fracture area of Carl's leg. He takes cells that would normally do one thing, like make blood vessels, and wonderfully changes them into cells that make a fracture scar that looks like a glob of putty. This acts as a temporary splint to hold the bone ends together. And then, at just the right time, the cells that have been making the scar change again and begin to layer on sheets of bone. It isn't the fracture that heals itself. It's cells that haven't been damaged that effect the cure. And these cells must change from what they have been to realize the potential for healing that has been locked inside them.

It would be the same for me. If I stayed as I was, focusing mainly on my grief, I couldn't expect to see healing.

I knew what it would take to change me. Prayer.

For many years, Sally and I prayed each morning for our three children. Now that prayer was for two, and that the two of us would feel God's unseen touch. We needed to prolong our time with Him. We needed to ask why, and we needed to be willing to wait and wait and wait for His answer. And, yes, we needed to thank Him as well for twenty-six years of being loved by Ann. And for His assurance that Ann was now even more radiantly beautiful in His Presence.

And like the imperceptible healing that occurs in fractures, the change began. Ever so slowly. Too slowly.

And not only did I change, but so, it seemed, did He Who was making those changes.

Unchanging, eternal Father, You have shown me so much more of Who You are, that I barely recognize Who I thought You were. Perhaps You can say the same?   —Scott Harrison

---

THU
5

Day 4: Leaning on God
But the Lord was my support.
                              —PSALM 18:18 (NIV)

Carl lunged down the hospital corridor, careening off the wall, crutches flailing. By awkwardly landing on his good leg, he was protecting the fractured one from touching the ground.

"You're almost ready to go home!" I shouted over the cacophony as the dinner cart he'd just grabbed spilled dirty dishes to the floor. "Just one more lesson. You have to learn how to put some weight on your broken leg. It will do two things. It will make the bone heal faster, and help you not to break the other one as you struggle with those crutches."

"But I don't want to hurt it," he responded quickly. "I'm being careful."

I laughed, "It's a balancing act. And I don't just mean your attempts to walk on crutches. If you protect a fracture too much, it heals slowly, sometimes not at all. Of course, if you're too rough on it, the bone ends move and rupture the new tissue bridging the fracture. But most people are too timid and don't put enough stress on the fracture."

It had been that way for me after Ann's death, I thought. At first, I didn't want to do anything. Everything seemed too stressful. But as the pain abated ever so slightly, I was able to resume work part-time. Then I made some business trips. First with Sally, because she was going through the same process, and we needed the stability that leaning on each other could give. And just as I've observed in patients, there were often setbacks. Like the time in church when we saw the young girl sitting in the first row who looked exactly like Ann. The pain seemed to choke the air from us. We ran outside to gasp the fresh air. But the tearing open of such a deep wound, not yet healed, slowed our healing.

So we hobbled on, little by little finding where Ann now fit in our lives, and where we fit as well. I was absorbed by a picture of her with her arms around bead-bedecked mountain people she had gone to help, goats and chickens lounging in the background. Even through misty eyes I could see that hint of pride in her face. She was going to make a difference. *Was that where she slept when she lived with them?*

Even answering the simple question, "How many children do you have?" (I'd never realized how often it gets asked) became painfully complicated. It also charted the healing as I became more comfortable giving the answer. And when a handmade quilt she'd sent arrived three months after her funeral, I was able to take this as her last embrace for me, and rejoice.

My "spiritual limp" is still there and, perhaps, like some of my fracture patients', it's permanent. But my Physician hasn't discharged me yet.

Father God, guide each step of my healing, but may I never feel so "cured" that I stop leaning on You.   —Scott Harrison

---

FRI	### Day 5: Removing Our Scars
6	*To him who is able to . . . present you before his glorious presence without fault. . . .* —JUDE 24 (NIV)

"Carl, the way you bounced in here today, I'd never guess it was just four months ago that you broke your leg," I said to the bearded man who handed me his X ray. "Let's look at your film. See that white area? That's all the new bone you've layered around the break. It's so smooth that you can barely see where the fracture was. And it will get even better. An X ray in a few years may show no sign of this fracture."

As Carl's fracture healed, the bone had responded to the forces generated by walking, getting up from chairs, all the activity that is part of each day. God's sculptors were at work. Earnest "osteoclasts" were chewing away at the primitive bone that first knit the fracture together. Their cousins, the osteoblasts, then began laying mature bone at just the right places to reshape the bulbous scar of fracture bone, making it perfect. Bones are unique among body tissue: They alone have the potential to heal without a trace of scar. But it depends on how bad the original injury was.

My loss of Ann was like a gash perforating my heart. No, it was worse than that. Perhaps like an arm mangled by a grinding lathe. No, far worse than that, for it affected every cell of my being. More like—well, my words really can't describe it. Having seen patients torched by phosphorous grenades, run over by trains and mutilated by suicide jumps from fifth-story windows, I assumed that somewhere in that thirty years of carnage would be an analogy that was adequate. Not even close!

Each of us carries scars, some perhaps worse than I've described. We see them every time we picture some event in our past. Or we feel them bind us when we try to do things, but we can't because we've failed similar challenges before. We sense them and know that they are there even when others can't see them.

But we are unique, just like bone. God continues to sculpt us: chewing away pieces of anxiety; laying on new strengths. Like the healing of a bone, the process takes time. But we are different in this special way: We need the hand of His Son to erase the last vestige of scar.

Father, by Your Son, we who believe on Him will *be perfect, just as Ann now is.*   —*Scott Harrison*

SAT

7

Day 6: Strength to Trust

The Lord gives strength to his people; the Lord blesses his people with peace.   —*PSALM 29:11 (NIV)*

"Carl, I didn't expect to see you again," I blurted in surprise. "Is something still wrong?"

"My leg isn't strong yet, even though it's been nearly a year," he responded. "I can't run on it. It feels like it's goin' to give out."

I held the recent X ray to the light. "Look, your tibia is thick with new bone where the fracture once was. Let me examine your leg."

When I had finished, Carl was shaking his head, "See, I told you it wasn't right."

"Wrong," I answered. "It tests fine. It's your confidence that isn't right. You don't trust your leg yet. That bone is now *stronger* than the other one. The problem isn't in the fractured tibia, it's in your head. You need to accept that your leg is healed and act accordingly. I'll give you some graded exercises to do, each one tougher than the last. Once you've progressed through them, you'll be able to trust that leg again." Carl left the office mumbling that he couldn't believe that his broken leg was now his stronger one.

For a few years after Ann's death, I still grumbled that the healing that had occurred in my life sure hadn't made me stronger either. How could I think that I was stronger when I still cried on days— her birthday, her wedding anniversary—that marked milestones of her life? Or driving past the school where she was valedictorian. Or remembering her galloping across a springtime pasture, her face alive with the joy of being one with her pony.

Was the process the same for me as it needed to be for Carl?

God's healing could make me strong, perhaps stronger than before that terrible day, if I trusted Him. I began testing myself by taking progressive steps to demonstrate just how strong that healing had become. I became more involved in church by rejoining the elder board. I read some of those books on grieving that I'd been afraid to tackle. And, finally, I even began to write again.

What will be next?

Master Physician, You promised to make us strong in our weakness (II Corinthians 12:10), and You are faithful.
—Scott Harrison

EDITOR'S NOTE: Dr. Harrison is now building a hospital for crippled children in Kenya, and still seeing the miracle of God's healing.

SUN

8

Seek ye first the kingdom of God, and his righteousness. . . .   —MATTHEW 6:33

In more than four decades of flying, the airlines have never lost one of my bags, though occasionally my luggage and I have arrived at different times.

Once, when Billy Graham was conducting a crusade in Manila, Philippines, I flew out to be a part of it. The plane was on time, but my bag was not on it. By the time I had filled out all the forms and had been assured by the airline that it "would be on the very next flight," I had to go directly to the meeting place to begin the conference.

When I presented Dr. Graham to the group, I breathed a prayer of thanksgiving that I had worn a jacket, slacks, shirt and tie for travel, rather than jeans and a knit shirt. My black cowboy boots didn't seem to bother anyone. What I didn't know was that this would be my wardrobe for the entire week. My bag never came. So each night after a long day, I washed my socks, underwear and shirt in the sink, and got a few hours sleep while they dried.

When I returned to the airport for the trip home, a happy airline agent announced to me, "Your bag just arrived!" I settled into my seat on the flight and had a good laugh about the whole experience.

Later, somewhere over the Pacific, a little voice inside me said, "Kenneth, you always carry too much stuff—in your suitcase and in your life." I knew that the voice was right, and I decided to do something about it. Some days I manage better than others, but trying to lighten up has been a wonderful adventure, whether I'm packing for a trip or deciding what to schedule for next year.

Dear God, help me to be more realistic about how I pack my suitcase and my life.   *—Kenneth Chafin*

MON	*Therefore all things whatsoever ye would that men*
9	*should do to you, do ye even so to them. . . .*

—MATTHEW 7:12

Not long ago, visiting a kindergarten where there were lots of small children, I was impressed by a mysterious disciplinary technique that the teacher used. Whenever squabbles arose, or a child became too pushy or aggressive, she would say gently to the offender, "Don't be a WAM!" and usually the disturbance stopped.

Finally, curiosity made me ask, "What's a WAM?"

"Initials that stand for the most self-centered phrase in the world," she said. " *'What about me?'* Almost every time there's a quarrel, it's because somebody wants something that someone else has, or some

priority on the swing or the sliding board. *'Me, me, me,'* they're saying. *'What about me?'* We try to make them see that they'll never get
a gold star that way. The gold stars we hand out at the end of the day
have initials on them, too."

"Let me guess," I said. "WAY?"

She laughed. "That's right," she said. "Go to the head of the class."

*Dear Lord, the world is Your kindergarten. Teach us to look
at others and ask, "What about you?"*   *—Arthur Gordon*

TUE
10
*When your words came, I ate them; they were my
joy and my heart's delight. . . .*
—JEREMIAH 15:16 (NIV)

Our fast-paced society emphasizes productivity and efficiency. But
in many other countries of the world, people and relationships still
take priority over everything else.

The Maasai people of East Africa, for example, have a charming
tradition called "eating the news." This standard greeting is expected
whenever friends meet; it's a leisurely, detailed exchange. It's common to see two old men leaning on their sticks, taking turns relating
information about their families, the weather and their animals (not
necessarily in that order).

On one particular afternoon when we were living in Tanzania, I was
rushing to complete some household tasks so I could hurry off to do
some errands before the market closed. Glancing out my window, I
saw a woman coming up the porch steps. I couldn't suppress an in-
ward *Oh, no, Lord, not now.* I struggled to set aside my own agenda
as I welcomed her into the house and prepared tea.

We had never met before, but I knew who she was. Our husbands
worked together, and I had been told she would be coming "someday" to welcome me to her country. Neema and her husband lived
up on the mountainside, about two hours' walk from our house.
They had many children and very little money.

Unwrapping her small bundle, Neema handed me a gift of maize
meal that she had grown and ground herself, and some fresh vegetables from her garden. For the next hour we drank tea and "ate the
news," using a lot of sign language and becoming comfortable with
long pauses.

By the time Neema left, my self-imposed schedule was in shreds, but I had made a new friend and learned an important lesson. As one of my African friends put it, "In America, everyone has a watch but no one has time. Over here, few of us have watches, but we all have time."

Help me, Lord Jesus, to have time today for the things that are truly important.   —*Mary Jane Clark*

WED

11
Therefore, since we are surrounded by such a great cloud of witnesses. . . .   —*HEBREWS 12:1 (NIV)*

One cold February day two years ago, my husband Bill and I drove to Leesburg, Virginia, to attend a funeral. As the minister, the stepson of our departed friend, reminded us that Jesus had said, "He who believes in me will live, even though he dies" (John 11:25, NIV), I had a strange experience. It was as if his mother, father and stepfather, all now dead, were there, just above and behind him, smiling on him and all of us with joy. I shook my head to clear it, but the sense of their presence remained for several minutes.

Later that day, taking the long way home, Bill and I swung through Western Maryland College to see our son David. After a brief visit, David hugged us good-bye and raced back into his dorm, disappearing up the stairs toward his fourth-floor room. Bill put the truck in gear and I stared out my side window as we moved slowly past the ivy-clad buildings.

Look up! The thought startled me. I often forget that the truck has a sun roof and I can do that. But the thought was so strong that I did look up, and there, high above me, David hung out of his dorm window, waving gleefully. Suddenly, the "cloud of witnesses" (Hebrews 12:1) around me became real—I just didn't have the faith to see them before. What I had sensed earlier that day, the happy presence of those we were remembering, was as real and true as seeing my son wave us off from high up in his college dorm.

Lord, thank You for those who live in Your presence now as witnesses of Your love.   —*Roberta Rogers*

12 *"But as for me and my household, we will serve the Lord."*   —*JOSHUA 24:15 (NIV)*

In my sideline work as a magazine photographer's stylist, I've learned a lot about people through the things they display in their homes. Take Barbara Burcham, for instance. From the outside, her Barboursville, West Virginia, bungalow, built in the 1940s, looks like every other house on Central Avenue. But step inside, and you take a trip back in time to the nineteenth century.

Barbara, a resourceful single parent, decorated with antiques that aren't just for show, but serve a real purpose: braided rugs, cozy quilts and old tinware she picked up for pocket change at early morning yard sales. Best of all, Barbara has filled her walls with framed pictures and quotations of Abraham Lincoln. One hanging over her fireplace reads: "I like to see a man proud of the place in which he lives. I like to see a man live so that his place will be proud of him."

When I asked Barbara what she admires most about Lincoln, she told me: "I like the way he lived his life—simply. He knew what was really important. He was a deeply spiritual man who had the courage of his convictions."

Today, as we celebrate Lincoln's birthday, it's good to remember the godly principles that directed our sixteenth president. It is said that Lincoln kept a Bible on his desk and consulted its pages for comfort and guidance. Yesterday and today, God's Word is an unsurpassed foundation for living.

Dear Lord, help me to put the Word that Lincoln lived by to work in my life.   —*Roberta Messner*

13 *How good and pleasant it is when brothers live together in unity!*   —*PSALM 133:1 (NIV)*

Like every set of brothers, our boys sometimes fight, and fight bitterly. Sibling rivalry boils over to the point that I begin to wonder if they love each other at all.

During a family ski vacation last spring, heavy snow drove us inside one afternoon and kept us off the roads that evening. Disappointment and close quarters sparked an argument that only ended when I threatened to confiscate driver's licenses and tell a few well-chosen stories to girlfriends.

The next morning a sullen mood prevailed as we rode the ski lift together to the top of the mountain. It didn't help that the boys' favorite run, a steep glade where turns twist between groves of trees, was closed because of broken branches on the trails. Looking at the damage done by the heavy snow, one of the boys noticed that the trees across the mountain were not affected. "Why is that, Dad?" he asked.

"Well, on this side, they cut down a lot of the trees to give the skiers room," I replied. "On the other side, the trees grow close together and have each other to lean on, so the snow doesn't break them."

"Oh no, I hear a sermon illustration in there, guys!" Nathan teased.

"Right, Nathan," I said. "Brothers who stay close can weather life's storms much better than brothers who push each other away with cutting comments and angry attitudes."

"Let's go before we get the whole sermon," Nathan exclaimed. And with that they headed down the mountain together.

Lord, let my sons grow leaning and not pushing, and let me follow their example.   —Eric Fellman

---

SAT
14

And now these three remain: faith, hope and love. But the greatest of these is love.
—I CORINTHIANS 13:13 (NIV)

I was sitting in my office on a mid-January day a few years back when Pastor Jones, the new youth pastor of our Mendenhall, Mississippi, church, came in to talk to me.

"Pastor Weary," he said, "Valentine's Day is coming up. For some people—the single, the widowed, those without somebody special in their lives—it can be a very depressing day. We have a lot of faithful people in our congregation who get left out, year after year. They could use some cheering up. I'd like to have the youth host an Agape Banquet this Valentine's Day, so we can share our love and appreciation for everyone, single or married, who helps in our church and ministry."

Valentine's Day has become such an important secular celebration that I'd been looking for a way for us to celebrate it as Christians. I was overjoyed to hear Pastor Jones' suggestion, and told him to go ahead.

Our youth group spent the next few weeks in furious activity. Cooks were recruited, music was arranged, invitations were sent out, and our church hall was decorated.

On the night of Valentine's Day, our young people greeted our guests at the door of the hall and escorted them to their tables. They seated them, making sure that everyone had friendly dinner companions, and lit the candles in the floral centerpieces. Dinner was accompanied by gospel music, with a few love songs added in honor of the day. After dinner, we asked people at each table to share their feelings for each other.

The Agape Banquet has a become an annual event at our church. It's a great way to expand our vision of love from the two-person model of romantic love to the all-encompassing love Christ shares with each of us.

Lord, help me today to understand love from Your perspective.   *—Dolphus Weary*

<table>
<tr><td>SUN
15</td><td>*And thou shalt rejoice in every good thing which the Lord thy God hath given unto thee. . . .*
                                        —DEUTERONOMY 26:11</td></tr>
</table>

Dave Sweeley, a Presbyterian pastor friend, dropped by my office one afternoon. "I'm arranging a going-away party for members of Ministerial Alliance who are leaving the community," he said. "It's short notice, and I'm a little concerned. Would you pray for the food?"

"Sure," I promised. And I did. The restaurant where the party was being held wasn't known for quality, so I prayed the food would be edible and that no one would get sick. I prayed that there would be a respectable crowd. I prayed for Christ's blessings on those who were moving.

My prayers were answered. There were at least twenty people present, the salad looked tasty, and the honorees were genuinely excited about their new opportunities for service. When we were ready to eat, Dave said, "I've asked Penney to give the blessing."

I was caught by surprise! "No, you didn't," I contradicted him, "but I'll do it anyway. Please bow your heads."

"I know I asked you pray for the food," Dave said right after Amen. "Last Wednesday, when I came to your office."

"I did pray for the food!" I answered. "I prayed every day! And twice on the weekend."

The room erupted with laughter. I looked around, still puzzled, when it finally dawned on me what Dave had meant. As I started to laugh at myself, I said a private prayer of thanksgiving for the privilege of praying before meals, whether we called it a blessing, giving thanks, grace or even praying for the food.

Thank You, Lord, for filling our mouths with food—and with laughter.   *—Penney Schwab*

Herald of Healing

He speaks; and, listening to His voice,
New life the dead receive,
The mournful broken hearts rejoice,
The humble poor believe.

Hear Him, ye deaf; His praise, ye dumb,
Your loosened tongues employ;
Ye blind, behold your Savior come;
And leap, ye lame, for joy!
                    —CHARLES WESLEY

MON

16 *He who pursues righteousness and kindness will find life and honor.*   *—PROVERBS 21:21 (RSV)*

My daughter's school welcomes parents' help, so this Presidents' Day I shared with her class some delightful stories I had discovered in an antique book of sermons for children.

When I asked the kids if they knew a nickname for President Lincoln, most said, "Honest Abe," but none knew that he was fondly called "the American Great-heart," a well-earned description. As a young lawyer, Abe once astonished his traveling companions by turning back, getting off his horse and putting a fallen bird back in its nest. One day, on his way to work, he stopped to carry a trunk for a little girl and helped her catch her train.

As president, his office door was open wide—to soldiers of any rank, to widows and children, to anyone needing his help. Once, in the middle of a crucial meeting, his young son Tad interrupted, and Lincoln astonished the officers with his patience. He took time to write sensitive condolence letters to grieving women who had lost husbands or sons in the war.

After reading the stories, we spilled out to the playground. It was a bleak, cold day. Lately I'd felt like a failure, falling short in all I attempted—whether homemaking, parenting or teaching. But as I watched the children running and kicking balls across the frozen ground, I found encouragement. Although each child had potential to achieve much, few, if any, would be "great" athletes or scholars or presidents. Yet they could each be "a great-heart."

I can't meet my unrealistic standards of perfection, but I *can* show kindness more often—write a note of encouragement or be patient with my children or notice someone needing help. Like Lincoln, I can be "greatly alert" for anyone needing kindness.

Father, fill my heart with love and compassion today.
                                                        —Mary Brown

TUE

17 *"I tell you the truth, I have not found anyone in Israel with such great faith."   —MATTHEW 8:10 (NIV)*

I woke up with a slight feeling of unease. What was wrong? Oh, yes, I remembered too quickly. Today, my three children were setting out on a canoe trip up the Napo river in the Amazon Basin to explore the rain forest. At 23, 21 and 20, it was a great adventure, the greatest adventure of their lives. They had saved and planned, chattering about piranha fishing, butterfly farms, monkeys, bug sprays, rubber boots and flashlights.

Now they were gone. And I was in New York City with absolutely no way of reaching them. *If only they had a cellular phone*, I thought, *or a fax machine.* A fax machine in the rain forest! That was pretty silly, even for an anxious mom. But I just wanted some proof that they were all right, that they were together, not lost or separated, or hacking their way through the steamy green jungle far from rescuers.

"Wait a minute," I said to myself. Words from Matthew 8:8 (NIV) I had read only a few days before came back to me: "Just say the word, and my servant will be healed," the worried Roman soldier said to Jesus, Who replied, "It will be done just as you believed it would." The centurion didn't ask Jesus to take time from His busy schedule to go to his house and heal the sick man. He didn't whip out his cellular phone to check if a miracle had indeed happened. He asked for no proof, only for Jesus' assurance that all would be well.

Where did that Roman Centurion two thousand years ago find such faith in an unknown teacher in what was for him a foreign land? I took a deep breath, looked myself in the eye and said aloud, "Jesus, please keep a close watch on the Amazon River basin today," got dressed and went to work. Honestly, my thoughts that day in quiet moments were only of adventure and learning, not of threats and danger.

The children (young persons, I should say) came back whole and I am now the proud owner of a very sinister-looking piranha skull.

Lord, help me to remember that faith in You is the best answer to anxiety.   —*Brigitte Weeks*

WED
18
And God said, "Let the waters bring forth swarms of living creatures, and let birds fly above the earth across the firmament of the heavens."
—*GENESIS 1:20 (RSV)*

"Judging by the wings He gave them," someone said, "God must have loved birds almost as much as angels."

I thought of that while I was visiting Ding Darling National Wildlife Refuge on Sanibel Island in Florida last year. With my wife Shirley, I spent the better part of a day exploring the refuge's six thousand acres of trails and wetlands. Ding Darling provides a haven for nearly three hundred species of birds, fifty types of reptiles and amphibians and thirty-some mammals. Of course, we saw only a small portion of its offerings, which is why I intend to return again.

But what we did see was memorable—plovers, willets, dowitchers, curlews, dunlins, anhingas and more. In one slough, dozens of roseate spoonbills waded among the mangroves. I'd never seen the flamingo-colored birds with the flanged bills before, so I watched them through binoculars for half an hour.

We found the biggest congregation of wading birds in a shallow bay where they were busy feeding on the black silt, rich in sea creatures. I could identify most of them with the aid of my bird book, but I wasn't sure about one black-and-white specimen that was out of range of my binoculars.

"Is that a stilt or an oystercatcher?" I asked a white-haired man nearby with a more powerful spotting scope.

"See for yourself," he said, offering his lens. "The bird you're look-ing at is a black-necked stilt. It has a white eye patch, black bill, longer legs and is more sleek than an oystercatcher, which has a yellow eye-ring and a red-orange bill."

"You know your birds right down to the last tailfeather," I said ad-miringly, adding, "God is in the details of birds, too."

"God is in the details of everything," he responded.

It was the perfect benediction to a perfect day.

> *Thank You, God, for giving us birds,*
> *Beauty that mutes redundant words.*
>   —*Fred Bauer*

THU
19

The word of God is living and active . . . it judges the thoughts and attitudes of the heart.
                                       —*HEBREWS 4:12 (NIV)*

I had taken a job with the Association of Christian Schools Interna-tional to help write Bible curriculum that would be used in their schools worldwide. And it was turning out to be even harder than I expected! How could we take the Word of God and turn it into work-book pages and class activities?

I wasn't the only one feeling dwarfed by the project. Finally, at one of our devotional sessions, I asked our director Sharon how we could accomplish this. "How," I asked her, "can we defend the Bible in such a simplistic format?"

Sharon laughed and pointed to her open Bible lying on her lap.

"The Word of God is like a lion. You don't have to defend it; you just have to let it out of its cage!"

I've long since finished my part in that curriculum writing, but I've never forgotten Sharon's advice. How can I "let the lion out" in my daily life? Well, I'm writing Scripture verses on all the cards and thank-you notes I send. I often quote an appropriate verse in conversation, even to non-Christian friends. I'm even considering including a tract in the bills I pay or buying checks with preprinted verses. After all, you never know what might happen with such power on the prowl!

Thank You, Lord, for Your mighty Word. Make us bold—and creative—in sharing it.   —*Mary Lou Carney*

FRI

20 *Making the most of the time, because the days are evil.*   —EPHESIANS 5:16 (RSV)

As part of the hectic swarm of office workers making their way down Madison Avenue every morning, I pass a little flower shop on the west side of the street. In the window there usually lounges a big, fat, fluffy, indolent-looking cat colored like agate. There are days when I've wanted to shake this smug creature by the scruff of his neck and tell him to make himself useful.

One particular Friday recently, when I was feeling harried and behind, as if the week had skidded by without my getting anything useful done, I found myself stopping to glare through the window at this puffy loafer. There he was, flat on his back in a pool of appropriated sunlight, legs splayed, a furry mockery of the work ethic. "You good for nothing . . ." I started to mutter when an elderly woman, immaculately dressed, appeared at my side. "Yes, isn't he wonderful?" she said. "I love to watch him enjoy his rest after a night of chasing mice."

"He doesn't look as if he's chased a mouse in his life," I snorted.

"On the contrary," she shot back. "I know the owners of this shop. They had a terrible problem with mice until they got Clancy. He saved their necks!"

I continued on my way down Madison, but slowly, giving some thought to what she'd said. I'd been hasty about the big cat, letting my own aggravations color my perceptions. How often did I do that with other people, friends and colleagues, even strangers? After all, as the woman pointed out, God has given all of us a job to do, even Clancy. I should remember that.

Help me keep your world in perspective, Lord, and take a well-earned breather every once in a while, like Clancy.
—*Edward Grinnan*

SAT
21

"You strain a fly out of your drink, but swallow a camel!" —*MATTHEW 23:24 (GNB)*

Hank seemed to bring my critical nature to full bloom. He headed a charity where I did volunteer work, and Hank's chronic disorganization drove me crazy. One day when he again failed to return my call, I decided the best thing to do was to quit.

That Saturday I found an ornate, antique mirror at a garage sale. Over the years the mirror silver had deteriorated, leaving the reflection hazy and badly streaked. I decided to have a new mirror cut to fit the vintage frame. When I unwrapped the new mirror, I was disappointed to find that it wasn't flawless. My eye kept returning to an eighth-of-an inch scratch on the silver and a tiny crater in the glass about the size of a pin head. "This will never do," I decided. I rewrapped the new mirror and promptly returned it.

While I stood awaiting my refund at the glass shop, a worker carried the mirror back to the workshop. Suddenly, I heard a loud crash, followed by the tinkling sound of shattering glass. "How awful!" I said to the clerk. "It sounds like they had an accident back there."

"Oh, no," she answered, "that's what we do with all returned pieces."

"Oh," I said meekly. I suddenly recalled the three feet of perfectly serviceable mirror, not the minute scratches. *If I'd known they were going to smash the whole thing, I wouldn't have been so picky,* I thought. *Would I want to be treated that way for some small fault?*

When I got home, I called Hank. Not returning phone calls wasn't such a big deal after all. Certainly not enough to shatter a friendship.

Father, please keep me from turning minor irritations into major forces of destruction. —*Karen Barber*

22 *"Select capable men from all the people—men who fear God, trustworthy men who hate dishonest gain—and appoint them as officials. . . ."*
—EXODUS 18:21 (NIV)

Some years ago, before the fall of the Soviet Union, a friend of mine invited me to attend a weekend celebration in honor of St. Vladimir, the prince of Kiev who is regarded as the apostle of Russia. The weekend's activities included church services on Saturday evening and Sunday morning, a dinner on Saturday night, and a Sunday luncheon.

Most of the people at the celebration were Russian-American immigrants and their children and grandchildren. Many of the older men wore medals they had earned in the brutal civil war that followed the Bolshevik Revolution. The ushers at church wore Cossack uniforms, cartridge belts crossed over their chests. The services were sung in Old Slavonic, a precursor of modern Russian, with fervor and devotion, tinged with sadness for the suffering of Mother Russia and for a way of life that was passing away.

At the luncheon after the Sunday service, a short man with a long white beard came over to where I was standing. He looked up at me, smiled, and said something in Russian. I smiled back and shook my head no. His smile broadened. "You American?" he asked.

"Yes," I answered.

Grinning now from ear to ear, he took my hand and shook it vigorously. "America!" he exclaimed. "George Washington! George Washington!"

Although we lacked the linguistic skills to take our conversation further, I think I knew exactly what he meant. In the stern visage that peers up at us from the dollar bill and down from the portraits in our public buildings, he saw more than cold rectitude and a powdered wig: He saw the founding father of a country where you don't have to storm the Winter Palace to change the government; where victorious generals put down their swords and go home instead of turning their troops on the capitol; where leaders leave office with a handshake and a parade instead of a show trial and a firing squad. He saw the man who, more than any other, showed us how to be free.

Lord, as I remember George Washington, help me to use my freedom for the common good.   —Andrew Attaway

23
O bring thou me out of my distresses.
                                        —*PSALM 25:17*

I had just finished my rookie month as a financial consultant. It had been an incredible success. I felt positive about every meeting I had had with my new customers and closed almost ninety-five percent of my sales.

But in the first week of my second month, my business dropped like a ton of bricks. I made virtually no sales. My mentor from church, Sam Oakley, had told me to expect business to fluctuate quite a bit, but I had arrogantly dismissed his advice, thinking I was an exception. Believe me, I was not. To top it all off, one of my most recent customers had made a very conservative investment and then decided she wanted to back out.

How quickly misery had swallowed up my optimism! That night I went to my parents' house for dinner. I was determined not to tell about my recent troubles, but thirty seconds after I stepped through the door, I started my complaints. "I'm a flop," I whined. "A one-hit wonder. My business is at a virtual standstill, and I think I'm gonna get the boot."

My father laughed warmly. "C'mon, Brock," he said, "don't be silly. You're always saying yourself how cyclical the investment business is."

I continued my complaining, and Mom and Dad continued their comforting. Halfway through dinner, I was feeling better. "I'm sorry I came over here with such a negative attitude," I said when it was time to leave. "I didn't mean to dump all of my problems on you. But I have to admit, I feel a whole lot better than I did three hours ago, and it's not just because the food was so good. It's having someone to listen and care that did the trick."

"Brock, I'm glad you were honest with us," Dad answered. "It would be awfully disappointing to learn you had problems and hadn't shared them."

Driving back to my apartment, I realized that talking to people who loved me had driven the blue funks away. "That's how my relationship with God should be," I said out loud, and then I prayed:

God, I know You want me to talk to You about my worries and concerns. I know You're always waiting, ready to listen and offer Your comfort. Does it hurt You when I forget? Could You help me remember?   —*Brock Kidd*

TUE

24 *Do ye look on things after the outward appearance?...* —*II CORINTHIANS 10:7*

Our committee spent months preparing an evening at our library in observance of Black History Month. Life-size photographs were borrowed from the Boston Public Library. We had received unexpected funding, and we invited an expert on W.E.B. Du Bois, educator and author. Dr. Du Bois had been the first African American to earn a Ph.D. from Harvard University. I had never met the speaker, but I'd formed a mental picture of him.

When that February evening came, I waited at the library door to greet the speaker. While I was waiting, I noticed a stranger studying the photographs. Just before program time, the librarian rushed up and said, "Oscar, the speaker is waiting for you!" I blinked. How could I have missed him? I'd seen everyone who'd entered.

I hurried into the hall, where I was introduced to the stranger I had seen studying the photographs. I was shocked! I'd expected the speaker to be black, and he wasn't. I'd made assumptions based on stereotypes, a trait I disliked in others. But another jolt awaited me: Only eight people attended the lecture.

The speaker appeared not to notice as he held us spellbound for two hours. He had known and loved Dr. Du Bois. After the lecture, I apologized for not greeting him at the door and for the disappointing attendance. He smiled and said, "You prepared, you invited others, and you were here. What more could you do?"

Well, for starters I could try harder not to jump to conclusions about people based on prejudgments or superficial observations. And I could remember that it's the quality of the listening, not the number of listeners, that makes a successful lecture.

Lord, today let me try harder not to be deceived by appearances. —*Oscar Greene*

WED

25 *To whom also he showed himself alive after his passion by many infallible proofs, being seen of them forty days....* —*ACTS 1:3*

Nine of us were gathered in bleary-eyed silence. A bell rang. The priest entered. The winter sun rose just in time to cast a weak gray

light into the small chapel. I'd started going to church regularly following a ten-year absence, and this was the first Ash Wednesday service I'd ever attended. I wasn't quite sure what to expect.

After a sobering description of how the first Christians prepared
themselves for celebrating the passion and resurrection of Christ, we
were asked to do the same. Self-examination . . . repentance . . . prayer
. . . fasting . . . self-denial . . . all were to be combined with reading
and meditating on God's Word.

Do people actually do all this? I wondered. I barely knew any practicing Christians, much less anyone who approached their faith with
rigor.

Then we knelt to receive ashes made by burning the fronds from
Palm Sunday the year before. I happened to be first in line, and so
the priest's words hit me like a blow, "Remember that thou art dust,
and to dust thou shalt return." With his thumb he traced a cross on
my forehead, and moved on. I staggered back to my seat, stunned by
the gritty truth of what he'd said. And yet God loved me enough to
die for me.

On the way to work, I was quiet and thoughtful. The busy world
went on as noisy and unruly as usual. I was momentarily distracted
from my meditations by the odd sight of a businessman striding toward me with a dirty face. I shook my head in amusement. A moment later I saw a woman with a briefcase—and a splotch on her
head. And a delivery boy with a dark spot high over his nose. *What's
going on?* I wondered.

My heart leaped as I figured out the answer. Ashes. All around me,
everywhere I looked, there were people with ashes on their fore-
heads. Yes, people did take their faith seriously. On this one day of
the year, it was obvious that New York City was filled with Christians,
many of whom wore a mark of humility on their brows.

*Father, help me as I set aside these next forty days to pre-
pare for Your son's death and resurrection.*   —*Julia Attaway*

THU

26   *Bear one another's burdens, and so fulfil the law of
Christ.*   —*GALATIANS 6:2 (RSV)*

When I underwent surgery in 1964, friends were wonderfully helpful—chauffeuring the kids, running errands, preparing meals. But it

was a co-worker at Guideposts, Jacquie Lake, who speeded my healing in another way.

"I know you're anxious about your work," she told me over the phone. "But you have enough on your mind. I'll take over worrying about your assignments."

Is this possible? I wondered. *Can one person take on the worries of another?* But sure enough, in the weeks following surgery, every time I looked at a desk piled with unfinished projects, I'd think, *Jacquie's fretting about those. I don't need to.*

It worked so well for me that I've used it ever since as a form of intercession: taking on a specific area of concern for someone else. Just recently a friend, let go by the company where he's worked for sixteen years, confided to my husband John and me the anxieties that were keeping him awake at night. We couldn't solve his career problems, but we could help him get the sleep he needed to solve them himself.

"Let us take on the night-terrors," we said. John chose the loss of the family's health insurance, while I focused on the fear that money set aside for his daughters' college educations would be spent meeting bills. At bedtime and in wakeful moments throughout the night, we let our minds dwell for a while on these situations, then turn them over to Jesus.

Jim hasn't found a new job yet, but his mood is different. "I'm sleeping like a two-year-old," he told us last week. "I tell those anxious thoughts, 'That's being handled elsewhere.' "

Remind me, Father, each time I see a need today: When I pick up another's burden, Your hand lifts it with me.
                                                              —*Elizabeth Sherrill*

FRI

27 *Happy is the man that findeth wisdom, and the man that getteth understanding.*   —*PROVERBS 3:13*

The first time it happened I thought it was a fluke. I got on a crosstown bus at Seventy-ninth Street and was angling to the back when a pleasant-looking woman smiled, stood up and said, "Please, sit here." I turned around, looking for the person she was giving her seat to. To my amazement, she meant me.

"Oh, thank you, no," I blurted clumsily in embarrassment. In the next several weeks, the same thing occurred three more times: one boy on the subway and two women on buses. I declined all their offers.

"You shouldn't have done that," advised my friend Joe. "You robbed them of a chance to do good. Probably made their day a little darker."

I thought about that and decided I just couldn't refuse if it ever happened again, but to myself I said, *Do I look old? Or was it because of last year's stroke? Or was it both?* After all, I was only seventy-three. I say "only" because nowadays that's nothing. Why, a lot of my friends are in their eighties and nineties and look upon me as their junior. As for the stroke, it principally related to difficulty with speech. Besides, I didn't *feel* old.

But suppose the women and the boy were correct, that I *was* old. It was a shocking moment. At first I tried to ignore its implications, but slowly I came to accept that they had been giving me a little advance warning of what was to come. That I didn't feel old was immaterial. Should the pleasant looking woman offer a seat again, I will accept gallantly. The trouble is, since I've come to appreciate age, no one has offered.

Oh, Father, I always have something to learn. If that is one way to keep me young in spirit, I thank You. —*Van Varner*

SAT
28
Now learn a parable of the fig tree; When his branch is yet tender, and putteth forth leaves, ye know that summer is nigh. —*MATTHEW 24:32*

When I was sixteen, my father bought a new luxury car. I begged him to let me take it out for a spin. He agreed, and the whole family came along. And what did I do? I promptly backed down the driveway into an old maple tree. What a jolt. Everyone jumped out to inspect the damage. I was mortified. I couldn't stop crying. I was sure I'd never drive again.

My father, rubbing the bump on his head where it had collided with the dashboard, helped me out of the car and put his arm around me. "Everybody makes mistakes," he said. "But the wise person learns from his mistakes. There's a lot to feel positive about here. We're not hurt. The car is still drivable. We can fix the bumper. And the dent in the tree will remind us to be more careful next time. Let's just say this maple is our family's training tree."

Once I knew my father had forgiven me, I forgave myself. Forgiveness healed my wounded pride. In the same way, God's forgiveness heals me when I've hurt someone's feelings or forgotten to do something I promised. My heavenly Father gives me the confidence I need to start over. God knows I'm in training, and next time I'll try to do better.

Lord, help me to remember I can always try again.
—*Susan Schefflein*

My Healing Journey

1 _____

2 _____

3 _____

4 _____

5 _____

6 _____

7 _____

8 _____

9 _____

10 _____

11 _____

12 _____

13 _____

14 _____

15 _____

16 _____

17 _____

18 _____

19 _____

20 _____

21 _____

22 _____

23 _____

24 _____

25 _____

26 _____

27 _____

28 _____

MARCH

S	M	T	W	T	F	S
1	2	3	4	5	6	7
8	9	10	11	12	13	14
15	16	17	18	19	20	21
22	23	24	25	26	27	28
29	30	31				

And he showed me a pure river of water of life, clear as crystal, proceeding out of the throne of God and of the Lamb. . . . on either side of the river, was there the tree of life . . . and the leaves of the tree were for the healing of the nations.

—REVELATION 22:1-2

SUN

1

THE TOUCH OF THE HEALER
Healing Our Minds
This kind can come forth by nothing, but by prayer and fasting. —MARK 9:29

My good friend Beth is a psychiatrist. She is well-educated and extremely bright, but she remains down-to-earth. In fact, as a member of our church's "Prayer Can Change Your Life" class, she's tops at making a thoughtful phone call or writing a timely note to another class member.

There's one more thing about my friend that I'd like to tell you: Beth had a major mental illness a few years ago.

"People who are mentally ill suffer so much," she said. "Depression is terribly painful, and when you're there, you just can't see a way out."

Beth explained that twenty-five percent of us will experience a biochemical change in the brain sometime in our lives that may be diagnosed as mental illness. "As new medications are introduced that can correct these chemical imbalances, people need to recognize that mental illness has a physical basis, like cancer or heart disease. People who are mentally ill or who have friends or family members who are experiencing this illness need to know that there is hope for recovery. They need to know they're not alone."

There's one more thing about mental illness that Beth stressed. It has to do with prayer: "It's almost unbelievable to think that four years ago when I was hospitalized in New York and not yet a Christian, this church in Nashville, Tennessee, was praying for my healing. Today, here I am, a Christian and a member of this church, praying for others.

"Mental illness taught me that I can get *really* ill relying on myself. Acknowledging God as a power higher than myself was all-important in my recovery. There's no doubt that God had a hand in the medication and the psychotherapy that helped me recover. But beyond such treatment, I have come to realize that prayer is where all healing begins—healing of the mind, the body, the spirit or the heart."

Father, teach us to pray for Your all-encompassing healing.
Make us truly well. —Pam Kidd

2   *His flesh upon him shall have pain. . . .   —JOB 14:22*

One morning when I was about eight, my mother and I were sitting at the breakfast table. I was not in school that day because my friend Jimmy had thrown a pampas grass spear at me during a mock battle and had struck me between my right eye and right eyebrow—miraculously missing putting out my eye, which was now almost swollen shut and hurting like crazy.

"Why would God invent something as awful as pain?" I wondered, wishing mine would go away.

Mother raised her eyebrows and looked out the window behind me a few seconds. Then she said, "Well, feelings like pain are God's way of sending helpful, even life-saving, messages to us about dangerous or harmful things we're doing that we might not notice until it was too late."

I scrunched up my face and asked, "What do you mean?"

She continued, "You might say that pain is like a fire alarm system God's given us to help us pinpoint the exact place where our personal 'fires,' our injuries or sicknesses, are. And if we don't pay attention, the pain usually gets 'louder' until we do. So pain can be a life-saving friend. And God uses all kinds of pain to teach us to change our lives, if we pay attention."

"You mean like my deciding not to play spear-fighting chieftains anymore?"

She smiled and nodded her head.

Thank You, Lord, for using my pain to call me to You.
—Keith Miller

3   *To every thing there is a season. . . .*
—ECCLESIASTES 3:1

On this oppressive winter day, I dragged about the house carrying the weight of the lead sky. I had so much to do—church work, paperwork, housework—it felt like I'd never come out from under. The phone rang. It was my friend Penny. "Kathleen and I are going to Oram's Diner for lunch. We want you to come."

I heaved a dutiful sigh. "I wish I could. But I have so much to do."
I hung up, took two aspirin and turned to the desk full of paperwork.
Outside, thick, wet flakes of snow began falling, sticking to the window like lacy invitations. *Come out and play*, they seemed to say. I pictured my friends in our favorite diner. I *was* hungry. And my headache was getting worse.

Ten minutes later, I was in my car, heading to Oram's Diner, windshield wipers slapping, slush hitting the fender, guilt weighing me down. As I pulled into the parking lot, I could see my friends through the window. They were laughing. "Hey, look who's here! The busy one," they chuckled as I sidled into their snug booth.

Penny said, "I was just telling Kathleen about the time . . ." I leaned in to listen to my friend whose bubbling laughter cannot be resisted. We ordered colas and steaming bowls of clam chowder, and shared funny stories till the tears ran down our cheeks. My headache was gone.

Two hours later, I walked into my house to the same pile of work. Yet it looked different—not as high or foreboding. Perhaps because I was seeing it through a fun-washed spirit that had scrubbed duty down to manageable size.

Lord, when I'm overwhelmed, help me to slough off guilt, give in to playtime and go back to work refreshed.
                                                              —*Shari Smyth*

<u>WED</u>

4

. . . A great multitude that no one could count, from every nation, tribe, people and language, standing before the throne and in front of the Lamb."
—*REVELATION 7:9 (NIV)*

As a teacher, I prize those occasions when students are struck simultaneously by an encompassing insight. I call these "agape moments," earthly manifestations of that divine love that enlightens and binds humankind.

Yet at the huge, New York suburban community college where I teach, agape moments are rare. With students of diverse colors, cultures, ages, nationalities and backgrounds careening together, encounters on campus and in classrooms can be divisive, even explosive.

Or so I thought until I went to the first annual Club Day at the

Campus Center and discovered hundreds of students happily tearing down the walls of custom and decorum out of a shared passion
for learning. Young women from the African Culture Club were
teaching a Ghanaian folk dance to passersby. The Irish Club was
handing out pieces of savory soda bread to a knot of curious fresh-
men. The Honor Society was corralling volunteers for an impromptu
performance of Walt Whitman's "I Hear America Singing."

That day, I learned to say "I love you" in Tagalog, hummed along
to a catchy tune from South India, added my voice to a choral reading of Martin Luther King, Jr.'s "Letter from a Birmingham Jail." We
were many and one. And growing beautifully together.

In Christ there is no East or West, in Him no South nor
North; But one great fellowship of love throughout the whole
wide earth.   —Linda Ching Sledge

THU

5   *The Lord is in his holy temple: let all the earth keep*
         silence before him.   —HABAKKUK 2:20

There are days when I open my Bible to read and fall into the middle of a desert. This morning I was standing outside the walls of
Jerusalem with the fiery prophet Jeremiah, lambasting the callous
high priest. The biblical scene, set in an ancient world six hundred
years before the birth of Christ, seemed foreign and irrelevant to my
life and needs. I nearly stopped reading. I did not want to stroll
through the arid dust of history.

When I finished my Bible reading and began to write in my journal, I found these words flowing across the page: "Sometimes I read
the Bible and there is nothing there. Only silence. Yet, even in that
still silence I am strengthened; I am drawn to a holy presence. It's
like two good friends who sit quietly alone, content in each other's
company."

God is such a friend. He is often silent. He does not speak at my
demand. But as I grow older, I find I need less of His voice and more
of His presence. Just to know that He is with me is enough. Perhaps
that's why the ancient Psalmist wrote in his journal, "Be still and
know that I am God" (Psalm 46:10).

Dear Father, may I be still with You today.   —Scott Walker

FRI

6
Make love your aim. . . . —I CORINTHIANS 14:1 (RSV)

Growing up, I envied large families because they all seemed to look out for each other. But, I used to tell myself, by coming from a small family I was learning some lessons in self-sufficiency.

Recently, though, I discovered that self-sufficiency isn't enough. I needed surgery on my right hand, which meant I wouldn't be able to use it for several weeks. If I couldn't drive, how would I get to my physical therapy sessions? How would I shop for our food? Who would look after my stepfather and my animals the night I was in the hospital? Oh, if only I could turn to a big family for help!

It turns out that I have a big family after all. When word of my predicament got around, many hands reached out to me. A church-supported community organization referred me to a retiree named Harold Hieter, who volunteered to drive me to the hospital and my physical therapy sessions. My neighbors the Johnsons brought my dad and me wonderful meals and kept our walks shoveled during the worst winter in local history. Another neighbor, Mel Haas, took me along to the supermarket when he did his family's shopping. A delightful and competent woman, Gladys Smith, took such good care of my stepfather and my animals while I was in the hospital that they hardly realized I was away. And a dear friend, Joyce Hardigg, saw that I needed a trip to the hairdresser and found time in her busy schedule to make it happen.

It doesn't matter whether we come from a big family or a small one. As long as we're willing to give some of our time, our attention and our care when one of us is in need, we can make each other feel like family.

Lord Jesus, help me to find opportunities to help my brothers and sisters in You. Amen.   —*Phyllis Hobe*

SAT

7
And David said with longing, "Oh, that someone would give me a drink of water from the well of Bethlehem. . . ."   —I CHRONICLES 11:17 (NKJV)

At a low time in his life, King David longed for the familiar sweet water he remembered from his boyhood in Bethlehem. I understand that feeling, only it's pizza I long for, the kind we made on Saturdays when our two girls were still young.

At four o'clock Saturday, the four of us converged on the kitchen. I kneaded the spongy dough onto pebbled steel pans, because it took strong hands. My wife Sharon mixed sweet tomato paste, olive oil and herbs in a chrome bowl. Older daughter Teresa grated a chunk of white cheese into a pie pan, then sliced pepperoni with a serrated knife. Natalie chopped onions, green and black olives, and fresh mushrooms.

As we worked, we laughed at each other's nutty jokes and nibbled on stolen pieces of cheese or olives. Each of us custom-designed his or her own slices. Finished, I slid the heavy pans into a heated oven. The long wait was so hard because the entire house tingled with the pungent fragrance of dough and cheese. At last, the buzzer went off, and the girls sat impatiently at the table while I sliced the pizzas.

Oh, that I could have a slice of that pizza right now! Everything about the pizza was ours, from the recipe to the toppings and even the corny jokes we told.

It's a recipe for life, really. The more of me I invest, the more I participate, the more the flavor in my life.

When life is flat and tasteless, Lord, show me how to enhance the taste by putting more of my heart into it.
                                                    —Daniel Schantz

---

SUN

8   *For do I now persuade men, or God? . . .*
                                    —GALATIANS 1:10

After I became a Christian and started to attend a prayer group, I discovered that I had a small problem. I'm hearing impaired, and I depend on lip-reading for communication. If I closed my eyes and bowed my head as everyone else did during the prayers, I wouldn't know who or what was being prayed for. Yet, if I kept my eyes open, I feared that someone watching me might think I wasn't sincere in my prayers.

One day I suggested to a friend that perhaps I should drop out of the group. "Why?" she asked. I told her.

"That's rather self-centered of you, isn't it?" she answered. "Everyone in the group knows you lip-read. We understand your problem.

And, after all, when we pray we are concentrating on God, not on you."

For a moment my friend's blunt honesty shocked me. Then I saw how right she was. So ever since, in any prayer group, I keep my eyes open to watch the person who is praying. I get a lot more out of it this way. And I am able to put much more into it.

No one is watching *me*. Just God.

Lord, hear my prayer.

—Eleanor Sass

MON
9 *Have mercy upon me, O Lord; for I am weak. . . .*
—PSALM 6:2

I hauled Elizabeth down the stairs so we could go to my three-month obstetrical checkup. Some women get diabetes when they are pregnant; oddly enough, I get asthma. It was bitterly cold, and I was having trouble breathing.

Halfway down the block, as I began to gasp for air, I realized I wasn't going to make it to the subway, much less to the doctor's office. I couldn't speak. Could I even walk back to the house? I wasn't sure.

Elizabeth began to cry. Not thinking, I unbuckled and lifted her out of the stroller. Immediately, I put her down. Her weight against my chest was suffocating. She cried harder, with real distress. I didn't know what to do. I couldn't lift her, and I couldn't breathe well enough to push the stroller home. I couldn't even console her with words. And I began to panic. I'd never had an asthma attack this severe before.

I sat down on the icy sidewalk. The street was bereft of Good Samaritans, since they were all sensibly snug at home. *Oh, Lord, please help me.* Elizabeth slid out of her stroller and curled up in my lap. Together we cried in the freezing cold, rocking back and forth, mingling tears and heaving gasps of steamy breath. Over and over I mentally cried, *Jesus, help us. Jesus, help us*, until we both calmed down. Then somehow we made our way home.

When I could, I spoke with an asthma specialist by phone. He prescribed various medications, which would do far less harm to the baby than oxygen deprivation. That night as I gave thanks for the simple but profound gift of air, I learned more about my need for God.

I cannot see or touch or hold God, or air, but without either one neither I nor my baby can live.

Father, You blew Your own spirit into the nostrils of man to give him life. Do not let me forget that each breath I take is a gift of Your love.   —*Julia Attaway*

TUE
10
Search the scriptures; for in them ye think ye have eternal life: and they are they which testify of me.
—*JOHN 5:39*

The Bible speaks to me through the guidance it gives about personal problems. I have found it truly "the Book of the solved problem."

It is my habit to search the Scriptures for answers and insights when I need to solve a problem. If I come to a passage that seems to be germane, I write my problem on a piece of paper and put it at that particular place in the Bible. Sometimes I have had as many as a half-dozen problems in my Bible at the same time.

Then, every day, I hold the Bible in hand and ask the Lord to guide me. And the heavenly Father always answers that prayer—not necessarily quickly, nor for all the problems at the same time, but always ultimately and surely. As I gradually remove each slip from the Bible, how amazing, how wonderful it is to find the number of problems that have been solved. Today I have a large file marked "Answered Prayers." That file is proof that the Bible has really spoken to me.

O Lord, thank You for Your guidance and answer to prayers.
—*Ruth Stafford Peale*

WED
11
Be kindly affectioned one to another. . . .
—*ROMANS 12:10*

Recently, when I was at my daughter's house, she and I had some ruffled feelings to deal with. I had work deadlines to meet, so I needed to set some boundaries on the amount of time I spent babysitting my granddaughter Saralisa. Karen responded with hurt feelings and then with anger, and I countered with the same.

Right in the midst of all this, her pet hedgehog Mickey got out of his box and went scooting across the floor and behind the bookcase. "Oh, no," said my daughter, "when he gets back there, I have a *terrible* time getting him out! He gets scared, bristles out and then he's stuck! If only he'd relax, those spiny quills would smooth out and he could easily scoot on through."

After we'd moved the bookcase out and Mickey was safely back in his box, Karen started to laugh. "Know what, Mom? You and I've been acting like a couple of hedgehogs ourselves! We get upset, bristle out and then we're stuck behind our own defenses."

I thought about it a bit and then saw what great truth there was in it. "That's exactly what we've been doing," I said. "Mickey's a pretty good teacher for us!" As we laughed together, we relaxed and were really able to listen to each other, so we ended up with a good solution we both thought was fair.

I hope the next time I feel threatened in a disagreement, I'll remember the lesson of the hedgehog: *Bristling gets you nowhere but stuck!*

Heavenly Father, You know my tender spots, the ones that make me bristle. Please help me to override them by relaxing and then truly listening. —Marilyn Morgan Helleberg

---

THU

12 *Be devoted to one another in brotherly love. Honor one another above yourselves.* —ROMANS 12:10 (NIV)

Long before he became a U.S. senator from New Jersey, Bill Bradley distinguished himself on the basketball court. In high school, he led his team to a state championship in Missouri. In college, at Princeton, he starred on a team that made it to the finals of the NCAA tournament. And as a professional, he played on a team, the New York Knicks, that twice won the NBA championship. The common denominator of all those experiences, he would say, was the word *team*.

I'll never forget a conversation I had with him many years ago during his all-American days at Princeton. Though I tried to get him to talk about his own accomplishments, he preferred to focus on the sense of fulfillment he got from a good team effort. "I get more satisfaction passing the ball to a teammate who scores a basket," he admitted in a character-revealing statement, "than I do in scoring one myself."

It is indeed amazing what can be accomplished when no one cares who gets the credit. Next time I'm tempted to take a bow for something that others at home, at church or on the job have shared in, I hope I can remember that.

Teach me, God, when telling my story,
To spread the credit and share the glory.
                                                —*Fred Bauer*

FRI

13

The snare is broken, and we have escaped!
                                —*PSALM 124:7 (RSV)*

My husband's grandmother and mother had each died when their fourth, and youngest, child was twelve years of age. Thinking about unlucky sequences of three, I became convinced as a young mother—also of four—that I was next in line. I honestly did not believe I would outlive my youngest daughter's twelfth year.

Then, one morning before school, the children began questioning me about death. I immediately opened my Bible to Psalm 139 (RSV) and showed them verse 16: "Thy eyes beheld my unformed substance; in thy book were written, every one of them, the days that were formed for me." God, as our maker, I told them, has the exclusive right to say when our days will end. They trotted off to school satisfied with my answer, and I sat down to reread the verse I had just quoted.

Suddenly, the foolishness of my superstitions fell away. It didn't matter about sets of three, black cats, broken mirrors or what had gone before. My days were established before my life began, written with a divine finger and held firmly in God's grasp. They *predated* my superstitious beliefs! A dark weight seemed to lift from the edges of my consciousness.

Then I began to laugh heartily. Never have I appreciated the Lord's supreme sense of humor in quite the way I did that day. For I had just realized the date: Friday, January 13, 1984.

Father God, You break the chains of all superstition. Heal me
of my hidden torments and set me free.   —*Carol Knapp*

The words of a wise man's mouth are gracious. . . .
—*ECCLESIASTES 10:12*

"Only two days till my birthday!" I announced to Mom as I came into the kitchen.

But she had other things on her mind. "Brock," she said, "I heard you teasing Keri just now about her mussed-up hair. You could have made her happy by using kind words. Don't you know that kind words are presents that you can give people whenever you want?"

Presents! Just what I was thinking about—but I was a lot more interested in receiving than giving. The next forty-eight hours seemed an eternity. But finally my seventh birthday came. My grandfather and grandmother drove down from Chattanooga to Nashville to celebrate the day with us. And they brought gifts. The largest was wrapped in red, white and blue paper. It was a bank, shaped like Uncle Sam, that would grab a coin when you pulled a lever on its back. I thought it was one of the most marvelous things that I had ever seen. I played with it for hours.

As the day went on, I began looking forward to dinner. Every year on my birthday, we invited some of my older friends from church over for dinner. It was a great opportunity to share a special day with our extended family, but more important to me, it was a chance for more presents. Especially from Mai Davis, a retired teacher and my first baby-sitter, whose gifts to me had become legendary. So what would it be this year? A magic set, Lincoln logs, sea monkeys? As I ran a penny through Uncle Sam for the hundredth time, the anticipation was unbearable.

Dinner seemed endless. But at last the birthday songs were sung, the candles were blown out, and cake and ice cream were served. Finally, it was time. I grabbed the box Mai had brought me and eagerly ripped away the wrapping.

Oh, no! I thought to myself. *This can't be!* It was a second Uncle Sam bank!

My first reaction was to tell Mai that she had made a terrible mistake. But when I opened my mouth to speak, I suddenly remembered what Mom had said: "Kind words are presents."

"Thank you, Mai," I said with the biggest smile a depressed seven-year-old could possibly muster. "I've always wanted an Uncle Sam bank. You always give the neatest presents."

And a second later, when Mom's eyes met mine, I could tell that she thought I gave pretty neat presents, too.

Dear God, everywhere I go there are people who could use kind words. Give me the wisdom to offer them freely.
—*Brock Kidd*

SUN

15   *Let not your heart be troubled. . . .*   —*JOHN 14:1*

George, my doctor husband, claimed he had two partners: Dr. God and Dr. Love. During his fifty years of practice, he prescribed fewer drugs, tests or hospital stays than his colleagues, and most of his patients lived longer—mainly because nobody left his office without a hug, a prayer and a little song.

But George himself had circulation problems, and after a long struggle, one of his legs had to be amputated. Joking, he went into surgery, and groggy but singing, he returned. Quickly, he mastered his prosthesis. We were even dancing again when the other leg was doomed.

This was almost too cruel. The day of the operation, his family gathered as he tried to comfort *us*. "Don't cry, honey," he told me. "I still have eyes to see you. I still have arms to hold you."

"Yes, and you still have a beautiful voice to sing to me," I reminded him.

"You bet!" he replied and burst into our love song.

Eventually, Dr. God called George home. But these memories have been a wonderful help in healing my grief. Instead of feeling sorry for myself, I, too, count my blessings. I still have eyes to see the beauty all around me, arms to hold those I love. And like George, I don't want anybody to leave my house, or even put down a letter I've written, without feeling they also have received a hug, a prayer and a little song.

Dear Lord, please let all the words I write or speak be a source of joyful healing for others.   —*Marjorie Holmes*

Herald of Healing

O Love that wilt not let me go,
I rest my weary head on Thee;
I give Thee back the life I owe,
That in its ocean depths its flow
May richer, fuller be.

O Joy that seekest me through pain,
I cannot close my heart to Thee;
I trace the rainbow through the rain,
And feel the promise is not vain
That morn shall tearless be.

—*GEORGE MATHESON*

MON
16
And my God will meet all your needs according to his glorious riches in Christ Jesus.
—*PHILIPPIANS 4:19 (NIV)*

I was taking a Sunday afternoon drive and already fretting about the start of another work week. There was so much to do and only one of me. How would I ever get it all done? Then, as I passed a church in my neighborhood, I noticed a new message on their sign: "Prepare by Pre-Prayer."

As I glanced at my appointment book in the passenger seat beside me, those words seemed to have an urgency about them. Somehow, I'd managed to neatly separate my work self from the rest of my life. Prayer seemed natural at home or in church, but not in the workplace. Now I decided to give it a try.

All afternoon and evening, I found myself thinking about the people and situations represented by each entry in my book. "Help my fellow workers to have a relaxing weekend and come to work tomorrow refreshed and energized," I prayed. Before I knew it, I was asking God to meet the needs of a co-worker with debilitating depression, another with financial woes, another who seemed to thrive on chaos. "Be near and dear to my patients, too," I prayed. I scribbled their names on sticky notes and placed them on my steering wheel so I could pray on their behalf on my way to work.

And you know what? Work was different because *I* was different. Of course, there were the usual challenges and irritations. But by quietly inviting God into my workplace, I began to see people and situations in a new light.

Many people will merely get through this work week, yet never really live it. But I've found a little "pre-prayer" can change all that.

Dear God, prepare my heart and hands for a new work year serving You.   —*Roberta Messner*

TUE

17   *God will accept all people in every nation who trust God as Abraham did. . . .*   —*ROMANS 4:17 (TLB)*

St. Patrick, the missionary patron saint of Ireland, always reminds me of my days at St. Dennis, the Catholic grammar school I attended in Philadelphia. Like the block I lived on, the school was heavily Irish and Italian, the roll call full of names like O'Malley, Zerelli, Thompson, Nordone, O'Hara and, of course, Grinnan—since there were four of us Grinnans growing up on Hillcrest Avenue.

Over on Oakmont Street was the public—read "Protestant"— grade school, a hated place. We fought those kids after school or crossed to the other side of the street when we saw them. They called us names, and we screamed names back. I had no Protestant friends, not one. No one directly taught us to hate, but it didn't help that on weekends when my Aunt Cass Gallagher instructed me on the "real" history of Ireland she would admonish, "Never trust an Englishman." She also hated a new music group called the Beatles.

Imagine my shock when my family moved to the Detroit area and I landed in a *public* school in suburban Birmingham, Michigan. The neighborhood was so fresh and recently settled that our new parish, St. Owen, hadn't even erected a permanent church, let alone a school. There were plenty of Catholics at Meadow Lake Elementary, but there were even more Protestants, and a number of mysterious Jews, including the Greenes, who lived next door to us. We all loved the Beatles. When St. Patrick's Day arrived that first year, it was a revelation. The halls of Meadow Lake were decked out in green construction paper shamrocks. Protestant and Catholic alike gaily wore green. And Mark Greene, my neighbor—well, he had his name and he knew how to sing "Danny Boy."

Today, when I hear about the serial ethnic slaughter in different parts of the world, I sometimes remember my first St. Patrick's day in public school. Hatred is an acquired taste, and prejudice a lie each generation learns from its predecessor. We human beings have far more in common with one another than not. After all, Aunt Cass never told me what historians well know: St. Patrick was born an Englishman.

God, Father of all people, teach us to live and love as one family, Your family.   —*Edward Grinnan*

<u>*WED*</u>
18

He answered their prayers, because they trusted in him.   —*I CHRONICLES 5:20 (NIV)*

"We're going to start a paper prayer chain," Elisa Morgan told us with great enthusiasm as she handed out colorful strips of construction paper during our regular prayer time at MOPS International, where I work. Elisa is president of MOPS, a ministry that reaches out to mothers of young children across the country, and as a staff, we spend time praying regularly for the specific requests of these moms in our groups.

"When you have a prayer request, a personal one or one from a mother, write it out on one side of these strips. Then when you get an answer to that prayer, put it on the other side and staple it into a loop on the end of the chain."

With that, she made the first loop: a prayer that fifteen hundred moms would be able to attend our annual convention. That morning our registration went over the fifteen hundred mark. She wrote the prayer and answer, and taped the loop to the wall.

Over the next few weeks and months, the colorful chain grew, loop by loop, answer by answer, across the ceiling of the conference room. Prayer: for a mom's difficult pregnancy. Answer: She was home with her healthy baby. Prayer: for a husband to grow in his faith. Answer: He's been voicing a desire to do so. Prayer: that a son would go the right way at a turning point in his life. Answer: Last night, he prayed and rededicated his life to the Lord.

The other day, I passed the conference room on my way to my desk to make a difficult phone call. I prayed for God's words and that I would surrender my desire to be right in the face of a disagreement. "Give me Your righteousness instead, God." The sight of the colorful paper prayer chain reminded me that God hears and answers our prayers, and gave me a sense of trust as I sat down to dial the number.

That afternoon, I added a loop to the chain with these words:

Thank You, Lord, for answered prayers, and that You gave me Your patience when I ran out of mine. —*Carol Kuykendall*

THU

19 *My soul shall be satisfied . . . when I remember thee . . . and meditate on thee. . . .*   —*PSALM 63:5-6*

I was nine the first time I was really scared. My father lay across the bed, clad only in his boxers, his face ashen. He moaned as if gored, alternately clutching the bedpost until his knuckles turned white, then grabbing his head, pulling at his short, military-style haircut. The phrase *writhing in agony* is not, I learned, a cliché.

I thought my father was dying. He wasn't. He was passing a kidney stone. At that moment, he probably thought of dying as something much less painful.

He survived, but I've never forgotten that scene. And here I am, a father myself now. Occasionally, the two older kids—ages four and five—call me "Big Guy," an ironic title since I'm five-eight dripping wet. But I'm big to them, and if I stub my toe or cut myself shaving, they seem completely flummoxed—they can't imagine the Big Guy feels pain. "Does it hurt, Daddy? Can we kiss it to make it better?" They hate to see me suffering, just as I have worried away half my stomach on their aches and hurts.

When I was nine, I didn't think there was anything to learn from watching my father's pain—other than that I didn't want a kidney stone. But looking back, I remember that I prayed for my father, perhaps for the first time I *really* prayed, in the frantic voice of a desperate child. I was on my knees in the bathroom, thinking, *Please, God, don't let my daddy die.*

So maybe my kids *are* learning something, the same thing I learned about that strange animal called empathy—that Big Guys get hurt just like little girls, that sometimes all of us could use a little prayer to ease the pain.

Lord, when I feel helpless to relieve suffering, let me re-
spond with prayer.   *—Mark Collins*

FRI

20

Worship him [the Father] in spirit and in truth.
                                              —JOHN 4:24

When my parents invited us to a Christian "family camp" and a
lakeside sunrise service on Easter weekend, I refused. "Oh, I'd miss
our church service too much—the beautiful Easter lilies, the choir
and trumpets, the sermon—all the tradition I'm used to." I felt a little bad disappointing them, but after all, it was Easter!

The next fall I attended Cowboy Church after a "Ranch Roundup
Weekend" where we'd visited with friends from ranches around
Texas. Folding chairs served as our pews under a canvas big top. The
congregation wore jeans and boots or shorts and tennis shoes. There
was no cross, no altar. A straw cowboy hat served as an offering
plate. Our carpet was grass.

An ex-rodeo cowboy and his wife, who had a lovely voice, led
songs, prayer and testimonies. Their message made up in power for
what it lacked in proper grammar. I found myself laughing and even
crying as people shared from the heart. A gnarled cowboy with a guitar sang a song telling of Jesus "at the windmill" instead of at the well.
It was simple, refreshing, beautiful.

I couldn't wait to call my parents and suggest we try the lakeside
service next Easter. Who needed trappings and scholarly teaching to
be inspired? Like Jesus' followers of old, I could learn a lot by a lake.

Father, thank You for the wonderful variety of ways in which
I can praise You.   *—Marjorie Parker*

SAT

21

"What God has cleansed, you must not call
common."   *—ACTS 10:15 (RSV)*

When told that our son and his wife had scheduled the baptisms of
their two small boys for the Saturday before Easter, I knew what I
wanted to bring back from a trip to Israel: water for the sacrament
from the Jordan River.

Near where the Jordan flows from the Sea of Galilee, I scrambled down a bank with a half-liter bottle, climbing back with wet shoes and a full container. On the flight home, the bottle never left my shoulder bag. Two months later, cradled in bubble wrap, it accompanied my husband and me on a three-month car trip.

The week before Easter, we arrived with the much-traveled bottle at Scott and Raena's home in Nashville, Tennessee. That Saturday five children were presented for baptism at St. David's Episcopal Church. *A good thing,* I thought, *that I brought enough water for them all.*

"This water," the Reverend Eric Greenwood announced to the congregation as he emptied the bottle into the baptismal font, "was carried here from the River Jordan."

But . . . what was he doing now picking up a pitcher and pouring some other water into the font? "We'll just add some good Nashville tap water to it," he went on.

Tap water! Ordinary kitchen-faucet water, when they had water from the Holy Land? Why would the minister spoil the symbolism by mixing it with. . . . Then I caught myself. By mixing the holy with the everyday? Wasn't that just what Jesus did when He came down from heaven to live the daily life of ordinary people? Tap water and water from the Jordan; our grandsons were baptized, after all, with the most fitting symbol of all.

Father, teach me to see the holy in the common gifts of this day. —*Elizabeth Sherrill*

SUN
22

Your zeal hath provoked very many. . . . and he which soweth bountifully shall reap also bountifully.
—*II CORINTHIANS 9:2, 6*

Most people think of Thomas Edison as a man who achieved one success after another. The truth is, some of his experiments turned out to be dead ends; but he was not easily discouraged. For instance, he tried hundreds of times, without success, to develop a storage battery. When a friend sympathized with him over his failure, Edison exclaimed, "But I haven't failed. I've found ten thousand ways that don't work!"

Eventually, he found a way that *did* work.

I thought of Edison when my husband Larry decided I should learn to use a computer. I tried for weeks to memorize the commands and execute them properly, but to no avail. The showdown came on the day I hit some wrong keys and wiped out thirty-seven pages, which I hadn't saved.

"That's it! I quit!" I yelled.

"Why quit now?" Larry asked. "You've just learned which keys *not* to punch in this situation, and that's very useful. Keep trying. You're gonna get it."

No way, I thought rebelliously.

The following Sunday an elder in our church read aloud from the sixth chapter of Galatians, where Paul says that in due season we shall reap if we faint not. That's when I remembered Edison and his storage battery. If he could try ten thousand times, then surely I could try once more.

Father, help me to realize that every honest effort is in itself a success, no matter what the results.   —*Madge Harrah*

MON
23   *Hold thy peace. . . .*   —*ZEPHANIAH 1:7*

For twenty-one years, the Monday-morning incident had troubled me.

It began with my performance appraisal the previous Friday. The economy was tight, and I wasn't expecting a raise. I knew I wasn't doing well, even though I enjoyed my job as a technical writer on aircraft engines. I wasn't applying myself.

Norrie, my manager, was talking about my problems on the job. "The other writers look at a problem, teach themselves and come up with answers. But you seem slow to learn." All weekend my anger grew as I thought about his words.

On Monday morning, I sat across from Norrie feeling as if I were going to explode. All my past struggles and difficulties seemed to flash before me. I lost my temper and for the first time, I lashed back. My words were cold and meant to wound. I could see that Norrie was deeply hurt. As I went back to my desk, my anger gave way to remorse, but I said nothing.

Norrie let the incident pass. I worked for him for another ten years. I worked hard, and my job performance improved. There were other annual appraisals, and Norrie was always fair. But I never said I was sorry.

I retired in 1981. Norrie and his wife attended the celebration and greeted me warmly, but I still felt unable to apologize to him. Then, about twelve years later, I received a newsletter about some of my fellow-retirees. It included an item about Norrie: He had retired and moved out of state.

I wrote to Norrie, apologizing for my outburst. He answered at once. He had felt for years that he had done something wrong, because I was usually polite and pleasant.

Why had I waited so long to admit I was wrong? Why had I taken twenty-one years to ask for forgiveness? I'll never really know, but I do know that God has patience with slow learners.

Lord, I am still slow to learn. Be persistent in Your teaching.   —*Oscar Greene*

TUE

24   *How hast thou helped him that is without power? . . .*
—*JOB 26:2*

I love to help people. It makes me feel needed. In fact, sometimes I wonder if I'm not a "foul-weather friend," rushing in when I'm needed and then leaving people alone when they are doing well.

On the other hand, it's very hard for me to acknowledge that I need help. I think I need to be the strongest one around, and on the occasions when I'm not, I sometimes used to think that I had failed or was at fault.

On one such occasion, a good friend and mentor grew impatient with my trying to do it all myself and told me I was being selfish. When I protested indignantly that taking care of myself and not imposing on another was the very opposite of selfishness, she asked calmly, "How do you feel when you get to help other people?"

"Well, it makes me feel very good," I said honestly, unable to see what she was getting at.

She nodded. "Then why would you want to keep that experience from other people?" she asked. "Not letting other people feel very good sure sounds like selfishness to me."

Now when I need help, I try to let other people do things for me. It's still hard, but it's easier than it was.

God, thank You for letting me recognize Your love in the hands of those around me.   —*Rhoda Blecker*

25   *Jesus wept.*   —*JOHN 11:35*

Not long ago I heard a fable, an imaginary story, about a giant computer, the greatest ever assembled. It was designed to answer any question that could possibly be put to it, and the inventor was given the honor of asking the first ones.

He wrote down a list of tremendous questions. "Why is there so much injustice in the world?" "Why do wars continue to rage?" "Why so much racial strife and religious bitterness?" "Why so much crime and senseless violence?" He fed all these questions into the giant machine and waited while lights flashed and circuits hummed. He kept his eyes fixed on the slot where the printout containing the answers would appear.

But no printout came. Instead, a drop of water. Then another and another. And with a desolate sense of shock, the inventor realized what those drops were. They were tears. The computer was weeping.

A powerful fable, isn't it? And the message is so plain. God gave us free will. When we abuse it, God will not prevent us. The mighty Creator of the universe can only weep.

Lord, You cannot stop me from grieving You, if I choose to do so. But perhaps You can help me to choose otherwise. Please do.   —*Arthur Gordon*

26   *Let your conversation be always full of grace. . . .*
—*COLOSSIANS 4:6 (NIV)*

Several years ago, I shared a cubicle at work with Benita, a new worker who was a compulsive talker. From nine to twelve and from one to five, she chattered.

At lunch with my boss (and friend) Betty, *I* went on and on. "I feel like a deer trapped in the headlights. She's so irritating I want to scream, 'Be quiet!' or worse. Do me a favor: Change my cubicle."

"I could, I suppose," Betty said thoughtfully. "But I prayed before I decided to put her with you. I knew she'd be difficult, and I thought you'd be able to handle her. I once read that compulsive talkers are fearful people. They're afraid of being alone, of the unexpected, so they want to control everything that's said. Tell me, what *does* she talk about?"

"I don't really know," I admitted. "I usually say '*mm-hmm, mm-hmm*,' and tune her out while I do my work."

The next day, I made it a point to listen to Benita. I learned that she lived alone, that her children lived two thousand miles away, that her elderly mother had Alzheimer's disease and that during her long period of unemployment her phone had been disconnected. "But it's been so wonderful to have someone who's a deep listener like you!"

My face aflame, I asked, "Would you like to have lunch? We could get to know each other better."

God, is there someone in my life who "talks too much"? Today, with Your help, let me "listen deep." —Linda Neukrug

FRI

27 *When the cares of my heart are many, thy consolations cheer my soul.*   *—PSALM 94:19 (RSV)*

I had one kitten left from my cat Samantha's first litter. I had been able to place the other two kittens in loving homes, but this one was fast outgrowing the cute-kitten stage when adoption is easily arranged. And now another litter was on the way. In desperation, I took little Brownie to the animal shelter to see if they could find her a good home. It was the hardest thing I had ever done, and I cried as I left her.

All that night I fretted about Brownie. *What will happen to her if no one chooses her for a pet?* In the darkness, I decided to go back the next day and rescue her from the shelter.

The phone rang early the next morning. "Good morning," a pleasant voice greeted me. "This is Elaine at the animal shelter. Are you the lady who brought Brownie out to us yesterday?"

"I am," I answered, "but—"

"I'm calling to tell you," she cut in, "that Brownie is getting a wonderful home. A couple are here to adopt her, and they love her!"

"I'm delighted," I fairly crooned. "I hated so badly to leave her with you, uncertain of her future."

"I know you did. In fact, I saw your tears. That's why I called. I want you to know that right now she's happily purring in her new owner's arms."

I thanked Elaine and hung up the phone. And then I thanked God for this young lady who cared enough about my pain to take a moment to ease it.

Keep me alert, dear Lord, for opportunities to ease another's suffering.   —*Drue Duke*

SAT

28   *Thou preparest a table before me. . . .* —*PSALM 23:5*

"Be foolish to ship that thing halfway across the country. Must weigh a ton . . . cost a fortune, too," said several friends.

Sound reasoning. But the old, round oak table had been in my family since long before I was born. Whenever relatives had gathered at our house, the table was pulled apart at the middle and leaves were inserted so everyone could be seated together. Grace was said at every meal, whether we had company or not.

At that table I told my parents about school happenings, sports scores, the latest boy I thought was neat. My stories—especially during my early years—were often interrupted by manners training: "Not such a big bite, Isabel." "Use your napkin, not your sleeve." "Say please."

After most evening meals, my mother donned her apron—she called it her "apern"—and told me she'd "worsh" dishes while I did homework. If an arithmetic problem was a stickler, Dad sat there, too, insisting the answer must be in the back of the book; it always was when he went to school.

The table's generous forty-eight-inch top provided space for working jigsaw puzzles, or playing dominoes or Old Maid. Sometimes it became Mom's ironing board or a surface to cut out patterns for my school dresses.

Just before bedtime, Dad would open Hulburt's *Story of the Bible* and read, using a coal-oil lamp for light because back in the twenties electricity had not yet arrived on our farm. Then we bowed our heads and prayed together around our old oak table.

So despite the cost, I had the table packed and shipped. Today it sits in our home, reminding me to be faithful to the things I learned at it so many years ago.

Father, help me to remember—and pass on—the values I was taught during my growing-up years.   —Isabel Wolseley

29 *"I have found David son of Jesse a man after my own heart...."*   —ACTS 13:22 (NIV)

Many a father dreams of having his son take him for a model and follow in his footsteps. And I'm no different. I would like to see Reggie, my firstborn son, become involved in the outreach of Mendenhall Ministries. Periodically, we have a conversation like this:

"Reggie, what do you see in your future? What do you think God has in mind for you?"

"Well, Dad," he answers, "I think I'd like to major in business and then start a business of my own."

Each time I respond, "Think and pray about it, son. Maybe God wants to use you right here in the ministry."

Recently, Reggie and I attended a Promise Keepers meeting in the Superdome in New Orleans along with forty-five thousand other men. We heard a message about fathers and sons. The speaker talked about supporting and encouraging our sons, spending time with them, not criticizing and, more specifically, allowing them the privilege of being molded and fashioned in God's image rather than that of their fathers.

In the middle of that tremendous crowd, I bowed my head and repented to God for trying to make Reggie in my image. And then I asked Reggie for his forgiveness. "I want to support you," I told him, "in whatever profession you go into and wherever God leads you." There was a big sigh and a smile on his face as we hugged.

I still have a nagging desire to see Reggie working beside me in ministry. But when I'm tempted to bring up the subject, I remember what I learned that day in the Superdome: My son needs to seek to be a man after God's heart, not mine.

Lord, help us all to let go and to give our children to You.
                                                           —Dolphus Weary

<u>MON</u>
30
"It is the Lord who goes before you; he will be with you, he will not fail you or forsake you; do not fear or be dismayed."   —DEUTERONOMY 31:8 (RSV)

How well I remember those first really hard times in junior high school. I'd developed asthma and a severe skin condition, and to change classes in the prescribed five minutes was an ordeal. I had to navigate the crowded hallways, sometimes race up and down three flights of stairs, and still have enough time left to hide in the bathroom nearest my next class so I might slow my wheezing and scratch. For fifty-five minutes, all through the preceding class, an intense itching would have built up, and my only relief was to rake a comb over my raw skin.

This is when I first felt God's continuous presence in my life. I was thirteen, and He watched out for me in ways that matter to a teenager. He never let me be late for a class. There was always an open stall for me to use. And I was never picked on by students who like to make life difficult for misfits.

Over the years I've never felt abandoned by God. Indeed, He uses my afflictions to create an awareness of His wondrous presence in my life.

Lord, when I'm not feeling well, help me to see the many ways in which You go before me, and to rest in Your continued, very real presence.   —Brenda Wilbee

<u>TUE</u>
31
When pride comes, then comes disgrace, but with humility comes wisdom.   —PROVERBS 11:2 (NIV)

I switched off my desk light and stretched, brushing away the cobwebby equations, freeing my thoughts for that last unfinished physics problem. I flipped my notebook shut and tipped back the chair.

"I'm going down to the courtyard."

"Okay, Kjerstin. What's up?" my roommate asked.

"It's almost five-forty-five. The prayer group is meeting."

"The physics homework is pretty bad. Maybe I should come along and ask for divine guidance." She laughed.

I smiled, used to her kidding, and said what I always did: "You're welcome to come along."

Reaching for my coat, I paused. The late-night whispers between our bunks—echoed, I was sure, in the hundreds of other rooms by the hundreds of other students at the college—often turned to God.

"How can you get past the big questions, the unfairness and cruelty of the world?" she had asked. "What about your caring God, Kjerstin?"

I hadn't been able to reply. I hadn't been willing to admit I didn't have an answer. Whether it's the physics homework or the mystery of suffering, I find it hard to say, "I don't know." And I don't know why people suffer, why life isn't fair; I simply know that Jesus is my Savior.

One arm in my coat sleeve, I said, "I was really hoping you would come along today. You always ask such good questions. I don't always have the answers. Maybe the group can help us both to find some."

"I probably shouldn't," she replied, looking up from her textbook. "I still have number thirty-seven to figure out."

"When we come back, let's work on it together. I don't know how to do that one, either."

Lord Jesus, You are the answer to all my questions.
—Kjerstin Easton

My Healing Journey

1 _____

2 _____

3 _____

4 _____

5 _____

6 _____

7 _____

8 _____

9 _____

10 _____

11 _____

12 _____

13 _____

14 _____

15 _____

16 _____

17 _____

18 _____

19 _____

20 _____

21 _____

22 _____

23 _____

24 _____

25 _____

26 _____

27 _____

28 _____

29 _____

30 _____

31 _____

APRIL

S	M	T	W	T	F	S
			1	2	3	4
5	6	7	8	9	10	11
12	13	14	15	16	17	18
19	20	21	22	23	24	25
26	27	28	29	30		

*He was wounded for our transgressions, he was
bruised for our iniquities . . . and with
his stripes we are healed.*

—ISAIAH 53:5

WED   THE TOUCH OF THE HEALER

1   Healing Our Past
         Surely he hath borne our griefs, and carried our sorrows. . . .   —ISAIAH 53:4

Following a tradition started by a group of brethren in the Taize Community in France, on Good Friday our pastor lays a rough-hewn, life-sized cross flat on the platform in the church sanctuary. Around the cross, beside small kneeling cushions, he places little yellow stickum notes, each with a pencil. From six in the morning until six that evening, our church is open to anyone who would care to come and lay whatever pain they have in their hearts upon the cross.

For a good part of my life, I have carried a pain that will not go away. It woke me in the middle of the night and twisted me up with grief for my father, for all that was and all that could have been. It is a pain I cannot change. "I'll never divorce," my mother said, and she didn't. Instead, I lived with her in a faraway separation from a daddy I adored.

"I'll come to see you," he promised. Week after week in years of broken promises, he never came. Then he died.

Kneeling at the cross, I wrote my pain on a yellow stickum note and gave it to my suffering Lord. The pain did not go away, but it became an okay pain, because now Christ was carrying it for me.

Lord Jesus, take all those things that twist me up with hurt. I lay them at the foot of Your cross.   —*Fay Angus*

EDITOR'S NOTE: How have you been experiencing God's healing touch in your life? Take time to review your monthly "My Healing Journey," and let us know. Send your letter to *Daily Guideposts* Editor, Guideposts Books, 16 East 34th Street, New York, New York 10016.

THU

2   *For our heart shall rejoice in him, because we have trusted in his holy name.*   —PSALM 33:21

Today is sonogram day. We've awaited it with excitement and dread. Andrew and I are thrilled about meeting our baby for the first time. But we're afraid of what we might learn.

For me, the fear mostly outweighs the excitement. We've bypassed the amniocentesis and the other major prenatal tests: God knit this child together, and in His eyes our baby is perfectly made. To me, this means that our job is to love and accept this child as he or she is created, no matter what the circumstances. But I am weak; I still fear the circumstances.

Yet when the picture appears on the monitor, I am immediately transfixed. Andrew appears at my side and holds my hand. Together we watch as the doctor zeroes in on the baby's head, arm, leg, heart. He goes quickly, freezing the pictures and measuring body parts, grunting out the name of each organ or bone. These simple words transform what looks like a weather map into a little baby, our own flesh and blood. Never before has the word *femur* sounded so beautiful to me. Nor have I ever heard the glory in *ventricles*.

Suddenly, the baby's hands move toward its little mouth. Andrew and I both gasp in awe. My entire being seems to sing, "God is so good, God is so good." I turn to Andrew for a moment. "This is such a beautiful baby," I say. He nods and squeezes my hand. I know now that no matter what happens, this baby is lodged as firmly in our hearts as in my womb.

The doctor says, "Well, the baby looks okay." His words were reassuring, but were nothing compared to the peace we have found by seeing this child that God has created.

Giver of life, help me to trust You in all things, especially Your plans for my life and my children.   —*Julia Attaway*

FRI

3

Do not think of yourself more highly than you ought. . . .   —*ROMANS 12:3 (NIV)*

Every year, on the first weekend in April, it was my husband Mark's job to make sure our clocks were changed to daylight saving time. But this year it was going to be different; I was going to do my part, too. On Saturday evening, I watched Mark dutifully reset the grandfather clock, the mantel clock and the clock on the microwave. Then I efficiently took care of the alarm clock, my watch and the clock in my car.

On the drive to work at the hospital Monday morning, I'd never felt more on top of things. I'd taken new initiative and now my growing expertise included clock setting. But when I turned on the radio, I was startled to find unfamiliar programs on two different stations.

When are they going to get their acts together? I secretly sneered. And I couldn't help but wonder how many people would be late for work.

Yep. Just as I'd predicted, staff members were straggling in from the parking lot. I was growing more smug by the minute. But when I got inside, I didn't get it. Why were all these people on the 8:00 A.M. shift already here at seven? And why were all the clocks two hours ahead of my watch? And, wait a minute, wasn't that parking lot awfully full for so early in the morning?

Then it hit me. Mark, as usual, had set all his clocks ahead. I'd unknowingly set mine back. But I'd been so busy looking at everyone else that I'd failed to see that *I* was the one who was out of sync with the world. Why, I'd been on "Roberta Time" all day Sunday as well. "I'm going to take a long vacation from finger-pointing," I vowed as I humbly signed away two precious hours of vacation time.

Lord, You have a great sense of humor when it comes to pointing out my foibles. Thank You for Your gentle redirection.

—*Roberta Messner*

KEEPING VIGIL

SAT **Saturday before Palm Sunday**
4   *And they were in the way going up to Jerusalem; and Jesus went before them . . . and as they followed, they were afraid. . . .*   —MARK 10:32

Every year of my adult life I confess I have met the prospect of Holy Week with a combination of anticipation and dread. I'm a coward when it comes to sorrow; part of me would rather ignore the sad, tragic aspects of Christ's story. And yet, when I have truly celebrated Holy Week, worshiping in some way each day, I have been given great spiritual gifts, walking out of church on Easter Sunday with a surfeit of joy—even on a gloomy day.

Several years ago, my wife Carol and I went through a terrible month that began in the middle of Holy Week. On Maundy Thursday, our four-year-old son Timothy broke his femur in two places. The next day, Good Friday, seven-year-old William came down with chicken pox. Ten days after that, I entered the hospital to have a large tumor removed from my parotid gland.

"You're not going to write about that, are you?" Carol said. "Why do you want to relive the horror of it?"

Maybe that's the point, I thought to myself. After I go through a trial—somehow surviving, rarely triumphing—I prefer to forget about it. When a crisis is over, it is easiest to file it away as a distant memory, never to be thought of again. After all, why relive the pain? And yet our faith is one that sees triumph in travail, lessons in our struggles. "No cross, no crown," says a framed postcard in our kitchen. That's what happens during Holy Week. Each year we relive the horror of it fully to understand and appreciate the glory.

Lord, help me to see Your godly lessons in my struggles.
—*Rick Hamlin*

SUN
5

Palm Sunday

Go your way into the village over against you: and as soon as ye be entered into it, ye shall find a colt tied . . . loose him, and bring him.   —MARK 11:2

When I received the telephone call at the office I was in the best of moods. My career was going well, the family seemed fine, the warm rain outside brought a promise of spring. But then I heard Carol on the phone saying, "Timothy was hurt at nursery school. It sounds bad. He's getting X rays at the hospital."

It can't be as bad as all that, I told myself. But as I stepped out of the hospital elevator, the first person I saw was a doctor telling a colleague, "A kid hit by a tricycle . . . the worst break I've seen in a child that young."

Timothy was white and shaking with shock. I rushed home for a change of clothes and spent the night with him, a little four-year-old tossing and turning in his orthopedic bed, his leg in traction, his mind full of nightmares. "Daddy," he cried out, shaking the steel bars, "we're stuck!"

Yes, we are stuck, I thought, and for the first time in many months I felt angry with God. Was this the promise of spring? Was this how

I would spend my Holy Week? If God had any lesson to teach me, why was He doing it through the misery of my son?

I couldn't hear the answer then, but if I had listened carefully or remembered our celebration of Palm Sunday, I would have realized God doesn't always expect us to understand. It is enough if, like the disciples fetching the colt, we trust and follow.

I will follow You, Lord. Show me the way.   —Rick Hamlin

MON

6 Monday of Holy Week
Heaven and earth shall pass away.   —LUKE 21:33

The second disaster in this string of family trials arrived the next day when William came down with chicken pox. Now Carol and I had to alternate duties, one of us at home, the other at the hospital. "How are we going to survive?" I asked her on the phone. I desperately missed the daily delights that kept us together as a family. No gatherings around the dinner table, no playing catch, no breakfast cereal quizzes, no precious conversations between my wife and me after the children had gone to sleep. I told myself this was only temporary and that we would all be under one roof again soon, but I struggled to believe. Fear had taken over.

"It will be all right," Carol reassured me, but the tremor in her voice revealed her fear, and I could already picture the stack of paperbacks at her bedside. When she is afraid, she retreats into the world of historical fiction, and I retreat into silence. I couldn't get over my dread that the world I loved was coming to an end.

While Timothy watched a dancing purple dinosaur on TV from his bed, I picked up my Bible and turned to the Holy Week chapters. This would be my pattern. I would immerse myself in Jesus' story. That day I was startled by the imagery in the Gospel prophecies of a violent world going awry. Christ's words weren't comforting: "Ye shall hear of wars and commotion . . . nation shall rise against nation, and kingdom against kingdom." There would be "earthquakes, famines, pestilence." But amidst the apocalyptic mayhem was this reassuring promise: The words of Christ would not pass away. "Watch ye therefore, and pray always" (Luke 21:36).

I would cling to Him even now, especially now.

I bow my head and watch, Lord, knowing Your Word will not
pass away.   —*Rick Hamlin*

TUE	Tuesday of Holy Week

7 *A new commandment I give unto you, That ye love one another; as I have loved you. . . .* —*JOHN 13:34*

"The tumor has to come out," the doctor said to me, running his nimble fingers along the side of my face, studying the mass below my left earlobe.

"But not now!" I argued. "I have to take care of my kids. We have one in the hospital with a broken femur, and we have another at home with chicken pox."

"It can't wait." He was equally insistent. "It's been growing for a long time. We'll schedule you for surgery next week."

He must have read the fear in my face. *Tumor, cancer, surgery*—those words sounded like a premature death sentence to me. *Not this. Not now.* He held up one finger, like the statue of a medieval saint, attempting to silence my protests. "In most cases like yours, the tumor is benign. Do not worry." But being told not to worry when you're upset is fruitless.

The night before my operation, I was back at Timothy's bedside. As the spring sky darkened, I pulled down the blinds, turned off the TV, put away the toys and read him a short book. We sang his usual bedtime song and said a prayer, "Jesus, tender shepherd, hear me, bless this little lamb tonight. . . ." And then it was lights out.

I might die, I thought. The streetlamp cast a rippling shadow through the blinds. I sat on my cot, took out my Bible and turned again to Holy Week. One week of Christ's life and it fills over a third of each Gospel. Almost every move of His last few days was accounted for, the preaching, teaching, praying. It was as though Christ's ministry, under the threat of death, suddenly moved at a faster pace. *Maybe it's not such a bad idea to live every week as though it were your last.*

What would I want to do if I knew I were dying? I pulled out the sheets, made up the cot and then lay down on it next to my sleeping son. *Just this,* I decided. *Keeping watch beside a loved one.*

Each day, Lord, I will live with the fervor as though it were my last.   —*Rick Hamlin*

<u>WED</u>   **Wednesday of Holy Week**

8   *If I then, your Lord and Master, have washed your*
     feet; ye also ought to wash one another's feet.
                                                    —JOHN 13:14

I was in a cheery mood the afternoon I checked into the hospital for surgery. "You'll only be here one night," the staffers told me. One night seemed nothing compared to the twenty-six-night vigil we'd been maintaining with Timothy in his hospital a couple blocks away. I could see his building out my window. I felt I could wave to him and Carol there with him, and William at school further uptown. Surgery, I convinced myself, was a routine procedure. Even as I went under the anesthesia in the operating room, I joked with the doctor.

Six and a half hours later I woke up in a hospital bed, disoriented, retching, my head swathed in bandages. "Rick, it's Margaret," said the woman at my side. *Margaret from church.* "She's been waiting here for hours," said a nurse. "She needs to go home now." It was already late. "Thanks," I tried to say. *So nice of her.*

I dozed fitfully all night, feeling miserable and lonely. First thing the next morning, Colleen from the office showed up. "Morning," I mumbled, my face in partial paralysis from the surgery. "I brought you the paper," she said, pulling up a chair by my bed. "You should go to work," I urged. "No," she said patiently, "you need someone to help you check out of the hospital and get home." *So nice of her.*

Then at home, Emily, another friend from church, showed up with chicken stew and an apple pie. "Look at you," she said, glancing at me with a professional eye. A veteran nurse with years of hospital experience, she decided I needed a better bandage. Soon she was unrolling gauze and creating more efficient headgear for me.

Only as I was falling asleep did I think of the Holy Week incident when Christ washed the disciples' feet in a supreme demonstration of Christian service. In twenty-four hours, three friends had dropped everything they were doing in their busy schedules to do mundane things for me—wait by my side, help me to the car, cook, clean, change bandages. As Christ urges us, "For I have given you an example, that ye should do as I have done to you."

Thank You, God, for the kindness of friends. May I give as I have received.   *—Rick Hamlin*

THU   Maundy Thursday

9   *Father, if thou be willing, remove this cup from me: nevertheless not my will, but thine, be done.*
—LUKE 22:42

For days I struggled to find my equilibrium. I spoke to Carol on the phone, but couldn't see her because she was taking care of Timothy. When I slept, I would sink into nightmarish delusions that I was still in surgery, the bright lights shining over my draped body. When awake, I hobbled slowly from bed to chair to bathroom. The muscles on one side of my face remained paralyzed. My smile was half a frown, I could only open and close one eye, and I made sucking sounds when I ate. All the while in the back of my mind I wondered, *What did the surgeon take out of me? How big was the tumor? Was it malignant?*

The doctor, when I called him, was quietly reassuring. "It was a very large tumor going through your facial nerves; it must have been growing for a long time. But don't worry, your nerves are only bruised. The feeling will come back to your face. Give it time." And the biopsy? "Don't worry. We will know in ten days."

I could not wait. I did not want to wait for the lab test results or the natural healing of my nerves. I had no patience with ill health. And I felt I had a very good reason to get back to normal quickly. I could hear myself argue with God: *Get me well now! My family needs me!* Here was a moment, more than any I've ever had, when I could readily empathize with Christ in the garden, suffering, in agony before His mockery of a trial and crucifixion: "Father, remove this cup from me."

And yet, I couldn't imagine saying the words that followed those: "Nevertheless not my will, but thine be done." Everything in me screamed out in objection, *Don't I know, Lord, what's best for me? I can't wait!* Where could I find the strength to persevere?

Then I looked again at the scene of Christ in the garden: "And there appeared an angel unto him from heaven, strengthening him" (Luke 22:43). God doesn't always remove us from suffering. He walks right through with us, lending His superhuman strength.

Give me strength, God, when mine is gone.   —*Rick Hamlin*

FRI
10

Good Friday

Then said Jesus, Father, forgive them; for they know not what they do.   —LUKE 23:34

"Were you there when they crucified my Lord?" we always sing on Good Friday in the three-hour service I both need and dread. It seems the saddest moment of all Holy Week, worse than having to call out, "Crucify Him! Crucify Him!" in our reenactment of the Passion. "Were you there when they nailed Him to the tree?" goes the plaintive spiritual. "Were you there when they laid Him in the tomb?" What makes it so sad is the unspoken, unsung answer: *Yes, I was there. Yes, I did nothing.* I'm always reminded of my own selfishness.

During that month of trial, as my health gradually returned, so did a self-centered enjoyment of the attention it brought. One evening when I was at the hospital by Timothy's bedside, a friend called up with sad news of her own. And she wanted a bit of advice from me, something that would have been easy for me to give. *Can't you see,* I wanted to shout into the receiver, *I've gone through a hellish month? My child is still in the hospital and I don't even know if my tumor is malignant. How can I possibly help you?* I couldn't bear her claim on my time. I'd had a hard enough time as it was.

Only when I hung up, offering little help, did I recognize this blind egotism for what it was. Were you there when they crucified my Lord? Yes, like Peter, I would have betrayed my Lord. Like the disciples, I would have fled. Like Pontius Pilate, if I had been in a position of power I would have washed my hands of the whole nasty business. It makes it all the more remarkable that Jesus' last words were ones of forgiveness. Only He knows how much He has had to forgive.

Forgive me, Lord, for all the small and large ways that I have betrayed You.   —*Rick Hamlin*

SAT
11

Holy Saturday

On the sabbath they rested according to the commandment.   —LUKE 23:56 (RSV)

Waiting. Waiting. Maybe I'd gotten used to waiting—waiting for the biopsy, waiting for Timothy to get out of the hospital, waiting to go home to be with William and Carol, waiting for life to return to what it had been. (Would it ever?) And all the while there were still insurance forms to fill out, telephone calls to return, nurses' and doctors' advice to follow, office visits to make. On a warm sunny day, a day before Timothy was supposed to be released, I went outside to the park in front of the hospital and sat down on a bench. I was tired of the interruptions of the hospital room and fed up with forms. Sitting there, I took out my pocket New Testament.

Suddenly, I noticed that others around me were also reading, Hebrew scriptures in small black books that went from back to front. The women were in conservative cotton dresses that covered their arms and wigs or hats that covered their heads, the men wore dark suits and had full beards. I recognized them as part of a Hasidic Jewish sect that I'd read about in the newspaper. They were gathered outside the hospital because their leader was inside, dying. There was nothing better to do than keep vigil beneath the leafing plane trees, praying for a dying man.

I thought of how terrible it must have been for Jesus' followers after His death. What could they do after their Lord was killed? We read that Joseph of Arimathea took the body, laid it in a tomb and then rolled a great stone over the door so no one would get in. Hope was dead. All the events of the previous week had been a false alarm. On Sunday the disciples would return to their fishing, their nets, their work. But on Saturday they followed the commandment and honored the Sabbath.

That's the best thing to do when you have to wait—to worship, read and pray, making a space for God to fill.

Lord, help me through the down times when all my hope seems dead.   *—Rick Hamlin*

SUN

12

Easter Sunday
Jesus saith unto her, Mary. She turned herself, and saith unto him, Rabboni; which is to say, Master.
—JOHN 20:16

Good news came all at once: The biopsy was negative; the tumor was benign. And Timothy, bound in a cast that went from his hip to his toes, was coming home. My expectations were modest. *Things will be like they were,* I thought.

On a beautiful spring day, Timothy and I took an ambulette ride from the hospital back home where his mother and brother waited. "Look at the flowers!" he exclaimed. "Look at the trees! There are leaves on the trees!"

He missed spring, I realized. He went into the hospital when the trees were still rough, brown branches scratching the sky, and now they were in their full glory, pink buds dropping from the cherry trees, white flowers like snow on the apple trees.

As we drove up the highway, bouncing over potholes, driving along the surging river, he kept saying over and over again, "It's so beautiful! I knew I would like it! But it's so much more beautiful than I thought!"

So much more than I thought! That's what Easter was. That's what Easter is. It often takes me by surprise, like the sight of spring to a boy who was deprived of it for nearly a month, like the return of good health after a period where it seemed to be gone forever. The disciples thought they were getting a king to free them from the Romans. Instead, they received a King Who freed them from death for all time.

When I think of the women at the tomb or the disciples meeting Jesus on the road to Emmaus and not even recognizing Him until He sat down with them and broke bread, I realize that Easter was so much more than they expected, so much greater, so impossible. Not back to normal. It was the end of life as they knew it. It was the beginning of a new world. That's what happens to us when we're at the end of a time of trial. That's what happens to us again and again when we embrace the new life we find in Christ.

Hallelujah, Christ is risen indeed.   —Rick Hamlin

<u>MON</u>
13
"You must put aside your own pleasures and shoulder your cross, and follow me closely."
                    —MARK 8:34 (TLB)

Grandsons Ryan, six, and David, four, were excited about Easter—and concerned that perhaps I didn't know about it. "Did you know that bad people killed Jesus by nailing him on a cross?" Ryan asked.

"Then some people put a rock on his grave!" David added. "But Jesus didn't stay dead! He got alive again on Easter."

I was delighted with their theological knowledge. "On Easter Sunday you're going to my church," I said. "During Children's Time, Pastor Lloyd will give you a little cross. It will remind you of how Jesus died and rose again."

Ryan was excited about getting his own cross. David wasn't. He thought for a moment, then said "I think I'd rather stand outside with my basket and wait for the Easter bunny."

It was funny—until I took an honest look at my own life. How often did I talk about following Christ, then get sidetracked? Were there "Easter bunnnies" in my grown-up world? Oh, yes! Watching television instead of attending Bible study; ordering a terrific (expensive!) dress I don't really need; short-cutting prayer time for a trip to the mall. "Goodies" that distracted me from the Cross of Christ.

"We'll think about the Easter bunny after church," I told David. "On Sunday, maybe we can plan to go get our crosses together."

Today, Lord, fill my heart with the glory of Your Resurrection.   —*Penney Schwab*

TUE
14   *Truly, truly, I say to you, unless a grain of wheat falls into the earth and dies, it remains alone; but if it dies, it bears much fruit.*   —*JOHN 12:24 (RSV)*

Each spring my husband and I looked forward to visiting our friends Bill and Jean Brown on their farm Oakland Green, near Leesburg, Virginia. That was when the grape hyacinths along their brook raised their blue exclamation marks in a spectacle to rival the sky.

One spring, however, instead of glorious life, a spectacle of death awaited us. On stream banks and lawn, only sodden brown mud. "Just look at this place!" Jean lamented as we made our way over the muddy ground to where she waited at the door. Record April rainfall, she explained, had turned the normally docile brook into a torrent, sweeping the hyacinths away.

Driving toward the farm the following year, therefore, we expected no welcoming blaze of blue. As we reached the Browns' mailbox down by the road, I caught my breath. Hyacinths . . . hyacinths everywhere . . . tumbling down the hillside, carpeting the meadow across the road, stretching out of sight toward Crooked Run. Clusters, patches, swaths of brilliant blue. Far from killing the flowers, the flood had renewed them—divided the bulbs, multiplied them a hundred-fold, and spread them far and wide.

I thought, as we gazed at that glory of color, about the "deaths" in my own life. Three years writing a book that was never published. A lifelong friendship broken off. And I thought of what followed. A new understanding of my craft. A deeper love built on mutual forgiveness.

Death, burial, rebirth. Each time what looked like the end was simply a good laid down to flower more abundantly at another time.

This Easter season, Father, teach me to ask, "What new growth will you bring from the grain that is buried?"

—*Elizabeth Sherrill*

WED

15 *Suffer the little children to come unto me . . . for of such is the kingdom of God.*   —*MARK 10:14*

I was feeling resentful and frazzled as I entered the little family restaurant for a quick bite. I had come from one meeting in White Plains, New York, and was soon to rush to another in Tarrytown. No time to go home, no time to catch my breath. I wolfed down a sandwich and was gulping my coffee and making some notes when a little, rosy-cheeked fellow came in with his parents and marched right up to my table.

"Boons!" he cried ecstatically. "Boons!" he said again when I didn't understand. He pulled my sleeve and insisted that I share his joy.

Lifted out of my self-absorption, I smiled at his enthusiasm. My eyes followed the little hands pointing to the wall above me. I hadn't noticed it at all, but there, perched gaily over my table was a picture of a rocking horse with brightly colored balloons tied to its saddle. At last, I joined in the child's laughter. "Yes," I agreed, "balloons! Beautiful balloons!"

We smiled at each other as I left the restaurant. *Amazing*, I thought, *how much lighter I feel.* In fact, I practically floated out the door. Only later, quite by accident, I found the word *boon* in the dictionary. It's defined as a favor or blessing, and it comes from the Old English word *ben*, which means prayer.

Dear Father, thank You for the many ways in which I may lift my heart and spirit through prayer.   —*Susan Schefflein*

Herald of Healing

It is finished! Christ is slain,
  On the altar of creation,
Offering for a world's salvation
  Sacrifice of love and pain.
Lord, Thy love through pain revealing,
  Purge our passions, scourge our vice,
Till, upon the tree of healing,
  Self is slain in sacrifice.

—*GABRIEL GILLETT*

THU

16 *He saved us through the washing of rebirth and renewal by the Holy Spirit.*   —*TITUS 3:5 (NIV)*

Have you ever seen a Jericho rose? It looks like a balled-up fist or a small tumbleweed, dry and brittle as a closed mind. Its spindly, tightly curled branches wear the mask of death, and its tiny bundle of roots seems hardly enough to have held it in place anywhere at all. The Jericho rose seems to be the sun-baked corpse of a desert weed.

A friend of mine brought one of these pitiful plants to my house one afternoon. She fished it out of her handbag as I started making tea. We had planned to prepare for the next week's Bible study and I remembered her suggestion of baptism or forgiveness of sins as a topic, but I couldn't see how a lifeless, potless runt of a shrub had anything to do with it. Smiling, she excavated a shallow bowl, which she filled with tap water and set on the dining-room table. Extremely curious by now, I started to ask what she had in mind, but she simply sat down and looked at the plant. Ever so slowly, its limbs began to straighten and unfurl. I forgot the tea as I watched the scraggly little branches spread. And was it becoming just a little bit greener?

Fifteen minutes later, the teapot was whistling insistently. The Jericho rose was unfurled now, and I understood its role in the upcoming Bible study. This is my freshman year in college, and the hectic pace often leaves me feeling spent and exhausted. It's all too easy for me to neglect to set aside quiet time for prayer and worship. My faith can get as dry and shriveled as a desert plant. But within it are the seeds of life, and by His forgiving grace, God will awaken it, as His gift of water awakens the Jericho rose.

Lord and Giver of life, in the dry times, help me to remember the Jericho rose.   —Kjerstin Easton

FRI

17 *Two are better than one....*   —ECCLESIASTES 4:9

My name is Shep. I am a Belgian shepherd, expected to herd sheep, but in the year and a half of my life I haven't seen any. You see, I've had trouble finding a home. First there was Heidi, who turned me over to a couple in New York City, but when the woman had a baby I went to Betty Kelly to await adoption. *Why didn't they want to keep me?* I was nervous when I was told a man was coming to look at me. *Suppose I didn't measure up? Suppose I didn't like him?* And then Van arrived and, in an instant, none of the worries mattered. I bounded to him and he took me in his arms and I knew that I was his.

So another New York apartment. Very cozy. We got right into a routine: Up at five, he fixes my breakfast at the same time as he does his, then forty-five minutes in Central Park where he unleashes me, but I keep an eye on him as I scurry around. There are more walks during the day, but outside the dog run, the rest are on the leash. I've heard from country and even suburban dogs visiting the park that I was lucky to have so much freedom. I don't know, but who cares? I am with him.

Van hasn't had a dog since his pointer, Clay. Ten years. Imagine going so long. But I have inherited Clay's leash and bowl and have tried in every way to be a worthy replacement. Sometimes I feel I am better, since I do not shed the way he did and I have a more beautiful tail. Yesterday Van took my head in his hands and spoke to me.

"You know, Shep," he said, "God's wisdom is phenomenal. I don't know why He formed this alliance between man and dogs, but I am awfully glad He did. I've been lonely. I've missed a wagging tail when I come home and the regimen you bring to my life. You and I are partners, yes?"

I gave him a big, fat lick.

Van's God, Whoever, wherever You are, thank You.
                                                —*Van Varner*

SAT

18 *Train up a child in the way he should go: and when he is old, he will not depart from it.*—PROVERBS 22:6

Seated amid the congregation at Broadway Presbyterian Church here in New York City one Sunday morning, I watched as my god-daughter Neva and her husband Tom carried their infant son Nikolas to the front of the church, where their minister waited.

"Is it your intent," he asked Tom and Neva, "to raise this child as a follower of Jesus Christ?"

"It is," they answered.

Then, taking Nikolas from Tom and lifting him high, he turned to face the congregation. "And is it your intent, as members of Christ's church, to accept the responsibility for helping these parents raise this child to be a follower of Jesus Christ?"

"We do," we answered.

As the minister placed his hand on Nikolas' head and began the prayer of dedication, my thoughts drifted back thirty years to when—as one of Neva's godmothers—I promised to help her parents raise her in the Christian faith. And I thought about all the times Neva and I had spent together, playing, going on trips, talking over dinners, laughing, consoling, counseling. Oh, there'd been difficult times, too, with disagreements and stubbornness, but we'd ended these sessions with prayer, thanking God for our special relationship.

Suddenly, my heart surged with joy. *With God in her life, she turned out all right,* I thought. *And with God in his life, Nikolas will too.*

Dear Lord, thank You for the tremendous difference you make in our lives.   —*Eleanor Sass*

SUN

19 *Be of good cheer; I have overcome the world.*
                                                —JOHN 16:33

It's the Sunday after Easter, and there's plenty of room in the sanctuary that was filled to overflowing last week. The colorful explosion of spring flowers has disappeared, as have the fancy hats that dotted the congregation. At home, my new, flowered-print dress is already moving toward the back of the closet. Our one day to celebrate the Resurrection of Jesus Christ is over, and now we return to the way things were.

Would you be surprised to learn that it wasn't always this way? I was. *The Joyful Noiseletter,* published by the Fellowship of Merry Christians, explains that for early Christians, forty days of Lent were followed by a joyful Easter season, fifty days of thanksgiving and celebration. They considered this Eastertide the most important time in the church calendar and, unlike modern Christians, continued to celebrate Christ's Resurrection throughout the year.

The good news of Easter morning—Christ is risen—doesn't disappear when Monday comes, but as I work through life's daily grind I sometimes push that message toward the back of my spiritual closet and lose sight of it. So, what do the Merry Christians suggest to keep the Easter spirit alive?

1. Start simply with a smile for a stranger in church. Perhaps it will encourage him or her to return the following week.
2. Suggest a "Happy Hymn Day" in your church, an opportunity to sing jubilant songs to the Lord. (Then be sure to sing them with gusto!)
3. Seek out the joy of the Bible. The New Testament has more than 280 references to gladness, merriment, rejoicing, delight, laughter and joy. I'm collecting these verses, and when I need lifting up, I tape one to my kitchen cabinet or above my desk to continually remind me of the joy at the center of my faith.

Who knows, I might even wear my Easter dress in the middle of August!

Dear God, let me live each day with a "Happy Easter" heart, and share the joy of the risen Christ with everyone I meet.
—*Gina Bridgeman*

MON	*We have a building from God, a house not made with*

20 *hands, eternal in the heavens.*
—*II CORINTHIANS 5:1 (RSV)*

My father-in-law Bill never owned much. Yet he created sublime dwellings of unparalleled magnificence. A huge timber mill in the redwood forests of northern California complete with cabins of every size. An immense marina along the San Joaquin River dotted with sailing vessels and boathouses. And houses! Victorian mansions towering up to the very sky. Sprawling stucco villas crowned with Spanish tile where herds of cattle came to feed. White marble palaces spilling across the Piedmont hills.

None of these actually got built, mind you. But they did exist in the divine landscape of his dreams. He drew pictures of them, described them over pie and coffee, consulted with his sons and grandsons about specific embellishments. And when each dwelling was finished to his exacting taste, he would give its picture away to someone he loved, for he never built anything for himself. The glory of each dwelling was in the abundant imagining and the generosity with which it was bestowed.

"Dreams are free," he emphasized. And he kept on dreaming dwelling places not made with human hands.

Earthly dwellings fall away, Lord, while Your house stands, eternal in the heavens, freely given. Let me abide there with You.   *—Linda Ching Sledge*

TUE
21   *Love your enemies. . . .*   *—MATTHEW 5:44*

My father was not a teacher, he was a cotton merchant. But he had his own quiet way of conveying lessons to my brother and me. Once, I remember, he showed us a piece of paper with a few words on it:

> The length of our lives is not at our command, however much the manner of them may be. If our Creator enable us to act the part of honor, and to conduct ourselves with spirit, probity and humanity, the change to another world, whether now or fifty years hence, will not be for the worse.

"A soldier wrote those lines in a letter many years ago," Father said. "What sort of man do you think he was?"

We said that he sounded like a brave man, someone worthy of admiration and respect.

"Yes," said Father, "I think he was. He was also our enemy. His name was Patrick Ferguson. He was a colonel in the British army that fought against our ancestors in the Revolution. Not long after he wrote that letter to his mother, he was killed at the Battle of King's Mountain, along with most of his command."

Father looked at us thoughtfully. "One of the most difficult commandments the Bible gives us is to love our enemies. It's difficult because so often we're urged, almost required to see nothing good in them. Just now you had a different reaction. Admiration. Respect. Not love, perhaps, but little steps in that direction. Remember that, will you?"

After all these years, I remember it still.

Lord, keep us mindful of the humanity we share with all people, even those who seem to be our enemies.—Arthur Gordon

---

WED

22

Then God spoke to Noah and to his sons . . . saying, "Now behold, I Myself do establish My covenant with you, and with your descendants after you; and with every living creature that is with you. . . ."

—GENESIS 9:8-10 (NAS)

I grew up on a farm, loving animals, especially dogs and cats. I can still remember the delight of watching my cousin spray milk in the cat's mouth as he milked the cow, and the thrill of going to see Uncle Lawrence, who had promised me the pick of the litter for my first pup. But you didn't keep those pets in the house. And when they got sick, you didn't take them to the vet. Times have changed.

A few years ago, when our daughter Nancy bought her first house in Houston, an urban cat came with it. She named it Porch Cat and began putting food out for her. Porch Cat later gave birth to two kittens, which were named Peter Wyatt and Emma Louise. Then Porch Cat disappeared. Nancy put food out for the kittens, and when she discovered they were sick, she took them to the veterinarian. When Peter Wyatt died of a host of complications, it was like a death in our family. Despite her allergies, Nancy determined that Emma Louise would not suffer the same fate, and so moved her into the house. There have been many trips to the vet during the past year, but Emma is now a healthy, contented member of the family and even gets remembered with gifts at Christmas.

Out of my Great Depression background, I once said to Nancy,

"Please don't tell me how much you have spent on Emma." My wife Barbara and I both know that it's probably more than we spent on Nancy during her first year, but we also agree that it has enriched Nancy's life as well as saving Emma's. There is something about caring for a cat or dog, or feeding wild birds in winter, or nurturing a plant, that makes us partners with God.

Lately, I've been thinking about getting a Jack Russell terrier. I may even keep it in the house!

On this Earth Day, help me, God, to be a faithful steward of all the life that surrounds me.   —*Kenneth Chafin*

THU

23 *But I have called you friends. . . .* —*JOHN 15:15*

There is a woman whom I follow everywhere in New York. Her name is Aileen, and she cuts my hair. I first encountered Aileen when she worked at the salon in Bloomingdale's, and I had a half-price coupon for hair-styling. I liked what she did with my obstreperous locks—somehow she got them to behave. So, when Aileen moved from Bloomingdale's to a little shop on East 58th Street, I loyally followed. When she left that job without another to go to, she came by my apartment and cut my hair over the kitchen sink. Later, she was hired by what I was told was *the* trendiest salon in Manhattan, where patrons booked weeks in advance and paid a pretty price for the privilege. Aileen and I didn't feel comfortable there. We moved on.

Aileen was quite young when we started, and I was, well, young*er*. She lived an exuberant nightlife back then, sometimes showing up for her first appointment without having gone to bed. I saw her meet the man of her dreams, get married and join a venerable old Dutch Reformed Church in the East Village. Her work area used to be covered by postcards from downtown art galleries and dance clubs. Now she keeps pictures of her young son and his grandmas.

We're settled in now, the two of us, at another department store salon. It's funny to think I've known Aileen longer than I've known my wife or been at my job. My hair is starting to show just a touch of gray. I've never socialized with Aileen outside of her work and I've never seen her without a pair of clippers in her hand, but yesterday while she was finishing up by disciplining my cowlick with some hair gel, she said, "You know, you've changed." I thought she was going to tell me my hairline had eroded some since last visit, but no. "You're mellower," she said.

I don't quite know what that means, mellower. But I've been thinking it over and the next time I see this woman—not exactly a friend but certainly not a stranger—I have something to tell her: We've mellowed together.

I am thankful, God, not just for the people You bring into my life but for those whom You keep there as we journey on Your path.   —Edward Grinnan

---

FRI

24 *And whosoever shall compel thee to go a mile, go with him twain.*   —MATTHEW 5:41

I spent the night in a Washington, D.C., hotel and in chatting with the manager, I complimented him on the hotel's service, which had been noticeably efficient and warm.

"Thank you," he said. "We do make an effort. We even have a name for it among ourselves. We call it 'Plus One Service.' "

Then he explained that the staff had been instructed to add one additional courtesy to each duty they performed. For instance, if a guest requested his or her key at the desk in the evening, the clerk would not only reach for it, but ask if a wake-up call was desired. When the operator called in the morning, she would not only tell the visitor what time it was, but give a quick report of the weather. If the guest telephoned for breakfast, room service would ask if the guest wanted a newspaper as well. And when the tray arrived, in addition to the food, it held a tiny vase with a bright flower in it.

"Always thinking about the extra something keeps us on our toes," the manager said. "It not only makes for better service, but somehow or other I think it makes us better people. It's kind of a secret of successful living, isn't it?"

Yes, I thought to myself, *but it's not really a secret.* Upstairs in my hotel room, lying open on the bureau, was a book (another facet of the hotel's thoughtful "extra something"). In it, Jesus Christ makes His own recommendation for Plus One Service. It's there in Matthew 5:41.

Jesus, today I'll try to add to my service: plus one . . . plus two . . . plus three. . . .   *—Ruth Stafford Peale*

<u>SAT</u>
25   *The race is not to the swift. . . .*
                                    —ECCLESIASTES 9:11

I love to walk for exercise. I find it helps lift my spirits, so I've been pretty regular about walking a mile or so a day for the last year. But two friends kept urging me to try aerobics. "You'll get a much better workout," they insisted.

As soon as I entered the gym, I felt out of place. Instead of looking at mountains and buildings, all I saw was my sweaty reflection flailing about in a wall mirror. And I'm no fan of rock music, so I felt like plugging my ears as we danced to a noisy tune blaring from the instructor's tape recorder. *How will I ever keep up for an hour?* I thought, longing for my quiet morning walk. I eyed the door . . . and, suddenly, I ran toward it, opened it and bolted!

Freedom! I leaned against the door of the gym, panting, and then ran to the corner, giggling like a child. My run slowed to a jog and then to my usual relaxed walk, which I enjoyed more than ever.

Later that day, I chatted with my two friends. "Didn't you love aerobics?" one of them asked. Red-faced, I confessed, "I didn't exercise!" I explained briefly how I'd run out.

"But you did exercise," she replied. "You exercised your right to change your mind. You knew what was right for you and you did it, even under pressure from two bossy friends like us!"

Today, God, let me "exercise" my freedom to do what I know in my heart is right.   *—Linda Neukrug*

<u>SUN</u>
26   *The Spirit himself pleads with God for us in groans that words cannot express.*   *—ROMANS 8:26 (GNB)*

It's 6:30 A.M. Sunday, and I'm driving north to speak at an area church, filling in for the minister who is on vacation.

The sky is dark, and a cold April rain smothers the car. My sinuses throb, and my bones ache. I feel angry at God about a recent loss, and I'm exhausted from nine months of classroom teaching. It depresses me to think about all the paperwork yet to do, and I'm in no mood to minister to others this morning. I need someone to minister to me.

I arrive at 9:00 A.M., park near the back of the lot and sneak in the side door to avoid the crowds. I sit in the front pew and try to sing, but my mouth refuses to open in praise of God. I stare at the songbook and feel only resentment.

> There is sunshine in my soul today,
> More glorious and bright
> Than glows in any earthly skies,
> For Jesus is my light.

The song seems to mock me. *What sunshine?* I wonder. In a few moments I will have to become professional, to stand up and inspire others to godliness, maybe even crack a joke or two to warm up the audience.

I can't do it, Lord. I simply cannot do it.

On the second verse, the words seem to leap out at me. "And Jesus, listening, can hear the songs I cannot sing." My eyes overflow, and the raw emotion strengthens me for my task.

Are you in one of those times when you don't feel too wonderful about God? When you can't seem to praise or give thanks? If so, try to relax and let the spirit of God turn even your pain into a prayer.

Lord, it's hard for me to talk to You right now. My spirit is heavy, and I need Your Spirit to speak for me.

—*Daniel Schantz*

MON

27 Be ye of an understanding heart.   —PROVERBS 8:5

I was on the telephone, a long way from home, trying to deal with a school crisis one of my sons was having. In the heat of conversation, he shouted, "I hate it, Dad! Hate it, hate it, hate it!" Then the phone went dead as he slammed down the receiver.

Helpless to call him back because he was calling from a pay phone the number of which I did not know, I took a walk around the neighborhood where I was staying. As I passed a vacant lot, the piercing cry of a killdeer caught my attention. I had not seen many of these interesting, long-legged birds since I was growing up in Minnesota, where they are plentiful. Remembering that killdeer nest on the ground and would rather run than fly, I walked toward the bird and watched in fascination as it flopped through the grass, apparently the victim of a broken wing. It never let me get close enough to touch it, and after leading me across the lot, it suddenly took flight and circled back to where we started.

I laughed, recalling the "broken wing" trick killdeer use to keep intruders away from what is really important—their nests. It didn't take God long to nudge me to see that maybe my son, like the killdeer, was using a "broken wing" to deflect my attention from the real problem. For the bird, it was hiding its nest. For my son? . . . Later that night we talked, and I listened for what was really bothering him: insecurity at making friends and finding his place.

The next time you face a strong emotional response, look closely at the "broken wing" and listen for the real problem.

Lord, give me ears to hear, eyes to see and a heart to understand what is behind the pain I see today in other people's lives.   —*Eric Fellman*

TUE
28 *Blessed are all they that put their trust in him.*
                                                  —*PSALM 2:12*

"What a wonderful crop you have this year!" I exclaimed to Aunt Emma as we stood at the edge of a prairie wheat field admiring the broad expanse of grain rippling in the wind.

"Yes, but it's not in the bag yet."

She was right. Drought, hail and grasshoppers still posed very real risks. Only God Himself knew the outcome.

The next spring I went home to visit my mother. "Don't bang the screen door," she cautioned as I stepped inside. "It might disturb my visitor." She pointed to the covered front porch, where a new clothespin bag was hanging among the Virginia creepers. Printed on the side were the words, "Cheer up! It's in the bag."

"A gift from Aunt Emma," Mom whispered. "As you can see, she's feeling much more optimistic since her good harvest last fall."

"But what's in the bag?" I asked. Tiptoeing over, I cautiously peeked inside. There peering back at me with beady, black eyes was a little house wren. Unruffled, she sat securely on her nest.

As my husband Leo and I begin our retirement, I often wonder about what our future will be like. Will inflation undermine our financial nest egg? Will we become infirm and need constant care? What will our children's and grandchildren's lives be like? Instead of fretting, I try to look back at the harvest of blessings God has faithfully given us in the past. That way I can confidently say of the future, "Cheer up! It's in the bag."

Father, thank You that the past, present and future all fall within Your sovereign love. —Alma Barkman

---

<u>WED</u>
29
"Work for the good of the cities where I have made you go. . . . Pray to me on their behalf. . . ."
—JEREMIAH 29:7 (GNB)

Our church was going through a difficult time, and many families had decided to leave. At times I felt like giving up myself. I wondered if the time would ever come when I would feel at home there again after so many unwelcome changes. Then two women in the congregation, Cynthia and Glenda, proposed something radical. Would I meet with them at 8:30 every weekday morning at the church to pray? They explained that there would be no chitchat. We would simply come in, sit down together and pray for our church for about fifteen minutes without hashing over any of the details or trying to solve any of the problems.

At first it was a battle of will for me to get up and go every day. But as the weeks went by, getting up became easier and easier. If I was discouraged on a particular morning, my ears would perk up as someone thanked God for a good report from the men's Bible study, the choir program on Wednesday night or a word of wisdom from the minister.

One morning as I turned into the church driveway, I nearly forgot where I was. The daily routine of making a right turn after the stand of pine trees had become so familiar that I had the same sensation that comes with pulling into my own driveway. Although the problems at church had once made me feel like a stranger, prayer had slowly but surely cleared a welcoming path back home.

Thank You, Lord, that no matter how inhospitable the place
I endeavor to pray, prayer itself fashions it into Your home
and mine. —Karen Barber

THU
30
A good measure, pressed down, shaken together and
running over. . . . —LUKE 6:38 (NIV)

This was my first trip to the market, and the delightful chaos swirled around me: babies wrapped snugly to their mothers' backs with bright *kikois*; exotic sweet-spicy smells; low tables heaped high with fruits and vegetables, dried fish, rice and beans. Flies buzzed happily over piles of discarded fruit, and chickens cackled noisily on the backs of bicycles. Women glided by, heavy baskets balanced gracefully on their heads.

Timidly, I approached a mountain of rice on a low wooden table. Struggling to remember my numbers in Swahili, I also recalled the warnings of well-meaning friends that I was an obvious target for the unscrupulous. I bypassed the heaping tin sitting there. (Does it have a false bottom? What's underneath the nice stuff at the top?) Reaching for an empty tin, I filled it with rice and carefully leveled it off. But just as I was about to dump it into the plastic bag that I had brought with me, a brown hand reached out to stop me. A woman— the proprietor—took the tin and set it down, tapping the sides lightly to settle the contents and make more room at the top. Again and again she dipped her hands into the pile, heaping rice into the tin until it cascaded over the sides. Placing the plastic bag over the top, she gently tipped the rice into it. Then, with a warm smile, she scooped another handful into the bag before handing it to me.

I'm embarrassed now to remember my suspicions and her generosity. But in our four years of living in East Africa we found that to be the norm rather than the exception: generosity, even in the midst of poverty. I still sometimes struggle to remember my numbers in Swahili. But I have never forgotten the lesson of my first marketing day.

My God, help me to give generously today, in thanksgiving
for all You have given. —Mary Jane Clark

My Healing Journey

1 _____

2 _____

3 _____

4 _____

5 _____

6 _____

7 _____

8 _____

9 _____

10 _____

11 _____

12 _____

13 _____

14 _____

15 _____

16 _____

17 _____

18 _____

19 _____

20 _____

21 _____

22 _____

23 _____

24 _____

25 _____

26 _____

27 _____

28 _____

29 _____

30 _____

MAY

S	M	T	W	T	F	S
					1	2
3	4	5	6	7	8	9
10	11	12	13	14	15	16
17	18	19	20	21	22	23
24	25	26	27	28	29	30
31						

*Their soul shall be as a watered garden; and they shall
not sorrow any more at all. . . . for I will turn
their mourning into joy, and will
comfort them, and make
them rejoice from
their sorrow.*

—JEREMIAH 31:12-13

FRI   THE TOUCH OF THE HEALER
1   Healing Our Families
         God setteth the solitary in families. . . .—PSALM 68:6

My daughter Melanie is recovering from cancer, thanks to good doctors, thousands of prayers and her sister Mickie, whom she scarcely knew for years.

They were born almost a generation apart. Mickie, my first child, was graduating from high school when, to my own initial dismay at forty, I gave her this baby sister. Melanie started kindergarten the same year Mickie graduated from college, who after a year in the dance world, married and moved to Hollywood with her filmmaker husband. In time, Melanie, too, graduated from college. A dancer like her sister, she married a Greek musician and moved with him to Athens, Greece. Except for letters, phone calls and rare visits, the two girls were almost strangers.

Then God's will and our different needs brought us all back to Virginia, where we could enjoy and help one another. Mickie and her husband now live next door; Melanie and her family only an hour away. Making up for lost time, the girls quickly became best friends. And at the news of Melanie's cancer, her sister rushed to help her husband and others drive her to all the tests and appointments. Despite Mickie's own busy career as an inventor/writer, she didn't miss a day during the long, hard struggle, and always felt richly rewarded. Especially after giving her blood when Melanie needed a transfusion.

"It's thrilling, Mother, almost like giving birth. Mine was the blood type she needed!" And it helped her sister so much that Mickie has volunteered to become a regular blood donor for others.

For me, the thrill is in how God used His healing power, not only to deliver us from our agony, but to weave a scattered family back together after so many years apart.

Dear Lord, when the way seems darkest, help us to remember that You have lessons of love to teach us, we will all be better for this, and to put our trust in You.
                                                    —Marjorie Holmes

2

"Show mercy and compassion to one another."
—ZECHARIAH 7:9 (NIV)

Last May is etched in my memory as "chicken pox month." My daughter Elizabeth was confined at home all week with itchy, blistery spots. By Saturday afternoon she was begging to play outside, and I was "itching" to work in my garden. After settling her little brother Mark down for a nap, we headed outdoors brimming with eagerness—she, to play with her friends, and I, finally to get my flower beds ready for planting.

But I forgot that it was opening day of the East Lansing Art Fair. We stepped outside to find many neighbors going to town. As the last of Elizabeth's friends left, we felt deserted. With my husband Alex at work, I was stuck at home with a disappointed child.

I started pulling weeds in the perennial bed by the driveway, trying to interest Elizabeth in bike riding or roller blading. That lasted ten minutes, during which time my neighbor Donna came out to talk, telling me about her health problems and upcoming surgery. I listened half-heartedly, impatient to get back to weeding. When Donna finally left, Elizabeth pleaded to go to the art fair. "Maybe later when Mark wakes up, honey."

She whined, "It's so boring. The sun is making me itch more."

"Then go inside and play."

"There's nothing to do inside."

I hoed furiously. *But I want to get this garden done!* I was about to explode when I looked at her teary, red-spotted face.

Dropping the hoe, I put my arm around her. "Let's go inside and cool off with some ice cream." Later we curled up in the rocking chair to read together. And I gave thanks for all the young growing things that need my special care.

Father, help me to see when spending time with others, listening to a friend or playing with my children is the gardening I ought to be doing.   *—Mary Brown*

3

In him we live, and move, and have our being . . . For we are also his offspring.   *—ACTS 17:28*

On a gray, drizzling Sunday, my daughter Karen and I visited a church we'd never attended before. Usually, I'm quite comfortable in churches of various denominations, but this time I found myself strongly disagreeing with the gist of the sermon. I felt my stomach muscles tighten; I was angry about the pastor's interpretation of the Gospel passage (it didn't agree with *my* viewpoint!). I grumbled to myself until I'd formed a little black cloud that hovered over my heart as the service continued.

When it was time for the Lord's Prayer, the woman next to me took hold of my hand, and I saw that people all over the large congregation were holding hands for this shared prayer. As my other hand clasped Karen's, I felt a twinge of guilt about my critical thoughts on the sermon. And when I addressed God in those familiar words, "Our Father," I thought, *We really are all children of the same Father. Siblings!* By the time we came to "forgive us our trespasses," I remembered that our faith is, above all, a matter of the heart.

At that moment, the cloud over my own heart began to release its dark water. I felt it behind my closed eyelids. And when I opened my eyes, I saw that the sun had broken through, streaming in the stained glass window above the altar.

As I shook hands with the pastor on our way out, I said, "I'm so glad we belong to the same family!"

Loving Father, though our styles of worship are different, and though we often disagree on interpretations, we truly are all children of Your love. Bless all *my siblings this day!*
—Marilyn Morgan Helleberg

<u>*MON*</u>
4   *"My grace is sufficient for you, for my power is made perfect in weakness."* . . .
                                        —II CORINTHIANS 12:9 (RSV)

Tonight, while picking blackberries across the street, I remembered a conversation I'd had with my daughter three years before. I'd wanted to rip out the vines and plant something prettier. "But I like the wild look," Heather had objected. "You don't have to tame everything!"

I've come to realize she's right. Some things *are* better left wild. In nature, and *human* nature as well. It's important that I do my best to meet the many expectations around me. But there are times I need not rise to each challenge. Some things aren't worth it. Sometimes the energy just isn't there. Sometimes I need just to "let the weeds grow," let things run a little wild and not worry about taming everything.

As with blackberries, in time such honesty can produce its own fruit. An "I don't know" gives people a chance to share what *they* know. When I get to the "end of my rope," letting go allows others to step in and help. Admitting to a cranky day enables friends to be more gracious and forgiving—and teaches me patience whenever I'm part of someone else's cranky day.

Across the street grow plump, sweet fruit, a reminder that whenever I'm honest about my imperfection, good things can and do grow.

God, You created all things—the cultivated garden and thorny thicket. Out of both, You always bring Your fruit.
—Brenda Wilbee

TUE
5
"You will know the truth, and the truth will make you free."
—JOHN 8:32 (RSV)

I've been afraid about many things as far back as I can remember—even after I became a Christian and asked God to fill me with His Spirit.

For example, one morning last week, I was finishing a book project. I woke up afraid about it, though nothing negative had happened. My first thought was to put it aside and run away to live in Mexico. Realizing that was a ridiculous fantasy, I prayed that God would remove the fear. But He didn't. In fact, it got worse. So I worked really hard and practically redid the whole thing. When I still felt uneasy, I remembered that Dr. Paul Tournier had once said that fear is sometimes a message from God telling us to listen and find the meaning of it so we can grow spiritually.

So I asked myself, "What am I afraid will happen when this book comes out?" And the answer to that question came almost at once: I'm being very open about my imperfections, and I'm afraid that some Christians are "imperfection-sensitive" and may reject me.

Now I had something concrete to think about. Although I still felt the fear, I decided that I would rather be rejected by some than not try to help people in pain. I surrendered the outcome to God.

God's Gospel truth for me is that I'm still afraid to be honest if it might cost me esteem from others. I must learn to trust God and offer Him my fears today.

Lord, thank You that courage is not dependent on our getting rid of all our fear, but on trusting You and offering You the fear. —Keith Miller

6 *And when the people complained, it displeased the Lord. . . .* —NUMBERS 11:1

Do you know who invented the Q-Tip? A man named Leo Gerstenzang thought of it while watching his wife's frustration at trying to clean their baby's ears using toothpicks and cotton. Likewise, Charles Strite was angry about the constantly burnt toast in his factory's lunchroom, so he invented the automatic toaster. And Ole Evenrude got so mad when the ice cream in his rowboat melted before he got to his island picnic spot, he invented the outboard motor.

Reading these stories of ingenuity reminded me of the phrase, "Necessity is the mother of invention." Unfortunately, when things don't work the way I think they should, often the only thing born of my frustration is complaining. For example, when Ross started school one September, the system for dropping off and picking up the kids was a chaotic mess. I complained about it to my husband, other parents, the teachers, anyone who'd listen. When another parent came up with a simple solution for easing the traffic jam, I wondered, *Why didn't I think of that?* Probably because I'd put my energy into complaining instead of acting.

It's no surprise that the ultimate role model for taking action is Jesus Christ. When a Canaanite woman begged for His mercy for her demon-possessed daughter, the apostles complained, "Tell her to get going . . . for she is bothering us with all her begging" (Matthew 15:23, TLB). But Jesus was moved by the woman's faith and healed the girl. Not long after, Christ took pity on the crowds that had followed Him, telling the apostles not to send the people away hungry. "And where would we get enough here in the desert for all this mob to eat?" they cried (Matthew 15:33, TLB). Again Jesus acted, turning a few fish and loaves of bread into food for thousands.

Following Christ's example, I can first ask, "What can I do?" instead of "Whom can I complain to?" Simply taking a positive step has to make a difference.

Lord Jesus, help me do one thing today that brings someone farther away from a problem and closer to a solution.
                                                    —*Gina Bridgeman*

THU

7   *After this manner therefore pray ye: Our Father. . . .*
                                                    —*MATTHEW 6:9*

"Please, let's not talk about this anymore," I said to my mother. Then I hung up, angry. A relative with a fondness for misery had said some mean, hurtful things to Mother. No matter what kind deed my mother might perform, Aunt Nana will find some way to criticize her. No matter what good thing happens to her, Aunt Nana will find a way to dampen Mother's happiness. "She's not like you," I had said to my mother. "Why can't you shut her out of your life?"

Now, I sought out a comfortable corner of the living room and sat down to pray away my irritation, but no words came. Finally, I settled on reciting the Lord's Prayer: "Our Father," I began.

I imagined a father with his children gathered about him. Some of them loving and kind, others bickering and fighting. Sometimes they even hurt each other. And does the good father love one child more than the other? No. The father loves each of them, even the misery-makers, as if he or she were his only child.

Today has been set aside as the National Day of Prayer, and all around the country, many of God's children are praying, "Our Father." Their differences might frighten, even irritate me. But no matter what their political choices, language or style of dress, all of them, rich and poor, well-educated and unlettered, are praying, "Our Father."

I want to be a part of this day of prayer. I want to pray for understanding, forgiveness and peace. I want to ask our Father to show me how I can love all my brothers and sisters, the way He loves. But, first, I must go back to the beginning:

Our Father, I need to remember that You're not only my Father, You are Aunt Nana's Father, too. Let me live as though I know that's true.   —*Pam Kidd*

FRI

8

"What is impossible with men is possible with God."
—*LUKE 18:27 (NIV)*

I tried to appear brave, but I was shaking in my sneakers as we stood within five feet of a six-ton elephant. My second-grade mind didn't understand the laws of physics, but somehow I knew that the short red and white stake ol' Jumbo was tied to was no match for his brawn. In my mind, I can still see him rocking back and forth, tugging against the stake, but never pulling it up.

My dad took my hand and told me I didn't need to be afraid. Then he asked, "Billy, do you know why such a little stake can hold a big elephant like that?" He pointed to a baby elephant nearby who seemed to be pulling with more determination than the big guy and explained, "When the big elephant was little, he was chained to a stake just like that baby. He pulled against it over and over again, but it wouldn't budge. Then one day he gave up. He decided it was no use, he was just not strong enough. And an elephant never forgets."

I've thought about that elephant a lot. The one thing that keeps that six-ton animal from getting away is not a two-foot stake. It's a thought.

That elephant reminds me a lot of myself sometimes. I live within limits that come nowhere close to my full potential. Some of my limits are self-imposed; some I've allowed other people to impose on me. No matter what their source, these limits make a difference in how I see myself.

In order for me to move toward becoming the person God created me to be and fulfill the purpose He created me to fulfill, I must pull some stakes and jump some fences. After all, I'm not what people think I am. I'm not what I think I am. I am who Christ says I am.

Lord, let me ignore any "stakes" but Yours.   —*Bill Peel*

SAT

9

The end of a matter is better than its beginning, and patience is better than pride.
—*ECCLESIASTES 7:8 (NIV)*

Families change, grow up and move on with incredible flexibility, like amoebas under the microscope in biology class: oddly beautiful, never still. But what to do, when the family moves on and the family home stands still? With three children out of college, it didn't make sense for us to endure long commutes and support a big, old house with empty rooms.

But then come the questions. When is the right time to sell? When we retire? When the children finish college? When they get jobs? When they, perhaps, have families of their own? If the "home" is gone, will the family drift apart?

After worrying, arguing with all family members and listening to everyone I know giving different advice, suddenly while buying a large, family-sized bundle of socks, I figured it out. It was so simple. *There's a plan here,* I heard myself saying. *The only problem is that you haven't been told yet what it is. You will. Patience!*

"It's a deal," I said to my inner voice. "I'll quit trying to interfere." And I did.

Several times a week, men, women and their families walk through the house—imagine being neat all the time! But I am waiting for God to send along whomever He has chosen to succeed us in this home. There's lots of fine spirit under this roof of love, loyalty, fights fought and resolved, crises survived and laughter shared. I'll be proud to hand all this unseen real estate on, when the right moment comes.

Today, as we ate lunch in the sunny kitchen, a young family with a boy who looked about five walked through, peering around with interest. The boy wanted to check out the trees in the garden, perhaps for future hair-raising exploits. The dad was asking questions about the bathrooms. Maybe this is the family. If so, I'm sure that both the real estate agent and the Lord will let us know.

Give me patience, Lord, to wait for Your decisions and to trust in Your judgment.   —Brigitte Weeks

---

<u>SUN</u>
10
Reject not your mother's teaching.
                                    —PROVERBS 1:8 (RSV)

A LOVE LETTER TO MY MOTHER:

Mother, this year, when you'd be ninety-nine if you were still alive, I want to express my love and appreciation for you and your life, perhaps more genuinely than I ever did when you were alive.

You were always giving, always thinking about what you could give your family and many friends—nothing expensive, just a note or some little thing to show you cared and were thinking of them. I've been going over the many gifts you gave me for which I don't think I really thanked you. Here are some of them.

You gave me the *gift of memory.* "Do you remember?" was a game you played often while I was growing up in China. Because we recounted the experiences and looked at pictures, I remembered much of the car trip across the United States and Canada we took when I was only two and three. They are memories I treasure.

You gave me *my wider family.* "These are your uncles and aunts," you'd tell Flora Nell and me as we looked at snapshots, "and these are your cousins." And then we had to name them! It was particularly hard to remember all of Uncle Nathan and Aunt Olive's eight kids! You'd always read the letters from relatives to us, so the connection would remain alive. We're still in touch.

You continue to give me *my history,* through the various scrapbooks of photos and mementos you created for me. Your handwritten notations about the people in the pictures, some of whose faces are familiar but whose names have long since left me, are gifts for which I continue to give thanks.

Thank you for your example of a *God-centered life of prayer.* Some of my early memories are of you and Daddy at your desks before sunrise reading your Bible and praying.

Thank you, too, for your love of *poetry,* which I am only now discovering in your scrapbooks, and your love of *jokes.* Thank you, Mother, for being you.

Dear Lord, thank You for putting me in my family . . . and into Your family, too.   —*Mary Ruth Howes*

MON
11

Most gladly therefore will I rather glory in my infirmities, that the power of Christ may rest upon me.   —*II CORINTHIANS 12:9*

Seven months into my pregnancy, and after several weeks of feeling as if the back of my left leg was bruised, I looked at it in the mirror. I flinched in horror. Huge, bumpy blue lines wobbled like a meandering river down my leg. I raced to the book about having a baby. It couldn't be true! But it was. Pregnancy can bring on varicose veins.

That night I morosely told my husband Andrew about my dreadful discovery. He smiled gently and said, "Aw, honey, I noticed those weeks ago. I didn't say anything because you're having a baby, and things like that happen. Besides, I'll love you no matter what your legs look like." His words were so sweet that, ashamed of my reaction, I resolved to forget my distress. But it was harder than I thought.

A few weeks later, as the weather turned warmer, I began to debate whether or not to wear shorts in public. By now I had blue blotches on my left calf too big to ignore. If the weather were sweltering, I knew I'd swallow my pride and wear whatever was comfortable. But there was more than just vanity behind my reluctance. Somehow these varicose veins made me feel, well, old. I wasn't used to that. And it didn't feel good.

Finally, I confessed again to Andrew. He was quiet for a minute, and then said thoughtfully, "I see. You probably feel the way I felt when I discovered I was going bald at age twenty-four." I had not known him when he was a young man; he was bald when we met, and it was touching to think of how hard it must have been for him to lose his hair at such a young age.

I looked again at my leg. Even if it was streaked with blue, it was still the leg God made especially for me. I gave Andrew a kiss on the top of his beautiful, shiny head. Then I hauled out my maternity shorts and put them on.

Lord Jesus, help me face the symbols of my mortality with the faith that leads me to life eternal.   —*Julia Attaway*

TUE

12

May he [God] give you the desire of your heart and make all your plans succeed.   —*PSALM 20:4 (NIV)*

It was my favorite birthday present the year I was six. A miniature fishing pole with a big plastic hook and three bright blue plastic fish, their mouths perpetually open, waiting for the imaginary bait. I'd climb over the garden gate and run through the field to the creek. There I'd place the three fish upstream. Then I'd run like crazy to a spot downstream, plop myself down on the bank and wait for the fish to come by. I'd pretend I'd been there for hours, waiting for the big bite. Soon, here they'd come. Bumping through the rapids, sliding over the mossy rocks. My fish. I'd toss the line out to them and—with the skill of a seasoned fisherman—snag my catch.

"How was fishing?" my mother would ask when I got back to the house.

"Great!" I would always beam. Always. I never had a bad catch. Why? Because I planned it that way!

Sometimes when things aren't going the way I wish, I remember those fish. Have I planned my current ventures as well as I did those trips to the creek so long ago? Perhaps I could take a class now that would help with a promotion next year. An extra half mile added to my daily walk could have positive long-term results. And kindnesses bestowed today may come back to me in my own time of need.

Very little in life can be as sure as those fishing trips long ago, but I can still do my part to bait my hook for success.

You, God, are the Source of all success. I will do my best and leave the rest to You!   —Mary Lou Carney

13 *For I trust in thy word.*   —PSALM 119:42

"The X rays are negative. Your mother is going to be okay," the calm, professional voice on the long-distance phone said when I called Mom's nursing home. I found myself confused by the impromptu reassurance. The word *negative* immediately threw me. *What X ray? And why* wouldn't *my mother be okay? What was going on?* I'd called just to say a quick hello to her.

Before I could get any answers, I found myself thrust on hold, that uniquely modern limbo, while someone fetched Mom. In that short but amazingly interminable wait, I was swept up in a damburst of worry. *Had my older brother and sister shielded me from something? Had a serious situation developed that I simply didn't know about? Why would they X ray her if nothing was wrong, and can't they think of a better word than* negative *to give you good news about an X ray?* I wanted to pray, but I was too busy worrying.

At last, I was retrieved from limbo by the nurse saying, "Hang on, she's on her way."

"Wait!" I practically shouted and demanded an explanation.

It all came out. Mom had been dancing when she took a spill and sprained her wrist. The nurse was new and as such had confused me with my local brother, who'd already been apprised of events. I felt myself sag with relief. All I could say was, "Dancing?"

When Mom got on she had very little recollection of hurting herself, though she allowed she might have been overdoing it. (In fact, she had been jitterbugging at a birthday party for another patient on her Alzheimer's unit.) "You know me," she said. "Always on the go."

Just like my imagination. My gut response to a situation isn't always the right one. When the nurse said everything was okay, I immediately assumed something was wrong. Instead of reaching for faith, I reached for worry. Often I am too quick to assume the worst, but if I truly allow myself to trust God with my life, then I must believe that He wants only the best for me.

Lord, teach me to turn to You rather than to myself in moments of crisis.   —*Edward Grinnan*

THU
14

Whatsoever things are honest, whatsoever things are just, whatsoever things are pure, whatsoever things are lovely, whatsoever things are of good report; if there be any virtue, and if there be any praise, think on these things.   —*PHILIPPIANS 4:8*

"Few people can go twenty-four hours without saying something negative. As an antidote, two U.S. senators have introduced a resolution proclaiming May 14 as a positive-speaking day."

I snorted and put down the newspaper. *I don't need a day like that. I'm a positive thinking/speaking person if there ever was one!*

Less than half an hour later, a friend greeted me with, "That's a pretty blouse you're wearing." I answered, "Oh, this old thing? I've had it for years!"

Well, that was an accident. It won't happen again.

Later that morning I spotted my neighbor, so I called across our fence, "Come on over for coffee." I'd just made a thirteen-egg angel food cake, my specialty, and I was sort of proud of it. Yet, when I served her a slice and she exclaimed, "Your cake is so light, I almost have to nail it down to take a bite!" do you think I graciously answered, "Thank you"? No, I shrugged and said, "It turned out heavier this time than usual."

Oops, miss number two . . . I'll have to do better.

The opportunity came that afternoon when a jogger paused near our driveway and said, "Your roses are beautiful!" I shrugged again. "They were much nicer last year."

My third deprecating remark in as many hours. If this were a baseball game, I'd have struck out.

Why must I downplay any compliment, implying that the person giving it is wrong, that what he or she says is untrue? Laugh if you like, but how long do you think *you* can go without saying something negative about yourself? Or worse, about someone else?

Father, help me to think and speak positively about every-one—myself included.   —Isabel Wolseley

---

FRI

15

But when Jesus heard it he said, "This illness is not unto death; it is for the glory of God, so that the Son of God may be glorified by means of it."
—JOHN 11:4 (RSV)

My friend Kimi carries a great sadness. Her arms are empty. Four months ago, her daughter Mari died.

When she was just a toddler, Mari was stricken with meningitis. Kimi, a woman of profound faith, prayed for her child and believed that a passage from John 11:4 was a word for her situation, as well: "This illness is not unto death; it is for the glory of God."

Mari lived, but not to grow as she might have. Kimi would tell me in glowing words of love how Mari weighed over sixty pounds now and was getting too heavy to hold in the shower and how she was so happy, always laughing. Mari was twenty-five when she died.

Sometimes Kimi couldn't come to my home because there was no one to stay with Mari. Diapers, baths, feedings . . . she did them willingly for all those years. And never one word of thanks, for Mari could not talk—only smile. Kimi once said to me, her eyes alight with joy, "How is it God has chosen me to care for Mari—to be given such a privilege?"

My friend Kimi is grieving, but in her sorrow I know one thing. She was right. Mari's illness so many years ago has worked "for the glory of God." To all of us who have humbly beheld Kimi's devoted love for Mari, it is Kimi herself who has shown us the glory of God.

Loving Lord, comfort all the Kimis and through them let me learn less about myself and more about You.   —Carol Knapp

Herald of Healing

We may not climb the heavenly steeps
    To bring the Lord Christ down;
In vain we search the lowest deeps,
    For Him no depths can drown:

But warm, sweet, tender, even yet
    A present help is He;
And faith has still its Olivet,
    And love its Galilee.

The healing of His seamless dress
    Is by our beds of pain;
We touch Him in life's throng and press,
    And we are whole again.
         —JOHN GREENLEAF WHITTIER

SAT
16

There is the sea, vast and spacious, teeming with creatures beyond number—living things both large and small. There the ships go to and fro. . . .
—PSALM 104:25-26 (NIV)

One of the best blessings of the past year is that my husband Bill is sailing again. Our "new" (1972) sailboat has become a peaceful haven where we can assess more clearly what the Lord is doing in our lives.

One Saturday recently I was sitting on deck, the spring sun warm on my shoulders. Bill took a break from his joyful puttering and stretched out on the other shelf-seat. We talked quietly about the challenges facing us and our mostly grown sons. Talk of the present gave way to concerns about what the future might hold. Before long my peace had given way to worry, and worry to fear. I was wishing I could stay safe in the present, avoid going on into a future that seemed so uncertain.

We fell silent and watched as a graceful, two-masted sloop raised her white sails and dipped past the cove entrance, headed for Chesa-peake Bay, maybe on to the sea.

"You know, honey," Bill said quietly, "boats are only completely safe when they are in harbor, but boats weren't built to stay there."

Instantly, I understood—Bill and I weren't built to stay "safe." We were built to follow wherever the wind of the Holy Spirit blows us. My peace returned as Bill started the boat's motor and we headed out into the river.

Lord, thank You for the sweet, strong wind of the Holy Spirit to guide my small ship through the seas of life.
                                                    —*Roberta Rogers*

SUN

17   He died for all. . . .   —II CORINTHIANS 5:15 (NIV)

My wife Rosie and my son Ryan accompanied me on a speaking trip last spring. As we arrived at the church where I was to speak, Ryan told me he wanted to go into the pastor's study with me. After we greeted the pastor, Ryan sat in the study and watched me go over my sermon notes for a while. Then he asked me what I would be preaching about. "I'll be speaking on Second Corinthians five fifteen," I answered, "where Paul tells us that Christ died for all."

Ryan began writing on a piece of paper. As we got ready to go into the sanctuary, he handed me the paper and said, "Use this in your message, Dad." I took the paper and put it with my notes. Ryan joined his mom and the pastor, and I proceeded to the pulpit.

When I got up to speak, I saw Ryan sitting happily next to Rosie. As I neared the end of my sermon, I noticed that tears were rolling down his cheeks. *Had Rosie disciplined him for some reason? Did he hurt himself, or was he not feeling well?*

Then I remembered his note. I quickly found it and said to the congregation, "My eight-year-old son wanted me to give you a special message." It read, "Luke 10:27 [NIV]: Jesus answered, 'Love the Lord your God with *all* your heart and with *all* your soul and with *all* your strength and with *all* your mind.'" The word *all* was underlined each time.

Dear Lord, You died for us all. *Today, help me to give my* all *to You.*
                                                    —*Dolphus Weary*

MON
18 *He changeth the times and the seasons: he removeth*
kings, and setteth up kings. . . .   —DANIEL 2:21

Change is difficult. That's why when lightning struck our telephone lines this weekend, requiring us to replace our phones, my husband and I were disappointed to learn we'd have to trade our familiar rotary phones for new push-button models. The young repairman said our phones were antiques. They had served us well, but we couldn't stand in the way of progress.

Gazing at the slicker, smaller object on my kitchen wall, I found myself missing the sturdiness, the solid presence of the old phone. What conversations had hummed through that receiver! What loving words had been transformed into sounds to warm my heart! Just as I was ruminating on the coldness of technology, I heard a mellow ring. It was the new phone. I picked it up. It felt odd in my hand, but the sound of Marta's voice was pure and rich.

"Hi, Susan. I've missed talking with you. What are you doing?"

"Mostly feeling sorry for myself about why things have to change," I confessed. I was pleased to hear her voice. I hadn't noticed, but the cord on this model was longer. I could walk into the living room. I could pull up a chair and sit down, kick off my shoes.

"Well, let me tell you about my new phone," I said. "Maybe I am ready for the twenty-first century. . . ."

Dear Lord, help me to appreciate Your ever-changing world.
                                               —*Susan Schefflein*

TUE
19 *Incline your ear, and come unto me: hear, and your*
soul shall live. . . .   —ISAIAH 55:3

I have noticed that when conversation between two people is sparse, it helps to give their hands an occupation. Men seem to talk easier when holding fishing poles, for example. And I imagine words flow easier for women when they're working together on a business report at lunch or sharing ideas for a church potluck.

Whenever I want to have a deep discussion with one of my three sons, we go to the backyard and play catch. I doubt that the founder of baseball, Alexander Cartwright, had any idea that this game would prove such a boon to father-son relationships, but others confirm its contribution. A career decision was troubling one of my guys recently, and when I sensed his struggle, I gathered gloves and ball and led him out beneath the spreading maple where our game of catch is always played. For a long time neither of us said much of anything. The only sound was that of ball hitting leather—*smack, smlat, smack, smlat.* Eventually, his concerns surfaced, and between *smack*s and *smlat*s, I got in a few reassuring *uh-huh*s and *yep*s.

Soon, Shirley called us for dinner. Nothing had been resolved by the ballplayers, yet I could tell by my son's body language and from the expression on his face that he felt better. It reminded me of the feeling I get when, confused and uncertain, I bare my soul to my heavenly Father. I don't always come away from those conversations with every care answered, but the fact that He hears my prayers is usually enough to dampen my doubts and reassure me that tomorrow will be a brand-new ball game.

School me, Lord, in the art of listening for Your Word,
Buttoning my lips until Your voice is heard.
                                                    —*Fred Bauer*

WED
20   *I am thy servant; give me understanding. . . .*
                                                    —*PSALM 119:125*

Back in the days when I was dating, I was afflicted with envy of happy couples. I recognized that I was lonely, but I didn't seem to be meeting the right men. I had a lot of unrewarding first dates.

On one particular first date, I knew in the first ten minutes at the restaurant that this was not a man with whom I could spend the rest of my life, that this would be another wasted evening. And at another table, behind my date's back, I saw what appeared to be a blissfully happy couple. The woman was radiant, smiling, holding the man's hand. I felt consumed with envy.

They were seated when we arrived and finished their meal first. After the man had paid the check, he returned to the table and stood by the woman's chair, waiting for something. As I watched, one of the waiters brought a wheelchair to the table. The woman reached up, and the man put his arms around her waist and lifted her into the chair.

I stared, ice cold; I had just been blessed with an unforgettable lesson at a time when I most needed it. I couldn't trade my life for only a part of someone else's—I'd have to take it all. I should treasure what I have instead of wasting time coveting what I didn't have.

And about two years after I learned that lesson, I met the man I have been married to for more than eighteen years.

Dear God, thank You for my life. Amen.   —Rhoda Blecker

THU	*"It is to your advantage that I go away; for if I do*
21	*not go away, the Helper shall not come to you. . . ."*
	—JOHN 16:7 (NAS)

It must have baffled the disciples. Just when Jesus was getting started, He said good-bye and went back to heaven. And yet, He had to leave, for He was a distraction, and He knew it. People looked to Him for free lunches, medical treatment and education. But Jesus didn't come to set up a local social services club. Instead, He was introducing a worldwide kingdom of faith. When He left, the Spirit came with His gifts and gave us the church and helped spread the written Word of God for everyone on earth to enjoy.

As a teacher, I can see how easy it is to be in the way. I've always liked the discussion method of teaching, but when I was a beginner I was unskilled at it. My discussions were too structured, with hand-outs and procedures. Whenever there was a dead spot, I felt duty-bound to jump in and say something to fill the awkward silence. Students were intimidated by my presence.

Then one day I came to class totally unprepared due to an emergency. Desperate, I introduced the topic of discussion, then let students go with it. To my delight, it turned out to be one of those rare classes where virtue came out of all of us. I went away feeling like a real teacher, and I hardly did any of the work!

It's ironic, but sometimes the best way for me to be a good friend, a good husband, a good teacher is for me to keep a proper distance. So I have been praying:

Lord, help me to be more concerned about the growth of my friends than I am about my own visibility.   —Daniel Schantz

<u>*FRI*</u>
22
Let your light so shine before men, that they may see your good works and give glory to your Father who is in heaven.   —*MATTHEW 5:16 (RSV)*

It's a mere strip of sand near the eastern end of the long Bahama archipelago. I've never been to Castle Island—few people even in the Bahamas know about it—but I think of it whenever I read this verse from Matthew.

Tiny and isolated though it is, Castle Island is important for the lighthouse that is its sole human trace. Sailing in the area, my brother Donn anchored there one evening and swam ashore to stretch his legs on the beach. The lighthouse keeper, Cedric Hanna, surprised and delighted to have company, insisted that Donn join him for fresh-caught lobster and a tour of the building. What astonished my brother when they'd climbed to the lantern room at the top of the stairs was the size of the light that signaled safe passage through a maze of shoals and reefs.

"It was a *tiny* kerosene flame," Donn told me. "Barely bright enough to read by." Yet with the aid of mirrors and reflectors, it was visible twenty-five miles out to sea.

I think often of Cedric Hanna and his stewardship of that feeble flame on his scrap of sand. "Let your light shine," Jesus instructs. But what if my light is a very dim one? What if my good works are few and small?

Perhaps, I think, my little light is magnified in the immense mirror of God's love. Perhaps His reflectors are human hearts, spreading the flame of kindness one to another. Castle Island tells me that even the most insignificant act of mine—ceding my spot in the grocery check-out line to a mother with a fretful baby, a two-line note dropped in a new neighbor's mailbox, a smile and a "hello" to a toll booth attendant—even such faint candles as these can be multiplied by Him to shine like beacons in a dark world.

Father, what simple act of mine will spread Your light abroad today?   —*Elizabeth Sherrill*

<u>*SAT*</u>
23
A cord of three strands is not quickly broken.
—*ECCLESIASTES 4:12 (NIV)*

Recently, our goddaughter Kelly asked us to give the blessing in her wedding ceremony. At first, it sounded like a nice opportunity to be part of her special day, but as that day drew nearer, it felt like an awesome charge.

"What can we possibly say to two people on their wedding day?" I asked my husband Lynn one Saturday morning as we sat together, drinking coffee and eating scones at our kitchen table.

The search for an answer got us to talking about what we'd learned since our own wedding day twenty-nine years ago, when I had hardly heard the words spoken in our ceremony. I was too distracted with worries about whether I could get up from a kneeling position without tripping on my dress or get Lynn's ring on his finger without dropping it. As I looked back on that day, I realized how clueless I had been about the meaning of our wedding vows. I'm sure I assumed that our romantic feelings would carry us through the challenges of living them out.

"I think we should tell them . . ." I stammered, searching for the right words as Lynn poured us both another cup of coffee, ". . . that marriage gets better with time."

"When you keep God in the center of your relationship," Lynn added, finishing my sentence and then my scone. (Those things happen after twenty-nine years of marriage.)

Finally, we began writing down our thoughts in the form of a prayer, which we read at Kelly and Mike's ceremony. Here is part of our prayer:

Father, we know that love starts with romantic feelings, but a marriage is built upon the intentional choice to be committed to each other as couples try to live out their wedding vows. We pray that this young couple will keep You in the center of their relationship, and learn that they will love each other more when they love You first . . . because You are the source of selfless love. —Carol Kuykendall

SUN
24 *They shall run, and not be weary; and they shall walk, and not faint.* —ISAIAH 40:31

In the days when I worked on many projects with Norman Vincent Peale, I was always impressed—astonished, really—by the energy and discipline that made him achieve so much. An endless stream of sermons, talks, magazine articles and books flowed from him. How did he do it? Where did he get such inspiration?

The other day in some old papers, I came across something Norman had written in his clear, legible hand on the stationery of a London hotel more than a dozen years ago. He called it "An Affirmation." Here it is:

> I affirm that God's power is rising in me.
> Renewing and healing my body
> Giving power to my mind
> Giving me success in my work
> I affirm health, energy, enthusiasm, the joy of life.
> All this I owe to Jesus Christ, my Lord and Savior.
> He has given me the victory principle for which
> I thank Him every day.

Would not this affirmation strengthen any of us who chose to make it? If we believed it as sincerely as Norman did, I know it would.

Lord, help me to mount up with wings as eagles when I wait upon You.
                           —*Arthur Gordon*

MON
25

When he came ... he was glad; and he exhorted them all to remain faithful to the Lord. ...
                    —*ACTS 11:23 (RSV)*

At the end of my first year of graduate school, I was ready to quit. When Dr. W.D. Wyatt, my pastor back home, came to Fort Worth, Texas, for the trustees' meeting, I planned to ask him to find me work back in New Mexico.

Before I could say anything at lunch, Dr. Wyatt said, "Kenneth, Jesse Northcutt tells me that you did great work in his class."

I gulped and responded, "He did?"

"Yes," he said. "He also told me that he may ask you to grade for him in the spring semester." While I was trying to absorb that amazing news, Dr. Wyatt continued, "He's hoping you will stay for doctoral work, and maybe consider teaching."

I was so amazed by his words that I never mentioned that I had considered dropping out. Instead, I spent the next five years studying as I had never studied before, did doctoral work and taught seven years on the faculty.

In 1995, Dr. Wyatt died at age ninety-three. I flew to Albuquerque, New Mexico, to preside at his funeral. As I stood with Mrs. Wyatt and the family at the visitation, I thought once more about how different my life would have been if, on that morning when I had been ready to quit, he had not said those powerful words of encouragement.

Our son's middle name is Wyatt, as a remembrance. But mostly I try to show my gratitude by being sensitive to those around me who need to be encouraged.

Thank You, God, for all those people whose encouragement has changed my life.   —*Kenneth Chafin*

TUE
26

Clothe yourselves with compassion, kindness, humility, gentleness and patience.
—*COLOSSIANS 3:12 (NIV)*

When my daughter Sanna told me she had found a job as a waitress, I waited with dread and hope to hear how her first day went. Success was crucial. Newly out of drug and alcohol rehab, she was on the mend in spirit, body and mind. That night, after her first day, she phoned me. "Something awful happened at work," she said.

My stomach churned. "Tell me about it, Sanna."

"I was carrying a pitcher of iced tea to my very first table when I had a panic attack. I began shaking and sweating. I put the pitcher down and ran to the ladies' room, praying. I felt God telling me to go out and try again. So I did. The couple at that table was still there. They'd waited a long time."

"What happened?" I asked, gripping the phone.

"Well, I started pouring the iced tea for them, and I was so nervous I spilled it all over the table."

By this time I could scarcely breathe. "Go on, Sanna."

"Here's the thing, though, Mom. They were so nice. The man said, 'Honey, don't be afraid. We're just folk like you.' The woman took my hand and told me to take all the time I needed, that they weren't in a hurry. So I slowed down, took deep breaths and got through it. The rest of the night went fine. I think I'm gonna make it, Mom."

From the bottom of my heart, I thank this anonymous couple who showed mercy to their "inept" waitress, never dreaming how crucial their response was.

Lord, in this hurrying, exacting age, may I, too, give others the benefit of the doubt and show mercy. —*Shari Smyth*

WED

27 *"This is My beloved Son, in whom I am well-pleased."* —*MATTHEW 3:17 (NAS)*

Today, my fourteen-year-old son Drew finally beat me in a tennis match. And not barely. He shellacked me real good!

Eight years ago we walked out on the tennis court for his first lesson. The racket was bigger than Drew. I had brought a whole case of balls in a hopper, knowing that more balls would fly over the fence than land in the court. But Drew showed early promise at the game. He's worked hard over the years and now, as a high-school freshman, he's made the varsity tennis team.

I've got to admit that though my middle-aged ego stings a little in defeat, I'm proud of my boy. It's a great thing to see your children forge ahead, succeed and surpass you. Yet I want Drew and Luke and Jodi to know that they never have to compete for my love or respect. They don't have to get good enough to be loved and accepted; I love them simply because they're my children.

Maybe one day I'll fully understand this truth about my heavenly Father: I don't have to earn His love or finally make the team after long years of effort. God loves me simply because I am His child.

Father, help me to accept Your love for me today and every day. —*Scott Walker*

THU

28 *Whoever loves his brother lives in the light, and there is nothing in him to make him stumble.* —*I JOHN 2:10 (NIV)*

An eight-year gap separates my husband Gary from his younger brother Rob, which left them perennially out of sync while growing up in California. When five-year-old Rob was playing Davy Crockett, teenage Gary was listening to rock 'n' roll. By the time Rob was old enough to drive, Gary was a married man in New York, a continent away. Thirty years flew by, widening the gap.

So when the chance came for both brothers to take a trip together,

Gary and Rob began to lay elaborate plans for a reunion. Rob would fly from California and Gary from New York to the tiny town of Sledge, Mississippi, their great-grandfather's birthplace. From there, they would take a weeklong journey to discover the original Southern roots of the far-flung Sledge clan.

Work schedules were rearranged. Plane tickets and hotel reservations were reserved months in advance. A complicated itinerary was created to satisfy Rob's passion for Civil War history and Gary's delight in old bookstores.

Then came disaster. Rob took ill. Refusing to disappoint Gary, who had worked long hours to clear his calendar, Rob got on the plane as scheduled. But by the time he arrived at the airport, he was worse. A worried Gary insisted on immediate medical care. Both brothers spent the first night in the emergency room. The next day passed waiting for Rob to sleep off the pain medication, the day after that sitting around until Gary recovered enough from jet lag to be able to drive. The itinerary was a shambles.

But not the relationship. A gap had been closed, a bond reforged in waiting rooms and coffee shops and a rental car. Whenever one stumbled, the other was strong. They were brothers in perfect sync.

Today, Lord, I will reach out and grasp the hand of my brother. —Linda Ching Sledge

29 . . . A time to mourn. . . . —ECCLESIASTES 3:4

The joy of my birthday on May 28 lasted until the telephone call on the morning of May 29. My dear friend Warren had died early that morning. As I rushed down the street to his widow's side, I remembered a day almost fifty years earlier.

It was bitterly cold on that afternoon in January 1948. I stood shivering on a corner, waiting for my ride to work. I looked up and saw Warren, on his way to work only a few blocks away. He smiled, and we began to talk. In those few minutes, my life was changed forever.

"Our apartment is available," he said. "Would you and Ruby be interested?" Would we be interested! There was a severe housing shortage, and for the past two years we had lived in two rooms plus kitchen privileges and a community bathroom. Warren's words seemed to chase away the chill.

In February, we moved into our first apartment, with our own kitchen and bathroom. Within that home we began to heal from the wounds of wartime separation, the disapproval of relatives and our poverty of spirit. Slowly, we regained faith, courage and hope. We also learned that Warren and his wife Eva were more than landlords. They were our neighbors, our friends and our family.

At Warren's funeral, as I stood near his casket and read some words of farewell, I still felt the warmth I received on that long-ago January day. Love, like God, is eternal.

All-knowing Lord, thank You for the gifts of love I have received from friends who have gone home to You.

—*Oscar Greene*

<u>SAT</u>
30

Wherefore I will not be negligent to put you always in remembrance of these things. . . .
—*II PETER 1:12*

Overheard at a counter where I was lunching:

She: We're going to the Hamptons on the three-day weekend.

Another She: We're going to the Jersey shore, but I wish we had more time.

She: We're lucky to have this. They used to have Memorial Day on the thirtieth. It was terrible when it came in the middle of the week.

Another She: What is it anyway, Memorial Day?

She: Some people call it Decoration Day.

Another She: Well, Memorial or Decoration, what is it?

She: I dunno.

I, smart fellow, intruded in their conversation. "Memorial Day," I said, "is a day set aside to honor the dead in the wars. It began by people decorating the graves of Civil War dead and . . ."

If looks could kill, I'd be as dead as a Civil War vet. "Thanks," she said, before turning away.

But they had started me thinking. I remembered back when I was in school, the marches we took to the town cemetery. They were a pain for us kids, something we had to do, but that was before World War II, before Bobby Stoddart and Slap Clarke and Bernie Lamont didn't come back. I remember them, and others, well. But on Memorial Day?

Yes, on Memorial Day. I, too, had other plans, but I would change them now.

And that's how it happened that I was at the Soldiers' and Sailors' Monument in New York City, standing at attention the way I hadn't done since school days. I was paying my respects because of two strangers who didn't know what Memorial Day meant.

Father, for all the Memorial Days I have neglected, forgive me.
                                                    —*Van Varner*

SUN

31   *"I will pour out my Spirit on everyone. . . ."*
                                        —*ACTS: 2:17 (GNB)*

On Pentecost Sunday, the minister read the familiar story in Acts 2 where the Holy Spirit shakes the whole house like the rush of a mighty wind and falls upon the believers in cloven tongues of fire. I was filled with enthusiasm for this mysterious Holy Spirit Who sweeps into lives with high drama, miracles, conversions, healings and irrefutable displays of power. But when I left church and got into my red minivan, I was back in a predictable world that seemed to have nothing to do with Pentecost.

That evening it was my turn to serve the youth snack supper. Afterward I faced a down-to-earth dilemma—what to do with the leftovers, fruit punch, pretzels, a quarter of a sheet cake and three bags of sandwiches. As I pulled out of the church driveway, a thought darted through my mind. *This food should be given to someone who needs it.* No one came to mind, as I stopped at the grocery store for some allergy medicine. The man in front of me at the check-out looked as if he could use more than the few items he was buying. Should I offer the leftover food to him? *No,* I thought firmly. *You don't want to seem foolish.*

On the way home from the grocery store, I passed an old woman with a stocking cap pulled down over her straggly gray hair. She sat on a dilapidated chair on the tiny front porch of an old sharecropper's house. In a second I was past the rusty tin roof. *You should have stopped,* I thought. *No, no,* I rationalized. *Maybe she can't eat sandwiches. Maybe she doesn't even like them. But Karen,* a calm thought answered, *If you don't do it now, you won't ever do it.*

I battled inwardly all the way to the turn-off for home. I finally gave in and made a U-turn. I pulled up in front of the little house, got out and introduced myself to the old woman. "You may think I'm crazy, but I have some food left from a church youth supper, and I thought you might like it."

The sun was setting as I finally drove home, this time in peace.

Father, thank You for the miracle of Your Spirit, Who enables me to say, "Yes, Lord."   *—Karen Barber*

My Healing Journey

1 _____

2 _____

3 _____

4 _____

5 _____

6 _____

7 _____

8 _____

9 _____

10 _____

11 _____

12 _____

13 _____

14 _____

15 _____

16 _____

17 _____

18 _____

19 _____

20 _____

21 _____

22 _____

23 _____

24 _____

25 _____

26 _____

27 _____

28 _____

29 _____

30 _____

31 _____

JUNE

S	M	T	W	T	F	S
	1	2	3	4	5	6
7	8	9	10	11	12	13
14	15	16	17	18	19	20
21	22	23	24	25	26	27
28	29	30				

Jesus went about all Galilee . . . healing all manner of sickness and all manner of disease among the people.

—MATTHEW 4:23

<u>MON</u> **THE TOUCH OF THE HEALER**

1 Healing Our Bodies
Heal me, O Lord, and I shall be healed. . . .
—*JEREMIAH 17:14*

Several years ago I was speaking at a conference at Laity Lodge, a retreat center in the hill country of central Texas. Almost as an aside, I mentioned that as a teenager I had suffered from juvenile rheumatoid arthritis. At the close of the session, a woman who knew that I lived a very active life asked pointedly, "Did God heal you?" I was tempted to say no, but as I thought about the question, I knew that the answer had to be yes.

At the time my arthritis was diagnosed, treatments were rather limited, and I didn't respond well to any of them. My doctor suggested that if I went to New Mexico or Arizona, my arthritis might respond to the drier climate. My mother's oldest sister, an aunt whom I had never met, lived in Albuquerque, New Mexico, and invited me to stay with her. My cousin Leah, who was a nurse, suggested that I see a doctor at the Lovelace Clinic. Eventually, I became a patient of Dr. Clarence Kemper, a renowned rheumatologist. When he was asked to conduct one of the early experiments on the use of steroids in human beings, I was one of the patients in the study. My body's response to the medicine surprised even Dr. Kemper, and my arthritis didn't return when the treatments ended.

Looking back, it seems that God had me at the right place at the right time, that none of it was accidental. Of course, there were other factors at work in my recovery—God's call, which had given me a new dream for my life, and a host of people who bathed me with their love and prayers. God used all these in my healing.

Today, if someone were to ask me if I believed in healing, my immediate answer would be yes! For I have discovered that God is constantly bringing healing in many different situations in life and through all sorts of means.

Thank You, God, for the healing You continue to do in my life.   —*Kenneth Chafin*

TUE

2 *By one sacrifice he has made perfect forever those who are being made holy.* —*HEBREWS 10:14 (NIV)*

My heart ached in church as I prayed for friends who were separating—friends whose twenty-year marriage had seemed like one of the "perfect" ones. Suddenly, I felt vulnerable. If this could happen to our friends, could it happen to Joe and me? Our marriage looked pretty "perfect," too. Could our problems one day become insurmountable?

I twisted my wedding ring and glanced at Joe, sitting beside me. I remembered the day we bought my engagement diamond, fifteen years before. We couldn't afford to spend very much so we chose a small flawless diamond over a larger one with a flaw that cost approximately the same. I felt proud of my small-but-perfect diamond. Years later, I learned from a dealer that nature does not produce a perfect stone. A "flawless" diamond is only perfect to a magnification of ten. A higher magnification would detect hidden defects.

And yes, I thought now, *our marriage is flawed—as defective as the two of us.* But like a diamond, our relationship has beauty, too: strong love and shared commitment. Joe and I could make it shine by magnifying each other's strong points, not our imperfections. Taking Joe's hand, I prayed God would help our friends do the same.

Bless this marriage, dear Lord. Amen.   —*Marjorie Parker*

WED

3 *When I sit in darkness, the Lord shall be a light unto me.* —*MICAH 7:8*

Andrea grabbed my hand, her frightened face lit for a moment by the flash of lightning, and asked, "Are you scared?"

I nodded in the darkness, thinking it was silly for two grown women to be afraid of thunderstorms. But the night was cold, the tent leaky, and the sounds penetrating the rain's steady tattoo unfamiliar. And we discovered that we were not alone! Two figures materialized in the next lightning flash, Dirk and Klaus, refugees from an even leakier tent. They called to us from across the drowned and steaming campfire.

We were camping in a beautiful region of the Czech Republic, meeting with Czech, German and American Christians to celebrate Pentecost. We rejoiced for the eleven apostles who had been filled with the Holy Spirit and had spoken in tongues so many centuries before. But at that moment we were only four cold, wet, worried people seeking warmth and company.

Dirk and Klaus joined us; Klaus had his guitar. The night seemed short as we four held hands in the darkness, sharing stories about our countries, about our faith. We sang to the muted tones of Klaus's guitar until the sky was no longer lit by forks of lightning, but by the coming sun. Klaus smiled as he followed Dirk into the sunlight, humming "A Mighty Fortress Is Our God."

Andrea squeezed my hand again. But this time her eyes were shining, and she whispered, "I think I finally know what that means, what Jesus said, 'Where two or three are gathered in my name, there I am among them.' I hope it storms again tonight."

Dear Lord, the miracle of Christian fellowship is everywhere. Help me to experience its wonders today.   —*Kjerstin Easton*

THU
4

But godliness with contentment is great gain.
    —*I TIMOTHY 6:6*

Our family trembled with anticipation as we boarded the Land Rover for our long-anticipated night ride through a wild animal reserve in South Africa. "Maybe we'll see hyenas hunting or even a leopard," my eight-year-old daughter Elizabeth whispered excitedly. We had heard tales about these night rides—and there was a rifle next to the ranger's seat, so there must be thrilling sightings!

Then our ranger Dan Pretorius gave his opening speech. "The only thing I can guarantee we will see are impala deer."

The group groaned collectively, and one man said, "We've seen at least a hundred today!"

"But have you seen any at night?" Dan shot back. He explained that many people are so focused on seeing big game, like elephants or lions, that they ignore all the treasures of the Kruger Park and leave disappointed. He urged us, "Put aside your expectations. Consider *any* wildlife we may see as a bonus—even an owl or rabbit. Go on this ride simply to experience the bush at night, and you won't be let down."

Soon we rolled out the camp gates, and I left behind my longing to see wild game. I breathed in the night air, listened to sounds of insects and birds, and watched the trees shimmer in the moonlight.

We did see many sights that night—jackals and hyenas and elephants—but the best gift was the reminder from Dan.

Dear God, help me "ride" through this day, enjoying whatever will be and appreciating every "bonus."   —*Mary Brown*

FRI

5   *"Listen to me, my people. . . ."*   —*ISAIAH 51:4 (RSV)*

I have a friend, Bill Criswell, who before his death in 1996 had an unusual kind of healing ministry. His business card read "Consultant to Husband-Wife Enterprises." These Mom-and-Pop companies—restaurants, specialty shops, various kinds of service businesses—would typically start out building on the couple's interests and skills, then in a few years begin to fail.

Bill would travel as much as a thousand miles to confer with the bewildered partners. He didn't carry organizational charts, growth graphs or even a calculator. His sole piece of equipment was an inflatable air mattress, which became his bed in some convenient corner of his clients' home. Often he wouldn't even visit their place of business. Instead he would settle down in the house, fixing his own breakfast and lunch, joining the pair at dinner. Day after day he would simply be there, until they almost forgot they had a guest.

"But what were you doing all that time?" I asked.

"I was listening."

Listening to husband and wife talk to each other. Listening for the assumptions, the different priorities. "Nine times out of ten," Bill said, "when these businesses fail, it's because the man and woman bring different expectations to them. If I can help them listen to one another—to listen with the heart as well as the ears—the business problems solve themselves."

If Bill installed his air mattress in my house, I wondered, *what would he discover?* Do I listen, really listen, to my husband John? To my neighbor? To my grandchild? Do I really listen to God? What healing would follow if I did?

Father, teach me to listen.   —*Elizabeth Sherrill*

As the deer pants for water, so I long for you, O God.
—*PSALM 42:1 (TLB)*

It had been a particularly difficult day. It started early in the morning on a sour note when I staggered into the kitchen to find an army of ants winding their way to cluster thickly around the sticky rim of a honey jar that had been carelessly put away unwiped. Then my daughter and I had locked horns over unwashed dishes, mildew in the shower and her papers scattered helter-skelter over the dining room table. To make matters worse, my husband joined in with several ill-timed suggestions as to how I could more efficiently keep up the household. Like lumbering turtles, the three of us snapped at each other for much of the day, until I wanted to pull my head into my shell, close my eyes and disappear.

Instead, I made a cup of tea, and as twilight threw purple shadows against the mountains and yucca nodded creamy white bells to ring down the night, I retreated to the glider at the end of the patio. My peace was short-lived. My daughter and husband came out, bringing me an argument that I had hoped had long since been put to rest. My heart sank under yet another harangue of words.

It was then I saw the deer. Three young bucks, the velvet still soft on their antlers, quietly grazed in the bushes on the other side of our fence. Deer roam our hills, but in all our thirty years of living here, they had never come to our backyard.

"Hush!" I whispered nervously. "Look . . . deer!"

In the miracle of the moment, harsh words fell away. Frowns and furrows became brows soft with wonder. Eyes seconds ago blazing with anger turned gentle. The three of us huddled together, arms now linked around each other as we looked at the three deer, frozen immobile, their high brown eyes looking just as intently at us.

"I guess even they lock horns once in awhile," John said quietly. Then he gave us each a kiss.

Lord, help me to see beyond the irritations of my daily life.
—*Fay Angus*

MY MOTHER'S HOUSE

Last year, Mary Lou Carney, long-time Daily Guideposts *contributor and editor of* Guideposts For Kids, *had a close-to-the-heart encounter with grief. Her mother died. "She was my best friend and my biggest cheerleader," says Mary Lou. Come share the difficult, meaningful moments as Mary Lou spends a week clearing out her mother's house—and learning about her legacy.*   —THE EDITORS

SUN
7

Day 1: Leaving a Legacy
A man's life consisteth not in the abundance of the things which he possesseth.   —LUKE 12:15

I sit in the car, staring at Mother's house, waiting for the rest of the family to arrive. My sister Libby. Her daughter Carol. My own daughter Amy Jo. The numbness is starting to wear off now, and I feel grief gripping my heart like a vise. Mother is dead. I look at the house and think about how much she loved this small bit of real estate. Home. She'd always said she wanted to go straight from here to heaven, and she almost had. Just a few days in the hospital after the stroke.

I gather my strength for the task at hand: cleaning out the house and going through Mother's stuff. I look at the cement goose on the porch, its purple bonnet askew and, through tears, I smile. Purple. How Mother loved that color! From the carpet on the floor to the kitchen cabinets, she had surrounded herself with shades of lavender. I sigh, thinking of the crowded knickknack shelves, the stacks of periodicals, the cupboards and cabinets stuffed with a lifetime of stuff.

But even as I wave to my sister and step out of the car, I know our legacy is not here. Not in the paltry possessions Mother left behind. We've already seen our inheritance: in the hundred people who braved last night's weather to pay their respects at the funeral home; in the eulogy of the young man who sang at the funeral, talking about how Mother had been his favorite Sunday school teacher; in the dozens of flower arrangements that now covered her grave. One card read, "To Nancy, who introduced me to Christ."

This was what Mother left to us. The things we have to sort and the decisions we have to make in the next few days are just details. The truly important stuff already has been taken care of.

Dear Father, give me the courage to leave a legacy of service. And thank You for those who have done so for me.
—*Mary Lou Carney*

MON
8

Day 2: Generosity
Give us this day our daily bread.
—*MATTHEW 6:11*

"The dishes are yours," my sister Libby says matter-of-factly as she opens the china cabinet door and begins wrapping plates and stemware. At some distant point, Mother had decided I should get these, since I often entertain. And every time we finished a big family meal, Mother would wave her hand over the dirty plates and half-filled bowls. "Some day, Mary Lou, all these lovely pieces will be yours," she'd say. "So you might as well get acquainted with them now." We'd all laugh as my sister and I cleared the table and I began washing "my" dishes by hand in the kitchen sink.

Now I gently place the newspaper-wrapped bundles in a big box. How many meals my mother had prepared! That had always been her hallmark: food. Plenty of it. Heaping helpings for anyone she could scurry to her table. But her generosity hadn't stopped there. As a child, I had helped her pack boxes for needy families, prepare meals for shut-ins, bake cakes for Christmas presents. Every summer I'd helped her can hundreds of jars of vegetables—and then watched her give them away all winter. In fact, her Christmas present to me last year had been two dozen jars of homemade vegetable soup. Nourishing. That was Mother's specialty.

I nest the dishes carefully on top of one another. I will use these for future family meals. And I will remember just how big my "family" needs to be.

Thank You, Father, for providing for me. Give me a spirit of generosity toward all Your children. —*Mary Lou Carney*

TUE

9

Day 3: Commitment
Better is the end of a thing than the beginning thereof.... —*ECCLESIASTES 7:8*

"Come look what I found!" my niece Carol calls from the back bedroom. We all cluster around a tiny white box she is holding. She lifts the lid to reveal two small circles of gold nestled on white cotton. Mother and Daddy's wedding rings. It has been twenty years since Daddy's death, since Mother slipped that ring off his finger before closing the casket. But Mother's ring comes as a surprise to us all.

"I didn't even know she had a wedding ring!" my sister says, picking up the tiny, frail band. "I never saw her wear it." We never saw Mother wear any jewelry. My sister places it back in the box and reaches for Daddy's. "I'll take this one," she says, slipping it on her index finger. "You take Mom's."

The sliver of gold feels cold and solid in my palm. Mother's marriage. I knew it had not been an easy one, yet she had remained faithful to Daddy and to the vow she'd taken when she was just seventeen years old. I look at my own wedding band—thick gold with circles of diamonds. "This ring represents love," the minister had said at our ceremony twenty-six years ago. "It has no beginning and no end." Nice words, but I had soon learned that feelings weren't enough. It took commitment. The kind my mother had had. That last month, when Daddy was dying of cancer, Mother hardly left his side, even to eat and sleep. Love? Certainly. But more than that. She had made a decision to do what she said she would do. "Till death do us part." It was a lesson I could use to make my good marriage even more secure.

I slip Mother's ring on the finger next to my own gold band. It fits just fine.

Dear Father, in a world of quick fixes and fickle promises, thank You for Your never-changing commitment to us. Empower me to apply that same steadfastness to my own relationships. —*Mary Lou Carney*

WED

10

Day 4: Assurance
I go to prepare a place for you.... that where I am, there ye may be also. —*JOHN 14:2-3*

"Anybody want this?" My niece holds up Mother's church directory, a small paperback book with pictures of the congregation and their addresses and phone numbers.

"Sure," I say, taking the book and leafing through it. How many of these people I remember from my childhood! Thelma, who always played the organ. Murl Weimer, a tiny, bent man with a huge heart. The Frame family. Nellie Fisher, who had been my kindergarten Sunday school teacher. Suddenly, I notice several of the pictures have words scrawled across them in pencil. The same words. I move toward the light so I can make them out.

Gone to heaven.

It's Mother's handwriting. I picture her here at the kitchen table—perhaps she had just come from serving the funeral dinner for the family—as she pens those three words. *Gone to heaven.* One more friend waiting there.

I rummage through a drawer for a pencil and then find Mother's picture in the directory. How confident she was of where her loved ones were! And her confidence helps make me sure, too. *Gone to heaven*, I write across her picture, in a script not unlike Mother's own.

It is enough, Lord, to know that our loved ones are at home with You.
                                              —*Mary Lou Carney*

THU   **Day 5: Humor**
11 *A merry heart maketh a cheerful countenance. . . .*
                                              —*PROVERBS 15:13*

"I'll get the stuff under the bathroom sink," I call as I bend to sort the shampoos and hair rollers and brushes. But before I can begin, I see the huge purple comb. I have no idea where Mother got it, but she'd had it for years—more than two feet of lavender plastic, complete with huge teeth.

I remember the last time she was in the hospital for surgery. I made the long drive and rushed to her side. Surgery was scheduled for the next morning. I arrived to find her propped up in bed, combing her hair with this giant, clownish comb. She winked at me and said, "A girl's got to look her best. Some of these doctors are quite good-looking!" Then she laughed, and I knew everything was going to turn out fine.

"What's that?" Amy Jo asks as she comes into the bathroom. I hold up the huge purple piece. She wrinkles her nose. "What would anybody do with that thing?"

Smiling, I say, "Don't people *play* combs? I've always wanted to become proficient on some kind of instrument."

"Oh, *pleeaase!*" Amy Jo says as she rolls her eyes and walks away.

Later, I toss the big purple comb into my box—a reminder not to take myself too seriously. And as it hits some glassware with a musical *tink*, I can almost hear Mother laugh.

You are the Author of laughter, Lord. I'll try to give You some to hear every day!   —Mary Lou Carney

---

_{FRI}

12 Day 6: Hope
But I will hope continually. . . .   —PSALM 71:14

We finish cleaning out the secretary and close its glass doors. Then, impulsively, I stand on tiptoe and slide my hand across the top. It's still there. The giant maple leaf, its points brittle and prickly.

When Mother visited me last fall, I took her out to Lake Michigan. While I did my three-mile walk, she sat in the car and watched the lake. How fascinated she was with all that water, all that power! "I have a present for you!" I said as I knocked the sand off my shoes and slid into the driver's seat. I handed her a huge, perfect brown leaf.

"And what does this gift mean?" she said, lifting the leaf so the sun illuminated its intricate veining.

"Well, I know how much you dread winter every year, so think of this as your own personal piece of hope," I said as I started the car. "Spring will come again and so will new leaves."

"I'll keep it always," Mother said, holding that small bit of nature lovingly to her chest.

I touch the leaf to my cheek. We have just come through one of the most brutal winters Indiana has had in a century. Mother was confined to her house for almost a month. Yet, when I visited her in February, she pulled this leaf down from the top of the secretary.

"See," she said, that familiar twinkle in her eye, "I still have hope."

I look outside at the new buds on Mother's trees. Gently, I place the leaf between two pieces of cardboard for the trip back home with me. Hope is a good thing to keep close by.

I will hope in You, Creator and Sustainer, during all the seasons of my life.   —Mary Lou Carney

13 Day 7: Love
Perfect love casteth out fear. . . . —*I JOHN 4:18*

My sister and I stand on the porch, exhausted by work and grief. "Have a safe trip," she says.

I nod. "Are you sure you don't mind if I take it?" I touch the scrap of paper in my pocket.

Libby shakes her head and hugs me. "Just send me a copy."

I climb into the car for the long drive home. Boxes and pictures, a piece of stained glass and stacks of books fill every inch of space. I reach into my pocket for the poem.

Libby found it. We were sitting on the floor in the laundry room, going through stacks of papers. Cards. Articles clipped from magazines. Suddenly, Libby began crying and handed me a scrap of paper. Mother's handwriting covered one side. It was titled "To My Children."

> When I must leave you for a little while
> Please do not grieve and shed wild tears
> And hug your sorrow to you through the years.
> But start out bravely with a gallant smile,
> And for my sake and in my name
> Live on and do all things the same.
> Feed not your loneliness on empty days
> But fill each waking hour in useful ways.
> Reach out your hand in comfort and in cheer,
> And I in turn will comfort you and hold you near.
> And never, never be afraid to die—
> I'm waiting for you in the sky!

Even when confronted by her own death, Mother had thought about us, her loved ones. Had sought to comfort us. To give us courage and purpose.

I place the poem on the seat next to me, beside a box of tissue. It's going to be a long drive—but I know I won't be alone. Not now. Not ever.

Thank You, Father, for perfect, undying love. Buoyed up by Your love—and Mother's—I'll face life with joy. And death with courage.
—Mary Lou Carney

14 *We . . . will lift up our banners in the name of our God. . . .*   —PSALM 20:5 (NIV)

Every year, it seems, I hear people bemoaning the fact that fewer and fewer people fly the flag these days. But when four British friends were visiting me some summers ago, I got to see flag-flying from a completely different perspective.

I took my friends to downtown Walnut Creek, California, where we set out in different directions—the visitors to explore, the "native" to do errands.

"Let's meet up in an hour," I said, "at City Hall. It's a brick building with the American flag flying in front."

We all went our separate ways. An hour later, when I got to City Hall, none of my friends were in evidence. Fifteen minutes, then a half hour passed with no sign of them. After forty-five minutes, I was ready to start scouring the neighborhood when my guests began to arrive.

"I was waiting at a school," said one.

"I got your post office confused with City Hall," another complained. "It has that tall flag outside."

"And I went up to what turned out to be a private home. After all, it had a huge flag out in front. The homeowner was kind enough to direct me to City Hall," said the third.

"I headed for the veteran's hall before I asked the way here," said the fourth.

"Lucky thing it wasn't Flag Day!" I said with a smile, picturing them stopping at every house and knocking on every door.

So as Flag Day rolls around this year, I think of all the places where flags do fly proudly. And this year, my house will be one of them.

Thank You, God, for this "grand old flag." Let it wave proudly at my house.   —Linda Neukrug

15 *Evening, and morning, and at noon, will I pray. . . .*   —PSALM 55:17

Being a part of the Sunday morning "Prayer Can Change Your Life" class at Nashville, Tennessee's Hillsboro Presbyterian Church includes a commitment to pray for each member throughout the week.

Prayer requests are written on index cards. These cards go with us on our daily walks, business trips and family vacations. We post them in our offices, on our dashboards, kitchen windows and bathroom mirrors. In class, we delight in each answered prayer that's reported and share the unexpected bonuses that come from praying for others.

"We're already in the middle of June," Nina, a lovely young mother, said, "and suddenly I realize time is getting away from me. Would you pray that this week I can slow down enough to enjoy the summer moment by moment?"

Monday morning I was out walking by 5:30 to beat the heat. As usual, I carried my prayer card and prayed for each class member as I walked along: *And, God, go with Nina today as she cares for her children and goes about her duties. Help her to see the touch of Your hand in the morning sky. Give her precious time with her little Olivia. Let laughter fill their lunch hour, and bless their evening meal with a sense of togetherness. Give her many joyful moments throughout the day, and tonight don't let her miss the lightning bugs.*

As I topped the last hill and headed toward home with my prayed-over prayer card tucked in my pocket, I looked up and saw the touch of God's hand in the morning sky. Later, when my daughter Keri called from work, I hung on every word. I found myself laughing with my husband David over lunch, and late afternoon found me humming as I prepared supper for my family. That night, instead of turning on the TV, my son Brock suggested we go out and sit in the backyard and watch the lightning bugs.

"What a wonderful summer day this has been," I said to David as we got ready for bed. And later, as I snuggled down for the night, I whispered my last prayer of the day.

Thanks, God, for hearing my prayers, and for answering in ways I wouldn't even think to ask.   —Pam Kidd

TUE

16   *A devout man . . . prayed to God always.* —ACTS 10:2

Back when I was cooling my heels between college and graduate school, stubbornly without plans for the future, I lit out on a long, vagabond adventure that took me from the mountains of Ecuador to the Amazon River basin of Peru and Colombia to the shores of Lake Titicaca in Bolivia. It was rare that I would find time to sit down and drop my mom a line. When I *did* write, I told her how at the little rural hotel where I was staying you had to inspect your shoes every morning for tarantulas. Or that guerrillas had menaced our bus in the remote Colombian countryside. One of the few times I phoned was to report that I was laid up in a La Paz hospital with dysentery. "Don't worry," I said, "they've decided it's not cholera."

My poor mother. I'd tortured her without meaning to. Like so many young adults I had mistaken self-centeredness for self-awareness, recklessness for freedom. The other day on the phone I asked her, "Do you remember when I was lost in South America?"

"Of course I do," she snapped. Even Alzheimer's hadn't erased that memory.

"I'm sorry I didn't keep in touch more, Mom. I know it worried you."

"Oh, I was frantic most of the time!" she agreed, as always clearer about the past than the present. "I prayed like the dickens. Everywhere you went my prayers went with you."

I thought more about that after we hung up. My mother had had a powerful secret weapon, and so had I without knowing it. Like a passport, prayers go with us wherever we go, across all borders and around the world. To keep us safe, and to bring us home.

Father, forgive me when I fail to keep in touch, and remind me that wherever I go, You go. —Edward Grinnan

---

Herald of Healing

Sometimes a light surprises
    The Christian while he sings;
It is the Lord who rises
    With healing in His wings:
When comforts are declining,
    He grants the soul again
A season of clear shining,
    To cheer it after rain.
—WILLIAM COWPER

<u>WED</u>

17

Thy righteousness is like the great mountains; thy judgments are a great deep: O Lord, thou preservest man and beast.   —PSALM 36:6

My wife Shirley spent much of last summer in Florida, walking the beach with a turtle patrol whose mission is to help protect endangered loggerhead turtles. When work permitted, I joined her and gave her a hand.

The sea turtle season runs from May through October. Each morning, turtle patrollers walk a designated portion of beach, looking for the tractorlike prints of a mother turtle and the mound of sand that indicates where she has deposited her eggs. Nests are marked with a numbered and dated stake so they can be checked later. An egg, about the size and color of a Ping-Pong ball, takes about fifty days to hatch depending on temperature and location. Nests closer to the tide line are cooler and take longer than nests farther back on the beach.

One of the most inspiring things about turtle patrolling is checking a nest after hatching. Tiny flipper prints (Shirley describes them as zipperlike) indicate that the silver-dollar-sized babies, sometimes a hundred or more, have emerged. What a sight to watch them race to the sea!

One morning after we'd uncovered half a dozen hatchlings, we followed them shoreward, hovering over them like mother hens so the gulls wouldn't grab them. Shirley and I marveled as we watched them scurry as fast as their flippers would carry them toward the beckoning waters.

"The same God Who created birds with the navigating skills to fly thousands of miles to their exact destination must have programmed baby turtles to seek the life-giving sea," I mused.

And after they had disappeared into the immensity of the sea, Shirley answered, "And the God Who cares for baby turtles must surely care for you and me."

> *Teach me, Lord, Your creations to respect,*
> *To nurture them, sustain them and protect.*
>   —Fred Bauer

<u>THU</u>

18

And I will strengthen the house. . . .
                   —ZECHARIAH 10:6

On a sun-bright day last June, my son Paul and his six children suddenly appeared at my house. They needed a place to stay, a listening ear, and someone to cook and care for them, for . . . well, we didn't know how long. Can you imagine the sense of panic that swooped over this sixty-five-year-old grandmother who had grown used to living alone, loves peace and quiet, and cooks as little as possible? It had been a long time since so much mothering had been asked of me. Was I up to it? I felt overwhelmed, the way I do when my normally neat garden has become overgrown. But, of course, I invited them in, managed to scrounge up a meal, and we talked and talked until the sun went down.

Then Paul helped me open the sofa bed, put sheets on the guest bed, roll out my sleeping bag, carry blankets and pillows from the basement, and fix a "crib" for baby Joseph in the inflatable kiddy wading pool. When everyone was finally bedded down and I entered my own bedroom, closing the door behind me, I was too tired to pray anything but, "Dear God, help!"

The visit stretched on for ten days. At times I thought I'd never make it, and I longed for my lost privacy. There were moments of irritation when our individual needs bumped up against each other in our now-crowded living space. And most nights, I fell into bed in exhaustion. But I'm still amazed at several things. Within a day or two, a power greater than mine took over as I swung into action as the maternal figure in a busy household, a role I hadn't held for many years. Though I was tired at night, I slept well and woke refreshed. I became reacquainted, on a deep personal level, with my son, and discovered again that Paul has the *sweetest* soul this side of heaven. My grandchildren, who have lived most of their lives in Colorado, have become real people for me in a deep new way.

Paul and the children are back in their own home now. All is well. And Grandma has discovered something: By the grace of God, weeds did not take over my inner garden. In fact, hearts have sprouted up anew all over the place!

My trustworthy God, help me to remember, always, that You will empower me in any challenge in which love is the labor.
                                           —*Marilyn Morgan Helleberg*

FRI

19 *Be without covetousness; and be content with such things as ye have. . . .* —HEBREWS 13:5

I'd spent several hours raking and digging and weeding when the mail arrived, bringing a magazine whose colorful cover announced, "You, too, can have a spot like this!"

I straightened my aching back and studied the pictured patio. A dainty coffee-filled cup and sweet roll topped a wrought-iron table. The matching bench, a wrought-iron rose molded into its black, lacy seat, invited me to sit and rest. *I wish I had a serene spot like that.*

Suddenly, Hebrews 13:5 popped into my mind. *Hey . . . maybe I can have a patio, too, if I'll "be content with such things as I have."*

In the garage, I found a plank and several concrete blocks. *There's my bench!* The table is just a discarded wooden spool that utility wires once wound around. I put them on my "patio"—a nook beneath a shade tree in the garden. All of this activity whetted my appetite and made me remember the cup of coffee and the sweet roll in the magazine photo.

In the cupboard was a box of banana muffin mix. I mixed the batter and scooped it into a ring mold. Before popping it into the microwave, I sprinkled its top with a combination of one tablespoon brown sugar, one-half teaspoon cinnamon and one-quarter cup chopped nuts. The three and a half minutes the batter was in the microwave was just enough time to pour coffee into a pretty cup.

God's creation is just as pretty at a makeshift table and plank bench as at an elegant wrought-iron one. I watch gray-blue, sun-rimmed clouds drifting across an even bluer background and listen to the music of a honeybee hovering over spirea blossoms. And I smile when I've sat so still that a fat robin hops up for a fallen crumb, then a bright-eyed chipmunk darts from a rock crevice and claims one, too.

Thank You, Father, for giving me everything I need to be content.
                                                                    —*Isabel Wolseley*

SAT
20
Fear thou not; For I am with thee: be not dismayed; for I am thy God: I will strengthen thee; yea, I will help thee; yea, I will uphold thee. . . . —ISAIAH 41:10

Several years ago, the lovely, old maple in the backyard of our farm in Pawling, New York, had died. Norman and I were both crestfallen as we surveyed it sadly one Saturday morning. "I guess we better call the tree man," Norman said, "it's too near to the house for comfort."

The tree surgeon came that afternoon, but instead of sawing

through the trunk immediately, as we expected, he began by trimming away small upper branches. Then he sawed the larger limbs off until just the lower trunk was left. This he sectioned too, until his final cut when the tree base toppled harmlessly to the ground. "On difficult jobs like this," he explained, "we always tackle the easy part first. That way, the rest of the problem gets simpler and simpler as we go along."

Norman scratched his head thoughtfully and went back to put the finishing touches on his sermon. And sure enough, the next day, Norman told the congregation at the Marble Collegiate Church about what he had learned from the tree surgeon. Now, whenever I am stymied by a sticky problem, I think back to that Saturday. Instead of trying to cope with the whole dilemma at once, I have learned to sort it out into little pieces that aren't so hard to tackle, after all.

When you're stuck with a problem that seems larger than life, you might want to think about our friend, the tree surgeon.

My problem, dear Lord, always seem to shrink once I've called on You. —Ruth Stafford Peale

---

SUN
21

Let every man be fully persuaded in his own mind. He that regardeth the day, regardeth it unto the Lord. . . . —ROMANS 14:5-6

When he was a young man, my father played semipro baseball with the Macon Peaches and, I'm told, was a star pitcher. Growing up, I was aware of his great love for the sport. He faithfully attended the Saturday games of the local team and took time off from work to keep up with the World Series each year, first by radio, then television.

As a teenager, I asked my mother, "Why did Daddy leave baseball when he still cares so much for it?"

"It was when they started having the games on Sunday," she told me. "He was ready to play ball anytime, but not on the Lord's day."

"Why not?"

"Because of his convictions. His Bible instructed him to keep the Sabbath holy and do no work on that day. He felt that if he played baseball for pay on Sunday, he would be breaking one of God's commandments."

I could see no harm in playing a ball game, even on Sunday. But something about it nagged at me. After all, we were talking about one

of the Ten Commandments. There are others that teach us not to kill
or steal or commit adultery. Surely I wouldn't be guilty of one of those
sins. But was I free to pick and choose which I would obey and which
ignore?

The following Sunday morning at church, I looked at Daddy sitting tall and straight in the pew beside Mother. *This is where he belongs every Sunday,* my heart reminded me, *and so do I!*

Some people said Daddy was making a mistake when he left baseball. But I know otherwise. He read his Bible, prayed to learn God's
way and committed himself to following it as he understood it. And
that's an example for me to follow, not just on Sunday, but every day.

*All this day, Lord, help me to honor my father by keeping
my mind on You and Your Word.*   —Drue Duke

MON

22   *For God alone my soul waits in silence, for my hope
          is from him.*   —PSALM 62:5 (RSV)

I'm sitting in the recliner at two in the morning, watching an in-
fomercial about golf. ("A complete video course for just three easy
payments of $19.95.") I can't move because my three-year-old
daughter has fallen asleep on my chest. This sleep has been hard-won
for Hope, and I'm reluctant to rouse her.

Her labored breathing and comalike slumber come courtesy of a
102-degree temperature. To see my daughter so docile is to see a miracle. Hope is the type of kid whom other parents kindly call "active,"
meaning she swings from the light fixtures and swings at her sister.
But this fever has tamed her. She's so hot she leaves sweat stains on
my dark shirt.

I am an American male. I change my own oil. I do my own taxes.
And I never, *ever* call the repairman. On nights like this, holding a
sick child, I'm rendered impotent. To just sit here and wait and wait
and . . . where's the owner's manual? What problem is this that I cannot solve? Just give me a pair of needle-nose pliers, a wiring diagram
and some duct tape, and I'll. . . .

I'll do nothing. Do nothing but wait. Because, I'm learning, it's all
I *can* do. Hold her here, spoon in some medicine, wipe her brow.
That's it. Wait.

By sundown tomorrow, my wife assures me, Hope will be back to her old self—a mixed blessing, by most accounts. But I will silently cheer her whining then, happy, at least for a moment, that she and I have survived this siege. We'll both live a little longer to learn more about each other.

I've learned, for instance, all there is to know about golf—about taking your time, about playing the lie, about reckoning the doglegs and occasional hazards. And when my daughter is old enough to read, she'll learn the metaphoric possibilities of her own name. She'll learn how Hope can teach patience, even to the most reluctant of students.

Lord, in all my trials today, quiet my heart and help me wait on You.   —Mark Collins

---

TUE
23
"Age should speak; advanced years should teach wisdom."   —JOB 32:7 (NIV)

My eighty-six-year-old stepfather has made me realize that one of the most uncomfortable things about aging is that you feel useless. My dad spends much of his time in a chair because he doesn't move around very well. He wants to help me unload groceries from my car, but I can't let him do that because the stairs between the garage and my kitchen are difficult for him. He can't do yard work because he doesn't have the strength to dig. He can't paint a wall or hammer a nail or put things together; he never used to do much of those things, anyway, but he forgets that. "I'm just in the way," he sometimes says, and nothing I say can change his mind.

But my neighbor Robbi Johnson can. Robbi is seventeen years old, the age when young people are supposed to forget that older people exist. Every now and then, Robbi pops in on her way to somewhere—just to "say hello to Ray," as she puts it. And my dad's eyes light up. Suddenly, he has a place in today's world because a young person considers him a friend. They talk, they laugh, they exchange advice, and then Robbi goes on her way.

A few weeks ago, Robbi and her boyfriend stopped by on their way to the senior prom. They were in formal clothes—Robbi in a long black gown and Adam in a tuxedo—and they wanted my dad to see how they looked. "It's a rare occasion," Robbi said, "and we don't want you to miss it!" Robbi's mother brought a camera and snapped a picture of the couple with my dad, who was beaming.

For a long time after that, Dad never mentioned being in the way. He was also more interested in everything that was going on. Perhaps he realized that just by being here among us he makes our lives better. It's a message that doesn't get through when some of our friends and I put it in words. But it's a gift that the very young can give to the elderly when they stay in touch.

Whatever our age, Lord, teach us to appreciate our elders. Amen.
                                                           —Phyllis Hobe

WED

24 *When Israel was a child, then I loved him. . . .*
                                                           —HOSEA 11:1

As a boy, I found deep pleasure in fishing. My entire tackle consisted of a bamboo pole, a white-enameled tin of golden hooks and another blue tin of lead-shot sinkers that rattled rhythmically in my pocket when I walked.

The pond I fished was nothing special: round and shallow, perched on top of a plateau in the middle of a pasture. The lime-soda water spawned only sunfish, none of them big enough to eat.

Yet I was in heaven. I loved swishing through the clover at dawn, making my way to the pond. I would turn and chase a giant swallowtail butterfly, or tiptoe upon a big-eyed mother rabbit and her sleeping babies. I would pause to stuff myself with the wild crabapples that grew along the fence row or chat with the browsing cows. When I tired of fishing, I would chase bullfrogs, skip rocks, wade in the shallows, then slowly savor my sack lunch, my feet dangling in the cool water.

As I grew older, my tackle grew also: a big metal box full of lures and baits; three spinning rods; an electronic fish finder. I fished bigger and better lakes, and brought home heavy stringers of lunker bass.

And then one day my love of fishing mysteriously vanished. I haven't thrown a line in the water for many years. What happened? I stopped being an amateur. I became too serious.

So this summer I'm going to fish with a bamboo pole. I'm going to play catch with the neighbor children, instead of hardball with the guys. In short, I'm going to pay a little more attention to the process of living and a little less to the results. I think I'm in for a pleasant surprise.

Lord, return to me the wisdom I enjoyed as a boy, when I knew how to live. —*Daniel Schantz*

THU
25

This one thing I do, forgetting those things which are behind, and reaching forth unto those things which are before. —*PHILIPPIANS 3:13*

Beth, our daughter-in-law, recently passed her General Equivalency Diploma exams at the age of thirty-five. She received her high school diploma at a graduation ceremony at the Kiva Auditorium in Albuquerque, New Mexico, along with hundreds of other G.E.D. recipients. We were all there to cheer for her: Larry and I; our son Eric, with his and Beth's four children; our daughter Meghan, with her husband Pete and daughter Kayla; Beth's mother. The graduates included people of all ages, races and ethnic backgrounds. As one elderly woman walked across the stage with her diploma, I heard a child's voice pipe, "Way to go, Grandma!"

Watching those graduates that day reminded me that it's never too late to turn one's life around. In college I majored in art, and I worked for years as a commercial artist. I was doing well in that career when I decided that I wanted to become a writer, instead. A scary decision! Nevertheless, I enrolled in a writing course for adults taught by Rod (*Twilight Zone*) Serling at Antioch College in Ohio. I was really nervous the first day of class, but I hung in there throughout the ten-week course, and I sold my first story a few months later.

Is there something you'd like to accomplish? A career move? A physical fitness program? Reconciliation with a relative or friend? There's no time like the present to begin!

Heavenly Father, guide me this day as I consider new directions in my life. Amen. —*Madge Harrah*

FRI
26

Command them to do good, to be rich in good deeds. . . . —*I TIMOTHY 6:18 (NIV)*

You would think that after twenty-five years of sleeping in the same bed, sharing the same tube of toothpaste and raising the same children, we would understand each other. Wrong. Bill and I are living proof that opposites may attract, but they might also write the script for *Murder in Texas—Part 2*. We are constantly reminded that we're in a lifelong challenge to meet each other's needs and desires. We expect it will take at least that long.

Recently, I fell into a familiar pattern. As Father's Day approached, Bill left a catalog on my desk conspicuously open to a picture of a 35 mm zoom lens. *How boring,* I thought, *to know what a present is going to be. Surprise is one of the finest aspects of life.* So the kids and I, knowing that Bill loves fishing, found him a fishing vest to rival any *Field and Stream* advertisement. On Father's Day, he was, of course, surprised. He loved the vest, but he admitted to me later that what he really wanted was a zoom lens. Once again, I had imposed my wishes on him.

Bill is catching on to this principle faster than I am. He had been listening for clues to my desires and learned that someday I would like to have a string of pearls. As fine jewelry is not in our budget at this point in our lives, I considered this a dream of late-life luxury.

Despite the fact that I keep all the checkbooks in my desk, Bill found a way to grant my wish. He secretly stashed money in his sock drawer for a year. When he gave me the pearls, I was dumbfounded—not only that he pulled it off without my finding out about it, but that he would plan this special surprise for me. I wondered if I would ever be as sensitive toward him.

Bill showed me that love makes anything possible—even knowing when no surprise is necessary. It's a lesson I want to learn well, no matter how long it takes.

Lord, let me learn to give for the other's deepest pleasure, not my own.   —*Kathy Peel*

SAT

27 But as for me, I watch . . . for the Lord. . . .
—*MICAH 7:7 (NIV)*

Last summer my two older sons, Jason and Nathan, worked as lifeguards at a couple of local lakes. Visiting Jason at work one day, I learned something about setting priorities.

As I approached the beach, I saw that Jason was working "the chair." He was sitting on an elevated platform, shaded by an umbrella and watching a section of the water roped off for swimmers. I was coming to tell him about some concert tickets that he had been waiting weeks to get. Knowing how important the tickets were to him, I called out as I approached him from behind.

"Dad," he said, not turning to look at me, "come around in front of the chair so I can keep my eyes on the water while we talk." As much as he wanted to know about the concert, Jason knew people's safety depended on him. He was keeping his priorities straight.

That's a good thing to keep in mind at home, where relationships have to come before the laundry, groceries or bills. Or at work, where it's quality that has to stay in focus in addition to budgets, computers and postal rules. Or in my spiritual life, where prayer and meditation have to precede church committees or social activities.

Keeping my priorities straight helps balance everything in life.

Lord, help me keep my eyes focused on You so that everything else in my life stays in balance.   —*Eric Fellman*

SUN

28

And you belong to Christ. . . .
                          —*I CORINTHIANS 3:23 (NAS)*

My husband Gene and I had been married just two days. We were honeymooning at my cousin's farmhouse near our home in northeast Georgia. On Sunday morning, we decided to attend church. It wasn't my church, but I'd been there before and knew a few of the people. Gene didn't know anybody.

The people were very friendly, and we mingled with the crowd out front before the service started. Gene gently pulled me toward a couple he'd just met and said, "I'd like for you to meet my wife Marion."

His words had such a powerful effect on me that I blinked quickly to make my unexpected tears vanish. Of course, I knew I was Gene's wife, but this was the first time I'd heard him use the word to describe me. I'd been a widow for four long years before marrying him. Hearing the word *wife* so lovingly and proudly spoken by Gene touched and smoothed over all the jagged places the word *widow* had left. I belonged to someone again!

I still think about that moment ten years later. It was a bit like the time I gave my heart to Jesus, and I discovered some of the special names He calls me as a believer: His sheep (John 10:3); chosen

(I Peter 2:9); beloved (Ephesians 5:1). I'm no longer lost, and I'm no longer a widow. I belong to Gene—and to Jesus.

So many call You Father, but You make me feel as if I'm the only one. Amen.   —*Marion Bond West*

<u>MON</u>
29

And Sarah said, "God has made laughter for me; everyone who hears will laugh with me."
—GENESIS 21:6 (NAS)

Oh, no, not a flat tire!

My day was not beginning well. Frustrated, I coaxed the car off the highway and gingerly made my way to George Grave's tire and battery store. George is a deacon in my church, as good a man as you'll ever find.

As I entered the store, George smiled broadly, and Sadie, his golden retriever, padded over to greet me. Her mate Rufus, a gangly, floppy-eared German shepherd, peeked around the corner but kept his distance. He was obviously having a bad day, too.

"Sadie's getting fat!" I said to George.

"Yeah, I know," he replied. "And I just found out why. Every morning I get here at six o'clock to open up. Sadie and Rufus jump out of my truck and disappear for thirty minutes. Then they come waltzing back with smiles on their faces. Turns out they're cutting through the alley down to the doughnut shop. Rufus trots up to the drive-in window like he owns the place, puts his paws up on the counter ledge and barks. The lady gives them half a dozen stale doughnuts, and they waddle back home. I found that out yesterday when I stopped for coffee. Can you believe it?"

I was watching Rufus, who was looking sort of sheepish, as if he'd been caught and was mighty embarrassed. Suddenly, I started chuckling, then laughing, then roaring. Rubbing Sadie's ears, I felt tears sting my eyes and I realized that I wasn't angry anymore. Good laughter had conquered a bad attitude.

Lord, place the healing spirit of laughter in my heart today.
—*Scott Walker*

TUE

30 *The earth is satisfied with the fruit of thy works. . . .*
                                      —*PSALM 104:13*

> Almighty God, I pray Thee to help me
> to fill up the vacant places in my life.
> Thou dost make the odd corners in nature beautiful.
> Teach me Thy way, O Lord!
> Let me plant flowers in the empty places.
> Make the very corners of my life centres of spiritual loveliness.
> Make me a wise gardener,
> and let my life abound in flowers and fruits.   —*J. H. Jowett*

I found this prayer for June 30 in a tiny book entitled *The Daily Altar* by J. H. Jowett, published in 1907. The book consists of a brief prayer for every day of the year. Praying that prayer has made me do a lot more thinking about surprises and corners and flowers. Corners have to be empty to be filled. That's why I turn over my garden every year and throw all the dead plants and weeds into the compost.

"But how do we plant flowers in our lives?" I asked my friend Eunice, after I read the prayer to her.

"Create a beautiful memory," she replied after a moment of thought. "Do something nice for someone else. Whenever someone does something nice for me, it creates such a beautiful feeling that I want to do that for someone else.

"And," she added, "for me I think it means not complaining or always focusing on the negatives, but focusing on all the good things in my life and thanking God for them."

Thanks, Eunice, for helping me understand that to be a wise gardener, I must create loveliness for others every chance I get. And I must take time to appreciate the beautiful gifts and people God has put in my life.

O Master Gardener, root out of my life the weeds of complaining and negativity, so that Your loveliness may grow in me and I may pass it on to others.   —*Mary Ruth Howes*

My Healing Journey

1 _____

2 _____

3 _____

4 _____

5 _____

6 _____

7 _____

8 _____

9 _____

10 _____

11 _____

12 _____

13 _____

14 _____

15 _____

16 _____

17 _____

18 _____

19 _____

20 _____

21 _____

22 _____

23 _____

24 _____

25 _____

26 _____

27 _____

28 _____

29 _____

30 _____

JULY

S	M	T	W	T	F	S
			1	2	3	4
5	6	7	8	9	10	11
12	13	14	15	16	17	18
19	20	21	22	23	24	25
26	27	28	29	30	31	

*The Lord is near to those who are discouraged;
he saves those who have lost all hope.*

—PSALM 34:18 (GNB)

THE TOUCH OF THE HEALER

1   A Covenant of Healing
     Let us not become weary in doing good, for at the
proper time we will reap a harvest if we do not give up.
                                              —*GALATIANS 6:9 (NIV)*

For people with terminal cancer, time is often measured in moments, not months. That's how it was for a patient of mine I'll call Rex, who had cancer of the esophagus and wasn't expected to live more than six months. The autumn Monday I met Rex, he charmed me with his big toothless grin and his contagious zest for life. Although he was having trouble swallowing and was in tremendous pain, Rex didn't complain. Rather, he wanted to know how *I* was doing.

As fall stretched into the holiday season, Rex dropped twenty-five pounds. He showed up at the clinic with a string threaded through his belt loops to hold up his jeans. "I heard your kids are all coming home for Christmas," I said, avoiding his eyes. "I hope you have a wonderful visit. Now, please, tell me how I can help you."

Without a moment's hesitation, Rex answered, "Nurse, if I could just have a candy bar, I think it would be about the best Christmas ever." His voice was hoarse and raspy from the tumor. It was the smallest of requests, and I happily obliged, although I doubted he would be able to eat it. But when he left, he was gumming that bar of candy with his characteristic gleaming grin.

I didn't see Rex again until July, when he reappeared with a surprise for me—the first tomato from his garden. It was the best tomato I had ever sunk my teeth into, for it was flavored with God's promise of hope in the worst of circumstances. And for four more years, we were blessed with a lovely little ritual, Rex and I: a candy bar for Rex at Christmas and his first tomato of the season for me.

There's no medical explanation for why Rex lived those four years beyond the doctor's grim prediction. But I like to think that he was just aided by love—and our simple exchange of gifts.

Dear Lord, with You on the job, we really can make a dif-
ference. Thank You.   —*Roberta Messner*

2   *Rejoice, and be exceeding glad. . . .*
—*MATTHEW 5:12*

As a child, I loved spending the night with my grandparents. When it was time to go to bed, my grandfather Pa would make me a pallet on the floor beside his bed. It was our custom to take turns telling each other stories until we went to sleep. We told stories of bear hunts and roundups out on the western range and just about anything else we could think up. Pa would always reach down and hold my hand, and I remember lying there long after he would go to sleep, trying to keep my arm up so I wouldn't have to let go of his hand.

Other times we would be on the road before the sun was up. It didn't matter whether we were going fishing or driving across the state on a business trip, the pleasure of being with Pa was enough for me. I can still smell the coffee sloshing in his cup as we drove and the weight of his big hand draped across my shoulder as we talked and sang and planned further adventures to who knows where.

My mom says that if ever there were two soul mates, it was my grandfather and me. He was one of the kindest, most gentle human beings I have ever met. He was strong enough and gentle enough to pick up a strapping ten-year-old boy when he was hurt and rock away his fears. But at the same time, Pa had another side:

"Harrison, I can't believe you're letting that child swing on a rope from that height!" I remember my grandmother Bebe calling out.

"Daddy, surely you're not letting Brock drive that big tractor all by himself?" my mom would fuss.

He had me eating oysters on the half-shell and ordering whole lobsters by the time I was five. I learned to swim, dive, run, jump and drive anything with a motor attached soon after. He didn't want me to be afraid of anything, even death. When someone died, he made sure we faced it head-on with visits to the funeral home and stories of God's heaven.

Pa passed on when I was twelve. But he hasn't ever been very far away. Even today, I still feel him nudging me on: Enjoy life. Taste everything. Notice flowers. Hold babies. Try anything new. Have conversations with children. Listen. Be generous. Talk to old people. Don't miss any sunsets. Find a hand to hold. And don't ever be afraid to love.

*God, keep my arms wide open to life and make my heart
merry.*   *—Brock Kidd*

3   *. . . A time to every purpose under the heaven.*
                                      —ECCLESIASTES 3:1

The day started with signs of early labor. I was excited and happy:
My doctor was on call; it was my mother's birthday; and because of
a long holiday weekend, my husband Andrew could be with me at
the hospital without using up precious vacation days. What luck!

But then—nothing. The contractions stopped. I was very frustrated. I was also in trouble: As Brooklyn turned into a ghost town
for the four-day weekend, all my baby-sitters disappeared. That's
when I got mad at God.

"What's wrong with having the baby today, God? It's so perfect!
Any other day this week is a disaster. Who will watch Elizabeth?"

No answer.

"I trusted You on this, you know. Even when my child care arrangements fell through over and over. You promised Elizabeth would be
taken care of. Now what?"

No answer.

"What's the point in having the baby born on a different day? Why
is another day so important?"

Still no answer. I gave up and went into a funk. It wasn't until late
that night that I finally admitted that although there must be a reason, God had not chosen to let me in on it.

Shortly after I fell asleep, Elizabeth woke up coughing violently.
Cries of "Mommy! Mommy!" roused me repeatedly, until at 4:00
A.M. Elizabeth was too sick to get back to sleep. I nestled her fever-
ish little body around my huge belly, and we rocked and rocked as
the morning light slowly filtered through the dark gray sky.

It was then that I thanked God that I wasn't in the hospital. For
now I understood: There is a time for all things, and this time was
not meant for having a new baby. It was meant for holding a sick little girl who needed her mom.

*Lord of all creation, help me to be patient with Your ways
instead of impatient that You don't follow mine.*
                                      —Julia Attaway

4 **Proclaim liberty throughout all the land unto all the inhabitants thereof. . . .**   —*LEVITICUS 25:10*

On a ferry between Dover and Holland in the early 1970s, I found myself sitting across from a woman from Romania. Her name was Daniela; she'd come to England for dental work and was now on her way home. She told me the Romanian government was holding her ten-year-old daughter as hostage against her return from the West. I was sympathetic, if not entirely able to understand her predicament.

As we neared our landing point, Daniela fished out a *leu* from her purse, the basic Romanian coin, and gave it to me. It had a tractor on it. I scrabbled around in my purse and found a quarter, handing it to her in return. She studied it for a moment, then looked up at me with tears in her eyes, and said, " 'Liberty.' You even put it on the money."

I was suddenly prouder than I had been in years to be an American. I've never forgotten that pride. It was a gift of awareness, of recognition that God did shed His grace on my nation, and that I was very fortunate to be part of it.

Thank You, God, for a country that stands for liberty and justice for all. May I do my part today to uphold Your blessing.
                                                                    —*Rhoda Blecker*

5 **May God who gives patience, steadiness, and encouragement help you to live in complete harmony with each other—each with the attitude of Christ toward the other.**   —*ROMANS 15:5 (TLB)*

After spending June in South Africa, we returned home to find our church surrounded by excavation. The grounds weren't the only thing torn up. Our parish had been divided by disagreements and the removal of our pastor.

As I stared at the mounds of dirt and machinery, I noticed the large flower boxes in front, brimming with weeds. I pictured them filled with bright red geraniums and white petunias to distract from the ugly construction.

Later, at the garden center, I found slim pickings. The scraggly petunias were pot-bound but cheap—three plants for forty cents. The geraniums looked lush, but not a red one was left, just an odd assortment at two dollars each. As I deliberated over the leftover flowers, I thought sadly about how our church family needed to be filled with peace again. And as I made decisions, God seemed to whisper encouragement.

I bought the geraniums, though they cost more. *Right now our church needs extra prayer and effort—spend it!*

I put aside my picture of neat red and white boxes. There weren't enough geraniums of one color left, but as I loaded my flat with salmon, fuchsia and pale pink, I saw they blended beautifully. *The differences, even the conflicts, in our church reflect our diversity. Pray for a harmonious blending.*

Back at church, I planted the geraniums in the center of each box and the borders with the weaker petunias, then poured on fertilizer. *With special care and watering with love, our frail fellowship can flourish again.*

Many people have left our church. I look at the boxes, now filled with vivid blooms from all that was left. We who remain can be enough; an unlikely assortment can be beautiful.

Father, help us weed out animosity and nourish our relationships. May harmony and peace bloom among us.

—*Mary Brown*

MON	*"Prepare for me the kind of tasty food I like . . . so that I may give you my blessing. . . ."*
6	—*GENESIS 27:4 (NIV)*

On the face of it, chicken stir-fry (with broccoli) should be a pretty simple proposition. "You just cut up the stuff and put it in a wok, Mom," said my college-aged daughter Charlotte.

Sure, I thought, *nothing to it.*

I confess I've never cooked much of anything—that's what happens when one is lucky enough to have a husband who is a truly gifted cook.

Charlotte was living with me temporarily in my small city apartment while going to summer school. She's been independent for several years, but suddenly here she was again: a grown-up, but somehow still expecting Mom to know everything! And tonight she wanted chicken stir-fry for supper.

So we cut the chicken into small pieces. "What goes in first?" she asked.

"No idea," I answered cheerfully, but we decided on the broccoli— it looked somehow as if it would need more cooking.

"I think we should put in some sugar. Someone told me that's the secret ingredient," she said. Then we had to stop all operation temporarily and run out and buy some teriyaki sauce. And so it went.

The result was a quite edible meal that we shared with considerable mutual satisfaction. And the empty nest was, temporarily, empty no longer. But the child who had left was no longer a child. There's a joy in raising, shaping and watching a child grow and a reward in feeling essential to the process. Over the sizzling wok that day, I realized there was a quite different joy in standing back and noticing the burden of responsibility had become lighter—because invisibly, Charlotte had begun to shoulder it herself. While I wasn't paying attention, so much had changed: She was suddenly an adult, a friend, a fellow adventurer and a co-chef.

Dear God, let me give thanks for the ever-changing joys of family.   —_Brigitte Weeks_

TUE

7   **_"Shake the dust off your feet."_**
                                        —_MATTHEW 10:14 (NIV)_

There's a sorry-looking, old brown dog with a gray muzzle that I pass every day during my morning walks. He's tied by a long rope to a tree in front of his house, and while he looks well fed, he also looks lonely and unhappy. I pet him every time I see him, and I'm always rewarded by an exuberant show of affection. If I scratch his ears, he rolls over and over, and his tail goes wild. I've had fantasies of untying his leash and freeing him—and frankly, vivid fantasies of walking up the long driveway, knocking on the owner's door and giving him a piece of my mind for allowing this creature to languish alone.

One day I saw a man walking down the street with the old brown dog on a leash. _I'll give him a piece of my mind,_ I thought. So I returned the man's smile and nod with an icy stare. "Are you this dog's owner?" I demanded, ready to chastise him for the way he treated his dog.

"No, I'm not," he said pleasantly.

"Well, I think that you—" I stopped abruptly, confused. "You're not?"

"No," he said. "I just saw the poor creature, lying tied up day after day, and finally I knocked on the door—"

"Yes, I've thought of doing that myself!" I said excitedly.

"—and I asked the owner if I could walk his dog every so often."

"You're kidding!" I said, nonplussed. While I'd been fuming and plotting revenge, this man had taken action to improve a situation he didn't like. It was something for me to keep in mind next time I had a complaint.

Dear God, is there an ongoing situation that I've been complaining about? Today help me do, not stew. —Linda Neukrug

---

WED
8

When Jesus saw her weeping . . . he was deeply moved in spirit and troubled. . . . Jesus wept.
—JOHN 11:33, 35 (NIV)

Last night I was at a youth camp with two hundred and fifty high school kids. The telephone rang, and my heart sank as I was told that a sixteen-year-old girl in our town had been killed in an accident. Some of her closest friends were at our camp, and I had to tell them the terrible news.

Four girls were called into the camp director's office. Although they didn't know why they had been summoned, one of them looked at me, her face filled with fear, and blurted out, "What's wrong? What happened?"

No one has ever asked me a question that was harder to answer. I had no healing words. All I could say was, "I was just told that your good friend Carol was killed in a car wreck this afternoon. Her family wanted you to know. I'm so very sorry."

A fierce sucking in of breath burned the air, followed by screams and gasps of pain. Then we cried and hugged and prayed together into the night.

Now, in these early-morning hours, I wonder if I could have done things differently, if I could have found words to make the blow softer, the pain more bearable. Probably not; there will never be words to soften the blow of death or explain a senseless tragedy. In such a moment, I could only give myself: a hand to hold; a shoulder to cry on; silent tears joining in a communion of grief.

Father, when I don't have the words, may my presence bring comfort to someone who grieves.   —Scott Walker

9   *Peace I leave with you. . . .*   —JOHN 14:27

A small pine cone sits in a basket on our buffet. It's much more than just a souvenir of our latest trip to Canada's west coast. Sealed inside it is God's blueprint for a sanctuary.

After our drive across the broad, flat prairies, the narrow mountainous roads in British Columbia put me on edge. Hairpin turns and signs warning about rock slides on the road to Ucluelet left me particularly tense.

I was relieved when my husband Leo parked the car at Cathedral Grove, a magnificent stand of tall Douglas fir trees. We followed the foot trail into the forest, our steps cushioned by cedar chips, our voices muffled by moss-green velvet. High above our heads, a light wind blew among the treetops, but where we walked there was cool, quiet calm. I inhaled the pungent smell of cedar and felt my tensions melt away.

On either side of us, tree trunks stood like tall pillars, some nearly nine feet in diameter and more than a hundred years old. We walked down the winding aisle toward the tallest tree in the grove. Standing before it, I felt a renewed sense of awe at the God Who can create a cathedral from some pine cones dropped on the forest floor. I reached down and picked one up to take home.

Yesterday I had a mountain of work to conquer, and somewhere among the twists and turns I seemed to lose sight of God's enabling power. Fearful and tense about an imminent landslide of problems, I reached for the little pine cone. Holding it in my hand for just a moment helped me put things in perspective and gave me peace— cathedral peace.

Thank You, God, for the tangible reminders of Your peace and power that are everywhere around me. —Alma Barkman

FRI

10 *"But they did not realize it was I who healed them."*
—HOSEA 11:3 (NIV)

Last July, I was invited to go to New Orleans to attend a Promise Keepers conference at the Superdome with a group of men from my county. There were eight of us in my van, four black and four white. On the way, we talked about what we expected from this all-male Christian conference, but as we talked I became aware that we were only communicating on a surface level. We weren't speaking about the barriers that keep us from being fully brothers in Christ.

At the conference, we were challenged to examine our consciences and our lives: "How many of you," a speaker asked us, "have a deep, intimate friendship with someone of another race? How many of you turn to someone of another race to share the joys and sorrows of your Christian life and to ask for spiritual advice?"

On the ride back to Mississippi, something remarkable happened: One of my white brothers began to talk about what he had learned at the meeting. "You know," he said, "so many of my relationships with black people are task-oriented—we work together on projects in church or in the community or on the job. We get along fine, but we don't have any relationship outside of that task. I know now that being a brother in Christ means a lot more than that. I want God's healing power really to change my life and attitudes. I want to live out our brotherhood every day."

As I listened to him speak, old feelings of isolation and separation began to change for me as well. I felt a freedom to talk honestly about my own feelings, and I began to open up. And I've tried to continue the dialogue today and every day.

Lord, help me to trust You enough to talk to others from my
heart.   *—Dolphus Weary*

SAT

11 *The Lord lives; and blessed be my rock. . . .*
—PSALM 18:46 (RSV)

I was hiking Alaska's Twin Peaks trail with friends one Saturday in July. It is fairly steep, but the three-and-a-half-mile effort is worth it. We passed a stunning overlook high above glacier-fed Eklutna Lake.

Behind us, the jagged rock face of Twin Peaks rose majestically across the narrow, tundra-cushioned valley. The whole effect was spectacular and whatever big words were in my vocabulary failed to describe it.

We continued to pick our own trail up the spongy tundra and across an occasional slide of loose shale, straddling the spine of the mountain and always climbing, climbing. Ahead, huge rocks jutted upward in a final, forbidding spiral. "I don't know about this," I mumbled nervously. I did try, but after I got about a third of the way up the rocks, I froze. The height was terrifying and the fear of slipping, paralyzing.

Urging the others to finish the climb, I fastened my arms around a flat shelf of rock and half-sitting, I literally clung to it. I couldn't look down, so I tried looking out. It didn't help. Being eye-to-eye with Twin Peaks and higher than three separate flocks of mountain sheep, with the valley a dizzying drop a few feet away, was not a glorious encounter.

"If I faint," I lectured myself, "I'll fall off this mountain for sure." I felt utterly helpless. Gone were all my big words. I hugged that rock shelf and sang a simple childhood refrain, "Jesus loves me, this I know. . . ." And somehow I held on until my friends returned to help me inch down. Backward, I might add.

Letting loose the security that rock ledge held for me was one of my bravest feats ever. I understood, for perhaps the first time, the significance of God being called "rock" in the Scriptures. Not a big word, rock. Just a solid one.

Lord, You are the only secure Rock. Keep me ever clinging to You.   —*Carol Knapp*

SUN

12

I thank thee, O Father, Lord of heaven and earth, because thou hast hid these things from the wise and prudent, and revealed them unto babes.
—*MATTHEW 11:25*

On a perfect summer day, I gathered with a tiny Episcopal parish near my home to dedicate an open chapel in the woods behind the church. Clearing the ground and the trails leading to the chapel had been an Eagle Scout project of one of the members, who'd also built the benches and the case housing a statue of St. Francis.

The inspiration for the chapel had come from a man named John, whom the church had housed and fed. John was well-known in our community for his friendliness and his love of nature. Every Sunday, he was a greeter in the church. "Hello. Welcome. Good to see you," he'd say with a hearty handshake and sunny grin. He tended the gardens at the parish house and spent hours tramping the woods behind it. He found treasure there while those of us with more complicated things to do and think about passed by. The shape of a leaf, the texture of bark, the squirrels and birds were all wonders John shared with others. At sixty, he died of a heart attack.

Now young and old from all stations of life gathered to dedicate the chapel to him. The Boy Scouts stood at attention. A toddler kicked her feet in a stroller. An aged, wrinkled woman sat on a bench, cane across her knees. A thirtyish professional man, starched and crisp, stood next to her. A cluster of teenagers huddled together. Even a dog pushed his nose through the crowd and lay in the center.

As the rector talked of God's glory, I thought of John, who saw the splendor of God in a leaf, yet couldn't read a book or do math. I looked from the tip of the tall trees where sky peered through to the low, scraggly brush, and was reminded how the great and small, the rich and poor, all come to God through the same door of faith. Only the proud and self-important are excluded. The paradox is that the deep things of God are often seen most clearly by the simple.

Lord, clothe me in childlike faith so that I can see You and cast off the heavy, wearying burden my pride brings.
—Shari Smyth

MON

13

Eye hath not seen, nor ear heard, neither have entered into the heart of man, the things which God hath prepared for them that love him.
—I CORINTHIANS 2:9

All spring semester, my daughter Keri had anticipated a glorious summer. Now she was in the doldrums. She took a hospital job to work with patients and found herself filing charts. Her night class in calculus seemed overwhelming. Her sentences were peppered with "wasting time."

Sleep isn't peaceful for a worried mother, so I rose early to work at my desk. My usual computer screen saver of a kitten chasing a butterfly had disappeared and had been replaced by something called, of all things, "Chaos." Blocks of cells multiplied and divided into a riot of colors and shapes. Their patterns of movement were pretty enough to inspire me to look into the matter.

"David," I asked my husband, "budding chaos is monopolizing my computer. Is it telling me the entire creation is out of control?" *Like Keri's life,* I wanted to add.

My husband started talking about "principles" and "predictability." I told him I needed "simple."

"Picture a drop of water falling into a river," he said. "It swirls about in the current and rushes downstream, bouncing off rocks and experiencing such turbulence it could go anywhere. But though its course seems chaotic, the principles of nature are steadfast: Out of seeming disorder comes regularity. Though it's impossible for us to predict where that drop of water will end up, God will send it where it's meant to be."

I looked back at the screen. Fragments of a rainbow were dancing there. I couldn't imagine how this "wasted time" would finally flower into something good for Keri, so I reminded myself of the underlying promises God has made to us as He unfolds a plan far too complex for our eyes to see. And I smiled and trusted Keri's summer to Him.

Father, help me remember that when the world seems chaotic, far beyond our seeing, You have established Your order.   *—Pam Kidd*

TUE

14   *Thou art my hiding place. . . .*   —PSALM 119:114

A tall, narrow house on a busy street in Haarlem, Holland. Here Papa ten Boom opened his home and heart to the Jews during World War II, while his daughter Corrie had the job of manning a complex team of secret police in a bold venture to help Jews escape. Before the war was over, though, the family was betrayed; the ten Booms were sent to a concentration camp, Papa and Corrie's sister to die there. But the eight Jews living at the hiding place at that time were saved.

Fifty years later, people come from all over the world to see this haven of hope. I made my own pilgrimage to the house on the busy

Barteljorstraat. I wound my way up the skinny, circling stairway to Corrie's wee room at the very top of the house. The room was just as she'd described, only today a cool breeze blew in through the open window at the foot of her bed. The soft, white sheers floated into the room, softening the back wall and the hole that had been gutted to reveal the famous hiding place.

I stepped inside and something happened. No words, no visions. I just suddenly knew, as I'd never known before, that God is very, very powerful.

I needed to know it, for I'd lived in fear of the world and its potential for evil ever since I was eight years old and the Cuban missile crisis frightened me badly. Yet standing in the ten Booms' secret hiding place, I came to understand I need never fear evil. God is more powerful. No matter what danger I face, be it war, poverty or any number of stresses in the world today, truly I can trust Him to be my hiding place.

Father, "Thou art my hiding place" wherever I might be.
—Brenda Wilbee

<u>WED</u>
15 *That he may bestow upon you a blessing this day.*
—EXODUS 32:29

Last summer my wife Pam and I visited the Zuni Indian community not far from Gallup, New Mexico. We knew a young priest there who ran a school for Zuni children, and we asked him if he could arrange for us to see the *Santo Niño*, the little carved image of the Baby Jesus that somehow survived when the mission church built by the Spaniards was burned in the pueblo uprising of 1680. Some Indians rescued the statue and hid it high up on a nearby mesa where it remained, carefully preserved and guarded, for generation after generation.

"The descendants of those Zunis who saved the statue still have it in their possession," our friend said. "The Santo Niño, or Holy Child, is an object of great veneration. They are glad to show it to anyone who will regard it with respect."

So we went to a modest Indian dwelling where two old ladies brought out the little statue, not more than two feet high, dressed in colorful robes with one hand uplifted as if in blessing. No one knows where the Santo Niño was carved originally, perhaps in Spain, perhaps in Mexico City, but there is an aura of great dignity about it. Here it is after more than three hundred years, having survived fire and destruction and the bitter cold of those high-altitude winters, still a reminder of the goodness of God in the gift of His Son and the power of faith to touch the hearts of men and women.

Time passes, the years pass, but some things remain the same.

Father, grant us the grace of faith that endures.
—*Arthur Gordon*

Herald of Healing

Be Thou our great deliverer still,
    Thou Lord of life and death;
Restore and quicken, soothe and bless,
    With Thine almighty breath:
To hands that work and eyes that see,
    Give wisdom's heavenly lore,
That whole and sick, and weak and strong,
    May praise Thee evermore.

—*E. H. PLUMPTRE*

THU
16

Pure religion and undefiled before God and the Father is this, To visit the fatherless and widows in their affliction. . . .   —*JAMES 1:27*

Last summer my wife Shirley and I did some pinch-hitting for a truly wonderful organization, Meals on Wheels. That is to say, we delivered lunches to people who needed the service while the regular volunteer driver was away. It was a revealing experience. Not surprisingly, most of the recipients were single, most were women and most were grateful not only for the nutritious meal but for the social contact. Living alone makes one hungry for conversation, too.

One day, after depositing her meal on the kitchen table, Shirley asked a frail, wan, disheveled woman in her eighties how she was doing.

"Not so good," she replied, pushing the runaway white hair back from her face. "You see, I'm going to need chemotherapy."

"Do you have anyone to look after you?" Shirley inquired.

"My children are flying in next week, but . . . but," she said tearfully, "I'm afraid I'll cry in front of them." Shirley assured her that they would understand, and that she would pray for her.

A week later we delivered lunch to her again, but the woman who met Shirley at the door had been transformed. Her hair had been done, she wore a colorful dress, and her smile was as radiant as the noonday sun. Her children had come, she reported enthusiastically, and it had been a wonderful reunion. "And," she said, beaming with an irrepressible inner glow, "my son said he would come back anytime I needed him."

How sweet to feel we're loved. How doubly sweet to hear it.

When the lonely cry at home or in the street,
Prompt me, Lord, to be Your giving hands and feet.
—*Fred Bauer*

FRI

17 *There is a time for everything . . . a time to weep and*
a time to laugh. . . . —*ECCLESIASTES 3:1, 4 (NIV)*

The night my husband Bill had asked if I'd like to take a trip to Colorado, I was too excited to sleep. *Now's my chance to plan some family adventures our kids will always remember,* I thought. We would stop to read, discuss and explore along the way, making the trip a stimulating educational adventure for our boys. We quickly learned that historical markers and geographic discoveries paled in comparison to expensive souvenir shops. And after nine potty stops, seven hours of whining, four packs of gum, three rounds of throw-up, two heated marital arguments and a broken fan belt, we finally arrived at our destination: a "fabulous" dude ranch.

Suffice it to say, the advertising for this dream vacation was highly exaggerated. Our "luxury" accommodations were cramped and ill-equipped. Saying the cabin had two bedrooms was a stretch. If you counted the living room/kitchen-turned-bedroom-after-9:00 P.M., there were two. The "fully equipped" kitchen consisted of a small refrigerator left over from the Ice Age, a hot plate with two settings—cold and scorch—and a Dutch oven for cooking and doing laundry. The only activity we participated in was watching dollars fly out of our pockets ($12.95 for a buffet that featured corn flakes!).

So what did we take home from our "dud" ranch visit, besides a couple of souvenirs? (The "snows in the Rockies" paperweight is my favorite.) We learned that laughing at the things we've endured together brings us closer, which makes even bad experiences good family memories.

Lord, please continue to season our lives with laughter.
—*Kathy Peel*

SAT
18
"You will surely wear out . . . for the task is too heavy for you. . . ." —*EXODUS 18:18 (NAS)*

One Saturday last summer, I was griping about all the people who were pressuring me to keep up with their pace. Reports for two committees at work were due on the same day, my church men's group wanted help with planning a retreat and a salesman wanted an answer about a new car. In the middle of my pity party, my youngest son Jon said, "Want to try a game of golf, Dad?"

It seemed like the best offer I would get all day, so we went. Now Jon and I are not regular golfers, so it was taking us a long time to finish each hole. About halfway through, Jon said, "Too bad high score doesn't win in golf, huh, Dad?"

About that time a foursome of good golfers came up behind us and had to wait while we putted back and forth across the green. Then they had to wait as we teed off and drove only fifty or seventy-five yards down the fairway. I could hear them grumbling behind us, and one finally called out, "Would you guys let us play through?"

I was getting peeved at the thought of being pushed aside by someone else, when Jon asked, "What does that mean, Dad?"

"It means we let them go by us, and then *we'll* play behind *them*," I replied.

"Good," said Jon. "What's the big hurry, anyway?"

With that, we relaxed and enjoyed the rest of the course. As we went along I began to wonder if there were other people I could let "play through." That salesman could sell the car to someone else; it's not like there's going to be a shortage of cars any time soon. And I could rearrange the schedule at work.

How about you? Got any pressures you could step aside for? I bet you'll enjoy the rest of the game a whole lot more once you let them "play through."

Lord, show me where I should step aside today so that I might do a better job where You want me to. —Eric Fellman

<u>SUN</u>
19   *Sing unto the Lord, O ye saints of his, and give thanks at the remembrance of his holiness.*
—PSALM 30:4

How I happened to be in St. Paul's Cathedral in London was something of an error. I got out of the tube at the wrong place and there it was, Christopher Wren's architectural wonder. I had "done" it years before, but . . . *well, a few minutes,* I told myself. *Why not?*

Those few minutes stretched into an hour, then two. Here was a vital part of English history, and I, a history major in college, wandering from statue to sarcophagus to scroll, felt refreshed. Why, of course, John Donne, the poet of "No man is an island," had been dean here, and Admiral Nelson and General Wellington, though they had met only once, and that briefly, now were entombed in this holy place. I wanted to get a look inside the dome, but was stopped by an informal barricade. "Are you here for the Evensong service," a young woman asked nicely.

"Oh, no," I replied, and turned away. And then, I thought a moment, *Why not?*

I took a program from her and passed through and found a seat. I stared up at the magnificent dome, losing myself in its baroque splendor, when from far off came music. Some thirty robed men gradually made their way to the choir stalls in single file, singing a capella, their voices making small the enormous reaches of the cathedral. For forty-five minutes I was held in the sway of a familiar service made fresh by song, in which we, the congregation, joined. Then the choir filed out again to be heard in benediction out of sight.

Did I say I had "done" it? That is the silly remark of a tourist, I fear. *Why not?* I'd asked myself. Why indeed? God's house is always keen, and some things are evergreen. Like Evensong at St. Paul's.

Father, let me not make the mistake of having seen once, then no more.
                                                        —Van Varner

<u>MON</u>
20
"Behold, I will bring it health and healing; I will heal them and reveal to them the abundance of peace and truth."   *—JEREMIAH 33:6 (NKJV)*

For me, the cure often seems worse than the disease, because I hate going to doctors more than I dread an IRS audit. I fear authority figures who will tell me, "Do this and don't do that and that will be a zillion dollars, please." I fear embarrassing tests and painful treatments. Most of all, I'm afraid the doctor will find something terribly wrong with me, something I would rather not know about. Ignorance is bliss, at least for a time.

This month I have made many trips to the doctor, who suspected I might have one of those unspeakably awful things wrong with me. Fortunately, the problem was not too exotic, and I'll be all right. But the hours I spent in his office were somewhat less than a party.

I sat there breathing like a runner, my skin hot and tight, my blood pressure setting Olympic records. Nurse Mary Twillman listened patiently to my complaints and anxieties, then she put down her stethoscope and stared straight into my eyes. "Dan, you should be more grateful for having a good doctor. The alternative is that you could die, you know?"

I hung my head, and when she left the room, I looked around and began to give whispered thanks, grudgingly at first, then freely. "Thank You for this air-conditioned room, for the light coming in the window, for these instruments of healing, and for the kind and gracious nurses. . . ."

In a few minutes I began to cool down and stop shaking, as I thought about all the healing figures passing through my life at this moment. And when I got home, I knelt down and gave thanks for all of them.

Thank You, Father, for doctors and nurses, for technicians and secretaries. I'm grateful for insurance companies and chaplains, and friends who wish me well, all channels of Your grace in times of distress.
                                                        —Daniel Schantz

<u>TUE</u>
21
"How long will you hesitate . . . ? I have created something new and different. . . ."
—JEREMIAH 31:22 (GNB)

I had looked forward to our beach vacation. I had pictured myself lying in the sun, free at last from anxiety over our impending move to Atlanta, Georgia. Instead, here I was on a park bench with my fears for company. We had moved our three boys eight times before, and I couldn't help but recall everything that had gone wrong. My throat tightened as I thought, *I just can't go through this again.*

Suddenly, my attention was drawn to a palmetto palm in a grassy field where several teenagers were tossing a lighter-than-air ring. The sea breeze caught the ring, and it landed with a rattle in the dense thatch of fronds high in the tree. An animated powwow convened around the limbless trunk. Finally, one of the girls pulled off her sneaker and tossed it underhand into the fronds. The ring didn't come down. Neither did the shoe.

A young boy came up behind the girl, hopping on one foot to pull off his own shoe. I wanted to cry, "Don't you remember what happened the last time?" The boy took his shoe in hand and put his whole arm into the throw. The fronds gave a frightened rattle, and down dropped both the ring and the boy's shoe. Another determined pitch and the girl's shoe fell to the ground as well.

The teenagers brushed the sand from their socks and went happily back to their game. The same action repeated several times— throwing a shoe—had had very different results. It could be the same with our move. I got up and walked briskly back to the room. We were moving. I was prepared to do it all over again—for the very first time.

Father, as I face a problem for the second or the eighth time, I thank You for using it to make me a new creation.
—*Karen Barber*

<u>WED</u>
22
Begin the music, strike the tambourine, play the melodious harp and lyre.   —PSALM 81:2 (NIV)

"We'll go here," Geoffrey announced as he scanned the playbill posted outside the church of St. Martin-in-the-Fields in London, England. "Mozart's Symphony 29!"

Gary and I regarded our teenage son with dismay. The last thing we wanted to do was spend Saturday night in a heat wave in a hot auditorium listening to music we did not have the background to appreciate. Yet, that evening found us seated on a hard wooden pew in the church auditorium, sweating through our summer clothes and waiting for the concert to begin. I was woefully conscious of the two hundred noisy individuals in the audience (one of whom was kicking the back of my pew), arguing, laughing, yelling across the aisles. Once the music started, there would be the interminable sounds of horns and violins. I doubted that my untrained ears could stand the two-hour assault.

The musicians filed in; the conductor wiped his face with a handkerchief and tapped his baton. The woman behind me gave a last desultory kick to my pew. And, suddenly, the auditorium was filled with the most glorious sounds I had ever heard! In a momentary lull, I saw that the delight on Geoffrey's face was reflected in every face in the audience, perhaps even in mine. Then the strings started up again, and two hundred strangers and I were lifted once more beyond the noise of our separate lives into a communion as sublime as prayer. We were, as the poet George Herbert wrote, a "world in tune."

Quiet the clamor within me, Lord, so that I might hear the joyful music of Your world in tune. —Linda Ching Sledge

---

THU

23 *And it shall come to pass . . . your sons and your daughters shall prophesy. . . .* —JOEL 2:28

I never wanted to be one of those fathers who enjoyed his children when they were small but didn't know how to relate to them when they were grown. But developing an adult relationship with children doesn't just happen. So I'm working on it.

Like most "empty nest" couples, Barbara and I spend time together with the whole family—Thanksgiving, Christmas, vacation time. And we stay in touch by phone. But two years ago I decided that I would invite each of our children on some special trip with me, just to create a block of time together doing something we would both enjoy.

My first trip was with my son Troy last summer. We spent almost a week together in Santa Fe, New Mexico. It was just a couple of hours by air from Austin, Texas, where Troy lives and works as a computer engineer. We focused on the wealth of art in the area. Troy has done some outstanding ceramic art and has growing skills as a blacksmith in metal sculpting.

There were predictable differences in our routines, and we each made adjustments that were good for both of us. I went to bed later than usual, and Troy got up earlier than was his habit. And I got used to being the passenger as he drove.

We had great fun exploring northern New Mexico together, but the most rewarding part of the trip was observing my son and the way people related to him, and experiencing the breadth of his interests and insights into the art and the culture. At a bed and breakfast where we shared our table with a lady who had attended a conference on health care, I listened as she and Troy discussed the information superhighway. In a shop on Old Canyon Road, I was fascinated as Troy gathered information from the owner about the early Pueblo woven baskets that the store featured.

When we flew home, I was very aware that not only did I know Troy better; I had looked at New Mexico through the eyes of my son and seen things I'd never noticed before.

Nancy and I are working on our trip for early next year.

Dear God, help me to know and love my children at each stage of their lives.   *—Kenneth Chafin*

FRI
24 *And the desert shall rejoice, and blossom as the rose.*   *—ISAIAH 35:1*

I first noticed it on a hot, July evening when the moon was full and bright. Several beautiful, large white flowers, emitting a fragrant perfume, were blooming on one of the cactus plants in our front yard. The following morning, when I took my family outside to show them this stunning sight, not a single blossom remained.

I soon discovered that this was a night-blooming cereus, called the "Queen of the Night." The flowers of this remarkable plant not only bloom just at night, but each one for only one night. Imagine—their one moment of glory and hardly anyone sees it.

I can relate to that. As a stay-at-home mom, I often feel I do my best work when no one's around to know. Such as when I find the magical combination of stain remover and elbow grease that saves my son Ross' favorite shirt from ruin. Or I call every Burger King in Phoenix finally to unearth the last remaining doll from the current Disney movie, the only thing Maria wants for her birthday. Nobody sees my moments of glory either, and sometimes I wonder about the merits of so much blooming in the dark.

But watching the Queen of the Night more carefully, I've noticed something wonderful. Come morning, after the flower closes, from it grows a bright red fruit, a delicacy for birds and small animals and the source of the seeds for new growth. It's the tiniest part of a great cycle, just as it's supposed to be, just as God has planned it.

It's the same for me. The little things I do for my family, the many tasks whose nearly invisible results help make our life together run more smoothly, are my contribution to the plan God has mapped out for us. And as I watch the fruits of my work grow strong, the rewards—a smile, a giggle, a thank you—are the tiny seeds that inspire me joyfully to begin the process anew each day.

Help me remember, Lord, that my accomplishments are not my moments of glory, but Yours.   —Gina Bridgeman

---

SAT

25   *Consider the years of many generations. . . .*
                                            —DEUTERONOMY 32:7

I just gave myself a new title. I'm a lifesaver! No, I haven't done anything heroic. It's just that I've saved my mother's diaries, as well as *The Story of My Life*, hand-scrawled by my paternal grandfather on now-yellowed pages in a loose-leaf notebook.

Granddaddy Morgan died sixty years ago, and Mother, twenty. Yet both of them have come alive again for me during this week, as I've been soaking in the written records of their lives. When I moved several years ago, I threw away many things, but these two treasures I saved. How else would I ever have known that my great-grandfather died when Granddaddy was only fifteen, leaving him with the full responsibility for the family and the large farm on which they homesteaded? My grandfather died when I was seven, so I barely remember him. Yet he became a real person for me when I read what he wrote about that fifteen-year-old boy: "Many were the nights I cried myself to sleep."

Reading my mother's diaries of the World War II years, I reentered the world of ration books and victory gardens and billboards warning that "Loose lips sink ships." I was reminded of the weeks without word of my father who was at sea, and of classmates' brothers being killed in action; and I knew, all over again, that war is a terrible thing. So I'm glad I've "saved these lives" to pass on to my children and grandchildren, along with my own journals. I hope someday they'll read them, and the generations will come alive for them.

Each day this week, after soaking in the diaries, I've spent a half-hour soaking in the Gospel of Mark, reading it as though Jesus were also a member of my family. It's made His life come alive in new ways for me, too. Did I say I'm a lifesaver? Make that a *life-savorer!*

Thank You, God, for Matthew, Mark, Luke and John, who saved in words the life of Jesus, so that all the generations might savor it.   —*Marilyn Morgan Helleberg*

SUN

26   *Yet now be strong. . . .*   —*HAGGAI 2:4*

Saying good-bye is less painful now. For years I dreaded all partings, no matter how small. Until recently, I never asked why.

Then one night, my thoughts edged back to my early years. I was almost six, and Mother, a nurse, was divorced. Until she remarried in 1925, finding work meant relocating. To spare me from the disruption of her frequent moves, she placed me in a foster home. Mother was unaware of the constant cruelty, the savage beatings and the meager meals I received from my foster family.

I survived because of Aunt Lillian. Aunt Lillian was Mother's aunt. She had raised Mother when Mother came north at age eleven after my grandmother's death. Aunt Lillian worked as a domestic ten miles away from my foster home. When Aunt Lillian's employers were out of town for the weekend, she would come to see me. Together, we would take the trolley to her house. Her meals were feasts! Then we'd have a quiet evening in her room, where she'd feed my mind with picture books and my spirit with her gentleness.

But the visits always ended with a sad ride back to the foster home. Aunt Lillian would lead me to the door and say good-bye. Parting was wrenching, and I wept and wept. From then on, whenever I had to say good-bye, I was saying good-bye to Aunt Lillian.

Why did this memory surface after seventy years? I believe God wanted me to see and admit my deep hurt, so I could better see when others are hurting and reach out to them.

Understanding Father, no matter how many times I say good-bye, You will always be with me.   —*Oscar Greene*

MON

27 *He had compassion on him.*   —*LUKE 10:33*

My wife tells me I am sometimes unsympathetic with other people's points of view. Yesterday I found myself in a situation that, I have to admit, made me think she could be right. I was waiting in line to rent a car, paradiddling my fingers on the counter as I watched the woman in front of me purse her lips and frown at the standard insurance waiver. "I hate renting," she muttered to no one in particular. "I wish I had my own little car with me, but it's back home in Illinois."

Hate renting a car? She had to be kidding. As a peripatetic Manhattanite, I *love* renting cars. I like to thumb through the book that has photos of all the vehicles I can choose from, the humble subcompacts to the luxury juggernauts. I love the smell of a pristine interior, and an odometer that has barely reached the speed limit. I relish commanding a car that's a little nicer, a little flashier than one I might actually own. Yet here was someone who feared doing something for the very reasons I liked to: novelty, adventure, the unexpected. And here I was, feeling impatient and, yes, as Julee pointed out, unsympathetic.

I slid over the book with the car photos in it. "Maybe they have your make," I said. "That might make it easier for you."

She smiled, flipped the book open and waved me on ahead of her.

Later, out in the lot, I saw her again. "Look," she said, "they gave me one almost identical to mine!"

"You'll do fine," I assured her. "Just remember, no right turn on red in the city."

"Thanks."

I beeped my horn and let her pull out in front of me. While I explored all the new gadgetry on the dashboard, I said a quick prayer that the woman and her temporary vehicular companion would get along okay—and added one of thanks for the unexpected reminder that there are many ways to see a situation and mine is only one.

Lord, I ask for an open mind to help open my heart to others.   —*Edward Grinnan*

TUE

28
Even in old age they will still produce fruit and be vital and green.   —*PSALM 92:14 (TLB)*

The children of Ray Johnson invite you to celebrate his ninetieth birthday at a reception on July 28 at the Copeland United Methodist Church. We believe that the loving memories he has shared with you, his friends, would be the most treasured gift he could receive. Please write one memory or experience for the book we are compiling.

At first I couldn't decide what to write. From the time he greeted our family at the door of Copeland United Methodist Church in 1969—our first Sunday in town—Ray has provided an example of simple trust in God and faithful service to others. He was school custodian until he was seventy. He shoveled snow from the walks and kept the church sparkling clean into his mid-eighties. His stories about farming during the Dustbowl encouraged us through tough times on our own farm.

But my best memory was an incident Ray scarcely remembered. We'd only been in Copeland, Kansas, a few months when our oldest son Patrick started kindergarten. I was concerned about that first day, afraid he'd feel lost and alone. Or maybe actually get lost since he didn't know his way around. But I needn't have worried. When I picked up Pat at noon, he had a big smile on his face. "I knew someone!" he told us. "You know that man from our church, the one who takes up the collection? He met my bus and said hi, and showed me the kindergarten room. He said he'd meet the bus tomorrow, too!"

Happy Birthday, Ray! Thanks for years of sharing Christ's love . . . and thanks for the memories.

Thank You, Lord, for the faithful examples of the many ordinary saints who have influenced my life. —*Penney Schwab*

WED

29   *My peace I give unto you. . . .*   —*JOHN 14:27*

Before coming here to our church in Mt. Kisco, New York, the Reverend Ralph Peterson was pastor of St. Peter's in Manhattan. A rundown 1905 structure on the corner of Lexington Avenue at 54th Street, St. Peter's had agreed to sell its site to Citicorp, which planned a skyscraper on the block, in exchange for a new sanctuary on the ground floor of the proposed building.

To accommodate the new St. Peter's, the architect designed a daring fifty-nine-story tower resting on slender stilts. Citicorp Center today is a Manhattan landmark (it's the building with the slanted top); the new St. Peter's is a handsome place of worship where on pressured days I often go to sit for a few moments.

What no one but a few engineers and company officials knew at the time, Ralph Peterson says, is that a year after the building was completed, new data revealed an unexpected problem in its construction. In a high wind, the kind that hits New York on average once every sixteen years, the whole immense edifice could sway badly. With hurricane season approaching, it was a nightmarish situation. Experts were hastily assembled, designs proposed for a complex system of bracing and reinforcement—along with a secret evacuation plan for the thousands of occupants, including the people at St. Peter's, should a windstorm threaten while the work was going on.

What fascinates me is the name given to that desperate time of round-the-clock design sessions. The effort was called "Project SERENE."

SERENE is the acronym for "Special Engineering Review of Events Nobody Envisioned." That's what I think about, sitting in the church at the base of the tower. Serenity, it tells me, doesn't mean the absence of problems. It doesn't vanish when trouble unexpectedly crops up. Serenity comes when I acknowledge my need and call on the best help available.

When crises come, Father, peace is knowing that Your help is a prayer away.   —*Elizabeth Sherrill*

THU
30
*The heavens declare the glory of God; and the fir-
mament showeth his handiwork.*   —PSALM 19:1

We were in the middle of dinner when our neighbor called. "Look
out the window right now—to the west. You can see the comet! It's
the brightest thing in the sky." We'd read about this astronomical
event in the newspaper and had seen reports on TV. A comet that
sailed by our solar system every ten thousand years would be visible
to the naked eye.

Putting down our forks, we rushed to the bedroom, turned off the
light and gazed to the heavens. There, indeed, was a star so bright it
illuminated the darkened room and seemed to cast shadows on the
grass outside, reflecting off the parked cars and bouncing off the white
tree trunks. With our binoculars, we peered through the branches and
admired the stunning blue light. How glorious! How monumental!
And to think, we were seeing the comet through our own windows,
across the Hudson River, lodged somewhere above New Jersey, so
close you could almost catch it by its tail.

Only later, after the children had fallen asleep, did our neighbor
call back and admit sheepishly, "That was Venus. I looked on a map
of the stars in the newspaper, and found the comet farther north, near
the Big Dipper."

"I can't believe it!" I said, more amused than disappointed. But
later, as I took my binoculars outside and scanned the heavens a second time, I was thankful for the mix-up. What delight we had taken
in seeing what was visible almost every evening of the year! What a
pleasure to appreciate the night sky! Not all wonders require a wait
of ten thousand years.

Lord, help me to see the undisguised glories of Your world.
                                              —*Rick Hamlin*

FRI
31
Thou didst make me hope. . . .   —PSALM 22:9

Some years ago, when unexpected illnesses took the lives of both my
dog and cat within a few weeks, I was devastated. Kate, my dog, was
nine years old, and Mr. Jones, my cat, was twelve, so we had been together a long time. Kate and I took long walks every day, and Mr.

Jones was always under my desk, curled at my feet, when I worked. We played wonderful games, but also enjoyed just being quiet while I listened to music or read a book. We knew each other's moods and needs.

My grief was so deep that it was hard for me to think about bringing another animal into my life. Yet I missed the special warmth and companionship that animals had brought to me. A friend of mine who had also lost a beloved pet some months earlier, told me about a nearby dog breeder who had a litter of puppies. He and his wife had chosen one for themselves, and he wondered if I would like to go and see them. "I'm not sure," I said. "Let's wait a bit."

The next morning, as I left by the back door for my early walk, I saw something bright out in the fields next to my house: four yellow daffodils. The ground was still winter-cold and nothing else was in bloom, and I had never seen anything like a daffodil there. But then I remembered that several years ago I had dug up some bulbs I thought were dead and tossed them into the field. Why had it taken all this time for them to bloom?

To me, they were a message of hope. They were God's way of encouraging me to bring new creatures into my life and to offer them my love. I went back in my house and called my friend. "Let's not wait," I said. "Let's go see those puppies!"

Thank You, Lord, for the animals who bring us joy, loyalty and love. Amen.
                                                    —*Phyllis Hobe*

My Healing Journey

1 _____

2 _____

3 _____

4 _____

5 _____

6 _____

7 _____

8 _____

9 _____

10 _____

11 _____

12 _____

13 _____

14 _____

15 _____

16 _____

17 _____

18 _____

19 _____

20 _____

21 _____

22 _____

23 _____

24 _____

25 _____

26 _____

27 _____

28 _____

29 _____

30 _____

31 _____

AUGUST

S	M	T	W	T	F	S
						1
2	3	4	5	6	7	8
9	10	11	12	13	14	15
16	17	18	19	20	21	22
23	24	25	26	27	28	29
30	31					

And he said unto me, My grace is sufficient for thee: for my strength is made perfect in weakness. . . .
—II CORINTHIANS 12:9

SAT
1

THE TOUCH OF THE HEALER
Healing Our Fears
I will not leave you comfortless: I will come to you.
—JOHN 14:18

I woke up in the middle of the night terribly afraid. It was pitch black in my room, and my brow was covered with cold sweat. I'd had a dream about going broke and winding up as an old man in shabby clothes on a tenement step, with no family or friends. The dream still seemed very real. I flipped on the light and glanced at the clock. It was 4:02 A.M.

Although we're not rich, we're certainly not bankrupt. Why, then, was I thinking, *There will soon be a total financial disaster!* If God was in my life, why was I fearful?

I thought about Jesus and His promises about fear. And in my half-asleep state, I began to dream about two little girls who reminded me of two of my daughters when they were little. The older one, Rachel, was consoling her three-year-old sister Janie, who had awakened scared and howling in the middle of the night after a Christmas play in which they both had been angels. In my dream, I heard Rachel say, "Janie, fear not! For I come to bring good tidings." And then she added, in a loud stage voice, "Jesus is right here in this room!"

"Oh," a tiny, tearful voice said, "okay," and Janie went back to sleep.

I smiled. What I needed there in the dark was not an answer to my financial problems but a Counselor, a Comforter to be with me through the long night. And, grateful that Jesus *was* right there in that room, I went back to sleep.

Thank You, Lord, for Your promise that the Comforter will be with me always.   *—Keith Miller*

SUN
2

The stranger did not lodge in the street: but I opened my doors to the traveler.   *—JOB 31:32*

I slid into an empty seat in the auditorium. The summer park concert had been moved to the school because of rain. As I opened my book to while away the time before the music began, a gray-haired man approached. "Young lady, isn't that Harrison's book on Shakespeare you have there?" He was tall and thin, and although his worn tweed jacket was fastened with a safety pin and he carried a battered shopping bag, he had a look of faded elegance.

"Yes, it is," I replied briskly, not looking up. I was uncomfortable speaking to strangers.

He persisted. "I love Shakespeare," he said. "I've seen *The Tempest* seventeen times. My great loves are Shakespeare, music and the Bible." He lifted the well-thumbed copy of the Bible he held in his hand. "They are my mainstay in every difficulty."

Just as I was about to say something, he was gone. I was suddenly sorry I hadn't been friendlier.

The following week I saw him again. As the musicians were packing up, the Shakespeare man approached my husband and me at our car. "Are you going toward the subway?" he asked. We weren't, but Ernie offered a ride anyway. We drove past the dark and lonely streets toward the station.

"You're good people," he said. "It's kind of you to take me. I'm an old man, and I don't get around so easily. I always look for kindness in people, and I usually find it." He laughed and patted my shoulder from the backseat.

"Here's the station," said Ernie, pulling up to the curb. "Will you be all right?"

"Oh, yes," he said. "I can always count on people to help me when I need it. We're all God's children, and we each have a measure of love to give."

With that he disappeared around the corner. We found ourselves smiling at each other all the way home.

Oh, Lord, let me have a full measure of love to give today.
                                                —*Susan Schefflein*

MON
3
Make a joyful noise unto the Lord, all ye lands.
                                                —*PSALM 100:1*

One late summer afternoon after working hard at my desk, I went out into my little backyard to clear my head and to bask in the sunshine. As my mind quieted, I began to listen—really listen—to the gentle sounds around me.

Tssp, tssp. Some tiny warblers flew out of my tall sunflowers. Cardinals added their contented *chuck, chuck,* as they scratched for seeds in the dirt. Sparrows chirped, and purple finches added a warble or two. The traffic on our usually busy street seemed especially light, and I began to relax.

Suddenly, the noise level increased. A car with double exhaust zoomed by with loudspeakers blaring a rap song. From the third floor above me, operatic arias began to drift downward—my renter must have turned on her CD player. Two doors away, my Italian neighbors turned on their radio, first for some popular songs by an Italian tenor, and then for a soccer game, while they chatted loudly and animatedly with each other and with friends over the phone. In the apartment house behind my backyard, the Hispanic family played their favorite music full force, joining in loudly with the rhythmic chorus.

What happened to the peace and quiet? was my first rather annoyed reaction. But as I kept listening, all the sounds blended into a multi-part, vibrant chorus. *This is what it means to live in a city, to hear many voices all making a "joyful noise,"* I thought.

My next-door neighbor came out to bring in her wash from the clothesline, and we both laughed at the din and joined joyfully in the chorus.

God, thank You for the many voices in the city. Help me to make all the noise in my life joyful.   —*Mary Ruth Howes*

---

4   *Do not forsake your friend. . . .*
                              —*PROVERBS 27:10 (NIV)*

The other day, I read in the newspaper that the father of one of my old high school friends had died. For a moment, I vividly remembered driving back and forth to school with her almost every day, sharing woes about homework and tests, boyfriends and family members. But that was some thirty years ago. She now lived in the East, and I still lived in Boulder, Colorado, where we grew up. Though we had stayed in touch for years, time and space had slowly separated us. In the last few years, she'd even disappeared from my downsized Christmas card list.

Her dad's funeral was scheduled for ten 10:00 A.M. on a Wednesday morning, just the time I was supposed to be attending an important meeting at work. I began to fight a battle of questions and rationalizations in my head.

Should I try to get out of the meeting and go to the funeral? Oh, I'm such an old *friend, would my being there really matter much? Couldn't I simply write her a note instead?*

A bit reluctantly, I made the decision, rescheduled my meeting and went to the funeral. After the service, I greeted my friend who seemed genuinely surprised to see me. We sat and talked and reminisced, and as I left, she took my hand. "Thank you for coming," she said, her eyes filling with tears. "You represent a meaningful part of my history with my dad, so having you here brings me great comfort."

As I drove back to work, I wondered why I had even questioned the importance of attending this funeral. We were *old* friends. It didn't matter that we hadn't seen each other for many years. It didn't matter that we no longer sent Christmas cards. What mattered is that we were like the threads of a tapestry, woven together for a time. And because of that, we would forever be part of the fabric of each other's lives.

Father, thank You for the gift of old friends who grow more precious through time. —*Carol Kuykendall*

WED

5

Little children, let us stop just saying we love people; let us really love them, and show it by our actions. —*I JOHN 3:18 (TLB)*

For eighteen years I worked in an office down the hall from Louise's office. We became close friends, and when I retired, we promised "to keep in touch." Somehow, though, as the months passed other priorities stole the time. Then I remembered that August 5 was Louise's birthday and called to wish her a happy one. We had a good conversation that ended in my open-ended invitation to breakfast out whenever her schedule permitted.

Where the next year went I can't tell you, but suddenly it was August 5 again, and I called Louise with the same greeting. We laughed and talked, shared bits and pieces of the last year's events, apologized for the lack of communication and vowed to meet for lunch soon.

After I hung up the phone, the room was very quiet. A sense of loneliness seemed to engulf me. *How many other dear old friends am I crowding out of my life?* I wondered.

I reached for a note pad and started two lists—one for telephoning, the other for writing notes. No better time than the present to begin "keeping in touch" with people I've neglected.

Is there someone who would delight in hearing from you today? Why not take a few minutes right now to make a quick call or write a short note. You might make a big difference in someone's life.

Dear God, my telephone and my pen are close by. Make me faithful in using them. Amen. —Drue Duke

---

THU

6 *The Lord make his face shine upon thee. . . .*
—NUMBERS 6:25

Not long ago, a woman from Pennsylvania told me about the nerve damage that prevented her from smiling. I sympathized because I knew how very much it means for me to be able to smile. For one thing, I like to be smiled *at*, and I find that all I have to do to get one is to give one.

And have you ever realized the power that lies in so effortless a gesture? I'll bet a smile, perhaps when you least expected it, has changed a day for you. I do know that a smile a stranger gave me in an airport once changed a whole week I had been dreading into one that was richly rewarding.

So my prayer that the woman in Pennsylvania regain her ability to smile is an earnest one. And so is our prayer that everyone who reads this will exercise that unique human gift of smiling today and every day. And here's a little secret about smiling. Even when you don't feel like it, go ahead and smile anyway. By the time you get one or two in return, the magical thing is that you *will* feel like smiling.

Dear Lord, today I'm going to try to give more smiles than I get. —Ruth Stafford Peale

---

FRI

7 *Let us encourage one another. . . .*
—HEBREWS 10:25 (NIV)

"When I grow up, I'm going to be in the circus!" I announced to my parents and my grandmother.

My grandmother chuckled, and my mother's "Ooooh?" seemed oddly unimpressed and quizzical to my ten-year-old ears. "Lots of children think that," Mom said. "The circus is exciting. But when you grow up, you won't think circus life is so wonderful."

Dad, however, listened and said, "Well, if you're going to be in the circus, you'll need good balance. I'll get an old barrel for you to practice rolling on."

A few days later a yellow and orange barrel showed up in our back yard. I spent hours on it. My friends and I learned to roll forward and backward, and even to jump rope on it. Even the dog and our pet goat would take a spin with us. We dreamed big-top dreams and put on backyard circuses for our neighbors. But soon, as mother had predicted, the circus lost its glamour for me. Still, I had had hours of fun and ended up with much better balance.

A few years ago, my eleven-year-old daughter Joanna announced, "I'm going to be the first girl to play major league baseball." I didn't laugh. Instead I said, "Great. Go for it! But remember, it'll take a lot of practice." Like Dad, I'm going to be a "barrel buyer."

Father, thank You for developing me as I dream.

—Marjorie Parker

8 *Let us not therefore judge one another any more. . . .*
—ROMANS 14:13

As I headed for the mall one Saturday morning, I reviewed an argument I'd had with my husband Larry at breakfast over the way he'd tracked mud from the garden into the den. Again. Anger surged through me, just thinking about it. Why couldn't he clean his shoes before coming into the house!

As I passed Christ Unity Church on Candelaria Avenue, I glanced to see if there was a new message on their announcement board. There was. It read: WHEN YOU BLAME OTHERS, YOU GIVE UP THE POWER TO CHANGE.

That set me back on my heels. Here I was, blaming Larry for his carelessness, but had I done anything positive to change the situation? No, all I'd done was complain.

When I reached the mall, I went to the housewares store and bought two mats, a ridged rubber mat for the patio on which to scrape one's shoes and a nubbly woven mat for inside the den door on which to finish the process.

"Oh, good!" said Larry when he saw them. "Those'll be a big help!"

And they were. As I looked at my clean carpet a couple of days later, I thought how simple the solution had been, once I stopped blaming Larry and assumed responsibility for effecting change—a major step toward conquering frustration. *And* healing a relationship.

Father, today I will set aside petty grievances and look for solutions.   —*Madge Harrah*

SUN
9

To the Lord our God belong mercies and forgivenesses, though we have rebelled against him.
—*DANIEL 9:9*

A story about golfing great Sam Snead tells how he, while playing with a friend, made a seven on the first hole, three strokes over par. As the two left the green and headed to the next hole, the friend was a little surprised that Sam wasn't bothered a bit by his bad score. "That's why we play eighteen holes," he said. Of course, when the round was over, Snead finished four under par and won the match.

Maybe that's why I like sports; it's the opportunity to try again, to follow up failure with success. There's always the second half, another time at bat, the next lap. After all, didn't Yogi Berra say, "It ain't over 'til it's over?" And, I guess, I'm a second-chance sort of person. I don't always get things right the first time. Sometimes I need another shot at saying the right thing to my husband Paul when we've quarreled or a second chance to keep quiet when friends indulge in a gossip session.

I thought about all of this earlier today in church as I, along with the congregation, silently confessed my sins. I remembered a friend who once told me how much she disliked that part of the service because she hated being reminded each week of all the things she'd done wrong.

"But it's followed by my favorite part," I told her, "God's forgiveness. And every week God forgives me, no matter what I've done."

I depend on that forgiveness because I know I will make wrong choices. I did today, as a matter of fact, snapping at my son Ross out of frustration and impatience. But God knows I'm not perfect and forgives me, and that says He wants me to take that second chance, to do better next time. I still may not succeed, but like an 0-for-3 hitter who steps up to the plate one more time, my "next time" is always there if I choose to take it.

Loving God, please give me more of what I need to make the right choice. But when I don't, please forgive me.
—Gina Bridgeman

MON

10 *And when a man shall sanctify his house to be holy unto the Lord. . . .* —LEVITICUS 27:14

The bus pulled out of the Port Authority terminal. The traffic was at its worst, honking, stopping, starting, leaving me plenty of time to observe the coarseness of the city I was suddenly grateful to be leaving behind. Finally through the Lincoln Tunnel, into New Jersey, and eventually forty-five minutes of Pennsylvania, and I was there.

"It wasn't so bad, was it?" said John, my host. "Let me take your bag."

"No, I read and enjoyed the view," I replied as we got into his car for the drive to his house. And what a house it was, too. So much done to it since my last visit. A new garage and a retreat built over the stream deep in the forest. There was the garden to see, and my room, spacious and friendly, and the dinner—*ah*, the dinner, but what could I expect from such a wonder of a cook? Just think, two days of this, with long walks and easy afternoons of reading or doing nothing at all. No noise. No crowds. No city.

Then came time to leave. I'd had a wonderful, restful visit, but as the bus neared New York and the skyline rose up, I was surprised at my excitement, a thrill that I've found nowhere else in the world. We roared through the tunnel and were in the city again with all of its lights and trash and confusion of human life. In the station, a man was begging and I uncharacteristically unloaded a spill of change for him—and a dollar for the man who sang and played his Yamaha as I waited for the subway. On the way uptown, I sat in a car chockablock with people of different races, and Mac in the token booth where I live waved a hand, "Hi."

It was good to be in my apartment again. I looked from my window at the city out there and said sincerely, "Thank God." Friends can have their country homes, and I understand their enthusiasm—and am grateful to be invited—but the city is where I feel I am home, thank God.

To be at home, Father, is what I wish.   —*Van Varner*

TUE

11 *"Tomorrow will be like today, only more so."*
—*ISAIAH 56:12 (NAS)*

I would not make a good prophet. I tend to assume that whatever is happening today will just get worse tomorrow.

Take this summer, for example. The month of June was miserably hot and humid. I dreaded July because I had a number of outdoor projects to do: painting the fence; replacing siding; gardening. "If it's this bad in June," I said to Sharon, my wife, "then it's going to be murder in July. I'll end up having a heatstroke for sure."

I was wrong. July turned out to be cool and dry. Nighttime temperatures fell as low as fifty degrees, and daytime temperatures seldom exceeded eighty degrees.

I've made this mental mistake many times. *If I'm this forgetful at thirty, what will I be at sixty? . . . If I'm this tired now, what will I be like by Friday? . . . If our finances are this bad now, I hate to think about next year. . . .*

I tend to forget that life is always changing. Trends fizzle out or even reverse. New factors come into the equation. Some dangers just dissolve into thin air. New opportunities appear out of nowhere.

"Most unhappiness," Bishop Sheen once said, "comes from dwelling too much on the past or the future."

He's right, I think, and I've decided that once a month I'll sit down with Sharon and work on our future, making plans and praying about it. The rest of the time I'm going to concentrate on making this day the very best day of my life. After all, it's the only day I have for certain.

Help me, Lord, to be humble about the future, and always to allow for Your providence to modify it for good.
—*Daniel Schantz*

WED

12 *Then our sons in their youth will be like well-nurtured plants. . . .* —PSALM 144:12 (NIV)

It was 2:00 A.M. on a muggy Virginia summer night. Bill and I were shaking our sons awake.

"Come on! Get up! Just throw on your shorts! Downstairs and out back in five minutes!"

"Why, Mom? What are we doing?" That was John, the inquisitive one.

"Mom, is that pizza I smell?" Tom, always hungry.

They grumbled groggily, fumbling for pants and slippers. I ran to lift David out of his crib. Meanwhile, Bill had set up deck chairs in the backyard. They faced southeast where the moon shone down between magnolia and oak trees. Already its light was dimming.

"Dad, what are we doing out here in the middle of the night?" Pete hopped excitedly from one foot to the other.

"Well, in a few minutes there will be a total eclipse of the moon. The experts say that the moon will turn red. And because when Mom and I were younger there was a silly song that started, 'When the moon hits your eye like a big pizza pie,' Mom thought we ought to celebrate with pizza."

For an hour, the six of us sat in the backyard, munching pizza, and watching the moon darken and redden and then begin to emerge from shadow to light.

Each boy has his own piece of the memory of that night, but Bill and I remember every detail. Not all the memories we built were for the children's benefit. Some have become ours, to tuck away for now, when our nest has emptied and there are just the two of us left to watch the moonrise.

Lord, thank You for the gift of memory. May our children's children give their parents precious moments to recall.
—Roberta Rogers

THU

13 *Offer to God a sacrifice of thanksgiving. . . .*
—PSALM 50:14 (RSV)

One summer, when we were living in a small apartment in Germany,

I got caught up in a bout of complaining. Hot, humid weather; no window screens; the smelly stable next door; flies constantly on the food and baby. . . .

I struggled to stop grumbling, but my irritability only increased. Then one day I read Psalm 50 and verse 14 struck me: Make a sacrifice of thanksgiving. *How about giving up my complaints and replacing each of them with something for which I'm thankful?*

I grabbed pen and paper and quickly listed negatives to sacrifice. Finding a replacement thanksgiving for each one took longer, but as I searched for positives, I found blessings that I hadn't seen before.

Sacrifice:	*Thanksgiving:*
Those flies! No screens! The horse stables!	The delight the children take in seeing the horses! The fields of wildflowers beyond.
The small sink. The hot water runs out so quickly.	The shower Alex improvised in the tub; his resourcefulness.
This tiny refrigerator. No freezer. Having to shop for groceries almost daily.	The kind clerk in the drugstore who translates labels for me. The friendly people in the shops.

I posted my list on a cupboard. Each time I started to sigh, "Oh, these awful flies," I said instead, "Thank You, God, for the beautiful horses and fields."

Now, back home in Michigan, you'll often see a list with two columns on my refrigerator. When I start simmering with grievances, it's time to make a "sacrifice of thanksgiving" list and keep it handy!

Father, whenever I start lamenting my lot, help me to sacrifice my complaints and offer thanksgiving.   —*Mary Brown*

FRI

14   *Let us lay aside every weight. . . .*   —*HEBREWS 12:1*

Yesterday I spent some time in the Museum of Nebraska Art. One painting in particular seemed to carry a special message for me. It was part of a series on the Oregon trail, and it portrayed a prairie scene with mountains rising in the background. In the foreground was a cedar chest with clothes and jewelry spilling out, an ornate chest of drawers and a full-length mirror in an elaborate gold frame. The painting was titled *Left Behind: Mountains Ahead.*

I've been thinking about those pioneers today. They could have given up, turned their wagons around and gone back when they saw mountains looming ahead. But their dream meant so much to them that they were willing to sacrifice some of their favorite possessions to fulfill it.

Now I think I know why that painting struck me with such impact. I've been working on a project for several months without making much headway. It seems overwhelming to think of the many tasks that lie ahead and the energy and hours required to complete them. There are also a number of unrelated things in my life that pull me away from my work. My friend Louise suggests we meet for lunch, and what I thought would be an hour stretches to three. I often do things for my grown children they could do for themselves. I belong to a couple of groups that meet regularly.

Perhaps, like those pioneers, my wagon is overloaded. Now I must ask myself: *Does my dream mean enough to make a few temporary sacrifices in order to fulfill it?* When I pray about it, the answer is simple and certain: *Yes!*

Lord, You've given me a dream. May I be infused with the pioneer spirit, undaunted by mountains, unafraid to shed some extras in order to fulfill it. —*Marilyn Morgan Helleberg*

SAT

15 *Ye shall be comforted. . . .*   —*EZEKIEL 14:22*

Thunder crashed. Lightning crackled. The wind blew the white lace curtains covering the open windows in my bedroom. It was a 2:00 A.M. summer storm, and as a child of four I was very much afraid.

Then I saw the shadowy form of my mother in the doorway. "There's nothing to fear, Eleanor," she said as she sat down on my bed and put a comforting arm around my shoulders. "The angels in heaven are bowling. And God is sending the lightning so that the flowers here on earth can see to take a drink."

I'd watched my daddy bowling and he'd seemed to have a lot of fun, so I smiled at the vision of angels hitching up their long robes, then sending their bowling balls hurtling down those heavenly alleys. As for the flowers—well, Mother and Daddy were both avid gardeners and beautiful flowers adorned the back and front yards of our house. And they needed regular waterings.

Today, I have no fear of storms. Oh, I certainly take precautions if I happen to be caught outside in one—like not heading for a tree or standing on a golf course holding an iron club!

My mother trained me well.

Dear God, thank You for the unique ways in which You guide parents to guide their children. —Eleanor Sass

---

SUN

16 *Truly God is good to the upright, to those who are pure in heart.* —PSALM 73:1 (RSV)

I was an altar boy when I was a kid, and I can still remember Father Walling rebuking me for racing through my Latin responses during Mass. "I'm going to give you a speeding ticket, Grinnan," he used to growl. Then came the transforming tide of Vatican II, a watershed event in twentieth-century Roman Catholicism.

Vatican II changed the lives of practicing Catholics around the world. My dad, however, did not want the way he practiced his faith changed. He loved the solemnity of the Latin Mass, for example, and he didn't want to say it in English. After 1965, he would come in from church on Sunday mornings and cloister himself in his study with his tattered Latin missal and a recording of the old Mass—skips, scratches and all. He said he never really felt as if he had been to church until that was done.

I had to get used to saying my liturgy in English. "It sounds like you're really praying now," my mom told me. It felt more like it, too, I had to admit. Though there had been something special about the Latin, something preternatural, as if God himself might have spoken in the language. It added to the sense of ritual I liked. Besides, I'd worked hard at my Latin. I had mixed feelings about the whole business. But Mom was adamant: These changes helped bring people into a closer relationship with God.

"Why destroy tradition and continuity?" Dad demanded.

"Why run from change?" Mom would counter.

There was no stopping Vatican II, and eventually my father came around a bit. He even allowed himself to be dragged to the occasional guitar Mass, though he persisted in playing his Latin record on Sunday mornings for as long as he lived. At his funeral, Father Walling, honoring my father's stubborn traditionalist streak, said a few prayers in Latin. My mom appreciated that.

Dad didn't want his way of worshiping God to be seen as irrelevant. Mom wanted it to be easier for people to know God. They both were right. Change is inevitable. But with God's guidance, it is good.

The other day I couldn't help but chuckle when I read that a new recording of Gregorian chants had made the *Billboard* top ten. I thought about my father. He would have said, "I told you so."

Dear Lord, I must remember that Your world is ever-changing, but You are constant.   *—Edward Grinnan*

Herald of Healing

Open now the crystal fountain
Whence the healing stream doth flow;
Let the fire and cloudy pillar
Lead me all my journey through:
Strong Deliverer, Strong Deliverer
Be Thou still my strength and shield.
—WILLIAM WILLIAMS

MON
17   *Be ye not stiffnecked . . . but yield yourselves unto the Lord. . . .*   *—II CHRONICLES 30:8*

I started running the Colorado River in 1976, so by the time I got tossed out of the boat in Lava Falls in 1990, I knew intellectually what the rapid was like. My first thought as I parted company with the raft was, *Uh-oh, I'm going to have to swim this sucker.* The power of the river pulled me deep underwater at once, and the sediment being carried by the current made everything solid black, so there was no telling which way was up. I felt the water jerk my paddle out of my hand, and then I was buffeted and tossed by its strength.

Automatically, I fought it. I knew I had to try to break the surface to get a lungful of air, but I didn't know where the surface was because no light was making its way through the crud in the water. All at once I became aware that I would never be as strong as the river. I deliberately made myself stop struggling, and the moment I held still, my life vest began to carry me upward.

It seemed as if I had risen a long time before I finally saw the red and black rocks of the canyon wall in front of me, took a deep breath and was sucked down into the darkness again. This time I just went with current until the river spit me out at the bottom of the rapid. The raft was waiting to pick me up.

I learned that faith is surrender. Just like the river, the world I confront every day is beyond my control. Faith is the life vest that brings me to the surface of the darkness. But I can't fight it. I have to let it save me.

Dear God, today I surrender my will to You.—Rhoda Blecker

TUE

18 *It is no longer I who live, but it is Christ who lives in me. . . .* —GALATIANS 2:20 (GNB)

I was having an ongoing difference of opinion with a co-worker, and my "Lord, help me" prayers concerning my critical attitude toward her seemed to be getting nowhere.

One day I was visiting the workshop of a woodworker named Gary Garner. Gary described how he had met the challenge of sculpting a nearly life-size crucifix using twenty-four different photos of an Italian sculpture as his model. He explained that he often used a mirror while carving, because the backward reflection told him instantly whether any distortion had crept into the work.

As Gary labored over the expression on the face of Christ, he must have often gazed back into the mirror, because when it was finished, his aunt had a startling comment. "Why, the face looks like your middle son!" Gary realized that he must have unconsciously incorporated some of his own features, glimpsed in the mirror, into the artwork.

As I drove home, pondering what Gary had said, I understood why my prayers for my co-worker had been ineffective: I was seeking vindication, not reconciliation. And so I prayed . . .

Lord, Jesus, when I try to remake You in my image, transform me into Yours.   —*Karen Barber*

WED

19 *"Be merciful, just as your Father is merciful."*
—*LUKE 6:36 (NIV)*

In the early years of my marriage, I was scared to death of my father-in-law Charles Speers. He was a tall, dignified airline executive whose standards seemed impossibly high. When I was around him, I felt that I would never be able to measure up. I felt especially inadequate when he and my mother-in-law visited our casual country home, where we had a spoiled, ornery goat named Tippy. The goat's hobby was to climb cars and sun himself on the roof, so when company came we locked him in the barn.

One day instead of flying down to see us, Mom and Dad arrived in their forest-green Mercedes-Benz. This car was Dad's pet. He kept it gleaming like a mirror, without a scratch on it. As they parked in the gravel space across our country lane, I ran outside to greet them. Tippy was wandering around, looking for new challenges. "Oh, I have to lock the goat up," I blurted to Dad, "or he'll climb your car." Dad paled. I dragged the recalcitrant goat by his collar to the barn and, in my nervousness, left one of the locks hanging.

An hour later, I looked out the window, and there was Tippy sprawled across the top of the Mercedes, his pale eyes squinting defiantly at me. When I saw the hoof scratches on the hood, my stomach plunged like an elevator. I wheeled around and there was Dad, jaw clenched, eyes burning. I braced myself. But when he looked at me, his face softened. He hugged me, a great big bear hug that made me feel like a million dollars. "Now get that goat off my car," he said with a grin.

As I ran out the door, Dad's hug followed closer. Its warmth melted the ice of my fear, opening a way to a closer relationship with him. That's what love does.

Lord, thank You for drawing me to You, not with fear, but forgiveness, so that I may do the same for others.
—*Shari Smyth*

THU
20
These see the works of the Lord, and his wonders in the deep.
                                          —PSALM 107:24

The friends who invited us for a boat ride in their handsome cruiser had also invited three nuns, Sisters of Mercy, who worked at one of our local hospitals. It was a sparkling summer morning, sea almost calm, sky a bottomless blue, gulls drifting by on the silver stream of the wind.

I was sitting up in the bow, talking with one of the sisters, when suddenly about a quarter mile away two streamlined shapes rose out of the sea, arched over in perfect unison high above the water, then disappeared with barely a splash. Dolphins. Big, seven-foot dolphins, good-natured, playful clowns of the sea.

A moment later they leaped again, still in perfect tandem, still racing toward us, almost as if they were saying, "Hey, look at us! We're here, too, you know, in this wonderful world!"

The third leap was so close that we could see their merry eyes watching us, mouths smiling as always, the grace and precision and power of their ballet so effortless and amazing that one felt like applauding.

Down they came in a swirl of green and gold, and were gone. Sister Mary Frances looked at me, eyes wide, and said the only thing there was to say: "Praise the Lord!"

And I murmured, "Amen!"

Thank You, Father, for those flashing moments when we know that because we are all Your creatures we are all kin to one another.
                                          —Arthur Gordon

FRI
21
Call to Me, and I will answer you, and I will tell you great and mighty things, which you do not know.
                                          —JEREMIAH 33:3 (NAS)

When I left bedside nursing to assume an administrative position, I suddenly felt like an outsider looking in on the front lines of health care. I sensed this alienation most keenly whenever the public address system announced a "Code Blue," signaling a dire medical emergency. All around me, confident staff members dropped what they were doing and flew STAT to assist the patient in distress. I missed the adrenaline rush of excitement, the camaraderie of teamwork, the intense joy of a successful outcome.

Then one evening when a Code Blue was announced, I found myself praying for the patient. "Get the team there fast, Lord. Let the first responder know exactly what to do. Keep everyone calm," I silently asked as I mentally went through the motions. "Let them find an IV line. Help them choose the right medications. And, please, comfort the patient and his or her family." Suddenly, I was filled with an incredible sense of purpose and belonging. I *was* there—in prayer!

Later that evening, I learned that the patient had experienced a life-threatening cardiac arrhythmia. The first respondent was a physician proficient in Advanced Cardiac Life Support. He immediately shocked the gentleman's heart, returning it to a normal beat before the rest of the Code Blue team arrived on the scene. The patient was now stable and resting quietly in the Intensive Care Unit.

And I learned an important lesson that has carried over into other areas of my life: Whatever my role may be, I have the privilege, through prayer, of being a vital participant in everything that happens.

Lord, You are only a prayer away in any role I play. Teach me to trust You more. —Roberta Messner

---

SAT
22
"And if, as my representatives, you give even a cup of cold water . . . you will surely be rewarded."
—MATTHEW 10:42 (TLB)

My friend Joan phoned just as I was about to leave the house. She was crying. For a moment, I considered saying that I really needed to run an errand, but instead I told her to come over.

When Joan arrived, I took her back to my small home office. She curled up next to Minnie, my cat, on our old blue-checked sofa. "Can I just sit here awhile and cry?" she asked. "I can't cry at home. I have to be Supermom and Superwife. It's so quiet and peaceful here."

I brought over a box of tissues. Joan cried while I watched silently. After a little while, we talked. Joan's problems were overwhelming. She was deeply depressed. I couldn't think of anything helpful to say, so mostly I listened. "Would you like something to drink?" I asked when she had finished.

"Just some cold water, please."

I went into the kitchen and grabbed a big red plastic cup, filled it with water and brought it out to Joan. She drank deeply. We talked, read some Scripture and prayed. Finally, we hugged good-bye and Joan left, still gripping my red cup.

In the silence after Joan left, I heard only the echoes of my failure to help her: *You did nothing. She's no better. She wasted her time coming to you.* The feeling lasted for days, but it vanished the day I received this note from Joan:

Thanks for listening to me Saturday and being there for me. I feel stronger today, and I praise God. I know this sounds silly, but I'm keeping that red cup you gave me water in. It sits by my bed. I call it my Care Cup. Every time people show they care, I'll write it down and put it in the cup. The next time my depression hits, I'll reach into my Care Cup and remember I have friends who'll try to help me through.

Love, Joan.

Oh, Father, the red cup was all Your idea. Thank You!

—*Marion Bond West*

SUN
23

And sure enough, as soon as she had touched him, the bleeding stopped and she knew she was well!
—*MARK 5:29 (TLB)*

My surgery was minor, but when I awakened in the middle of the night bleeding and feeling faint, I panicked. "If I were standing or sitting, and fainted, at least someone would notice and get me help," I muttered to myself. "But lying here in bed, I could faint and be in serious trouble and my husband wouldn't even know it!" I decided to prod him awake.

"Darling . . . darling," I called weakly.

"Huh?" John mumbled sleepily.

"I feel faint."

"So? You're lying down."

"You don't understand. I need help."

John raised up on one elbow and looked at me with half-closed eyes. Grumpily, he stretched his arm across the bed and placed his hand on my body. "Lord," he prayed, "Lovey needs some help. Lord, do it!" Then he flopped back onto the pillows. The bleeding stopped immediately.

I was grateful for God's healing touch, but I was irritated and puzzled by John's casual prayer. He didn't even get out of bed. He didn't come around to my side and kneel down. He didn't anoint me with oil or lift up a poignant supplication to the Lord. He was grouchy, and yet God used his hand and the simplicity of his "Lord, do it!" to heal me.

It was then I realized that what John had done was to touch the hem of the Lord's garment for me. The simple confidence of my husband's faith moved the healing heart of God.

"Forgive me, Lord," I whispered. "Give me that simple faith."

Thank You, Lord, for hearing my muddled, middle-of-the-night cries.   —*Fay Angus*

MON
24   *But God hath revealed them unto us. . . .*
                                —*I CORINTHIANS 2:10*

"Pam, do you have the chicken ready for the grill?" my husband David asked as he walked through the kitchen.

"Yes, it's ready—and I think I hear Keri's car in the drive."

Keri, our nineteen-year-old daughter, had just completed her last day at her summer job. Now she was home and ready for two weeks of freedom before she returned to Birmingham Southern for her junior year of college.

"So, cutie," I asked as she landed in the kitchen a few minutes later, "do you still see this summer as a 'waste'?" Keri had expected to spend her summer following doctors around the hospital and nursing their patients, but budget cuts had stuck her in a file room.

"Oh, Mom, don't be silly," she answered. "I learned a lot filing charts. Like how important it is to choose a career and work toward that. I learned that the chance to get an education is a gift that a lot of people never receive, and besides, Mom, without this job I never would have met Dionne. Don't you see? God wanted me to work at the VA this summer."

I was chopping vegetables and feeling amazed as Keri waltzed out of the kitchen and headed toward the backyard to join her dad.

"How clever, God," I whispered. "Three months of filing charts has made a good education all the more desirable. And she seems so focused. Forgive me for doubting!"

And then I thought of Dionne, a young African American girl who also worked at the VA hospital. Without any family support, this fine young woman worked not one, but three jobs, saving for her final year of college and hoping for a chance to go on to graduate school. Keri had made fast friends with Dionne, helped her find a support group that would see her through the year ahead, introduced her to a friend at church who was willing to help her with graduate school and submitted her name to a church scholarship fund that would provide financial aid for her senior year.

"And then, Father, there's Dionne." I smiled as I went to join my family in the backyard with this prayer in my head:

Even in the midst of human chaos, God, or should I say, especially in the midst of human chaos, Your plan unfolds in perfect order. You are, indeed, our Father!   —Pam Kidd

---

TUE
25   *To him who is able to keep you from falling. . . .*
                                          —JUDE 24 (NIV)

My mouth felt like it was full of cotton. My knees trembled, and I wiped my sweaty palms on my pants. This was my first attempt at rock climbing, and I was terrified. I hadn't been keen on trying it, but my husband Jim was insistent. "You'll be surprised at how it will build your confidence for other things. It's quite safe, and besides, you might even like it!" Swinging from the end of a rope off a cliff didn't sound like my idea of fun, but his persistence paid off. After watching our three young children do it, I felt I had at least to give it a try.

I stepped into the climbing harness and put on a hard hat. The belay-rope, which was secured to the rock and the mountaineering instructor at the top, was clipped onto the harness. I knew I was safe, but I was still terrified. Reaching up, my fingers clamped onto the narrow ledge of cold stone. After about thirty feet I was ready to give it up and turn back. "Don't get discouraged!" the instructor called down. "It's actually easier to keep going forward. Besides, I *know* you can do it." My concentration was so intense I hardly noticed the pain of my scraped elbows and knuckles. At times I groped in vain for the next secure hold, and then I would hear his reassuring voice, "Up a bit and a little to your left." Finally, I crawled over the clifftop—exhilarated, exhausted, amazed—while my husband and kids cheered from below.

Some months later, Jim was killed by a drunken driver in a head-on collision. When the news came in the middle of the night, my mouth went dry; I felt as if I'd been kicked in the stomach. But as I hung up the phone, my mind flashed back to that summer scene in Colorado. *God, I'm terrified, and I don't know the way up this mountain. But I know You're up there, and You have me "on belay."*

Help me to trust You, God, and to keep on climbing.

—*Mary Jane Clark*

WED

26 *Speak ye every man the truth to his neighbor. . . .*
—*ZECHARIAH 8:16*

Last summer, Shirley and I introduced our grandchildren—Jessica, Ashley and David—to golf. On a day when the course was nearly empty, we let them hit some balls. After some coaching, they all did surprisingly well and are now anxious to play again.

Something else they learned was how to keep score. In golf, scoring rules are very exact. Every shot is counted, and there are penalties for infractions like hitting the ball out of bounds. When I finished one hole, David asked me what my score was. "Five," I said.

"I thought you only took four swings," David said.

"You didn't see my whiff in the fairway," I told him. Then I told David and his sisters a story I had just heard about Tom Lehman, one of the top players on the PGA tour.

Before he joined the main tour, Tom went to qualifying school, as all players must. In the final round of the tournament that would determine who qualified and who did not, it appeared he had won a spot. But while Tom was preparing to hit the ball, it moved ever so slightly. No one but Tom saw the ball move, but the rules were clear. Tom called a one-stroke penalty on himself, and it proved crucial: He lost out by one shot.

"If I hadn't called the breach," Tom said, "I wouldn't have been able to look at myself in the mirror. You're only as good as your word, and your word isn't worth much if you aren't honest."

Integrity is a priceless value—on the golf course or off.

> *Teach me, Lord, there's naught but woe*
> *When I tell myself, "No one will know."*
> —*Fred Bauer*

THU

27 *What time I am afraid, I will trust in thee.*
—*PSALM 56:3*

"This scar tissue," the doctor held up a dye-enhanced X ray of my husband's heart, "indicates that you've had a mild heart attack."

Medication and exercise, he assured John and me, could prevent a recurrence. I hardly heard. At the words *heart attack*, terrifying images rose. Sickness. Disability. Death.

As we left the doctor's office, it was John who had the healing words for my fears. "Remember Willis Lee."

At Carlsbad Caverns, New Mexico, earlier that month, we'd heard about this writer who explored the caves for *National Geographic* in 1923. No paved walkways and electric lights then! Carrying lanterns, Lee and his guide descended rope ladders, inched along narrow ledges, squirmed through passageways two feet wide. Enthralled by the underground world opening before him, Lee felt no fear until, holding his lantern over a hole, he asked, "How far down is that drop?"

"Around ninety feet," the guide replied.

Ninety feet. . . . Suddenly, the rock beneath Lee's feet seemed less solid, the blackness of the cave filled with menace. For the rest of the underground journey, he related later, he groped on legs turned to jelly for the footholds that moments before had come so readily. *So far down! What if the lantern blows out! What if . . . what if? . . .*

Whatever the dangers along our path, John reminded me, we can look at the hole, at all the dread scenarios. Or we can look at the provisions for our safety. The lantern. The guide. The rock beneath our feet.

> *Jesus, You are the Light, the Guide, the Rock. Keep my eyes*
> *on You today and not on my fears.*   —*Elizabeth Sherrill*

FRI

28
So then every one of us shall give account of himself to God. —ROMANS 14:12

"Spend your birthday all by yourself? What in the world would you want to do that for?" asked my friend Jane, who could usually be counted on to understand my occasional crochet.

I could see why she was surprised. My life is very full of people: five in my immediate family coming and going with much ado; a busy office full of colleagues who are also my friends. I like people. But this was different. I was going to be fifty-three. I was tired and felt as if I hadn't had time to form a coherent thought in months or even to read a good book undisturbed. I knew I wasn't much fun to be around.

"It's what I'm going to do. I just feel like it," I answered rather defensively. So I took myself off for a few days to an old house in the country with no phone, no TV, no plumbing and no distractions.

That birthday morning in August was like no other. No packages to open, no candles to blow out or phone calls to answer. I looked out across the fields, half noticed the black cows making their collective way to whatever destination they had in mind. I thought of my life: the past and the future. I ate cereal on the porch and checked off my blessings—many. I made myself a cup of coffee and reviewed my sorrows—some.

I felt a bit like a company manager making an annual report to the board of directors, only in this case there was only one director and He wasn't judging me by the money I'd made for the shareholders. In fact, He wasn't judging me at all.

Thank You, Lord, for listening and for giving me Your strength to look back with thanks and to look forward with anticipation. —Brigitte Weeks

SAT

29
"Why are you afraid . . . ?" Then he rose and rebuked the winds and the sea; and there was a great calm. —MATTHEW 8:26 (RSV)

The lobby of the Hilo Airport on the Big Island of Hawaii was packed with tourists like my husband, son and me, all of us anxious about the weather. The prediction hinted at rain, a possibility that my over-

active imagination had magnified into a storm of dreadful propor-
tions although no cloud marred the horizon. Suddenly, exploding
into our midst came an *ohana*, a Hawaiian family, to bid a college-
bound son *aloha*, love and Godspeed. In minutes, the airport was
filled with the sounds of ukuleles strumming, voices raised in snatches
of song, children bantering in singsong island argot.

Without warning, the bustle ceased. *Was the airline canceling our
flight?* I wondered, listening for the loudspeaker.

But, no. The *ohana* was praying. Hands clasped, uncles, aunts,
brothers, sisters, cousins stood in a circle whose wobbly circumfer-
ence snaked around the waiting room and gathered strangers like ourselves into its center. The father's voice rose, offering up a blessing
laced with lilting Hawaiian words for a loved one bound for a distant
shore.

We prayed, too, one ohana embraced within the other. I felt fear
melting away.

"*Amene.* Aloha," came the benediction. The departure gate flung
wide.

"Amene," I echoed and went with my ohana through the gate,
across a wide and gentle sea toward home.

**Lord, calm the tempests, quiet the seas, surround our loved
ones with aloha and bring us safely home again. Amene.**
—Linda Ching Sledge

SUN

30 "Repent, then, and turn to God, so that your sins
may be wiped out. . . ." —ACTS 3:19 (NIV)

Have you ever hurt someone without knowing it?

Many years ago, we had an eight-year-old boy named Robert in
our summer tutorial program. Robert was very unruly in class. Day
after day the instructor tried to get him to do his math work on the
chalkboard, and day after day he refused. Out of desperation she
brought him to my office, and as director of the program, I gave him
a good, old-fashioned tongue-lashing and imposed a series of pun-
ishments for disobeying his teacher. I completely forgot about the incident and lost track of the boy.

Almost fifteen years later, a young man came up to me at a church
service I was attending. He related the whole incident to me and told

me that he was that young boy. He also told me that for a number of years he had hated me because I had punished him for being defiant, when he simply didn't know how to do math problems.

"Dolphus," Robert said, "if I had come in contact with you five years ago, I would have tried to hurt you. But now I'm a Christian, and God has enabled me to forgive you. Will you forgive me for all the years of anger I had built up inside of me?"

Even as I thanked God for Robert and his new life in Christ, I was shocked and ashamed that my unthinking actions of years before had caused Robert such deep pain. I promised the Lord not to jump to conclusions about people without trying to get all the facts. And then I asked God—and Robert—to forgive me.

Lord, today I need the healing power of Your forgiveness.
—*Dolphus Weary*

MON
31

On the third day there was a marriage at Cana in Galilee, and the mother of Jesus was there.
—*JOHN 2:1 (RSV)*

Two years ago when my daughter announced her engagement, I spent a year sorting through my own failed marriage. As her wedding drew near, I found myself puttering more and more in my garden, seeking solace. Pain, I thought long gone, was back.

I was mixing compost and last winter's ashes into garden soil when I saw a comparison. Just as I was creating a flower bed, rooted in manure and wood ash, was not God also creating something new in me *out of the manure and wood ash of my life?*

It was a simple analogy, perhaps trite. Yet something reminded me in a very poignant way that God is more than capable of transforming all that is bad in our lives. He takes the worst—the leftover, the burned-up dross—and uses it to create and give us new beauty.

Spring gave way to summer, summer edged toward fall. My garden burst forth, and on the last day of August my daughter married. It was the loveliest wedding I've ever attended. Not because old memories had vanished, or because the pain had ceased to sting. But because I realized that out of my past had come so much good. My daughter, for one. Wise beyond her years, kind, full of compassion for those less fortunate that herself. My two sons, proudly walking her down the aisle, pleased to be at her side. And my many friends and family come to help celebrate.

God, You do indeed take the very worst of our lives—the left-over, the burned-up dross—and use it to create for us something beautiful and good.

—Brenda Wilbee

My Healing Journey

1 _____

2 _____

3 _____

4 _____

5 _____

6 _____

7 _____

8 _____

9 _____

10 _____

11 _____

12 _____

13 _____

14 _____

15 _____

16 _____

17 _____

18 _____

19 _____

20 _____

21 _____

22 _____

23 _____

24 _____

25 _____

26 _____

27 _____

28 _____

29 _____

30 _____

31 _____

SEPTEMBER

S	M	T	W	T	F	S
		1	2	3	4	5
6	7	8	9	10	11	12
13	14	15	16	17	18	19
20	21	22	23	24	25	26
27	28	29	30			

I will not leave you comfortless:
I will come to you.
—*JOHN 14:18*

THE TOUCH OF THE HEALER
Healing Our Sadness
1   *Hope thou in God. . . .*   —*PSALM 42:5*

Somehow the subject of homesickness had come up, and I was recalling my struggles with it as a young boy sent off to school. "It was a sad, gray, empty feeling," I said, "with unshed tears behind my eyes and a dull ache in the region of my heart. I was yearning to be home with loved faces and familiar sights. As time passed, this desperate longing did diminish somewhat. But I was never fully free of it until I was back where I knew I belonged."

A doctor who happened to be with us nodded thoughtfully. "Every physician has patients with symptoms like the ones you're describing," he said. "When they're severe enough, we call it clinical depression. I can help such patients to some extent with medication, but sometimes I simply urge them to go to church, because often what they're suffering from is a kind of spiritual homesickness.

"Remember that poem of Tennyson's where he says that we come into this life 'trailing clouds of glory, from God who is our home'? Well, if God is our home and we lose touch with Him, there's bound to be deep uneasiness, a melancholy that's a lot like homesickness, even when the cause isn't recognized.

"Depression is very common in our society," the doctor went on, "but there's nothing new about it. Some of the great figures of the Bible had their share. In one of the Psalms, David cries out in anguish, 'Why art thou cast down, O my soul? And why art thou disquieted in me?' But then, almost in the same breath, he gives himself a remedy: 'Hope thou in God' (Psalm 42:5). That was a good prescription three thousand years ago. It's still a healing one today."

Lord, when I'm downcast, give me the wisdom to lean on You.
—*Arthur Gordon*

2   *The Lord hath his way in the whirlwind and in the storm. . . .*   —*NAHUM 1:3*

It had been a difficult day at the pottery fair in Dresden, Germany. We had escaped the sudden downpour after closing by ducking into a nearby pizzeria. The rain pounded the streets at a nearly impossible angle, and the wind howled across the marketplace, funneled by the tall downtown buildings.

Our booths offered pottery from all over Saxony, and despite the dreary weather, the crowds had been good that day. Christival, a convention of 33,000 young Christians from all over the world, had swollen the city to capacity, and between concerts and workshops, the enthusiastic participants had swarmed through the fair.

My friends Gabi, Conny, Hans and I had decided to attend the big Christival concert on the banks of the Elbe, and we were going back to the marketplace to pick up our jackets in case of more rain. But as we neared the market square, we stopped in our tracks. My jaw dropped, and Hans sank to his knees, moaning. Conny recovered first and braved what looked like a war zone. Our booths, shelves filled with the finest Bunzlauer ceramics, had been tossed across the square by the storm. Plates and teacups, jugs and vases lay crushed and scattered on the wet pavement.

Someone tapped my shoulder. I turned to see a group of four young people soaked to the skin. Their faces broke into hesitant smiles as one boy pointed and explained, "We saved some. . . ." Over by one of the market sheds, they had stacked crate upon crate of pottery. Out of the path of the whirlwind, more than half the booths' ceramics had been saved.

Hans stood and stumbled toward the stacked crates, staring in disbelief. Conny, Gabi and I descended on our sodden saviors with hugs of thanks. In the midst of the storm, God had been very active in the persons of four very wet, very kind, young Christians, who worked hard to save wares that weren't theirs, to help people they didn't even know.

Thank You, Lord, for Christian kindness in times of need.
—*Kjerstin Easton*

THU

3   *Preserve me, O God. . . .*   —*PSALM 16:1*

As I stepped into the morning and walked across the damp grass toward the garden, all I could think was *hot, hot, hot.* Living in the South, I'm used to summer's sultriness, but a busy day was pressing around me, and I wasn't sure I could stand the heat.

I seemed to be living in a pressure cooker. Four or five hours at the computer . . . then there's company coming and dinner to cook . . . the house needs straightening and I've got to make phone calls for the prayer group.

Laden with vegetables from the garden, I was heading toward the house when I noticed the magnolia tree. Overnight several big, white flowers had appeared on its branches, so delicate and perfect in spite of the hot, humid weather. I broke off several of the lotuslike flowers, took them inside and arranged them in a big bowl. I smiled, anticipating the lovely lemon smell that would fill the room by dinnertime. Yet, when I returned some hours later to the cool of the dining room, I found the blossoms turned an ugly brown.

Hurrying out to cut zinnias for a new centerpiece, I noticed that the magnolia tree's blossoms had not only withstood the heat, they'd actually grown more beautiful.

Back inside, I looked around: My work was done; the house straight; my phone calls made; dinner was in the oven and the table was set for company. In spite of the heat, motivated by the pressure, I was able to meet my responsibilities and provide a good dinner for family and friends.

I stood at the window and looked out into the summer green: Like the flowers out on the magnolia tree, I am where I belong. Sure, life is hectic, but I'd wither pretty quickly on easy street. And tonight when I look around the table and see my loved ones enjoying the results of my long day, you can bet a smile of contentment will blossom full across my face.

Father, let me flower in the middle of this busy life in which You have placed me.   —*Pam Kidd*

<u>FRI</u>

4   *A wise man's heart guides his mouth. . . .*
                                    —*PROVERBS 16:23 (NIV)*

As a preacher's kid, I used cuss words to convince my friends that I was a regular guy. I spoke one vernacular on the playground and another in the classroom, at home and especially in church. My problem became keeping my languages separate. One slip of the tongue could easily ruin my sterling image with the Sunday school teachers.

One thing I knew: No matter how angry I was or how bad my hammered thumb hurt, using the Lord's name in vain was strictly off limits—no matter where I was or whom I was with. "Religious" people like me made slight alterations using linguistic acrobatics. We came up with harmless alternatives like *tarnation, good golly* and *holy cow.*

In most circles I could get away with these alternatives, but one day I got caught. I was playing Ping-Pong with a friend in his backyard, and I was losing. He served, and I whiffed. I went for a safe enough phrase to utter. After missing the ball for three serves, I shouted my favorite pseudo-swear word. Repeatedly.

That's when my friend's mom came charging out of the house. I listened, blushing, to a short sermon that made Jonathan Edward's *Sinners in the Hands of an Angry God* seem tame in comparison. I saw the wrath of the Lord in her eyes and vowed never to profane that hallowed abode again.

That afternoon I began to learn that my speech was a reflection of my character, and if I spoke two languages, my character was just as divided. It became clear to me that I had to choose one language—for speaking and for living.

Lord, may my speech reflect a clean core.   —Bill Peel

SAT

5

The heavens declare his righteousness. . . .
—PSALM 97:6

One Saturday late last summer, my wife Joy and I got up with the sun and started in on several projects. Our two older boys Jason and Nathan were working that day, and Jonathan was off to a friend's house, so it was just the two of us. By afternoon, we were nearly exhausted. Finally, I said, "Honey, this is supposed to be a day off, and we're working harder than ever. Can't we take the evening off and go for a boat ride?"

With a wistful look at her to-do list, Joy suppressed her type-A tendencies and agreed. So we tossed out the fishing gear, put a couple of lawn chairs into the boat and drove it to the lake. The sunset was beautiful, and our conversation drifted back to all the tasks that needed doing before school started. The list was discouraging.

Darkness fell, and I turned on the running lights as we cruised the glassy surface in the nighttime quiet. As we bounced over the wake of another boat, a wire jiggled loose and our lights winked out. I shut down the motor and tried to fix them as we drifted in the darkness. My fumblings were interrupted when Joy exclaimed, "Look at that! The stars are brilliant."

I let the boat drift for a while and we just held hands and looked at the stars, which we couldn't see before because of the running lights. In those peaceful moments, it came to us that all the to-do items that crowd our lives need to be turned off once in a while. Then, like the stars, the quieter light of faith, family, love and hope can come into focus.

Lord, teach me how to turn off the glare of busyness so that the glow of eternal things can fill my life. —Eric Fellman

6 "And lo, I am with you always, to the close of the age." —MATTHEW 28:20 (RSV)

I am still playing the organ for our little church each Sunday, and each week seems to bring new problems. Though we spent thousands of dollars on a new roof, it leaks worse than ever! All of us are getting older, and some are no longer able to come out on Sundays. Others have moved away, so our numbers keep diminishing, and we few who are still active end up with multiple responsibilities.

When one of our more active members sold her house in Jersey City, New Jersey, this summer and moved, I was really discouraged. *Why don't we close up shop altogether?* I wondered. *Why do I keep on going here?*

Then our pastor asked me to preach for him on Labor Day Sunday. The Old Testament lesson for the day was Exodus 3, God's appearance to Moses from out of the burning bush. Moses had spent forty years in the desert not being able to do anything about his brothers and sisters in Egypt, while their circumstances were getting worse. *God has forgotten us,* Moses must have thought.

"I have seen . . . and have heard . . . I know . . . and I have come down," God told Moses (Exodus 3:7-8, RSV).

How reassuring! I thought, as perhaps Moses did. *God hasn't for-*

gotten us. He knows about our problems. And He's going to take care of everything!

But then came the curve ball. "I will send you" (Exodus 3:10, RSV).

Me? Is that my answer?

I believe it was. God changes situations through people, and since I'm in this situation, that means through me. So for now, my place is still with our little church and the multiple responsibilities. Fortunately, there's more to God's commission: "I will be with you" (Exodus 3:12, RSV).

Lord Jesus, help me to believe and act on Your promise that You are with me.   —*Mary Ruth Howes*

<u>*MON*</u>
7   *A good man . . . will guide his affairs with discretion.*   —*PSALM 112:5*

One typically hectic day at the publishing company where I worked, we were in the middle of an end-of-the-month push. People were sprinting from one room to another, and very few smiles were in evidence.

An administrative assistant in the editorial department always seemed much more serene than the rest of us. Yet she had to answer the phones, find and deliver files, type correspondence, keep up the status lists, mail out and check in proofs, and perform hundreds of other tasks on which the editors' work depended.

On this day, I saw one of the editors run up to her and toss a thick folder onto the top of her already stuffed in-box. "These contracts are late!" he almost shouted. "You have to send them all out today!"

She hung up her phone and looked at him squarely. "You're wrong about that," she said in a quiet voice. He stared at her; so did I. She continued calmly, "I don't have to send them out. I *get* to send them out." And as he continued to stare, and I grinned, she opened the folder and started working on the contracts.

It isn't the work; it's the way we look at the work that makes all the difference.

On this Labor Day, God, help me to face my work with a sense of appreciation and gratitude. Amen.   —*Rhoda Blecker*

<u>*TUE*</u>
8

A cheerful look brings joy to the heart, and good news gives health to the bones.
—*PROVERBS 15:30 (NIV)*

I live in a very beautiful place: Durango, Colorado. I'm grateful that I can look out my windows and see mountains and evergreen trees, clear blue skies, and sometimes even deer and elk. But at times I've wondered why God bothered to make all this beauty—it seems so unnecessary, so extravagant.

But now I have a theory about beauty. I think it's one of the ways God brings healing to our hurting world. In appreciating beautiful things, we experience healing for our brokenness, and by sharing or creating beauty, we can extend that healing to others who are hurting.

Some years ago, in a time of great brokenness and pain in my life, I was staying with friends in their comfortable home. Every morning I woke up early, unable to sleep. And every morning I would hear a light tap on my door, and open it to find a lovely tea tray: a tiny vase of flowers; a brightly colored napkin; a silver spoon and china cup; a pot of hot tea. While the tea warmed my body, the beauty of the tray helped to bring healing to my soul.

All of us aren't artists or architects, poets or composers, but we can still participate in the creation of beauty. It doesn't take a lot of money, either: a few green sprigs in a glass of water; a word of hope and encouragement; an invitation for a leisurely walk in the park; a lighted candle on the dinner table; tulip bulbs planted in a window box; a plate of muffins hot out of the oven. In a multitude of ways, we can be channels of God's healing, putting a little more beauty into our world and into our lives.

Lord and Creator of all, today show me how I can be a co-creator and healer in this broken world. —*Mary Jane Clark*

<u>*WED*</u>
9

"Remember the everlasting covenant between God and every living creature of all flesh that is upon the earth."
—*GENESIS 9:16 (RSV)*

My office desk is a zoo, filled with little animals that friends have given me. There must be fifteen of them, though fifteen doesn't sound like a lot when you consider that I have been working here for more than forty years. It's easy to see why there are dogs and horses—that's what I love—but the sea otter and the chick and the seal all have their reasons for being. So do the Santa, the bale of cotton (a music box that plays "Dixie"), and the teeth that people (too many) wind up and set to chattering. Every one of them has come from someone with a special message. I can't forget Alan who gave the "It's a Girl" cigar, or the koala bear from Ellie in honor of my trip to Australia. They go back a long way in time, and some of the people are no longer with us, but they are, here on my desk.

People have said, "What a conversation piece," as though that were necessary with me. I do recall the job applicant who seemed to open up once she came eye to eye with my yellow lab (she has been here for twenty-one years). I look forward to the current visitor who arrives with a cup of hot tea. When she leaves, the zoo is done over, the dogs and horses in circle-the-wagons stance, or the koala is mixing it up with the donkey, or the mounted horseman is jousting with the I Love You bear. I love it.

You probably have a desk arrangement of your own. I hope you have one faithful object, as I have. It's a paperweight from the time when our firm was forty (we're over fifty now). It has a bronze plaque on which there is an inscription from *The Book of Common Prayer*, 1928. No day goes by that I don't see it, and remember it:

> *O Lord, support us all the day long,*
> *until the shadows lengthen*
> *and the evening comes,*
> *and the world is hushed.*
> *Then in Thy mercy grant us*
> *a safe lodging,*
> *and a holy rest,*
> *and peace at the last.*
> —*Van Varner*

THU

10 *If any man walk in the day, he stumbleth not, because he seeth the light of this world.*   —*JOHN 11:9*

The other day I found Norman Vincent Peale's rules for a perfect day. They always worked for him, and you might wish to follow them today:

Try to strengthen your mind by reading something that requires effort, thought and concentration.

Try to do somebody a good turn and not get found out.

Try to do a task that needs to be done, but which you have been putting off.

Try to go for one full day without finding fault in anything.

Try to have a quiet half-hour by yourself. Think of God, read the Bible; you'll get a little more perspective in your life.

And, finally, don't be afraid to be happy; enjoy what is beautiful; believe that those you love, love you.

Dear Father, please help me concentrate on today and not worry about tomorrow or yesterday. Help me follow these rules for a perfect day.   —*Ruth Stafford Peale*

FRI

11

Man goeth forth unto his work and to his labor until the evening.   —*PSALM 104:23*

Resisting the tide of upscale espresso bars offering lattes, au laits, cappuccinos, mochaccinos, frappes and every other exotic hybrid of coffee concoction, I still prefer to wake up with a simple cup from George, an old Korean gentleman who runs a rickety little newsstand on my block. He serves it blistering hot in a short Styrofoam container with lots of milk. George's coffee is not very good, frankly. But that's not why I go there.

George is aware that I am a Detroit Tigers fan, so during baseball season he familiarizes himself with the baseball scores on the morning sports page so he can commiserate or congratulate me. He persists in calling me "Merit" after the brand of cigarette I used to smoke when I smoked. After all these years he still says, "You Tiger team did good last night, Merit!" Of course, George is not his real given name either, but we've grown quite comfortable with how we address each other.

It must have been fairly obvious the other morning that I'd had a rough night. I'd lain awake, tossing and turning, wrestling with my worries as I am wont to do. I mumbled for George to give me a large coffee, black. George shot me a look as he searched for a big cup. He said something I didn't quite catch through his accent: "Good worka night." I repeated my request. This time George laid a hand on my arm. "God work overnight."

"God works the overnight?" I guessed after a second.

"Yes!" George said. "God work the overnight. He take care of you worries, so you can sleep."

I suppose I could get used to those specialty coffee shops that dot my way to work in the morning, but I think I'll stick with George's watery brew to wake me up. He gives me something I can't buy . . . a little familiar conversation, a caring word and an occasional bit of spiritual advice that helps me get to sleep at night.

I'll try to remember, Lord, what George says: that You are there to carry my burdens when I need to rest.

—*Edward Grinnan*

SAT	*But concerning brotherly love you have no need that*
12	*I should write you, for you yourselves are taught by God to love one another.*

—I THESSALONIANS 4:9 (NKJV)

"Your attention please! Flight 703, scheduled to depart at 4:05 P.M., has been delayed and is now scheduled to depart at 4:36 P.M." *One more delay and it will be midnight before I get home,* I thought wearily. I shut my book and looked around. A harried-looking mother and four boys hurried past, no doubt rushing to catch their on-time connecting flight.

The youngest, about five, couldn't keep up. The others urged him to run. Instead, he stopped in his tracks. With tears running down his face, he screamed, "I hate you! I hate you all!" His mother tried to reason with him but to no avail. Her face flaming, she and the older boys turned away. The child stared at their backs for a second, then yelled, "Not only do I hate you, but you're all . . . STUPID!" With that, he threw himself face-down in the middle of the airport and began to howl.

I know how he feels, I thought. I'd like to cry, too. When his family walked on, however, I became concerned. Should I do something? As I debated, the just-older boy came back. He lay down beside his brother and patted him on the shoulder. After a few seconds, he got up and helped his younger brother to his feet. Side by side, hand in hand, they walked down the corridor and out of sight.

I wish I had stood up and clapped and cheered and said a hearty "Praise the Lord!" I didn't. I wish the scene has made me forever patient with airport delays. It hasn't. But I will carry with me forever the picture of Christ's love lived out: one person extending a helping hand to another, then walking along together as friends—and brothers.

Thank You, Lord of Love, for all the ways You show me Your love in action.   —*Penney Schwab*

SUN 13 · *I will show you lessons from our history, stories handed down to us from former generations.* —*PSALM 78:2-3 (TLB)*

Around eight o'clock on most nights when I was a boy, my dad would tuck me into bed. "How about a story?" he'd ask as he pulled a chair up to my bedside.

"Yes!" I'd answer eagerly. "Tell me a story about Grandpa." Settling my head on the pillow, I'd listen to Dad's gentle voice, with its ghost of a Southern accent.

"One summer, when I was a little boy, we moved to a new house. When we got to the new place, your grandpa noticed that Blue, his favorite hunting dog, was missing. He loved that old dog, and he was very sad that we had lost him.

"The next morning, your grandpa got up and hitched the horse to the buggy. 'I know where Blue is,' he said. 'I saw him in a dream, tied up on the porch of a farmhouse. I'll know it when I see it.'

"He was gone all that day and all that night. The next day after breakfast, he came back. Sitting next to him in the buggy was that old dog."

No matter how many times Dad told them, I never tired of hearing his stories about Grandpa. Grandpa Attaway died when I was a very small boy, but he's always been a very real presence in my life because of all those nights when my dad's voice made him live.

Now I have two children of my own, who will never know *their* Grandpa Attaway in the flesh; my dad died shortly after the first of them was born. When they're old enough to read them, I'll show them the letters he sent my mother during the war and the half-dozen yellow tablets on which he wrote his life story. But before that, every night I'll tuck them into bed, and when they ask me for a story, I'll tell them one about their grandpa.

Lord, on this Grandparents Day, help me to help my children know and love their grandparents, living and departed.
                                                              —Andrew Attaway

---

MON

14 *The Lord is near to all who call upon Him. . . .*
                                                    —PSALM 145:18 (NAS)

"I'll carry your pager while you're off from work having surgery," Cathy, a fellow nurse, volunteered.

"Can I take care of your dogs?" my friend Kim asked.

"Now don't you worry about cooking when you get home," my neighbor Kay reassured me. "I'm bringing over some casseroles."

It was my third major surgery in six months, and I'd never had so many offers for help. But I'd declined all of them. I'd been on the receiving end so much lately that I was almost embarrassed by the unending flow of kindnesses. On the way to the hospital, I mentally checked off my long to-do list. Sure enough, I'd taken care of everything myself, but I was utterly exhausted.

The night after surgery, I'd just gotten comfortable when my roommate moaned in severe pain. I pressed my call light to summon a nurse. "Bertha, you've just had a big operation," the nurse explained gently, "and this is no time to be brave. Push your button and give yourself a dose of pain medication."

Bertha was connected to a patient-controlled analgesia (PCA) pump, a device that lets patients give themselves pain medication through their IV line. But Bertha would have nothing of it. Frustrated, I joined in the nurse's petitions: "Push your button, Bertha. You don't have to suffer. And don't worry, that pump won't let you give yourself too much medication."

At long last, Bertha relented. Within a matter of minutes, she was sleeping peacefully. Her stoic self-sufficiency was fine, I thought to myself, but too much was wrong. Then I began to think of Cathy . . . and Kim . . . and Kay.

I had a couple of phone calls to make.

Dear God, help me to ask for help.   —*Roberta Messner*

_{TUE}
15

This is the day which the Lord has made; let us rejoice and be glad in it.   —*PSALM 118:24 (RSV)*

There's a pull-out on the Taconic Parkway in upstate New York where my husband and I used to stop to enjoy the view. Years ago you could see across a green and gold valley of fields and barns to the distant Catskill Mountains. But though the sign on the parkway still proclaims *Overlook*, a thicket of fast-growing ailanthus and locust trees now crowd right up to the stone wall.

We'd paused there for a moment to change drivers on a recent trip, when a car with Michigan plates pulled in. A young couple got out, looked about and, bewildered, came over to our car.

Oh, no, I thought, *they're going to delay us!* We were hurrying to an appointment in Albany, taking turns working on the laptop computer as we went.

The young man swept his arm around the viewless parking area. "What does it overlook?" he asked.

"You could see the mountains," my husband explained, "if it weren't for the trees. Too bad they don't keep a passage open."

You could see the mountains if it weren't for the trees. I thought of my fretful hurry, and decided the words applied to more than a roadside pull-out. The "trees" in my life that day were work pressures, but they could have been a dozen other things. All the little demands that multiply so fast and press so close, how easily they shut out the view—the face of God in every human being.

Lord, help me clear a passage today in my busyness through which to reach out to the people You bring my way.
          —*Elizabeth Sherrill*

> ### Herald of Healing
>
> There's a wideness in God's mercy
> Like the wideness of the sea;
> There's a kindness in His justice
> Which is more than liberty.
>
> There is welcome for the sinner
> And more graces for the good;
> There is mercy with the Savior,
> There is healing in His blood.
> —*FREDERICK W. FABER*

WED

16 *Our daughters will be like pillars carved to adorn a palace.* —*PSALM 144:12 (NIV)*

Last week I took my five-year-old, Faith, to the bus stop for her first day of kindergarten. We had the typical tears and quaking sobs, but then Faith told me to straighten up because I was embarrassing her.

The other parents offered hankies and sympathy. Then the conversation turned to "How Tough It Is to Raise Kids Nowadays"—a popular topic among young moms and dads. And God knows, I didn't argue. I needed the validation that I'm not crazy, that other people struggle with sleeplessness and worry and stretched finances.

But this idea about "nowadays," that we've got it tougher than our parents had it, that our parents somehow shortchanged us. . . .

Ummm . . . no. Not nearly. Not by a long shot. Our parents worked just as hard and had to deal with the same regrets, such as trading time for money. They tried their best. And we're no different.

Of course, "trying your best" doesn't ease the feelings of inadequacy ("If only I had done this or that, then little Johnny. . . ."). No matter what you did as a parent, it never seems enough. And you've got to deal with that uncertainty; you've got to trust that you've done what you could.

You've got to forgive yourself.

Correction: *I've* got to forgive *myself.* In Faith's five short years, I've let her down a million times. (That's 550 times a day.) This is the only penance I can offer, my *mea culpa* to her and her siblings when they're all old enough to read. To be a parent means to forever second-guess myself, so much so that I forget what I've done right.

And my wife and I must've done something right, because Faith came back from her first day of school full of laughter and stories, eyes bright with excitement, clutching the flower she had drawn just for me, running down the driveway into my waiting arms, her tiny hands circling my torso. And I swear to you there is a merciful, loving God because nothing else can explain such glorious math.

And the first thing I did then? I called Mom and Dad. They were anxious to know how it went.

"Great," I told them. "Everything turned out great."

Lord, help me to do the best I can for my children, and leave the rest to You.   —*Mark Collins*

THU

17   *He hath set the world in their heart. . . .*
—*ECCLESIASTES 3:11*

I read somewhere that humans are three different ages at the same time. There's our chronological age, based on the number of years we've lived; our biological age, based on the condition of our body; and our psychological age, based on how old we *feel*. Since the last of these is the only one I have much control over, I've been thinking about what attitudes make me younger or older. Here are some of the ways I can gauge how old I feel:

- I'm as young as the tap of my foot when my first love's theme song plays;
- I'm as old as the finger I point at the changeable ways of the youth.

- I'm as young as the wonder I feel when the first snow sugars my lawn;
- I'm as old as my moon-blind eyes on a sky-clear summer night.

- I'm as young as the games I invent when my grandchildren come to play;

- I'm as old as the guilt I feel about "shoulds" I've left undone.

- I'm as young as the choices I make for that which nurtures my soul;
- I'm as old as my neglect of the faith that makes me whole.

Father in heaven, the numbering of my days is in Your hands. Help me to enrich the quality *of those days by keeping my attitudes young.*   —*Marilyn Morgan Helleberg*

FRI

18
Let everything that has breath praise the Lord. . . .
—*PSALM 150:6 (NAS)*

"Mother," my daughter moaned over the phone, "I had the patio looking so nice for the party tonight, and then the dog chewed up one of my brand-new patio chair cushions. They don't have any more at the store."

I had extra time that day, so I asked Julie to describe the cushion and give me the stock number. If I could find a matching cushion, I'd bring it to the family gathering that night.

When I got to the store, a young salesclerk offered to help me. We went through all the patio chair cushions, but we couldn't find the one Julie needed. I had turned to go when the young man called after me, "Is this it, ma'am?"

I knew immediately from Julie's description that he had found the right cushion. Sure enough, the stock numbers matched. It was the only one they had, and it had been well hidden at the bottom of a stack. "Oh, thank you," I exclaimed.

In my heart I discerned a gentle but definite voice: *Praise Me. I knew you would come here today for that cushion. Praise Me out loud. Just say, "Thank You, Lord."* I reasoned that the young man helping me probably wasn't interested in spiritual matters. He'd most likely laugh at the idea that God would help me find a cushion. So I resisted the strong urge to praise God.

The clerk, a few steps ahead of me, carried the cushion toward the cash register. Suddenly, he stopped and turned around. Smiling, he said, "Our Father knows exactly what we need, doesn't He? Isn't God good?"

"Yes! Yes! God is *so* good. He knows our needs exactly," I answered, half in joy, half in regret.

Forgive me, Father, when I fail to praise You. Amen.
—Marion Bond West

SAT
19
And Jesus said unto them, I am the bread of life: he that cometh to me shall never hunger; and he that believeth on me shall never thirst. —JOHN 6:35

My parents had little money when I was young. They counted every penny and "made do" with what they had. As I got older, their joint incomes increased, and yet, out of habit, they continued to live very frugal lives.

One day when I was sixteen, I watched my father reach into a package of bread, lift a slice to his mouth and absently take a couple of bites. Suddenly, he straightened, a look of wonder illuminating his face. "We don't have to eat stale bread!" he exclaimed. He threw away that loaf and went out to buy fresh food.

Recently, I hit a snag in a project I was working on, and I couldn't get around it. I was unable to work for several weeks. *Was this it?* I wondered. *Would I never be productive again?* In desperation I prayed, "God, help me out of this slump."

Suddenly, I thought of my father on that day long ago. I heard him saying, "You don't have to eat stale bread."

Stale bread? Yes, I'd been feeding my spirit an unhealthy diet of doubt and fear. I got out my Bible concordance and began looking up verses on hope, faith and courage.

Thank You, Father, for Your "bread of life," which never grows stale. —Madge Harrah

---

SUN
20
For God hath not given us the spirit of fear; but of power, and of love, and of a sound mind. —II TIMOTHY 1:7

Jimmie's familiar voice whined, "Excuse me . . ." as he walked into the room where I was cleaning up after mass. I was startled to see a huge gash oozing copious amounts of blood on his forehead. Jimmie said he'd received the wound from a fellow street person who'd hit him with a baseball bat.

I quickly steered Jimmie into the parish hall and handed him a clean towel with which to apply direct pressure. Using warm water, I gingerly washed the dirt and matted hair from his bloody head. My ministrations were nearly complete when our priest appeared. His face was ashen, and he motioned to me to come with him. I stepped into the parish hall kitchen.

"Julia," he said quietly, "wash your hands well. Jimmie has AIDS." Oh.

We sent Jimmie off to the hospital for stitches. Then I walked home, feeling as if my life had turned into a surreal movie about someone else. I scrutinized each finger for hangnails and scratches. I considered how much blood there had been. Yet strangely, I wasn't terrified. Perhaps my mind was simply unable to grasp the nightmare I might be facing.

All afternoon I tried to understand the potential implications of wiping Jimmie's bloody brow. What I had done was in some ways simple, and in other ways rash. Confused, I got down on my knees. The words that came tumbling out startled me. "Lord," I prayed, "thank You for sending me Jimmie to take care of. You gave me the grace to care for him without fear. I trust that whatever the consequences, You will be there with me, too."

When I had a test for AIDS as part of a medical exam, it came back negative. Today, I carry a pair of surgical gloves in my bag, so that if Christ asks me again to wipe the blood from His brow, I need never be afraid to help.

Jesus, grant me the courage to serve You faithfully in every person I meet.   *—Julia Attaway*

MON

21   *"Be not afraid of them, for I am with you to deliver you, says the Lord."*   *—JEREMIAH 1:8 (RSV)*

We have a new gizmo on our phone called "Caller I.D." When my husband Lynn first suggested it, I resisted, but now I've grown to depend upon it. It works like this: When our phone rings, the caller's name and phone number flashes on this little screen, which opens up a whole new realm of choices for me. Do I answer or not?

Take this morning, for instance. The phone rang and I saw that it was a friend who talks on endlessly. I was busy, so I didn't answer.

About an hour later, the phone rang again and I saw that it was my daughter Lindsay, calling from Phoenix, Arizona, where she lives. "Hi, Lindsay," I said immediately as I picked up the phone.

"Mom, you're pretty hot stuff with that Caller I.D.," she responded. "What would you do if Jesus called? Would you answer or let it ring?" She loves to ask me teasing questions like that because, of course, I'm stumped for an answer.

"Well, He hasn't called yet this morning, so I don't have to worry about that."

Later, when I hung up, I realized I was wrong. Jesus had called while I was hurrying through my morning prayer time. I answered, but I put Him on "hold" several times. He called when my talkative friend called and I did not answer. In my busyness, I doubted that He would give me what I needed to respond to her appropriately, even if that meant honestly telling her I had to do something else. Finally, He called when Lindsay called.

The truth is I don't need Caller I.D. when it comes to Jesus, because I know that He is always calling, in every circumstance and every phone call. He promises to provide what I need, every time He calls. But I still have a choice, just as I do with Caller I.D. on my telephone.

Will I answer His call?

Lord, help me to recognize and respond to Your calls.
—Carol Kuykendall

<table>
<tr><td>TUE
22</td><td>Give me understanding, and I will keep your law and obey it with all my heart.
—PSALMS 119:34 (NIV)</td></tr>
</table>

"Looking forward to it. See you at twelve-thirty, usual place," my friend Bobbi said.

I was very punctual and sat down pleased with the quiet atmosphere, the pink tablecloths and the fresh flowers. I broke a piece off the warm bread, munched and waited in pleasant anticipation.

Five minutes passed, ten, then twenty. An unexpected phone call? Did I have the time right? Was it today? *Don't be childish*, I reproved myself. *Something has gone wrong. Order lunch. Behave like a grown-up.* Reluctantly I did, and a plate of fish and vegetables appeared before me.

As I ate, I calmed down considerably. *Too late to fix it now. I'll sort it all out later*, I told myself. Then I began hearing snippets of conversation from the tables around me. I wasn't exactly eavesdropping, you understand, but phrases floated past me, odd words, but sometimes whole sentences.

"It's not the money," said a very attractive woman lunching across from me with an elderly man. "But then there's my soul, but I guess no one can take care of that but me. . . . " And then the waiter was pouring fresh iced water, and the rest of her words were lost.

"I can't do that!" said a much younger woman to her girlfriend. "What would everyone think?" I'll never know what *that* was, but half a dozen possibilities passed through my mind.

Then the words "usual place" drifted through my mind. This was *my* "usual place," but had I heard what Bobbi had said to me? I hadn't noticed at the time that no name had been mentioned. It happens all the time—just miscommunication. But if I can't hear what my friend is saying about a lunch date, how will I hear the quiet voice of the Spirit? Words alone are not enough. It's the interpretation that matters.

And, by the way, Bobbi had been sitting, watching and wondering at *her* "usual place," a mere five-minute walk away. We rescheduled our lunch.

Lord, help me to hear Your message as well as Your words.
—Brigitte Weeks

WED
23
Wherefore comfort yourselves together, and edify one another, even as also ye do.
—I THESSALONIANS 5:11

When my father was diagnosed with terminal cancer, he begged to remain at home. He'd had a bad reaction to some medication at the hospital and dreaded going back there.

My friends responded readily. "Let me know if I can be of help," some said. "Don't hesitate to call if you need me," said others. "I'm standing by."

Only my dear friend Marie, who lived the next street over, was specific. "The time will come," she told me, "when you won't want the responsibility of Emily. When that time comes, just phone me and let me take her to my house. I'll treat her like my own and take good care of her."

There was no way I could imagine wanting to relinquish the care of my eight-year-old daughter! But when Dad's condition worsened and Bob and I took leave from our jobs so we could be at his bedside day and night, I knew the time Marie had prophesied had come. Reluctantly, I picked Emily up at school and explained to her why she would be staying at Marie's house. We spent a couple of hours with Marie, and I gave her a key to my house so she could get clean clothes for Emily. After hugs from each of them, I went back to be with my daddy.

From that experience, I learned a great lesson: Willingness to help someone who is in trouble is a wonderful way to serve God. But an even better way is to look for the *specific* need He would have me fill—and fill it.

Lord, help me to recognize the needs of the people I meet and give me the willingness to fill them in Your name.
—Drue Duke

THU
24 *"He has sent Me . . . to set free those who are down-trodden."* *—LUKE 4:18 (NAS)*

It was past midnight. I was sitting in the bench swing under the large red oak in our front yard. The wind was picking up, gusting in from west Texas, and I closed my eyes to enjoy the breeze in my hair. Then I heard a clattering sound. It was an aluminum can being blown through the street, a hollow clanking in the still night.

I suddenly remembered the recycle container in our kitchen, filled to the brim with cans. I had promised my wife Beth that I would take the cans to the collection center, and I had forgotten. Yawning, I stood up to go to bed. The can still clattered, the sound growing dimmer in the distance. Impulsively, I walked down the street and found the culprit. *I don't know where you came from,* I thought as I reached down to pick it up, *but you're going in our recycle bin. You're going to have another useful life.*

As I walked home, my feeling of virtue gave way to a sense of irony. Here I was, going out of my way to pick up a discarded can, yet often ignoring the people I see who are being blown about by poverty, sickness and despair. *It's a whole lot easier to recycle a can than to restore a human life*, I thought. *That's something only God can really do.* But it was a lesson I would not forget. God can use me to get the process started and help it along—if I'm willing.

Father, help me to reach out today to someone in need.
—*Scott Walker*

25 *Look up, and lift up your heads. . . .* —*LUKE 21:28*

The first job I got after college was on a mid-sized daily newspaper, and I was in over my head. I was new to the town and didn't know any of the people on my beat. If they said they didn't have any news, I didn't know what kind of questions to ask. Day after day I came back to the office with no stories to write.

My editor was a man with very little patience. If I did something wrong he called my attention to it immediately. I began to think I couldn't do anything right and was close to giving up my dream of being a reporter.

My desk was next to that of a veteran reporter named Phil Wright, who ordinarily wasn't much of a talker. But one day when I was feeling especially discouraged, Phil turned to me and said, "You know, you write good opening paragraphs."

"How can you tell?" I asked him. "I don't seem to write much of anything."

"Don't worry about that. You need time to learn the ropes. We all do. But when you get a story, you can write it." He had nothing more to say, and he turned back to his typewriter.

That little bit of praise meant so much to me! It made me more patient with myself. It also made me realize that I wasn't the only person who had to learn a job from scratch. Eventually, I saw that I had to get to know people better before I asked them for news, and I began coming back to the office with a pad full of notes. Even my editor was pleased.

"Thanks, Phil," I said one day after an especially interesting interview.

"What for?" he said.

"For the compliment about opening paragraphs," I told him.

"That was no compliment," he said. "I just told the truth."

I've always remembered his remark. It inspires me to give people praise when they're doing something well—even if they're not doing everything well. Praise gives us the encouragement we need to do better. Besides, it's just telling the truth.

Today, Lord, give me a helpful word for everyone I meet.
—*Phyllis Hobe*

SAT

26 *In his hand is the life of every living thing and the breath of all mankind.* —*JOB 12:10 (RSV)*

Our friend Richard was a librarian until he went blind at age thirty. Undaunted, he took up singing, only to have cancer claim his voice a few months later. His untimely death raised so many questions: *Why, Lord? Why him? Why now?* I was thumbing through my Bible for answers when I saw the butterfly wing.

Several years ago, while walking up the path to our summer campsite at Iskwasum Landing in northern Manitoba, Canada, I noticed something orange fluttering in a crevice between two big rocks. Looking closer, I saw the broken body of a monarch butterfly, the breeze ruffling one lifeless wing.

I picked up the butterfly wing to examine the intricate markings more closely. Various shades of orange were separated by black lines, the pattern edged in black and white scallops. The delicate wing lay in my open palm like a miniature stained-glass window reflecting its Maker's love of beauty.

That monarch butterfly would never again grace the northern woods. Had it lived out its full life span? Had it escaped its cocoon only to return to its Creator? I struggled to understand God's timing, only to conclude that, as a mortal, I never would. Instead, God was asking me to believe that even something as seemingly insignificant as a butterfly nevertheless fulfills His purpose in both its life and its death. As an act of faith, I tucked the butterfly wing between the pages of my Bible at Job 12:10: "In his hand is the life of every living thing."

When I lose a loved one, Lord, it's so hard simply to take You at Your Word. Give me the faith to hold fast to Your promises.
—*Alma Barkman*

SUN

27

Let us love one another: for love is of God. . . .
—*I JOHN 4:7*

When our Sunday school superintendent asked me to teach fourth grade, I wanted to say no. I hadn't visited a Sunday school class in thirty-five years, and I had been neither the brightest nor the best-behaved student. I knew youngsters were quick to recognize fear, poor preparation and lack of interest. What did I have to give to the children?

In spite of my reservations, I agreed to teach. I gasped when I was handed the Sunday school materials. When I was a boy, Sunday school lessons had centered around Bible stories. Now we were also expected to discuss contemporary social and economic issues. I had a lot of preparing to do.

One Sunday early in the school year, our curate tapped on the door and called me out of my class. "Oscar," he said, "I want you to know that the hour you spend with these children might be the only hour of love they receive all week."

His words reminded me that my relationship with the children was more important than the topics in the curriculum. I began to relax and to pay attention to each of the children. I listened as they shared their concerns with me. Although teaching was never easy, I came to enjoy it.

On the final day of Sunday school, one of the children, Nancy, stayed behind after class. She helped me gather up the papers, put them neatly on my desk, kissed me and fled. As she ran down the corridor, I could hear her weeping.

Thirty years later, our friendship has grown. When Nancy was married, I was a proud guest at her wedding.

Thank You, Father, for overcoming my hesitation and enabling me to give.   —*Oscar Greene*

MON

28

Lay great errors to rest.   —*ECCLESIASTES 10:4 (NIV)*

It was my first day of substitute teaching in the kindergarten class, and I didn't want the children to feel their routine was being disrupted too much. So as class began at 8:00 A.M., I smiled and announced, "If I do anything differently from Mrs. Currey today, just let me know and I will do things her way."

By 8:15, I was frazzled from hearing "Mrs. Currey uses a blue pen, not a red one," and "Mrs. Currey stands up when she reads us a story, she doesn't sit down," and "Mrs. Currey opens the top window, not the bottom one."

So I said more sharply than I'd intended, "Heads up, all!"

Thirty pairs of eyes watched me warily as I announced more softly, "Change of rules. When Mrs. Currey comes back, she will do things her way. But while I am here, I will do things my way. This means that I might not do things the way Mrs. Currey does, or I might make a mistake—"

A little boy's hand shot up in the air. "Teacher?" he said.

"Yes?"

"Mrs. Currey always says, 'If you make a mistake, just say, So what! That's what erasers on pencils are for!' Mrs. Currey says then you can just start over."

"That Mrs. Currey is one smart lady," I said.

God, is there a mistake I'm dwelling on today? Help me say, "So what!" and just start over. After all, that's what erasers on pencils are for.　　　　　　　　　　　　　　　—Linda Neukrug

---

TUE	*Think with sober judgment, each according to the*
29	*measure of faith which God has assigned him.*
	—ROMANS 12:3 (RSV)

Yesterday, I woke up with things to be done swarming around in my mind like bees looking for a place to sting me. I jumped up and made an "action plan" about these urgent tasks.

Once I'd completed it, the plan transformed "some things I could consider doing" to a list carved in stone and handed to me on a mountaintop by God. I felt that I had to do the whole list that day to be a worthy human being!

There were a couple of problems with the list—and the ones like it that I have made up every day for years:

1. It was twice what any sane person would try to do.
2. It was a grandiose projection of my own unreal expectations.

Recently, I heard a story about a man who routinely brought work home from the office. His little boy wanted his daddy to play with him, but his father always told him that he was too busy. Finally, in tears, the little boy asked his mother, "Why can't Daddy play with me after supper?"

His mother said, "Because he's behind with his work at the office."

The little boy asked through his tears, "Well, why don't they put him in a slower group?"

I realized that perhaps God wants me to get in a different group, too, the group of those who know that they are not God, and have seen that "sober judgment" includes seeing things as they really are, including how much they can realistically expect themselves to do in a day.

Lord, help me to be willing to live a sane life for You that includes taking time to love the people You've given me to love—even if I have to get in a slower group. —Keith Miller

---

WED | *God made us plain and simple, but we have made*
30 | *ourselves very complicated.*
  | —ECCLESIASTES 7:29 (GNB)

When our local library tied into the Internet, I decided to seek some answers to life's dark mysteries. For my debut, I wanted a world-class topic. Something philosophic, such as "the problem of pain," and yet something practical, too. A sharp pain in my left jaw suggested the perfect subject: "the cause and cure of canker sores."

Three hours later, after ransacking the electronic cracks and crevices of the planet, I gave up, having learned nothing useful about mouth ulcers. Oh, I found lots of interesting stuff: poems and jokes about the sores; Bible references that accused me of being under God's judgment; numerous ads for products that would both cure my mouth and at the same time improve my love life and get me a promotion at work.

Leaving the library, I spotted a small table covered with free booklets, one of them about mouth diseases. I picked it up. The booklet's suggestions were not complicated or expensive. I was told to cut back on sweets, get more rest and rinse my mouth with something alkaline, such as baking soda. I did, and the pain in my jaw soon disappeared. The rest alone was a great boost to my spirit.

I learned more from a few minutes with this booklet than from three hours of electronic globetrotting.

I have a feeling that I've often made things more difficult than they really are, and next time I'm faced with a problem I'm going to "think simple."

Lord, help me not to make life more difficult than it really is.
—Daniel Schantz

My Healing Journey

1 _____

2 _____

3 _____

4 _____

5 _____

6 _____

7 _____

8 _____

9 _____

10 _____

11 _____

12 _____

13 _____

14 _____

15 _____

16 _____

17 _____

18 _____

19 _____

20 _____

21 _____

22 _____

23 _____

24 _____

25 _____

26 _____

27 _____

28 _____

29 _____

30 _____

OCTOBER

S	M	T	W	T	F	S
				1	2	3
4	5	6	7	8	9	10
11	12	13	14	15	16	17
18	19	20	21	22	23	24
25	26	27	28	29	30	31

*But they that wait upon the Lord shall renew their
strength; they shall mount up with wings
as eagles; they shall run, and not
be weary; and they shall
walk, and not faint.*

—ISAIAH 40:31

THU

THE TOUCH OF THE HEALER

1

Healing and Hope
We are saved by hope. . . .   —ROMANS 8:24

With some trepidation, I approached the doctor's office. Since my stroke a year ago, I had followed Dr. Inra's instructions carefully. I had taken the Coumadin and Zocor tablets, had gone faithfully to the therapists, one for my numb right side and another for speech. Eventually, I returned to work three days a week, and gradually felt a resurgence of power in the right side, though it was still difficult to write. And the speech—well, people said it was vastly improved, but the frustration of not being able to say what I wanted was galling. I was depressed. "In time," people said, "in time."

Here I was about to take a stress test. I stripped to the waist, and a technician, Dawn, applied the wires to my body, then I climbed onto the treadmill. "Keep your eyes looking straight ahead," instructed Dr. Inra. Next, George, another technician, added the Thallium—for monitoring the arteries—to an IV on my right arm and had me lie down with my left arm behind my head, perfectly still, while a monster camera roamed over my chest for half an hour. Then I was unhooked and was told to come back at one for another half hour, and at four for an Echo exam.

"Your cholesterol is a little high, but outside of that you did better than I expected," said Dr. Inra in reviewing the results. "Especially your walking." I explained that the city was made for walking, and now that I had a dog— "A dog. You never mentioned a dog." I went on to say that Shep and I were out four times a day. This pleased the taciturn Dr. Inra. "Keep it up," he said.

What did it all mean? It meant encouragement. Despite the times when I had questioned my return to health, even knowing that a hundred percent back to normal was impossible, I had hope. That my office let me come back to work—and what a tonic that was—and therapists like Esther Blumstein who continued to work on my speech, and the untalkative Dr. Inra and, yes, even Shep, all these were God-sent. So what if it wasn't all the way back to where I had been. It was a healing, and there was more to come. In time, I say, in time.

Thank You, Father, for the healing power of hope.

—Van Varner

FRI

2

*The living creatures were lifted up from the
earth. . . .*   —*EZEKIEL 1:19*

Oscar, our gray and white mostly-sheepdog, was smuggled into our family eighteen years ago. My older son Paul had given the little ball of fur to John, then ten, just before Paul and his family left to return to their home in Colorado. Since we already had a dog, John was afraid we wouldn't let Oscar stay, so he hid him in his closet until they were gone. When John called me into his room and opened his closet, I gave him a lecture about sneakiness, and I tried very hard to look stern and disapproving. But the truth is that I just couldn't resist that little, floppy-eared, tail-wagging puppy, and by evening, it was settled. The Hellebergs had a new adopted "baby."

When John grew up and left home, he had no place to keep Oscar, so I got to have him a few more years. His faithful companionship helped me to get through empty-nest syndrome, a painful divorce and my move to a new house. My buddy was a quiet sort of guy, who liked to go for walks with me and lie on my feet during my evening prayer time. As I'd move from room to room, he'd follow and plop down with a huge sigh, as if to say, "Why can't you stay in one place?" But eventually he lost his hearing, his eyesight failed, and finally his liver and kidneys gave out. We had to say good-bye to our beloved pet.

Sometimes I wake in the night, thinking I've heard Oscar plop down by my bed, and I've caught myself saving leftover chicken scraps for him or looking to see if he wants in. Then I remember.

*O Great Creator, You must love animals very much, because
You created so many of them. Tonight I'm praying that
heaven has a whole backyard full of wet noses and wagging
tails!*   —*Marilyn Morgan Helleberg*

SAT

3

My steps had well nigh slipped.   —*PSALM 73:2*

It's a gorgeous fall day, perfect for fly-fishing on Tennessee's Caney Fork River. As Dad and I unpack our gear and put on our fishing vests, we notice two men on the other side of the narrow river unloading a canoe from their truck. I look at Dad, and we both grin.

We are true outdoorsmen, traveling light. On the opposite bank the two fisherman are struggling with the heavy canoe, lugging it down the steep forty-foot bank.

"Boy, you couldn't pay me enough to haul that big boat down that hill!" I say to my father.

We're still fiddling with flies and tying tippets as the men finally launch their canoe. They drift out midstream, and within minutes, one has snagged a nice rainbow trout.

"Let's get down that bank," Dad says. "Last guy to get a fish buys dinner!"

We both step in the water about the same time. I break into laughter as my father slips with his arms flailing wildly, his rod soaring skyward, and his feet now above his head, landing with an enormous, unceremonious splash.

I'm laughing so hard that's it's a minute before I realize I'm on equally slippery ground. I slip and slide and make a giant lunge forward, landing in a deep, cold pool.

As we stagger, still slipping and sliding, back to the bank, drenched to the bone, one of the men calls out from the now distant canoe, "Slippery bottom, boys. Didn't ya' read the sign?"

We look to where he's pointing: CAUTION: TREACHEROUS FOOTING.

Whether it's catching a trout on a vibrant fall day or striving toward a worthwhile personal goal, chances are the easiest way is not the best way. Shortcuts might get me where I want to be, but usually when I avoid the hard work necessary to do something right, I'm in for a dunking. And, of course, it doesn't hurt to read the signs that are posted along the way!

Lord, catch me when I slip and fall, and set me safe again on Your sure path.
                                                    —*Brock Kidd*

<u>SUN</u>

4   *I am with you always, even unto the end of the world. . . .*
                                            —*MATTHEW 28:20*

When my four children were young, there were days when all of them clamored for my attention at once, and I was hard-pressed to give it. My frazzled psyche, yearning for attention itself, began to question, *How can I have God's attention when this minute, all over the earth, His other children are crying out to Him?*

I began poring through the Bible, looking for answers. As I read the Gospels, I envied the people who'd had contact with Jesus, such as the woman who'd clutched His hem. *If only I could feel God's hem in my fingers and have Him turn to me.* Yet what caught my eye in this story was that the woman pressed on in her need. Though frail and weak from illness, she left her sickbed and pushed through an elbowing, shoving crowd till she reached Jesus. It was as if God were telling me to persevere through doubt till I touched Him.

It happened months later, on a Sunday morning. My husband Whitney, the children and I were squeezed into a packed pew. I was trying to answer four-year-old Laura's loud whispers while keeping two-year-old Sanna from coloring on the bench. Baby Jonathan was drinking from a bottle on Whitney's lap. Wendy, a grown-up six, was finding the number in the hymnal with Whitney's help. The congregation stood to sing "Break Through the Bread of Life." Tears sprang to my eyes at the words, "Beyond the sacred page I seek Lord; My spirit pants for Thee, O Living Word!"

The elders moved to the communion table. The minister held up the plate and said, "Take, in faith, your portion of Jesus' broken body." As the elder held the plate for me and I partook, I felt doubt slip away and the presence of the risen Lord enter, not just a grasp of His hem, a quick turn of His head or a half-tuned ear. *But Him.*

In His light, I saw what had been all along: Christ's risen body multiplied to give each of us His whole attention, as if he or she were the only one on earth. I receive this by faith—even through my doubt.

Lord, when a multitude of doubts and needs presses me in, may I persevere, through faith, to touch You. —Shari Smyth

HEALING THE FEAR OF OLD AGE

Roving Editor John Sherrill has worked for Guideposts for close to half a century. Now in his mid-seventies, John says

that he has the usual dread of the losses and indignities of old age. Indeed, these fears are present in most of us at any age. But John has developed a technique for dealing with these threatening specters. He stores a collection of healing memories, *which act as antidotes to specific anxieties. Here are five of his favorites.* —THE EDITORS

<hr/>

MON

5

A Memory of Beauty
My times are in thy hand. . . . —PSALM 31:15

I walked into the office of the New York ad agency and was struck by how young and healthy-looking all of the employees were.

Then I caught a glimpse of *myself* in a mirror. My face was lined, I was bald, even my clothes were out of date compared to what these young people were wearing. *I don't belong in this group,* I thought. *Who'd want to be around a wrinkled, bald, patched-up old fogy!*

But as I drove home that day I remembered visiting a Japanese rose grower some years ago. The Ishimaras' house was filled with lovely bouquets. Why not? In the fields behind their home were thousands of perfect roses ready for market: beautiful, just-opening blossoms.

I was puzzled, then, to notice that each bouquet was spoiled by having a few full-blown, wilted flowers in it. Mrs. Ishimara saw me staring at one rose in particular, a Talisman, some of whose petals had fallen onto the table.

"Isn't it lovely!" she said. "It has so much character now. I'm glad you like it."

I looked again. Mrs. Ishimara had found beauty where I had seen only the unpleasant signs of age. *Shouldn't I see myself, too, in a different light?* It had taken decades of experience in living and loving to earn these wrinkles! Shouldn't I be proud of them?

Father, help me appreciate the beauty of a wrinkled face.
—*John Sherrill*

<hr/>

TUE

6

A Memory of Acceptance
God . . . comforts us in all our troubles, so that we can comfort those in any trouble. . . .
—II CORINTHIANS 1:3-4 (NIV)

I could tell that the doctor was working his way up to some bad news.

My EKG was good, he said. Blood pressure fine. No problem with cholesterol. But sophisticated fluorescent-dye tests did show scar tissue on my heart, evidence of a "cardiac event" that had gone undiagnosed.

"In short," he said at last, "you've had what we call a silent heart attack."

The words filled me with terror. I was put on a rigid exercise program, medication, food restrictions. The prospect of being limited in this way appalled me.

Until I thought of my friend Barton Phillips. I hadn't seen Barton for over a year. But now, a few weeks after I'd found out about my heart attack, there was Barton, hobbling down the sidewalk on crutches! The right pant leg was empty.

"Diabetes," Barton said simply. "I lost one leg, but I've got one left and it belongs to God." He was even then on his way to a nearby VA hospital to talk with other amputees.

We never know what deficits life will impose on our bodies as we grow older. But Barton Phillips' bright face and eagerness to use his limitation to help others have given me a healing memory that serves as a model as I face restrictions of my own.

Lord, help me accept limits without murmuring and then use what I have left to the comfort of others.   —*John Sherrill*

WED

7

A Memory of Intercession
"Why have you been standing here all day long doing nothing?"   —*MATTHEW 20:6 (NIV)*

One morning after my silent heart attack had been diagnosed, I got into my car and headed resignedly for another of my thrice-weekly exercise sessions at our local Cardiac Rehabilitation Center. The very name was an unwelcome reminder that my body was wearing out.

All of us at rehab had something in common besides a heart problem: We faced hours of dead time. Endless sitting around in doctors' offices, interminable waits for test results, frustrating lines at the pharmacist. Our very exercises at rehab reflected our new lifestyle: We walked on treadmills; pumped stationary bicycles; climbed stairs that went nowhere. We did a lot of "marking time," and I, for one, chafed at it.

In that mood I arrived at rehab and climbed aboard one of the bolted-down bikes. To my right on another bicycle was a man who looked exactly as I felt—uncommunicative, frowning, clearly resenting this wasted hour.

On my left, though, was a red-haired fellow who must have detected my mood, because he launched into a description of what this regimen had done for him. He'd had a heart attack four years ago, he said, but now was feeling *great*. "I actually look forward to coming here," he said. Pumping pedals that propelled nothing, this man had nevertheless traversed the greatest distance any person can: He'd reached out to another human being.

I got down from my bicycle that morning, sure that I had a new healing memory. Dead time? Wasted hours? I don't know what they are anymore. Today, when life gets stalled—waiting for an X ray, standing in a line—I recall Mr. Redhead and turn to the person next to me. Whether I pray silently or offer a word of encouragement, I intercede for him or her as my red-haired friend did for me.

Father, none of the time You grant me here on earth is meaningless. Help me use each hour with a grateful heart.

—John Sherrill

THU

8

A Memory of Adventure

"When you were younger you . . . went where you wanted. . . ."   *—JOHN: 21:18 (NIV)*

I stepped into Joe's Barber Shop ready for another travel adventure. Joe was in his eighties yet he'd never really retired. Oh, he didn't cut hair from nine to five anymore; you never knew just when he'd be open for business. But those who knew him put up with the irregular hours just to hear the latest report on some far-flung part of the world.

Joe rarely left Nantucket Island, yet he traveled the globe in his mind. "That fellow just got back from Greece," he told me as I took the chair from the previous customer. Joe painted a picture of flying into Athens, visiting the Acropolis, sailing the Aegean . . . all of which he'd just heard from the last patron.

"And where have you been lately?" he asked me. I described a narrow-boat trip I'd taken through the English canal system. Joe was full of questions, and as I left I overheard him say to the next man, "Did you know the English still use their canals?"

I have always been very mobile, and one of my fears is that my world will get smaller and smaller in my later years. But Joe the barber showed me a way around that worry. Joe didn't travel, but he invited the world to come to him.

Lord, please help me learn to keep my curiosity forever reaching out.   —*John Sherrill*

FRI	A Memory of Giving

FRI
9

A Memory of Giving

"You have been faithful with a few things. . . . come and share your master's happiness!"
—*MATTHEW 25:23 (NIV)*

One morning in Grand Rapids, Michigan, where I was putting the finishing touches on the sale of my company, I took a walk. I was preoccupied. *What was I going to do next? Would new work be interesting and in any way important?*

After half an hour I came to a rather forlorn little doughnut shop. "Black coffee, half-decaf, half-regular," I said to the middle-aged woman rushing to fill orders behind the counter, humming as she worked. Her name tag identified her as *Anita*. She was the only person waiting on customers, and I grew fascinated watching her.

A pickup pulled in, and before the driver was out of his cab, Anita began filling a glass with iced coffee. "Did you get the contract, Rob?" she asked cheerfully as she handed him his drink. A double-cream coffee was waiting for another man she'd seen walking across the parking lot. "Your son better, Jorge?" So it went, a smile, a personal comment, the customer's taste remembered.

Next day, even though I'd been in the shop only once, Anita started drawing my half-decaf, half-regular order before I was through the door, as if I were one of her regulars. I asked her if she owned the shop. "Oh, no," she said. "I just work here."

I thought of Jesus' parable of the talents. One man was given only a single talent to invest. Perhaps he was resentful because he had not been given as much as others; he hid his talent and missed out on sharing his "master's happiness."

Not so Anita, and that's why she supplied me with a healing memory as I headed nervously toward some new work. Anita didn't have much to work with. Here she was, waitressing in a small, out-of-the-way doughnut shop, and yet because she invested herself completely, she was clearly sharing her Master's joy.

Lord, You may give me a lot to work with, or a little, but always help me to give every bit of myself. —*John Sherrill*

SAT 10 — A Memory of Welcome

Share with God's people who are in need. Practice hospitality. —ROMANS 12:13 (NIV)

When we moved to our present home almost forty years ago, it was traditional for some neighbor to throw a party to welcome new arrivals. We benefited from the gracious custom, and when our turn came, we held newcomer parties of our own.

But over the years, as houses up and down the street changed hands, the practice vanished. And as it did, anxious thoughts arose. *What will happen when Tib and I get old and must move to a new location, far from friends? Will anyone make the effort to know two older people?*

But I have another memory, a letter my wife and I received when we were living in Bolivia. Inside was an invitation from people we did not know, another American family who had just moved to La Paz. "Please Come to Our *New Kid on the Block Party.*"

In the midst of hors d'oeuvres and chatter, our hosts explained, "We lived in Berlin before coming here. In Germany, newcomers often do not wait for old-timers to invite them over. They throw a party to introduce *themselves.*"

What a wonderful idea—a spiritual principle of flexibility, of doing something in a new and unexpected way. God knows that older people suffer from isolation. If traditional means of becoming part of a community are no longer available, He is ready to show unexpected paths to fellowship . . . such as that wonderful "New Kid on the Block Party."

Lord, You don't want a lonely old age for any of us. Teach me to reach out with whatever new tools You provide.
—*John Sherrill*

SUN
11

A Memory of Glory
"I write these things . . . so that you may know that you have eternal life." — *I JOHN 5:13 (NIV)*

There is one aspect of aging that none of us likes to consider: the approaching end of life. Yet, because of one fragile experience, I shall never again look upon death in the same way.

At seven o'clock one dark October morning in 1993, I stepped into the side chapel of our church. Two days earlier, I'd lost a close friend and prayer partner, Bob Nardozzi, and I'd come here to wrestle with my grief.

I turned on the light, sat down and began to read the Bible as I had often done in this special place. The chapel was a favorite of mine because of a splendid Tiffany window that depicts St. Christopher crossing a river with the Christ Child on his shoulder. Today, however, the window matched my mood. In the dim artificial light the scene was sullen and lifeless.

For perhaps twenty minutes I immersed myself in the wonderful assurances of eternal life contained in the Book of John. When I looked up, a transformation had taken place in the window before me. The sun had risen behind the glass, displaying its colors in dazzling light. Christopher's face, his hands, the robes he wore, the river through which he walked that had seemed so dark and threatening, all pulsed with shimmering light.

In that moment, I glimpsed the end of life on this earth, Bob's and my own, too, with new eyes.

As long as I look upon death with my own feeble, man-generated lights, it appears bleak and forbidding. But when I see it in the light shining on it from the other side, then I see death from God's vantage point. Scripture provides that light. "For God so loved the world that he gave his one and only Son, that whoever believes in him shall not perish but have eternal life" (John 3:16, NIV).

Father, show me the passage we call death by the light of Your Word. — *John Sherrill*

MON
12

Come, take up the cross, and follow me. — *MARK 10:21*

I was the first to arrive, so the friendly janitor unlocked the chapel door for me. Some of Joanna's high-school teachers had begun a Monday-afternoon prayer time here, and a few of us parents were adding our prayers, too. Mine was for my then-fifteen-year-old daughter's peers who thought smoking marijuana was "harmless." I hoped Joanna and her friends wouldn't succumb to that mindset.

I sat down in a wooden pew in the plain chapel. In front of me was a small altar with a gold cross. The janitor gathered his cleaning supplies and commented, "This might sound strange, but I don't think of that as the real cross. Jesus' cross was rough. It had splinters. I don't think the cross Jesus asked us to carry was gold and beautiful."

I nodded my agreement as he rattled his supplies out the door. Yes, Jesus' cross must have had jagged edges: like some of my daughter's classmates at school whose lives were splintered by drugs, broken homes, gang violence.

Yet, with prayers for strength, this group of committed teachers was shouldering that rough cross, trusting God to provide opportunities for them to help the young people. My prayers, too, could smooth some splinters.

Lord, thank You for the privilege of sharing Your cross.
—Marjorie Parker

TUE

13 *The power which the Lord hath given me to edification, and not to destruction. —II CORINTHIANS 13:10*

I haven't punched anyone since 1967, when a kid named Tommy called my mother a nasty name. But last fall, when I overheard a young assistant basketball coach at my son's high school speak with scorn about Jonathan's ability and potential as a player, I was amazed at how the old feelings of protective anger boiled over. Fortunately, I have matured in thirty years, and I restrained myself. In fact, I channeled the anger into positive action: I put up a basketball hoop at home and practiced with Jon all summer. This season he made the team.

But the coach's inability to see Jon's potential nagged at me. I kept telling the story around the office until a colleague gave me an article about a rock and gem enthusiast in Tucson, Arizona, who paid ten dollars at a rock show for a stone that turned out to be a potato-sized star sapphire. It weighed in at 1,905 carets and was valued at

2.28 million dollars when it was cleaned and polished to reveal its true nature. The reporter wrote, "It took a true lover of rocks to see the gem under the rough surface of the stone."

I got the point. It took a father who loved him to see Jon's potential. Far from being disappointed in someone else's lack of vision, I became thankful for the privilege of being there to make the discovery and take pride in his hidden value.

Lord, let me see someone's potential today, that I might be used to bring it to fruition.   —Eric Fellman

<table>
<tr><td>WED

14</td><td>*Hear, O my people, and I will speak. . . .*
                                        —PSALM 50:7</td></tr>
</table>

It was a radiant mid-October day. Yet on that particular morning, I felt restless. *People tell me I'll hear from God if I just do my daily Bible reading. If I pray. If I have faith. . . . I've done all those things, and I still haven't heard from Him.* I glanced out the window. Maybe a drive in the country would make me feel better.

Soon I left paved highways behind to follow winding roads threading their way past farms and through wooded fields. On my left, men picked corn, snapping the tassel-topped ears from rasping stalks. On the right, bales of hay were being heaved onto flatbed wagons, bouncing across washboard stubble. A sign reading "Nature Trail" pointed out a winding, wooded path, which on that sunny autumn day was like a golden tunnel.

"Know where I can park?" I asked a hiking couple nearby.

"How about over there?" the man answered, pointing to a level place by the trail's entrance. "Nothing says you can't."

I was a bit apprehensive leaving my car there, but I shrugged off the feeling and started down the tree-lined lane. The sumac was turning red and the cottonwoods' yellow leaves slowly drifted down onto the trail. Squirrels scampered about, looking for nuts. A long-legged spider centered herself in a geometric web suspended between two trees. A two-toned caterpillar inched along a branch. A partridge added action, taking off from where she'd been camouflaged by undergrowth.

A glance at my watch reminded me it was time to head home. As I left the trail, my heart raced. A patch of red glared from beneath one of my windshield wipers. *Oh, no!* I thought. *A perfect day spoiled. Now I've heard from the park police!*

As I neared, I saw that the "ticket" under the wiper was a brilliant, red maple leaf. I'd heard from God.

How wonderful when You make me aware of Your presence, Lord.
                                                    —Isabel Wolseley

15 *Instead you ought to say, "If the Lord wills, we shall live and we shall do this or that."—JAMES 4:15 (RSV)*

Our silver wedding anniversary loomed enticingly on the horizon. Having never really taken a travel vacation, we started planning our dream trip. We'd catch the New England fall foliage, sample the quiet little inns, steep ourselves in a bit of history and maybe wander along the Atlantic seashore. It sounded wonderful—until our oldest daughter announced her engagement and upcoming wedding. We couldn't do both. New England would have to flaunt her autumn colors without us.

From then on, Terry and I embarked on the "incredible shrinking anniversary." Maybe we could travel somewhere closer to our home state. Northern Mexico? Southern California? What about San Francisco? Surely Seattle? The sad truth, we discovered, was *no* place is close to Alaska!

All right, we'd stay right here in the "Last Frontier." We booked reservations for Land's End Resort—an appropriate name by this point—on Alaska's famed Homer Spit—a six-hour drive away. Then unbelievably, two days before our scheduled departure, we suffered a major snowstorm. We'd have to stick even closer to home.

Where did we finally end up? Ninety miles away in Girdwood, a tiny community at the base of Alaska's popular ski slopes. Our two days together, an hour-and-a-half down the road, turned out to be terrific. It's true, our grand travel plans had shrunk considerably, but the most important thing—the love connecting us for twenty-five years—just kept on growing.

Lord, give me the positive attitude that expands and enhances every life experience.
                                                    —Carol Knapp

---

Herald of Healing

How sweet the name of Jesus sounds
    In a believer's ear!
It soothes our sorrows, heals our wounds,
    And drives away our fear.

It makes the wounded spirit whole,
    And calms the troubled breast;
'Tis manna to the hungry soul,
    And to the weary, rest.

—JOHN NEWTON

FRI

16
I consider everything a loss compared to . . . knowing Christ. . . .   *—PHILIPPIANS 3:8 (NIV)*

In the middle of a busy downtown street in Oxford, England, a simple cross is embedded in the tarmac. Some four-hundred-fifty years ago, when Broad Street was the ditch outside the city wall, three leaders of the Church of England were martyred here. Former bishops Nicholas Ridley and Hugh Latimer and Archbishop Thomas Cranmer were burned at the stake for refusing to deny their faith.

On October 16, 1555, Latimer and Ridley were executed as Archbishop Cranmer watched from his cell window. Latimer and Ridley were chained together and secured to a stake, and a fire was set beneath them. In the following months, Cranmer weakened under torture and wrote a recantation, denying his faith. But then his conscience overcame even the pain of torture and the fear of death, and he renounced the document that he had written. On March 21, 1556, he, too, was burned at the stake on the site where Latimer and Ridley had died. As the flames licked upward, he thrust his right hand first into the fire, crying out, "This unworthy right hand!" for that was the hand he had used to write his recantation.

During a recent trip to England, I stood on that site. I couldn't help recalling a phrase popular with advertisers in the last few years: "A dress [a car, a vacation, a bracelet] to die for."

Something to die for? Over the ages countless men and women, even children have suffered and died for their faith; they still do in some parts of the world. Given the place and time I live in, it's hard to imagine that I would ever have to make the choice between faith and life. But the possibility is always there. And I had to ask myself, standing on Broad Street that day: If I ever had to choose, would my faith be something to die for?

Faithful Father, strengthen my heart and my convictions, that I might live each day for You.   —*Mary Jane Clark*

SAT

17

Lord, thou deliveredst unto me five talents; behold, I have gained beside them five talents more.
—*MATTHEW 25:20*

Every fall, we empty our closets, drawers, bookshelves and toy chest for the church's annual rummage sale. It's a yearly reminder of how extravagantly we've been blessed—and a good opportunity to pare down. "Do I really need five sweaters?" I ask as I stand before my closet. "How often have I worn that suit?" my wife Carol wonders. "Do you want to keep the tractor and bulldozer?" we ask our sons Timothy and Willy. "You don't play with them anymore."

We take bags full of things to the church, and there we help sort, stack, pile, price. Of course, in the process, we see things that we might find useful. "Carol, have you ever read this biography?" I ask. "Honey, try this jacket on," she says. "It looks about your size. And wouldn't this snowsuit be perfect for Timothy?" At the sale, we buy almost as much as we donate.

Back home, as we read labels on clothes and books, we find that the biography belonged to a close friend, the jacket to another, the snowsuit to a favorite Sunday schooler who outgrew it. One year, I asked, "Wouldn't it have been easier for us to give one another these things without having a big sale?"

"No," Carol said. "This way the church raises money, we save money, and we do it by a fine biblical principle."

"What's that?"

"We make our talents grow."

Lord, make me a faithful steward of Your bounty.
—*Rick Hamlin*

18 *And Jesus said, Are ye also yet without under-standing?* —MATTHEW 15:16

Joel was a twelve-year-old boy in my Sunday school. He didn't participate in any of our discussions, he refused to read aloud, and he laughed when others did. I didn't know how to reach him, and frankly, there were times when I wished he just wouldn't show up. But he always did. And he always brought a spiral-bound notebook with him and scribbled in it all through class. If I tried to get close enough to look at it, he clapped it shut.

One day when he was concentrating very hard on his scribbles, I was able to come up alongside his seat and get a look.

"Joel," I said, "I didn't know you could draw."

He hugged the notebook to his chest angrily. "This is nothing!" he growled.

"It is to me," I said. "I don't have that kind of talent, and you obviously do. I wish you'd let us see your drawings."

For what seemed like a very long time, he considered my request. Then, very slowly, he handed me the notebook. Its pages were filled with sketches, and they were amazingly good for someone so young. The other students gathered around us and admired Joel's work. "Cool, Joel, real cool!" said one of the boys.

"They're just sketches," Joel said. "Then I paint them in oil."

"Do you think you could bring some in?" I asked.

"Maybe. I dunno."

The next Sunday, when I walked into the classroom, I was astonished to see six oil paintings propped up on chairs in the back of the room. Joel stood alongside them, shifting from one foot to the other.

"They're beautiful!" I said. "Joel, you're really an artist!"

As the other students arrived, they surrounded Joel and asked him questions about his techniques. In front of my eyes, he was changing from a sulky, hurt boy to a kid who was comfortable with himself and others.

Sometimes, when I want to communicate with someone, I have to put my own language aside and use the other person's instead. In Joel's case, we had to speak in pictures rather than words.

Lord Jesus, help me to hear what others are saying with their hearts. Amen.
—*Phyllis Hobe*

19 *Except the Lord build the house, they labor in vain that build it. . . .* —PSALM 127:1

"Mother," said our teenage daughter, "I don't want to ride the bus to school anymore! I'm too old for that. I want to take the subway to school, the way my friends do!"

I had qualms about New York City subways, and I said so. But Elizabeth begged and pleaded. "All right," I said finally, "you can go with a group of friends. But just remember this: My prayers are going with you every day, every step of the way."

And I did pray, placing Elizabeth in God's hands every morning and thanking Him for bringing her home safely every afternoon. Elizabeth knew this; she felt protected and loved. Once she did tell me that two men got into a noisy altercation not far from her group. "But we just got off at the next stop," she said, "and waited for another train" I was sure that the Lord, watching over her, put this simple and sensible idea into her head.

My point is a simple one: Of all the pillars that support and sustain a marriage and family life, this is the strongest—this willingness to bring God into every situation, every problem, every aspect of living. He loves us; He cares about us; He wants us to be happy. All we have to do is ask!

Be with us, dear Lord, in everything we do—this day and every day. —Ruth Stafford Peale

TUE
20 *I consider that the sufferings of this present time are not worth comparing with the glory that is to be revealed to us.* —ROMANS 8:18 (RSV)

The pain along my jaw began five days after removal of a parotid tumor. Of course, it was a Sunday—medical problems always wait for weekends. By Monday morning when I called my doctor, the ache was awful.

Over the phone I described the now-steady throbbing in the jaw: "Something must be wrong."

"On the contrary," the doctor said. "Something is right. Pain means life's returning to the tissue we had to cut. The nerve endings are responding. Healing has begun."

Healing has begun. . . . New beginnings, inseparable from pain. I thought of my friend Doris, who began to live again after her daughter's death only when, after months of numbness, she was able to cry.

I thought of Lucinda, a freshman classmate at Northwestern, several years older than I because her mother's rare nerve disease had kept Lucinda at home. Lucinda's mother could not feel pain. She could not tell when her fingers touched a stove, when water scalded, when she stepped on something sharp. A prisoner of painlessness, she needed somebody at her side night and day. Lack of pain meant lack of freedom.

Leaving home for the first time. Childbirth. Mastering a new skill. No growth without the pain that heralds life.

Let me see Your face of love, Father, in whatever pain comes to me today.   —Elizabeth Sherrill

---

<u>WED</u>
21
Set a watch, O Lord, before my mouth; keep the door of my lips.   —PSALM 141:3

Once while being interviewed on radio, I discovered that radio talk shows have a device that delays the transmission of callers' questions by seven seconds. The delay gives the host or producer the chance to pull the plug on any inappropriate comment before it reaches the air.

God already has given each of us a built-in mechanism to monitor our speech. It's called a brain, and if we employed it before engaging our tongues, many a conversational misstep could be eliminated. Unfortunately, at one time or another, we are all guilty of speaking first and thinking second.

This is especially true when we let our emotions take over. The other day I saw a fender bender in which the drivers nearly came to blows. "Why didn't you stop? Are you blind?" the one shouted. "Why were you driving like a banshee?" returned the other. Fortunately, calmer heads on the scene prevailed, and the most important question was asked: "Are you both okay?" After it was determined that neither was hurt, the two men became more civil and got down to the business of reporting the accident and exchanging insurance information.

One way to avoid foot-in-mouth disease when we're tempted to blow off steam is to speak quietly and slowly. One of my friends uses a variation on the "counting from one to ten" ploy. He repeats to himself the first ten words of the Lord's Prayer: *Our Father who art in heaven, hallowed be thy name.* "After that exercise," he reports, "I seldom get indigestion from words poorly spoken."

> *Teach me, God, my words to critique,*
> *To weigh their love before I speak.*
>   —Fred Bauer

<table>
<tr><td>THU</td></tr>
<tr><td>22</td></tr>
</table>

THU
22 *And let thy heart cheer thee. . . .*
                                    —ECCLESIASTES 11:9

I see a salesman named Mel in the locker room at my gym nearly every workday morning. He always one-ups the good-cheer brigade by exhorting me to "Have a perfect day!"

Invariably I reply, cringing inside, "If you insist."

This week, though, Mel is on vacation. Perhaps because I'm so accustomed to his hyperbolic salute, yesterday I found myself still grumbling, *Why does he always say that? Is it even possible to have a* perfect *day?* Naturally, we all have good and bad days, but nothing on earth is perfect, especially my typical day.

Like yesterday. I squabbled with a cashier, then upbraided her for being curt with me. I was testy with my wife on the phone and quite impatient with my dogs at their noon walk. I got off on the wrong foot on a work assignment and had to throw out everything I'd done. By four o'clock I was reaching for the aspirins and antacids and complaining to a friend on E-mail what a dismal waste the day had been. "When I feel that way," he typed back, unduly cheery, "I make a gratitude list."

Bah! I was more interested in making an ingratitude list. But almost involuntarily I found myself mentally checking off those things for which I knew I should be humble and grateful, even at the end of a horrible day: My friends were still my friends; my wife was still my wife; my health was strong; my job would still be there in the morning. My dogs—like all dogs—were the most forgiving creatures on the planet. And there was God, Who loves and hears me day after day, good and bad, no matter what.

I thought again of Mel's daily greeting. I've missed it this week. When he gets back and bellows it out, as I know he must, I'll be sure to reply, "I will."

God, help me realize that like all Your gifts, the days that You give me are perfect, even when I am not.   —Edward Grinnan

<table>
<tr><td>FRI</td><td rowspan="2">So Jacob served seven years for Rachel, and they seemed but a few days to him because of the love he had for her. —GENESIS 29:20 (NKJV)</td></tr>
<tr><td>23</td></tr>
</table>

Fridays are a treat at the little Bible college where I teach, thanks to Reta Ollmann, a member of our church.

On a long table in the hallway, she spreads out a banquet of goodies for students: platters of crisp crackers and moist, chocolate chunk cookies; bowls of tangy green grapes and kiwi fruit; and trays of rich cheeses, my favorites. Her compact form is always hidden behind the drove of students who come around to enjoy her treats and conversation.

"How can you afford to do this?" I ask her. "I mean, it must cost you fifty dollars a week, plus all that time baking, setting up, serving and cleaning up. These kids are taking advantage of you."

She laughs, her brown eyes flashing,. "No, no, they're not, not at all. I love these kids. This is more of a treat for me than it is for them."

I marvel at her attitude, and I'm convinced that she has found a valuable secret of happiness. After all, some burdens add weight, but other burdens add wings. Her secret? "I love these kids." Affection is the miracle ingredient that puts flavor in her cooking and in her personality.

I need to find ways to put her secret to work. If I'm fixing the brakes on our car (a dreaded chore!), I can remind myself that I'm making the car safe for my loved ones. If I'm mowing the lawn, I can make it an expression of my love for nature and beauty. Even if I'm filling out income tax forms, I can do it for love of country . . . well, let's not push it!

Above all, I can perform my work unto God, Who is my greatest love.

Father, lift up my motives into the realm of love, where I can hear music as I work.   —Daniel Schantz

EDITOR'S NOTE: One month from today, on Monday, November 23, we will observe our fifth annual Guideposts Family Day of Prayer. You can join our praying family by sending your prayer requests to Guideposts Prayer Fellowship, P.O. Box 8001, Pawling, New York 12564. Please enclose a picture if you can.

SAT
24 *"The wolf also shall dwell with the lamb. . . ."*
—ISAIAH 11:6 (NKJV)

Sometimes the act of reading my daily newspaper makes me wonder if there will ever come a time when people will learn to live together in peace. A bomb in London sidetracks peace talks in Ireland; a grave is uncovered in Bosnia, which tells of mass murder; unexpected election results reawaken fears in the Middle East; our police arrest members of a group who have plans for blowing up federal buildings.

When I feel overwhelmed by destructive divisions, I think about David and Anna D'Amico, close friends who live in New York City, just a couple of blocks from the United Nations. The two of them were born in Buenos Aires, Argentina, with parents and grandparents who migrated from Italy and Spain to South America. We were family to each other for the decade we worked together in Houston, Texas, and I watched them reach out across barriers—Anna training interpreters for the Kelsey-Seybold clinic and David directing an international ministry. The guests at their table always represent the diversity of the United Nations personnel. The sing-alongs around their piano reflect all the tribes and nations of our world, and the members of their weekly Bible study group experience a precious unity of spirit.

My wife Barbara and I will spend a long weekend with David and Anna soon. We'll probably see something on Broadway and visit a museum. But mainly we will enjoy being with good friends, whose lives remind us that God is at work through people creating small islands of peace.

Dear God, help me to find new ways of bringing people together.   —*Kenneth Chafin*

<u>*SUN*</u>
25 *"If you really keep the royal law found in Scripture, 'Love your neighbor as yourself,' you are doing right."*
                                        —JAMES 2:8 (NIV)

"See my finger!" my then-four-year-old son Brett said, shoving his outstretched hand toward me.

"Did you hurt yourself in Sunday school?" I asked, gingerly cradling his Band-Aid-wrapped index finger.

"No, silly!" he giggled.

That's when I noticed a heart-shaped sticker on the Band-Aid. "What's this?"

"It's to remind me that Jesus is the king of caring, and He wants me to be caring too!"

That afternoon as Brett napped, I thought about what he'd said. How simple life was to a four-year-old! But isn't simplicity what faith is all about? Jesus is the king of caring, and He wants me to be caring too.

So I used that philosophy all during the next week—when clerks were rude or neighbors long-winded, when my husband wanted to watch football (again), when a missionary spoke at our church of Russia's need for Bibles. Caring. What a wonderfully regal way to live! And if I begin to slip, I know just what to do. I'll create a reminder with one of the Band-Aids Brett and I bought for the medicine cabinet.

Dear Father, You are the king of caring. Make me like You today and every day. *—Mary Lou Carney*

<u>*MON*</u>
26 *For the eyes of the Lord are over the righteous, and his ears are open unto their prayers. . . .*
                                        —I PETER 3:12

When I received a summons for jury duty five years ago, I figured I would have two full weeks of nothing to do but read books. Instead, I quickly found myself serving on an eye-opening, federal drug conspiracy case. The nine men on trial ranged from ages eighteen to twenty-four; the forty-eight counts against them included money laundering, murder, kidnapping and assault. These were violent men, and we heard—and saw—evidence so appalling that I'll never forget it. There were days my eyes would turn toward the defendants, silently imploring, "Who are you? How could anyone even think of doing these things?" It seemed as if they were different creatures, inhuman.

Then one day a witness took the stand to testify about gun running. He was a store owner from Texas, a cheerful, white-haired man for whom coming to New York was clearly a pretty big treat. The prosecutor asked, "Mr. A., do you recognize anyone in this courtroom?"

Mr. A. flashed a big grin, pointed to one of the defendants and drawled, "Sure do! Why that's my friend Eddie right over there. How ya doin', Ed?" The courtroom chuckled. As the testimony progressed, Mr. A.'s good cheer was contagious. The giggles in the court grew louder. Even under severe grilling by Eddie's attorney, Mr. A. seemed plain happy to be there. At one point he looked straight at Eddie, shook his head and said, "Son, I don't think it happened that way." Eddie, along with his eight companions, laughed out loud. They laughed with genuine enjoyment, without cynicism, like boys instead of drug dealers.

That laughter was why, a month later, many jurors cried as we handed in our huge sheaf of guilty verdicts. Yes, these men had done unspeakable things and would pay for their actions with decades in jail. But for a few minutes one day, we saw through the toughness and horrors of their lives to the human beings God created them to be.

Lord Jesus, You hung with thieves on a cross and live hidden in the hearts of even the worst criminals. Help me to pray not only for victims, but for the souls of those who do harm.
—Julia Attaway

TUE

27 *A fool takes no pleasure in understanding, but only in expressing his opinion.* —PROVERBS 18:2 (RSV)

One of the biggest surprises I've uncovered in my family history research is that John Ross, my maternal great-grandfather, was fifty-four years old when his only child, my grandfather, was born.

"How strange," I remember saying when my mom and I made the discovery. I even rechecked the dates to be sure we hadn't made a mistake. "Imagine becoming a father when most of his friends must have been grandfathers," I said.

"I'll bet there's an interesting story there," Mom added.

Continuing to research, I learned that my great-grandmother Mary was John's second wife, more than twenty years younger. His first wife had died young, and when he married my great-grandmother, both longed to have children even though they were well past the typical age for first-time parents in the nineteenth century. They had good reasons for doing what I had considered so strange.

Their story made me wonder how often I fail to consider the circumstances that lie behind the actions of others. I thought of an angry boy in my son Ross' class whom I was quick to dismiss, not realizing his behavior may have been caused by his parents' sudden divorce. I also remembered an acquaintance who'd been mourning a close friend's death for many months and was still uninterested in socializing. I'd criticized her to others, not understanding that her pain was so great she simply needed more time.

My own way of seeing things often looms so large before me it eclipses other possibilities. But if I can push it aside long enough to see things from another's perspective, it's much easier to bridge the chasm between us. I can invite Ross' classmate over to play or call my friend just to talk. So it seems that one of the basics of genealogy, taking the time to find out *why*, serves me well in everyday life, too.

Lord, whether I'm looking back one hundred years or across the room at a friend, guide me to a better understanding, a greater compassion and a more loving heart.
—Gina Bridgeman

WED

28 *A good name is better than precious ointment. . . .*
—ECCLESIASTES 7:1

Once I heard a cynic say that ethics are what men live by until they conflict with self-interest. But not all men are like that. A friend of mine named Norman Beasley wasn't.

As a young reporter, Norman worked on Detroit newspapers and had several interviews with Henry Ford. The great inventor liked the young newspaperman and talked very freely to him.

During one on-the-record interview, Norman told me, they got on to the subject of reincarnation. Ford announced that he believed in it completely, and talked animatedly about the details of his belief. Beasley was astonished. He knew he had a scoop of considerable importance, one that would impress his superiors and quite possibly bring him a raise. But he wasn't sure that his editors would believe the story when he turned it in. So he asked Mr. Ford to look at his notes of the conversation and initial each page. Impatiently, the inventor did, and handed them over.

Beasley thanked him, hesitated, then handed the papers back. "Sir," he said, "I don't think publication of this story would do you a bit of good. I think it would do you and your company harm. People would jump to all sorts of conclusions. My advice to you, Mr. Ford, is to tear those pages up."

Ford stared at him for a long moment. "You're right," he said. "And, I might add, you are a remarkable young man."

And he tore the pages up.

Lord, give me the strength to do the right thing, especially when not doing it would be to my advantage.
                                                      —Arthur Gordon

THU

29   *Lean not unto thine own understanding.*
                                                      —PROVERBS 3:5

Several months ago while walking my dog Wally on the street where I live in New York City, I stopped to talk with a young woman whom I'd come to know only as "Dixie's mom." Dixie, a giant poodle, and Wally often nuzzled each other while her mistress and I chatted. But on this particular day she did not have Dixie with her.

"How are things going?" I inquired.

"Okay," she answered, and rushed away.

Hmmm, I thought, *that wasn't very neighborly.*

Then recently I saw her again, and she came hurrying toward me.

"I want to apologize," she said, "for the way I acted when we met last. You see, I was afraid that you'd ask about Dixie. She died just a few days before that, and I didn't trust myself to talk about it." Tears welled in her eyes. "You do understand, don't you?"

Understand? A woman who lived alone. A woman now lonelier than ever. Yes, I understood.

And silently I prayed for her, and prayed that she would get another dog soon. Like Wally and me.

Dear Lord, You told us to come to You in times of trouble. Teach me to be sensitive to others in their troubled times.
                                                      —Eleanor Sass

FRI

30 *Pray for us. . . .*   —*HEBREWS 13:18 (NIV)*

The train Texas Eagle moved slowly south from Chicago into the dark. "Bad storms ahead. Signals are out," the conductor said. I wondered how late we'd be getting into Little Rock, Arkansas, the next morning. We were due in at 8:00 A.M., and the seminar I was headed for started at 9:00.

Across the narrow corridor from our sleeper room, a white-haired woman sat knitting and smiling. Our eyes met, and we began to chat through the open sliding doors. Eventually, I told her of my concern.

"Honey," she said, "I'm gonna pray for you!"

I was soon snuggled into my berth and fast asleep. In the morning, the car attendant told us we would be at least two hours late getting into Little Rock. There would be plenty of time for us to get our breakfast before our 10:00 A.M. arrival.

"That's a good thing," my husband Bill said with a grin, "because we're number thirty-one in line!"

It was 8:35, and the steward was calling number twenty-four to the dining car when a conductor came by. "Sir, do you know when we'll be arriving in Little Rock?" I asked. "I'm going to be rather late for a meeting."

He glanced out the window and checked his watch against what he saw. "Should be there in ten minutes," he said.

Bill and I scrambled to get our baggage together. As I dragged my red daypack from the berth, the door across the aisle slid open and my new friend's face peered out. She broke into a great smile. "I asked God to get you there! I knew He would! Isn't He good?"

I arrived at the seminar just as the work began, disheveled and without my morning cup of coffee. But no matter, there I was, thanks to a stranger's caring prayer—and God's answer.

Lord, thank You for those who pray for me. Help me to be ready to pray for others.   —*Roberta Rogers*

SAT

31 *Love is patient and kind. . . . Love bears all things, believes all things, hopes all things, endures all things.*   —*I CORINTHIANS 13:4, 7 (RSV)*

Leaves are falling, swirling in muted colors, as I look out our breakfast room windows across our backyard. The previous owner of our house had transformed this green space into a place of beauty. The patio was immaculate, the rose garden lovingly kept, and the plants and shrubs under the large elm and hickory trees were green and trimmed. It has taken the Walkers only three and a half years to turn a showplace into a disaster zone.

It began when our children received a large trampoline as an anniversary present from our church. It has been their favorite plaything, providing endless hours of joy. But where do you put such a thing? Straddling the rose garden, of course.

And then my eleven-year-old son Luke wanted to build a tree house. After extended negotiations, we compromised. I didn't want to harm the trees, a treasure beyond price in arid Texas, so we settled for an earthbound clubhouse. I scavenged together scrap lumber, and the yard became a construction site. Luke and his buddies sawed and hammered and painted for weeks. Now as I gaze across our backyard, the focal point is an eclectic squatter's shack daubed in psychedelic colors.

I guess Beth and I will have to wait a few years for the lovely backyard of our dreams. To move the trampoline or tear down the clubhouse would create a major revolution. We are at the time in our lives when the ugly must be beautiful and when children must come first. Love is seldom nice and neat.

Dear God, give me the patience to live in the clutter of my world.
—Scott Walker

My Healing Journey

1 _____

2 _____

3 _____

4 _____

5 _____

6 _____

7 _____

8 _____

9 _____

10 _____

11 _____

12 _____

13 _____

14 _____

15 _____

16 _____

17 _____

18 _____

19 _____

20 _____

21 _____

22 _____

23 _____

24 _____

25 _____

26 _____

27 _____

28 _____

29 _____

30 _____

31 _____

NOVEMBER

S	M	T	W	T	F	S
1	2	3	4	5	6	7
8	9	10	11	12	13	14
15	16	17	18	19	20	21
22	23	24	25	26	27	28
29	30					

*The Lord sustains him on his sickbed; in his illness
thou healest all his infirmities.*

—PSALM 41:3 (RSV)

<u>SUN</u> *Live a life worthy of the Lord . . . giving thanks to the*
1 *Father, who has qualified you to share in the inher-*
itance of the saints. . . .   —COLOSSIANS 1:10, 12 (NIV)

All Saints' Day was coming, and I planned a small afternoon party
of women friends to celebrate the "cloud of witnesses" who have gone
before us. We would light candles to remind us of the Light of the
world and make stained-glass angels for our windows.

The day arrived with a sullen, rainy face—not the sort of clouds I
wanted. The ladies began to appear, and while rain streaked the windows my kitchen was filled with laughter. A new friend, Parry Grog-
gin, showed up carrying a blue bowl of sunflowers and ferns. "Isn't
God good?" she said cheerfully, setting down the exquisite present
in a space that looked made for it. "I had no idea of the colors in your
kitchen." The blue woodwork matched the blue bowl perfectly, and
the splash of yellow flowers was a burst of sun against the white walls
and green curtains.

Isn't God good? Parry's words filled me with renewed wonder at how
much God cares for us, even in the smallest things. It was His goodness that shone through the chilly, gray afternoon pressing on the windows, as, one by one, we shared stories of His presence in the lives
of friends who are now in heaven.

The stained-glass angels smiled at us. And we could almost hear
those saints from the other side lean in to whisper, "Amen."

Lord, the praise offered to You in the lives of Your saints
rings through the centuries. Help me to glorify You in mine.
                                                —Shari Smyth

<u>MON</u> THE TOUCH OF THE HEALER
2 Healing Our Broken Friendships
Restore us to yourself, O Lord, that we may return;
renew our days as of old.   —LAMENTATIONS 5:21 (NIV)

I became a Christian in 1964 as a junior in high school. John Perkins,
the man who led me to Christ, became my mentor and my model.
Spiritually and in many other ways, he became a father to me. He
encouraged me to go to a Christian college in California and allowed
me the privilege of coming back to Mendenhall, Mississippi, each
summer to work in the ministry he had started. After I graduated

from college and seminary, he encouraged me to join the ministry full-time in 1971.

We worked together, prayed together and shared together for three years. Then the ministry's central office was moved from Mendenhall to Jackson, in order to broaden its base. My wife Rosie and I, along with several others, remained in Mendenhall to carry on the work there. In 1978, with less than a month's notice, John decided to spin us off as a separate ministry, without access to the mailing list that was our funding source. I was devastated, and so was the ministry. We had no base of financial support and had to start all over again. By the grace of God, we survived and grew during those years, but my relationship with John was damaged and it needed healing.

I knew that this broken relationship had also affected my walk with God. Every time we had trouble paying a bill, I blamed it on John. And whenever I heard anything good about his ministry, I felt only envy. I longed to have my relationship with him back the way it was, but it took four years and much agonizing and praying before I had the courage to try.

In 1982, John and I sat down, and spent hours together sharing, praying, crying and seeking each other's forgiveness. God gave me back my model, my mentor and my spiritual father.

Lord, I need Your healing power to bind up the broken relationships in my life.   —Dolphus Weary

---

TUE

3

"Do not be afraid, for I am with you; I will bring your children from the east and gather you from the west."   —ISAIAH 43:5 (NIV)

A young boy, about twelve, with a thatch of hair that stood vertically on his head and finely sculptured Slavic features, stood facing the room. He looked proud but scared as he began, "I pledge allegiance to the flag. . . ."

Not a cough or a rustle. Everyone was caught up in this moment of change and affirmation. One hundred and ten people from all over the world sat that 1990 day in a Nassau County Courthouse. We were gathered to receive American citizenship. The presiding judge had asked this young man to speak for us all.

The paths that had brought us to that courthouse on that day would, I am sure, fill many volumes. I had arrived in the United States one cold gray morning as a third-class passenger on the *Nieuw Amsterdam*, a majestic ocean liner that docked in New York City's North River. I was twenty-one and wanted to see the world! The years slipped by, and the United States was good to me. It was past time, I realized one ordinary busy morning, for me to show my gratitude and to commit myself to a responsible role as a U.S. citizen. On that morning months later, the names were called, one by one. Mine was one of them. The clerk of the court struggled with names from Poland and India and Thailand. *Weeks* was easy.

Back in my seat I found that my hands were shaking. I felt overwhelmed with powerful emotions, unexpected and hard to explain: a feeling of joining so many great people who had gone before; of joining a big, new family; of taking on for the first time in my life the responsibility of casting my vote, shaping a government; and above all a realization that I belonged to a place that called itself "one Nation, under God, indivisible."

As You watch over this country, Lord, help me to use wisely the rights and powers I have as its citizen. —Brigitte Weeks

WED

4 *Truly my soul waiteth upon God: from him cometh my salvation.* —PSALM 62:1

When I was a boy in Kentucky, I was hooked on horses. Racehorses. I could tell you the winners of every Derby, their times and the bloodlines, say, of Gallant Fox or Broker's Tip. I've seen kids who made a saint of Joe DiMaggio, but they couldn't equal my worship of War Admiral. This son of champion Man O' War became my horse, and I followed him before the Derby, which he won, through all of his undefeated three-year-old season and his massive victories at four.

Came November 1938. I was in boarding school, and War Admiral was entered in a much-heralded match race with Sea Biscuit. I received permission to listen to the race in a master's room. I was excited and supremely confident as the raspy voice of Clem McCarthy led us through the false start, then back again and, at last, they were away. I was amazed when Sea Biscuit took the lead, but no matter, my little Admiral would collar him. And he did, in the stretch. I exulted, thrilled at my horse's superiority—but only for a moment. In disbelief, I heard Sea Biscuit pull away—and win. I was in shock.

I went to my room in a daze. I had never experienced such agony. Time went by. Evening prayers, then dinner had begun, when I heard a knock. It was Father Whitcomb, the headmaster. "May I come in, Van?" I couldn't say no. He didn't say he was sorry. He didn't try to console. He understood. By simple spiritual artistry he made me see things correctly.

As he was leaving, he said, "Come on down for dinner," adding, "There's this movie in Bennington."

That's how I saw Errol Flynn as Robin Hood on a school night—because Sea Biscuit had beaten War Admiral. But the movie only eased the pain. I had learned something from Father Whitcomb that day, something I have never forgotten: There is no sure thing—only God.

Father Whitcomb was right, Lord, as You know.
—Van Varner

THU

5   *The Almighty . . . shall bless thee with blessings of heaven above. . . .*   —GENESIS 49:25

There was a time in my life when my job was particularly stressful: I was going in early, working weekends and getting home late, unable to think of anything else but a TV dinner and the news and sleep.

Then one morning when the normal Los Angeles low clouds were absent and the sunshine was just beginning to reach the tops of the buildings, I was walking from the parking lot to my office when something made me look up. Against the clear, bottomless blue of the sky, three seagulls were wheeling and calling to one another, bright white against the background. Their motions were so lovely that my breath caught in my throat and I had to grab on to a parking meter to keep from falling down in dizziness.

Caught in the consciousness of beauty, I watched the three birds spiral and dart higher and higher until they were just specks. Then I let go of the parking meter and walked on to the office.

Somehow, that day, though the problems were the same, the stress was gone. I had been treated to a reminder of heaven that morning.

When things get tough, God, remind me to look up.
—Rhoda Blecker

FRI

6   *O taste and see that the Lord is good. . . .*
                                        —*PSALM 34:8*

I was midway through my morning errands when I neared the dough-nut shop. *I think I'll treat myself,* I thought, and promptly steered my car into the parking lot.

A small boy, probably six or seven years old, was at the counter as I entered. When the clerk asked for my order, I answered, "I believe this young man is ahead of me."

"He's still making up his mind about what kind of doughnut he wants," she said. "How about you?"

"A chocolate-frosted one, please," I answered, although a beauty smothered with pink-tinted coconut was a close runner-up. "And I'll have coffee, too."

I seated myself at a table. Other customers came, ate and left, but I ordered several coffee refills, which I really didn't want. You see, the little boy was still there, still trying to make up his mind. By then my curiosity had become intense. *Which flavor would he choose?*

Finally, I could wait no longer. As I left the shop, the child re-mained, two coins still clutched in one fist, nose still pressed against the glass case, where thirty-plus kinds of jelly-filled or frosted dough-nuts still beckoned.

I headed home, chuckling over the boy's indecision. Then I seemed to hear God speaking: "If you had to choose just one out of all the 'goodies' I put in front of *you* every single day, which would it be?"

Oh, Father, not only have You filled the earth with delights, but You've invited me to come and enjoy them.
                                        —*Isabel Wolseley*

SAT

7   *Blessed is he whose transgression is forgiven. . . .*
                                        —*PSALM 32:1*

When I was a child, my parents had a hard-and-fast rule about what films I could see. I was never permitted to attend a movie until it had been checked out in *Parents* magazine. If the magazine listed it as being suitable for my age group, then I could go; if the magazine ob-jected to the material, then I could not. It was that simple.

One Saturday afternoon, while my parents were away on a trip and my grandmother was taking care of me, a horror double feature was appearing at the theater. I had looked up the pictures and knew that both were deemed unsuitable for me. I also knew that Grandma was unaware of our movie rule, so ever-so-sweetly I asked her if I could go to the movies with two friends, she said yes.

Off I went, skipping all the way to the theater, where for three hours I shuddered and screamed along with the other kids as zombies came out of graves and a man turned into a werewolf at midnight. Afterward, I skipped home to dinner.

But my carefree attitude changed to worry when my parents returned. *What if Grandma mentioned the movies? What if one of my play-mates tattled? What if . . . ?* Finally, when I could bear the what-if's no longer, I confessed my guilt to my parents.

My father seemed surprised. "What movie did you see?"

"*Wolf Man of Paris* and *The Valley of the Zombies*," I replied. He seemed flustered, but my mother was more in control.

"Anybody brave enough both to see them and tell us about it is a good child."

She hugged me, and my father put an arm around my shoulder and said three wonderful words, "We forgive you."

Those words are with me still. They are the same with my heavenly Father Who forgives me my trespasses when I am sorry.

Dear Lord, let me never forget the things that I learned as a child.   —*Eleanor Sass*

<table>
<tr><td>SUN
—
8</td><td>*"The Kingdom of heaven is like this. A man happens to find a treasure hidden in a field. . . ."*
—MATTHEW 13:44 (GNB)</td></tr>
</table>

Because I had raised my son Chris in the church and had practiced my faith in our home, I wasn't prepared for the day Chris said, "I'm not sure what I believe about God."

I went for a walk, feeling like a failure. Suddenly, I looked down at the road and saw a shiny new penny. I bent to pick it up and then I remembered Grandpa's "found money."

When I was a girl, Mom kept Grandpa's found money in a yellowed tobacco pouch in her dresser drawer. On special occasions, Mom would take out the pouch and let me look at its contents. I'd loosen the drawstring, lay out the turn-of-the-century Liberty nickels and Indian Head pennies, and breathlessly pause over the large, slick copper penny with the faint eighteenth-century date. Then Mom would tell the story.

During his childhood in the 1880s, Grandpa came down with the measles and was confined to the loft of an old log cabin. One day he dug at a chink between the logs with his pocketknife and uncovered a small knotted rag. In the cloth was a treasure trove of old coins, including the quarter-sized penny. For the rest of his life, whenever Grandpa found a coin of any sort, he saved it with his cabin treasures.

I slipped the shiny penny I'd found on the road into my pocket. The coins in Grandpa's pouch had been so slick and worn that even today they would probably not be worth much money. Their enormous value to us came from Grandpa's joy in finding them. It was the same with faith. I had done my duty in raising Chris. Now it was up to him to question, seek and find for himself. I walked home, secure in the knowledge that in Chris' questions, God was wisely and wonderfully at work.

Lord, help me to welcome life's questions as an invitation to experience again the joy of finding Your treasure.
—*Karen Barber*

MON
9

And now I want to plead with those two dear women, Euodias and Syntyche. Please, please, with the Lord's help, quarrel no more—be friends again.
—*PHILIPPIANS 4:2 (TLB)*

In order to provide more effective health care for our area, the board of directors of my social service agency entered a cooperative agreement with another agency. After months of talks, the provisions were settled and the contracts ready to sign—I thought. Then the other agency's director, a friend of many years, wrote in major changes.

Because there were legal issues involved, I immediately met with our agency attorney, expecting him to share my outrage and concern. Instead, he asked, "Do you want to work it out?"

"Of course!" I answered quickly. "But these changes are totally unacceptable, and she wrote them without asking me, and—"

He interrupted. "Do you want to work it out?" he asked again. When I didn't reply, he explained, "Legally, nothing can be changed unless your board of directors approves. But I don't think legalities are the point here. If this agreement will be good for people who lack health care, then you and your friend need to sit down and talk until you reach an acceptable compromise."

Did I want to resolve the problems? Or was I more interested in venting my anger and hurt feelings at being left out? It was difficult, but I telephoned my friend, explained my concern over the changes and expressed the desire to reach agreement. Compromising was hard work: We spent nine hours talking and arguing and even crying. But today we are cooperating on several health care projects that benefit thousands of people in southwest Kansas. And we are closer friends than ever.

Dear Lord, help me put aside my pride and stubbornness and strive to "work things out" in every area of my life. With Your help, it can always be done.   —Penney Schwab

---

TUE

10   *Keep me as the apple of your eye; hide me in the shadow of your wings. . . .*   —PSALM 17:8 (NIV)

Our northbound train left Little Rock, Arkansas, near midnight. After settling into our seats, my husband Bill and I were soon asleep. At 3:30 A.M. I awoke to the throbbing of idle diesel engines and wondered groggily why we were not moving.

Suddenly, lightning began to flash around us. In its light, I saw that the train was sitting in a gully. The embankments on either side rose just above the tops of the double-decker cars. Overhead, I could see the outlines of swirling trees silhouetted against the black sky. Soon rain was pouring down the window, distorting my view, but I could make out rushes of muddy water flowing down and under the train. Thunder rattled the sides and roof of the car. Our great, heavy train did not seem such a safe haven anymore. I began to shake.

"Sir, please." I tugged at the conductor's sleeve as he passed. "What's going on?"

"Severe storms all around us, ma'am," he whispered. "We've sent a crew on ahead to check for washouts and trees or other obstacles on the tracks."

In the seat next to me, Bill awoke. He reached over and drew me close, tucking my head against his shoulder. We sat like that for almost an hour, praying.

Finally, the storm, and the train, slowly moved on. My shivering ceased. As we passed darkened towns and flashers warning of washed-out roads and downed trees, I thanked God for keeping us safe.

Lord, thank You for those who become Your arms to me. And thank You that all storms have an end.   —Roberta Rogers

11 *Freely ye have received, freely give.* —MATTHEW 10:8

The meeting of the American Legion post was reaching its conclusion. My friend Dick, leaning on his cane, was being installed as Post Commander.

I liked Dick from the instant I met him in 1965. He was tall, blond and rather shy. He was a senior technical writer on Project Gemini, the manned space-flight effort. I was on loan from the engineering test division to help him with the staggering paperwork. Secretly, I dreamed of working with him as a technical writer. When a job opened up, Dick encouraged me to take it, and he promised to train me.

Once I was on the job, the pace was exhilarating and exhausting. Reports, specifications, engineering changes and data were needed hourly. Our three-person publications team even compiled a 315-page engineering proposal in two weeks by working until three each morning and returning to our desks at 7:30 A.M. In the middle of all this, Dick remained calm and focused.

As the meeting at the Legion hall was breaking up, I made my way through the crowd to talk to Dick. "Oscar," he said, "you know the pressures we worked under. I've been retired for five years, and I have a bad leg. I ought to be sitting back and taking it easy. Yet I've accepted responsibility for this six-hundred-member post. Would you like to know why?" I nodded.

"It's simple. I joined the Legion and I found there was a need. Many of these vets need help—medical or financial or emotional. So now it's payback time. Through them, I'm thanking God for all the blessings He's given me over the years."

Father of mercy, on this Veterans Day, let me say thank you by sharing my blessings with those who fought to secure them.   —*Oscar Greene*

THU	And let us consider how we may spur one another

And let us consider how we may spur one another on toward love and good deeds.
—*HEBREWS 10:24 (NIV)*

THU 12

I woke up one morning recently, filled with concern for one of our nearly adult children who was about to make some important choices. Our long-distance phone conversations had grown tense, because I had some definite opinions about these decisions. As I got ready for work that day, I began to compose a letter in my head that would detail my concerns and give the kind of advice that a mother always seems to have on the tip of her tongue. Later, I told a younger friend in my office about the situation, and the letter of advice that I intended to write.

"Why don't you try writing a love letter instead?" she suggested simply after listening to my outpouring. "Grown children who are out on their own need affirmation from their parents. They need to know that you see some strengths in them, and they need to know that you love them. That gives them confidence and helps them make good choices."

"I'll think about it," I murmured, wondering if I could write a letter so opposite to the one already in my head.

That night, I sat down and composed a letter of encouragement, filled with reflections about this child's growth and gifts. Amazingly, the letter flowed out quickly and easily, as if those words were meant to be put on paper at that moment. I sent it off with a lighter heart.

My friend was right: A positive message of love was much better than criticism and advice. I realized it when I heard a warmer, more confident voice on the phone after that letter was received.

Jesus, I see power in Your words of love. Thank You for modeling that message.   —*Carol Kuykendall*

FRI 13

The eternal God is thy refuge, and underneath are the everlasting arms. . . .   —*DEUTERONOMY 33:27*

What a dreary morning. Although the sun was shining, I was filled with gloom. I'd found a lump in my breast, and I was going to have it checked. Worry poured over me. As I prepared to go to the hospital, I noticed my new gold earrings gleaming in their white box on the dresser. I hadn't worn them yet because the hoops were very dressy. Impulsively, I put them on.

During the drive, I tried to calm myself with prayer. Tilting my head a bit, I waited at the traffic light in downtown Danbury, Connecticut. In irritation, I realized the hoop on my right ear had gotten tangled in my trench-coat strap. *Oh, no,* I thought. The light turned green while I was trying to unhook the earring. At that very moment, a big truck came roaring across the intersection, the driver oblivious to the fact that he was going through a red light. My hands and knees began to shake as I realized I had just missed being killed.

"What's wrong?" the receptionist asked. "You look like you've seen a ghost."

I told her what had happened. "And if it hadn't been for that earring, I would have been hit. I wasn't even planning to wear them."

She smiled. "I'd say you've just experienced a miracle."

All of a sudden, I was filled with the most incredible joy. I had no fears about the check-up. I was safe in God's loving arms.

Dear Father, help me to remember that I am always within Your protecting arms.　　　　　　　　　　　　　—Susan Schefflein

SAT

14

Give, and it shall be given unto you. . . .
　　　　　　　　　　　　　　　　　　—LUKE 6:38

Frances Faulkner and I had just returned to her apartment after a long, happy lunch. Being with Frances is a pleasure. She's one of those people who makes others feel good about themselves. Though she's passed her ninety-third birthday, her positive approach to life turns every conversation into an upbeat experience.

"Frances, I've never noticed this pretty chair," I said, as I gathered my things to leave.

"Oh," she answered, "remind me to tell you the story of that chair sometime."

In no hurry, I set aside my coat and purse. "How about now?"

"My husband George was a great football fan. I never cared for football. But George just didn't enjoy watching the Saturday and

Sunday afternoon games unless I was sitting nearby. I tried to be enthusiastic, *oohing* and *ahhhing* at the appropriate times and making sure my comments favored George's team. Finally, I took up needlepoint, hoping George wouldn't notice my lack of devotion to his sport. That's how the chair came to be. Every stitch was done watching football on TV."

I looked at the chair. It was covered back and front in fine needlepoint, and I ran my fingers over the bouquet of roses so perfectly woven into its seat. Frances' life was also a work of art. She had given much: as an English teacher; a faithful church worker; as one who gladly cared for her ailing parents, her husband, then her sister and, finally, her brother—all with joy and without complaint.

I wonder if I might create a similar beauty in my time-giving? As I serve family, friends, employers, I can complain, lament, feel sorry for myself, or, like Frances, I can add roses to all that I do. Perhaps I'll learn firsthand that the beauty that decorates Frances' face is merely a return on a life stitched with love.

Father, make my giving beautiful. —*Pam Kidd*

SUN

15 *And his sleep went from him.* —*DANIEL 6:18*

What a wonderful fellow he was, my Uncle Cary Montague, a much-loved pastor in Richmond, Virginia. Through some hereditary affliction, Uncle Cary was very deaf and almost blind, but he never let these handicaps bother him. He went right on preaching (he saved some of his best sermons for the inmates of the city's jails), visiting shut-ins, helping people on welfare, telling funny stories, enjoying life immensely.

I thought of Uncle Cary the other day when I heard someone complaining dolefully about insomnia: "What a terrible night! Didn't sleep a wink! Oh, it was awful!" I remembered Uncle Cary because once when I was making a similar lament he set me straight.

"You couldn't sleep?" said Uncle Cary. "Lucky you! All that wonderful uninterrupted time at your disposal. When that happens to me, I like to pray for all the people I know who have problems. Then I think of possible topics for sermons. Every good sermon should have at least three jokes, so I try to recall some.

"The only trouble with that," Uncle Cary added reflectively, "is that I laugh so loud that I wake up Margaretta." (His wife Margaretta was my Aunt Gettie.)

Insomnia an affliction? Not necessarily. Not all the time. Uncle Cary saw it as an opportunity. Maybe someday, if I ever grow to be as wise as Uncle Cary, I'll think so, too.

Lord, make me grateful for Your precious gift of time all the time, at any time.   —*Arthur Gordon*

Herald of Healing

For Thou art our salvation, Lord,
Our refuge and our great reward;
Without Thy grace we waste away
Like flowers that wither and decay.

To heal the sick stretch out Thy hand
And bid the fallen sinner stand;
Shine forth, and let Thy light restore
Earth's own true loveliness once more.
                              —*CHARLES COFFIN*

MON

16 *Do not be overcome by evil, but overcome evil with good.*   —*ROMANS 12:21 (RSV)*

My husband John is seeing better than he has in years since the cataract in his left eye was replaced by a tiny plastic lens half the diameter of a dime. I'm grateful for the skill of his ophthalmologist, Dr. Mitchell Stein—and for a handful of British World War II pilots.

In the 1940s, Dr. Stein explained, these airmen presented doctors with a medical mystery. Bailing out of their shattered planes during the Battle of Britain, they suffered an injury never seen before: tiny shards of the aircraft's Plexiglas canopy embedded in the eye.

Ordinarily, the eye will reject a foreign body, working the intruder to the surface and expelling it. But in this case, Dr. Stein said, the eye failed to react to the Plexiglas particles. "It was a calamity for the injured pilots, but it led, a few years later, to the development of cataract implants."

I thought of those young men in their pain and loss of vision, and I thought of the millions since then, saved from blindness by the compatibility of plastic and the human eye. And I knew I was seeing a twentieth-century example of the Power that is always wringing good from evil, healing out of hurt.

How will You turn what distresses me today, Father, into healing for tomorrow?   —*Elizabeth Sherrill*

TUE

17   *Hearken to the sound. . . .*   —*PSALM 5:2 (RSV)*

I heard it off and on all morning as I went about the house. *Beep. beep, beep.* It was a sound that seemed distant yet distinct, subtle yet penetrating. Or was I just hearing things?

No, there it was again. *Beep, beep, beep.* Like a nagging conscience, the sound wouldn't go away, even when I tried to ignore it. I heard it while I was on the phone, gossiping with a friend. *Beep, beep, beep.* I heard it when I told someone I was too busy to keep a promise. *Beep, beep, beep.* I heard it as I juggled the budget and decided we should give less to church. *Beep, beep, beep.*

I could hardly wait for my son to come home from high school for lunch that day. "Lyle, do you hear a funny beeping sound, or is it just me?"

"Oh, that's just a big bulldozer working a couple of streets over. I watched it for a while on my way home. It makes that sound as a warning whenever it's going in reverse."

Going in reverse. . . . Had God used it that morning to remind me that in some areas in my life I was going backward?

Even now, years later, when I'm reluctant to do what's right or I'm taking the first steps to do something wrong, I sometimes imagine I hear a little *beep, beep, beep.* Yesterday, for instance, when I started running someone down with gossip: *Beep, beep, beep.* Time to stop, change gears and go forward in faith.

God of all truth, keep me sensitive to Your signals.
    —*Alma Barkman*

18

Seek ye the Lord while he may be found, call ye upon him while he is near. —ISAIAH 55:6

Because of my rheumatoid arthritis, I wear a special splint on my left hand at night to hold my fingers in alignment while I sleep. Without it, I'd wake up in the morning with a twisted, painful hand.

One night I forgot to put on the splint before I went to bed. I lay there in the dark wondering where I had last seen it. Was it in my office next to my computer? Was it in the kitchen on the sill above the sink? I knew I should search for the splint, yet I lay there for more than fifteen minutes, dreading to get up.

At last, with a sigh, I sat up and turned on the light. Right there on the nightstand within inches of my pillow lay the splint. I could have reached out at any time to pick it up.

Later, lying under the covers with my hand comfortably splinted, I thought about the many times I've worried over some personal problem while failing to reach out for God's comfort. Yet there He is, waiting always near at hand, in darkness or in light.

Do you sometimes forget to reach out, too? If you've got a personal problem that is causing you physical or emotional pain, maybe today is the time to say, "Okay, God, I'm reaching out. Please take my hand, and let's work on this together."

Lord, keep reminding me that You are always there ready to help, no matter when or where. —Madge Harrah

19

Therefore choose life. . . . —DEUTERONOMY 30:19

At the age of fifty, my friend Mona decided to leave the small town where she'd lived all her life, all of her friends and her extended family, to move to a distant city and start college for the first time. She had no solid means of support and no certainty that she was even capable of academic achievement after thirty-two years away from the classroom. But Mona trusted that faith could move mountains.

Not only did she earn her bachelor's degree in three years, but she went on to achieve her master's, as well as certification as a psychotherapist. Immediately after graduation, she was hired for a position of great responsibility—to set up and coordinate the entire therapy program at a newly built psychiatric hospital here in Kearney, Nebraska. She has since become one of the most eagerly sought therapists in the area.

"How in the world did you do it, Mona?" I asked her one day.

She thought for a few moments and then said, "Of all the things that helped along the way, I think the one thing that pulled me through was this: I had many decisions to make, some of them quite difficult, but every time a choice came up, I asked myself, 'Which option will make my soul stronger?' And I'd always choose that one. It was my sole criterion, and I've never regretted those choices."

I thought of Mona's "soul choices" today, because I've been debating with myself about whether or not I can afford to go to a spiritual growth workshop in Phoenix, Arizona. If I go, it will mean giving up buying a new TV set to replace my twenty-year-old set that has completely died and can no longer be repaired. I'll have to make some other spending cuts, too. Yet when I asked the soul-choice question, the answer was clear and the decision was easy. Though I'll be without TV for some months, I *will* be at the workshop.

I pray that You will guide all my decisions, Lord. Help me to make soul choices.   —*Marilyn Morgan Helleberg*

FRI

20

I will look to see what he will say to me. . . .
                              —*HABAKKUK 2:1 (NIV)*

I enjoy starting the day with a cup of coffee and have been fascinated by the proliferation of coffee emporiums across the country. Whoever thought one could make a thriving franchise out of offering a hundred different types of coffee? Who knew there *were* a hundred different kinds of coffee?

Anyway, the slogan of one coffee chain caught my eye the other day. It said, "Life is short, Stay AWAKE!" With a chuckle, I thought about how often I find myself drifting through the day without paying attention. I don't know if the coffee sellers would appreciate it, but I made a list of things worth staying awake to notice.

• The sunburst brilliance of yellow mums in full fall bloom.

• The giggle of my little niece in the background when my brother calls to give condolences on my birthday.

- The pride in my son's voice when he calls to say he made honors in a college course.

- The fear in another son's voice as he tells of an attempted suicide at his high school.

- The warmth of my wife Joy's smile when I arrive home tired out from five days on the road.

- The wonder of another morning, given of God not to be squandered, but lived.

Even if you don't like coffee, try making your own "Stay AWAKE" list today. You might be surprised by all there is to appreciate if you pay attention.

Lord, help me to notice everything You want me to see today.
—Eric Fellman

<u>SAT</u>
21   *"Do not be afraid; do not be discouraged."*
                              —DEUTERONOMY 1:21 (NIV)

"I have *pump-o-phobia*?"

I had asked my girlfriend to come with me to pump my gas, and she had used that pseudo-technical term. I'd overcome my fear of driving, but until today, I had always gotten a friend to pump my gas.

"Just pray and then ask someone at the filling station for help," she instructed.

"Ask a stranger for help?" I gasped. She didn't know to whom she was talking! If I go shopping and can't remember what aisle the grape jelly is in, I'll wander around for half an hour rather than asking a clerk to help me.

When I got to the gas station, I was the unwilling star in a comedy of errors. First, I drove up to the wrong side of the pump and discovered that the hose didn't reach to the passenger side of my car. So I had to move the car. Then I couldn't decide whether I needed unleaded or unleaded plus. After I'd chosen the gas and figured out which hose went with which pump, I didn't know how to get the pump started.

Humiliated, I walked to the glass booth. "This probably sounds ridiculous," I stammered out to the gray-haired man in the booth, "but I've never pumped gas in my life. I need help."

He gave me a steady look. "Had a feeling you did," he said.

"Oh. Why is that?"

"Never saw anybody trying to pump diesel fuel into a little two-seater before."

We burst out laughing, and then he showed me how to fill 'er up.

Is there some flaw I'm trying to hide from others, God? Let me "fess up" and accept the help You offer me through others. —*Linda Neukrug*

SUN

22

From childhood you have been acquainted with the sacred writings which are able to instruct you for salvation through faith in Christ Jesus.
—*II TIMOTHY 3:15 (RSV)*

I've had my Bible since high school. Its black leather cover is dog-eared, its binding sags, and its pages are wrinkled and yellowed, but I wouldn't exchange it for a newer one. It chronicles too much of my personal history—battles both won and lost—ever to let it go.

James, chapter 4 (RSV) is stained with tears from the many times I have cried in remorse over verse 17: "Whoever knows what is right to do and fails to do it, for him it is sin." And heavily underlined on the next page are those redemptive words that rescue me from despair, "Therefore confess your sins to one another, and pray for one another, that you may be healed" (5:16).

In the Psalms, an autumn leaf dated September 1992 marks a verse (71:18, RSV) that seemed to fit my mother's seventieth birthday: "So even to old age and gray hairs, O God, do not forsake me." And penned in the margin beside Ephesians 5:8, which urges us to walk as "children of light," is my niece's birth date and my biblical nickname for her, "Lisa-Go-Lightly."

Another meaningful passage for me is Philippians 4:19 (RSV): "And my God will supply every need of yours according to his riches in glory in Christ Jesus." It was here, in 1986, when our business was failing and we were in desperate need, that I discovered the "Father-lode" principle. God is our source of rich supply in everything.

One Sunday our pastor gave us a quote that I carefully copied in my old beat-up Bible. "If your Bible is falling apart, then you are most likely a person whose life is not falling apart!"

My Bible is an eternal Book, speaking words of truth and righteousness and forgiveness. It is both familiar and revered—and, yes, a little dog-eared.

Lord, on this National Bible Sunday, I honor You with a Book that is well-worn and well-loved.   —Carol Knapp

<u>MON</u>
23
For this reason, since the day we heard about you, we have not stopped praying for you and asking God to fill you with the knowledge of his will through all spiritual wisdom and understanding.
—COLOSSIANS 1:9 (NIV)

"May we pray for you?" we ask *Guideposts* magazine readers every month. Many people barely notice the offer. But over 11,000 on average every month do see and for a multitude of reasons respond by sending us a request. Letters come from all over the country and the world.

As we do our best to respond to this outpouring of need, we are always in search of how to do it better. "Improve prayer?" you ask in surprise or perhaps dismay. Of course, there's no such thing as a prayer more valuable or more urgent than any other prayer, but as an organization we always wonder if there are different things we could do to help, needs to which we could respond more effectively.

So we asked some small groups in different states, not "May we pray for you?" but "How do you pray?" and "What do you need from us?" Responses ranged from a schoolteacher in Charlotte, North Carolina, who told us "just knowing you're praying once a week is comforting even though I don't write to you," to a computer programmer in Kansas City, Missouri, who lamented "My prayer life is so disorganized. I can't seem to find enough time," to something I have felt so often myself: "Sometimes I feel my prayer doesn't get higher than the bedpost." We heard about praying in the car, in the shower, of prayers posted on the refrigerator, of prayers at dawn and prayers at dusk.

The most important thing we learned was that our Guideposts Prayer Fellowship is a part of a much larger group of many thousands, who don't know each other, who only know that they are part of this invisible, powerful network. We are still asking questions, still working on how we can be useful, still asking "May we pray for you?"

Lord, on this Family Day of Prayer, teach us always to listen to the needs of others and to bring those needs into Your presence.   —*Brigitte Weeks*

TUE
24

Though he brings grief, he will show compassion, so great is his unfailing love.
—*LAMENTATIONS 3:32 (NIV)*

When we got Duffy as a three-month-old pup, there were kids and lots of noise in the house. That was fifteen years ago. Now the kids had gone the way that kids go, the house was noticeably quieter, and Shirley and I were alone with our much-loved border collie, who was showing his age. First, it was arthritis that left him hobbling after our walks. Then his hearing and eyesight began to fade. Finally, he had kidney problems.

Amos Stults, who has been tending our animals for better than thirty of his eighty-five years, told us Duffy's days were getting short, but that with a special diet and tender loving care, he might be good for a few more months. And that proved to be the case.

Then one day after a business trip I came home to find him in bad shape. He had apparently suffered a stroke and could not get up to greet me with wagging tail and wet tongue. I phoned Shirley, who was visiting her mother in Florida, and reported Duffy's condition. She commiserated with me, then articulated what I had trouble saying: "The time has come."

"I wish you were here," I complained. "I don't want to do this alone." She made some understanding sounds before saying good-bye. I decided to wait until morning to make the decision.

"Could You take him tonight, Lord?" I prayed. Duffy's whining got me up several times during the night, and I knew he was suffering, but in the morning he was still alive. So I loaded him into the car and drove to the vet's office. There Amos and I put him on a gurney, and the white-haired vet turned away to prepare his needle.

"I love you, Duffy," I whispered, trying to hold back the tears. Then, as I petted his head and shoulder, something amazing happened: His shallow breathing stopped.

"Amos," I exclaimed, "I think he's gone!" The vet confirmed it. I had to smile. Either God had answered my prayers, or Duffy, sensing my agony, had done me one last favor. Maybe they conspired together.

Thank You, Lord, for loving pets, past and present,
And the memories they stir most pleasant.
—*Fred Bauer*

25 *Eat what is good, And let your soul delight itself in abundance.* —*ISAIAH 55:2 (NKJV)*

Almost nothing I grow in my garden resembles the luscious pictures in the glossy seed catalogs. Many of my tomatoes are deformed or blemished. The strawberries tend to be either green or rotten. The lima beans bore only a handful of pods, and the lettuce is tough to chew. Only the sweet corn is truly beautiful.

"Why do I even bother?" I ask myself, but I know the answer.

It's pure joy to participate with God in the creation of something unique. I bury a few seeds, and months later I pick buckets of delicious produce. "See what God and I did," I boast to my wife Sharon, who is grateful for the free groceries. I plant enough crops to be sure of at least some good fruit, and I cut out the bad parts. I don't dwell on the imperfections because the good parts are just so wonderful.

It seems to me I have the same choice about other "imperfections" in life. I can brood on the rotten parts of my job, the blemishes of my students, the inadequacies of my wife or the peculiarities of my minister. Or I can rejoice that this is my job, these are my students, this is my wife, my minister, and say "thanks" for them.

Here's a little pencil aerobic for you. Pick one of the following categories (or create some of your own) and see how many good things you can list about it.

1. My country: rich natural resources, variety of people, _____.

2. My church: hymns of praise, comfortable seats, _____.

3. Me: I try hard, I'm patient, I mean well, _____.

Lord, it takes no effort to be negative and cynical, but I want to be like You. Help me to see what is right and beautiful about the world You've given me. —*Daniel Schantz*

THU

26

Out of them shall come songs of thanksgiving, and the voices of those who make merry. . . .
—*JEREMIAH 30:19 (RSV)*

Sweet potato casserole has long been a favorite dish at Thanksgiving dinners in the South. Mine is a traditional part of our family's meal as we gather at my daughter Emily's house to celebrate.

My casserole tastes best straight out of the oven, so I like to prepare it at Emily's house. To make sure I have everything I need, I measure and package all the ingredients before I leave home and put them in Emily's refrigerator when we arrive. Then at cooking time, I mix them, pour the mixture into a baking dish and pop it into the oven.

Last Thanksgiving, however, something went amiss. I carefully rechecked the containers I'd brought. "Oh no," I moaned. "I forgot the sweet potatoes!"

Emily turned from basting the turkey. "Are you sure?"

"They were in a round red container," I recalled. "I cooked, peeled and mashed them and put them in a bowl. I must have left it sitting on the kitchen counter."

Emily stood silent before the yawning oven. Granddaughter Christy, a stalk of celery in one hand, a paring knife in the other, looked up from her salad making. My husband Bob and our grandson Bob came into the kitchen from the living room with quizzical looks on their faces.

"Mother forgot to bring the sweet potatoes," Emily told them.

Young Bob tossed his head back and roared a wonderfully happy, youthful laugh. "Grandmom," he taunted, "you can't make sweet potato casserole without sweet potatoes!" He threw his arms around me and hugged me. His glee broke the tension in the room, and everybody, including me, began to laugh.

"Don't worry about it," Emily said. "We don't need that casserole today."

At the dinner table, Christy's place was full, except for one round spot. "That," she announced, "is where my sweet potatoes were to go."

We all laughed at her gentle teasing. And joy and love prevailed in that house, and my heart overflowed with thanksgiving.

Father, accept our thanks today for Your many blessings, especially for family, for love, and for the ability to laugh at ourselves.   —*Drue Duke*

27   *Come before him with thankful hearts. . . .*
                                              —PSALM 95:2 (TLB)

This year we planned a gala event. We invited family and friends to our home for Thanksgiving. I could hardly wait. The dining table was to be elegant. Fourteen places were set with our fine china and crystal, accented by a centerpiece of gold and bronze chrysanthemums. I had made a special green apple sausage stuffing the night before, and now I needed my husband's help in getting the whopper of a turkey stuffed and into the oven.

"Let's go, darling." He put down the morning paper and followed me into the kitchen. Together we let out a wail. Our Siamese cat Shushi was crouched on top of the turkey. She blinked her bright blue eyes at us as she munched on a feline feast that had mangled the entire top of the bird.

"What on earth will we do?" I moaned.

"Don't panic. I'll rush out, find a store that's open and buy another turkey for our guests. Just cut away the gnawed parts on this one," John laughed, "and I'll throw it on the barbecue for sandwiches later."

The last-minute turkey, served on a platter garnished with chestnuts and spiced red apples, brought a round of applause. Then, much to my dismay, John brought in the cat-mangled bird.

"Have a go at this," he chuckled as he told our guests about Shushi's feast. "Smoked in mesquite chips. Delicious . . . tastes better than the other." It did. So much so that we all decided, from here on, we'd barbecue all our turkeys!

Thank You, Lord, for the unexpected good things that happen to us.   *—Fay Angus*

28   *This land that was desolate is become like the garden of Eden. . . .*   *—EZEKIEL 36:35*

When I returned to my former home in Virginia after losing my husband George, I was shocked by the tangle of vines and weeds that had overpowered the dainty English ivy I'd set out years ago, as well as most of my plants and flowers. At first, I told the man who cuts the grass to chop them down. And when he forgot his tools, I began to break them off with my hands or take shears along on my walks beside the lake and cut them myself.

And then I discovered the wonders of *God's* garden: garlands of white blossoms, like a bevy of brides on parade; tall, bowing golden plumes; a myriad of multicolored wildflowers too beautiful to throw away! In autumn, when the flowers were gone, I discovered the graceful shapes of dry weeds: treasures to stand like sculptures on my windowsills.

And just before Thanksgiving, I found another treasure. My neighbor Jeanette was in her yard, weeding. "I've got plenty!" she called out. "Take some of mine!" And for the first time since my return, we chatted—comparing *weeds*.

I had been deeply hurt that this once dear and caring neighbor hadn't come to see me. Now I saw that she was deeply troubled. Suddenly, she held out her arms and began to cry. "Oh, Marj, forgive me. I've just lost my best friend to AIDS!" And standing there clutching our weeds, we comforted each other. The next morning I called to wish her a happy Thanksgiving, but she was already at my door to bring me one of her apple cakes.

God had healed our estrangement. That was the most beautiful flower of all!

Dear Lord, let me always see the beauty in Your garden of vines and flowers and weeds—and people. —Marjorie Holmes

THE GIFTS OF CHRISTMAS

At Christmas, we share with others the joy God has given us in the gift of His only Son. For this special time of giving and receiving, we've asked Marion Bond West to share some of her own special memories of the ways in which she's come to know the true gifts of Christmas. —THE EDITORS

A Gift of Worship

29
"Where is he . . . ? For we . . . have come to worship him." —MATTHEW 2:2 (RSV)

In December, the little family had moved into the tiny frame house across the street from the First Christian Church in Perry, Oklahoma, where my husband Gene was interim pastor. There wasn't much heat, and Bea told her two small grandchildren to keep their coats on in the house. Gifts were out of the question this Christmas; Bea only hoped to keep the children warm and fed.

One day, four-year-old Paul noticed some activity on the lawn across the street. He found an old box and climbed up on it so he could look out of the drafty window. The church was preparing for its annual nativity scene. Paul almost forgot about the cold as he watched the bundled-up men build a little shelter, open in front so he could look right into it. Bales of hay were delivered and stacked. And then the animals arrived—a cow, a donkey and four sheep.

As night fell, lights suddenly illuminated the scene. Inside the shelter, people in colorful costumes knelt around a little box. Paul thought it looked like the box he was standing on. And high above the shelter hung a star of light—the biggest, brightest star he'd ever seen.

Paul called to his grandmother and sister, and the three of them watched the silent magnificence across the street. Bea told the children about the birth of a little Baby a long time ago. "They named Him Jesus," she whispered. "They almost didn't find a place to stay." Long into the cold night, after the children and their grandmother had curled up in bed together to keep warm, Paul and his sister asked questions about the Baby Who slept in a box.

After two days, the manger scene was removed from the church lawn. "Where is He, Grandma?" Paul sobbed. "Take me across the street so I can find Him." So Bea took her old, worn walker, and with Paul and his sister, shivering in the cold, came to church one morning in search of Jesus.

Oh, Lord, they came so long ago, and they still come to worship and adore You. —Marion Bond West

I command mirth . . . for that shall abide with him

30
of his labour the days of his life. . . . —ECCLESIASTES 8:15

I've been extremely frustrated all day, because sometime between last night and this morning, and somewhere in the vast quantities of paper in this house, I lost my booklet containing all my postage stamps. I had to make a special trip to the post office to buy stamps for the letters I'd written.

As I was berating myself for the umpteenth time, I remembered a similar occurrence a couple of years ago when my cousin Ruth was visiting me from Canada. "Look at this mess," I said to her one day, pointing to the stacks of books, papers, catalogs and magazines that covered desk, chairs, files and cabinets in my study-spare bedroom.

"I see you have your 'pilot's license,' " Ruth responded with a grin. At my puzzled look, she added, "You know, I have mine too."

"You don't mean you can fly a plane?" I gasped.

She laughed. "No, a 'pile-lots' license. You pile a lot and so do I. Piles of papers here, piles of catalogs there, piles of magazines elsewhere, and you almost need a license to maneuver between and around them or to find anything. And then you pile-a-lot more on!"

"Yes," I agreed, joining in the laughter. "And you tear your hair, because you can't find what you want in any of the piles. What can we do about it?"

"What sometimes helps me," Ruth said, "is to put everything in one pile. That way I'm sure to find whatever I might be looking for."

"The main thing," she continued, "is to remember that if we can laugh at ourselves, as we're doing now, and not let ourselves get frustrated, we can calmly sort through the piles and get rid of them!"

Tonight, that remembered laughter has helped calm my spirit and inspired me to do some filing. And just now I bent down to pick up some fallen papers and books—and there were my stamps!

Forgive my vexation of spirit, Lord. Help me to pilot my days with humor through the messes.   —*Mary Ruth Howes*

My Healing Journey

1

2 _____

3 _____

4 _____

5 _____

6 _____

7 _____

8 _____

9 _____

10 _____

11 _____

12 _____

13 _____

14 _____

15 _____

16 _____

17 _____

18 _____

19 _____

20 _____

21 _____

22 _____

23 _____

24 _____

25 _____

26 _____

27 _____

28 _____

29 _____

30 _____

DECEMBER

S	M	T	W	T	F	S
		1	2	3	4	5
6	7	8	9	10	11	12
13	14	15	16	17	18	19
20	21	22	23	24	25	26
27	28	29	30	31		

*Unto you that fear my name shall the Sun of
righteousness arise with healing
in his wings. . . .*
—MALACHI 4:2

THE TOUCH OF THE HEALER

1 Healing Our Prayer Life
You do not have, because you do not ask God.
—*JAMES 4:2 (NIV)*

"It's definitely a lump. We'd better take it out." The surgeon was calm and matter-of-fact as he laid down my mammography report. A month later, I was in the hospital, prepped for surgery. My family was in the waiting room downstairs.

"We'll just do one more shot for the surgeon," the lab technician said, wheeling me into the familiar room. And so we did. But something was wrong. After an hour of taking pictures of my left breast, the head of radiology entered.

"Mrs. Carney, we can't seem to find the lump. It's gone."

My family joined me on the way back up to my room. As I held my daughter Amy Jo's hand, tears flowed down my cheeks. *Gone!* I wondered aloud how that could be, questioned the skill of the hospital staff.

"I think I'm responsible for this," Amy Jo said softly. "I prayed that it would just be gone."

I looked up into her face and saw the simplicity of her belief. I had prayed that the surgeon would be skilled, that the facility would be adequate, that the pain would be minimal. But I had never prayed that the lump would simply vanish.

My health is fine these days. And my faith is strong. Thanks to my daughter, even my prayer life is thriving. You see, I've learned not to be afraid to ask for the biggest and best possible answers.

You, O Lord, have endless power. Give me the courage to ask boldly—and to believe.   —*Mary Lou Carney*

---

2 *Above all things have fervent charity among your-selves. . . .*   —*I PETER 4:8*

"Pauline just died," my cousin's voice said quietly out of the telephone from eight hundred miles away. "She wasn't in pain, and at the last she often didn't recognize us when we visited her. She was almost ninety, and we know she's with the Lord . . . but we'll miss her."

I felt very sad and wept, thinking how strange it was that I should feel so strongly about Pauline, since I had only seen her a few times. A schoolteacher, she had lived most of her life in a small town in Missouri.

But then I remembered a young Pauline who lived with us when I was a very small boy, while she was getting a degree at the university in our town. After she'd gone, she sent me Christmas presents until I grew up and married, and then she sent them to my daughters until they were grown. My children were amazed and felt they didn't deserve the presents, since they didn't really know Pauline. I told them that it was her way of saying thank you for what God had done for her.

As I thought about all of those Christmas remembrances, I realized that Pauline had taught me some things about quiet, continuing, unmerited grace. Even though we didn't "deserve" the presents, they kept coming year after year.

I still feel tearful about Pauline's going, but more than anything, I feel grateful for what she taught me by her faithful and giving life, and I'll miss her.

Lord, thank You for all those who have generously given me a glimpse of Your love. —Keith Miller

---

THU
3

"A woman giving birth to a child has pain because her time has come; but when her baby is born she forgets the anguish because of her joy that a child is born into the world." —JOHN 16:21 (NIV)

Last week my wife gave birth to our third child, Grace Marie. Mom and baby are doing fine, but we did have some anxious moments. After several hours of unproductive labor, my wife opted for a cesarean section. It was the way our first two children were born, so we were prepared.

What I *wasn't* prepared for was the sometimes odd reaction to our birth story. "Oh, a *C-section*," some acquaintances said. "Well, maybe next time . . . meaning maybe next time we'd have a child the *natural* way. Why is a C-section not quite respectable? I mean, we ended up with a beautiful baby daughter—what difference does it make *how* she was born? It's like judging a marriage by how well the wedding went.

But it's Advent now, and I'm taking solace in the story of Joseph, the foster father of Jesus. I can imagine him leaning against the rickety walls of the stable, exhausted from travel, trying to process the confused wonder of it all. No breathing classes here, no Lamaze. When the birth was over, the new parents wrapped their Babe in swaddling clothes and raised Him as best they could, on faith and instinct. And His life, it turns out, was even more remarkable than His birth.

It doesn't matter how kids are born, because this I know: They're all heaven-sent, and they're here to do His will—however they got here to do it.

Father, bless all the babies born this year, and help them grow close to You.   *—Mark Collins*

FRI

4

The place whereon thou standest is holy ground.
—EXODUS 3:5

Elisa Phelps, a young friend who is the curator of anthropology at the Museum of Natural Science in Houston, Texas, sent my wife Barbara and me an autographed copy of *Dialogues With Zuni Potters,* which she coedited. It's a wonderful book, with photographs of beautiful pottery and interviews with the potters, telling about how they got started, their early training, artists who had influenced them, and how they worked at their craft.

The potters were all good, but very diverse in background and style. I was especially impressed by the experience of Eileen Yatsattie. Although she had been doing well with her pottery, she felt that something was missing in her work. Her grandfather suggested that her problems came because she did not know the prayers of the potter, prayers for the various steps in the process—for gathering and preparing the clay, for forming the pot, for creating the patterns, mixing the colors and firing the pot. In the interview, she said that it was only after she had learned the prayers that everything in her pottery making fell into place.

I think I would find greater satisfaction in life if I were to "learn the prayers" that go with everything I do—whether it's earning a living, building relationships, preparing a meal, planting a flower or writing a note to a friend.

Dear God, help me to find Your presence in everything I do.
                                                    —Kenneth Chafin

<table>
<tr><td>

SAT

5

</td><td>

Anyone who is among the living has hope. . . .
                                —ECCLESIASTES 9:4 (NIV)

</td></tr>
</table>

A few months ago, I was sitting in our gymnasium talking with Kevin Jones, the youth pastor of our church, about various subjects. In the middle of our conversation, a well-dressed young man walked into the gym, and I turned to look at him. Pastor Jones told me that when he first came to our church eight years ago, he had tried on many occasions to tell this young man about Jesus. Every time, the young man would start cursing at him and then run away. Pastor Jones just kept on telling him that Jesus loved him.

"Eventually, I led him to the Lord," Pastor Jones went on to say, "and he spent many hours sitting on my porch talking about his broken family relationships. The more he talked, the more he revealed why he had been so hostile to me. He transferred his negative feelings about his own father on to me.

"I never gave up on Richard because God never gives up on us. And look at what God has done in his life—he has gone to technical school, has a job and is doing well."

How many Richards do I come in contact with each day? When I meet them, I'm tempted to turn off, walk the other way and hope that someone else will deal with them. But God is teaching me that He takes Richard—and me—and loves us the way we are because there is something greater in us that only He sees.

Lord, forgive me for all the "Richards" whom I have passed by. Help me to see what You see.   *—Dolphus Weary*

<table>
<tr><td>

SUN

6

</td><td>

THE GIFTS OF CHRISTMAS
A Gift of Generosity
"What I have I give you. . . ."   *—ACTS 3:6 (NIV)*

</td></tr>
</table>

I didn't like the old house we were renting. There were no younger couples in the neighborhood, and I hadn't gotten acquainted with the older people. There wasn't even a yard for the girls to play in. I'd put a wreath on the door and lights in the window, but there was no light in my heart that year. I sat on the sofa with our daughters Julie and Jennifer, ages three and one. We gazed at the tree together, but I didn't feel any Christmas joy.

I peered out into the night. My husband Jerry was late getting home from work. Suddenly, the doorbell rang. We'd never heard it in the four months we'd lived there. The girls ran to the door. "Mama, it's the lady next door!" Julie called to me.

I wonder what she wants. I got up and stuck my head out into the cold. "Yes?"

"Mrs. West, I'm Ruth Gardner, your neighbor next door. I brought you all something for Christmas."

"Ask her in, Mama," Julie prompted.

"Oh, yes. Please come in." Crystals of sleet clung to her dark hair and the wool scarf she had tied around her head. She had six children and worked somewhere all day. Her husband was rarely home. They lived in the small house next door.

"I work at the candy factory, and we're allowed to take home the broken pieces at the end of the day. I brought you some peppermint. Merry Christmas." She handed me a small, tinfoil-covered box with a green bow on top.

I asked her to sit down, and the girls entertained her while I ran to the kitchen, cut huge wedges of fruit cake and arranged them on a paper Christmas plate. I wrapped the plate in clear plastic and topped it with a red bow. Handing her the cake, I said joyfully, "Merry Christmas, Mrs. Gardner."

She stayed for perhaps fifteen minutes. Then the girls and I walked her out to the front porch. Mrs. Gardner had given me much more than a box of candy. Now all the beauty and wonder of Christmas filled the cold night air. And my heart.

You gave all You had that first Christmas, too, Father. Amen.
—Marion Bond West

MON

7　　*"Be on guard! Be alert! You do not know when that time will come."*　　　*—MARK 13:33 (NIV)*

There were eight of us crowded around the low table in Andrea's living room. It had grown late, and each member of our Bible study circle had work or classes the next morning. But we were shaken. We needed each other and weren't ready yet to part company. Doreen had posed a question two hours before, her voice quiet and hesitant, and it still hung in the air: "What if Jesus were to come tomorrow?"

At first, suggestions from the group flowed quickly:

"I'd spend time with my mother. I haven't been able to be with her much lately."

"I'd apologize to my girlfriend for not taking her to the concert last week"

"I'd tell my brother I love him."

"I'd go door to door and tell people the good news. I know I should be doing more to share my faith."

Our eyes sparkled, our enthusiasm growing with the scope of the fantasy. The rush of good intentions continued until Corrinna cleared her throat and said, "I think I've found something you guys should see." At her direction, we opened our Bibles to Mark 13. We read that we are servants left to watch over God's house, that we have responsibilities as His people and must be prepared for our Master's return.

Not one of us had been able to say he or she was ready. We all had something we had to do before He comes back. The contemplative silence set in.

Andrea broke the quiet; we joined hands and prayed:

Lord, Your coming is a joyous thing, but my heart grows heavy when I realize that I'm not prepared for Your arrival. Help me to become a ready, watchful servant. Amen.

—*Kjerstin Easton*

TUE

8   *Consider your ways.*   —*HAGGAI 1:5*

When I was invited to serve as a bank director, I was hesitant. My banking experience had been limited to making deposits and withdrawals—mostly withdrawals. But the kindly bank president said, "Oscar, join us. You'll learn from us and we'll learn from you."

I joined the board. There I learned two terms that resounded around the board room: *compliance* and *due diligence*. The question thundered from regulators and examiners: "Are you in compliance, and have you exercised due diligence? Are you observing the rules, and are you doing the best you can?"

There were volumes and volumes of rules that governed the way the bank did business. External auditing teams were conducting examinations the year round to see if we were obeying them. No matter how much effort I put in, it was impossible to learn them all. But I did find an area where I could do my best and that brought out the best in me—writing reports. There I could be clear and accurate, and help both the board and the examiners in their work. I was appointed to the auditing committee, and eventually elected chairperson.

I'm retired from the board now, but I still ask myself two questions every day: Do I strive to know and do God's will? Am I doing the best I can? Am I in compliance? Have I exercised due diligence?

Jesus, when the best I can do isn't enough, give me a share in Your perfect obedience. —Oscar Greene

---

WED
9

. . . Knowing that suffering produces endurance, and endurance produces character. . . .
—ROMANS 5:3-4 (RSV)

Ask my twenty-one-year-old son Phil which was the worst day of his life and he'll tell you about a fifty-degree-below-zero nightmare on Alaska's North Slope, just off the frigid shores of the Arctic Ocean.

He had been hired in December by a company involved in underground oil exploration. His first day on the job as a "juggy" required that he collect geophones—seismic sensors connected by cables—that crisscrossed the barren tundra in a six-square-mile grid. The crew had been "weathered in" for the previous twenty-four hours, and they were determined to make up the lost time.

Phil rode from the mobile camp to the field site in a track rig at 7:00 A.M. The recent ice storm had lacquered a brittle crust on the surface of the knee-deep snow. He had to kick through it, yank heavily on the geophones to pry them from their frozen cocoons, and then lug a hundred and fifty pounds of phones back to the track rig. The crew made twenty stops that day, all shrouded in the thick Arctic winter night. Phil wore a headlamp and tried not to think about being in polar bear territory.

For eighteen hours he toughed it out, finally finishing at 1:00 A.M. He kept telling himself, "Nothing is worth this misery," but he stayed on the job for another twelve weeks.

It did get better. And now, a year later, Phil's image of that dark day as a "worthless experience" has shifted. "It upped my estimate of what I could endure," he told me recently. "I'm going back this winter to earn some money so I can begin college. I *know* I can handle it."

Lord, You have endured everything for me and with me. Thank You for giving me Your strength to persevere.

—*Carol Knapp*

THU
10

What I want is not your possessions but you. . . .
—*II CORINTHIANS 12:14 (NIV)*

One of the things we liked best about our years in Africa was being in a culture that lives out its belief that people are more important than things. In Africa, Christmas isn't a time of frenzied shopping and lavish gift-giving; it's a time to enjoy family and friends, a time of "being with." For several weeks before the holidays, virtually all productive work ceases, and Nairobi becomes almost a ghost town. People go "up country" for the holidays, back to their roots, home to be with their families.

When we returned to the States we resolved to incorporate that African way of celebrating into our lives. We downsized our Christmas list by having each family member draw one name for whom to buy a present and setting a price limit. One year we rented a rambling old beach house at off-season rates and invited our families to join us for any part of the month surrounding the holidays. Money that would have been spent on gifts went toward transportation expenses and shared food costs. We decided to participate in a program at our church that allows us to share our holidays with a needy family from the community.

We have given up the obligatory gift-giving of Christmas, and it frees us to express our love for others in spontaneous ways and times. And sometimes we even stroll through the mall this time of year as spectators, our arms empty of shopping bags, no gift lists in our pockets and no avalanche of credit card bills anticipated in January. It's a fine sense of freedom and focus as we move through these days of Advent, anticipating Christ's birth—the *real* reason for Christmas.

Help me, Jesus, to rid myself of the distractions that keep me from the joy of celebrating Your coming into our world.
—Mary Jane Clark

11
Be strong and courageous, be not afraid. . . .
—II CHRONICLES 32:7

Napoleon Bonaparte is not remembered too kindly by history: his image is stained by bloodshed and all the horrors of war. And yet, in his day, the Little Corporal was adored by his troops.

One reason for such loyalty was Napoleon's understanding of human nature. In an era when commissions were considered a privilege of the upper classes, he said that every private soldier in his army carried a marshal's baton in his knapsack . . . and some of his greatest commanders did rise from the ranks.

On one occasion, at the siege of Toulon, Napoleon ordered a battery of cannon placed in such an exposed position that all his staff officers protested. To man those guns, they said, would be virtual suicide; no soldiers would obey such orders. Napoleon ordered a large sign to be painted and displayed beside the cannon: "The battery of men without fear." The guns were always manned.

Ask people for their utmost and hope to get it. That's what God does with each of us, isn't it? He wants the very best that's in us. He doesn't paint signs, and He never shouts. But for those who listen, His quiet voice is audible every day.

Including today.

Challenge me, Lord, today and every day. Challenge me!
—Arthur Gordon

12
Our mouths were filled with laughter. . . .
—PSALM 126:2 (NIV)

Stripe, one of our two cats, is in love with my husband. As soon as Paul settles into his recliner at night, Stripe races to the chair, jumps up on Paul's chest and gazes up at him with an adoring expression on her face that says, "If only some cruel accident of fate hadn't made us members of a different species." And, believe it or not, I was jealous.

The situation disturbed me so much that I waited in a long line one Saturday to explain the situation to a renowned cat expert at an ASPCA pet fair. "I even gave her some catnip. She still doesn't care for me!" I cried. "What should I do?"

I suppose I expected sympathy; I certainly expected some concrete advice (such as "feed her from your hand" or "brush her coat"). Instead, the woman stared at me for what seemed like a long moment, and then said, "Laugh!"

"Laugh?" I repeated blankly.

"You're jealous of a *cat*?" she said. "And you don't think that's funny enough to laugh about?"

I was embarrassed for a moment. And then it dawned on me—it *was* funny! So I laughed. And even though I'm still just a wee bit jealous of Stripe, I've learned to live with it.

Is there some situation, God, that I'm blowing up way out of proportion? Today, let me see the humor and laugh at myself.							*—Linda Neukrug*

SUN
13

THE GIFTS OF CHRISTMAS
A Gift of Comfort
Every good gift and every perfect gift is from above. . . .							*—JAMES 1:17*

I was on a mission trip in Bacolod in the Philippines. Christmas was approaching, but it was hard to believe it in the sweltering heat of a city halfway around the world from home. I was tired, not eating well and working long hours sharing the gospel with the poor. Now I'd come down with a painful throat infection. Our group was going to spend the day in an outlying village, but I would remain in town. "I'll be fine," I said, trying to sound matter-of-fact.

"Don't leave the hotel for anything, Marion," our Filipino leader said seriously. "There are guerrilla soldiers camped across the street in the plaza, and they don't like Americans."

I nodded, forced a smile and waved to the group as they left. Then I climbed into my bed. My throat throbbed, and my head ached with fever. I dreaded the long, lonely day. I almost didn't hear the gentle knock on my door. Slowly, I got out of bed, went to the door and opened it a crack. Looking out, I saw my sixteen-year-old friend Suzette. We'd met the day I arrived. She'd been a Christian for only six months.

She came in carrying a small bundle under her arm. "I couldn't go with the others and leave you alone." Desperately poor, rich only in her newfound faith, Suzette lived with her mother and father and six brothers and sisters in one floorless room. She handed me the package. "Merry Christmas, Mannie."

I opened the package, carefully wrapped in newspaper, and found—ice! Ice was a rarity in Bacolod because the guerrillas often cut the power lines. And I had been longing for something to soothe my burning throat.

"Oh, Suzette," I cried, "what a perfect gift!"

Father, remind me that good and perfect gifts come from the heart, not the mall.   *—Marion Bond West*

MON
14

These things have I spoken unto you, that my joy might remain in you, and that your joy might be full.
—JOHN 15:11

It was Christmastime, and the subway was crowded. I had to sidle my way into the car, but at last I found a space where I could grasp a bar to keep from losing my balance. I found myself looking directly at a seated woman who wore a pin that said JOY on it—and an expression on her face that was anything but. I gazed about to a woman next to her; she was glum, too, and the man next in line only made it appear that there was a contagion of unhappiness.

We stopped at Seventy-second Street. Three passengers squeezed on at my door. I returned to the woman with JOY. Her expression was unchanged. *Whatever prompted her to put on that pin when it's so obvious that she's joyless?* I thought. *Okay, maybe she's urging others to have what she doesn't.* Then something within me, some powerful force that I didn't understand, led me to speak to her. "I like your JOY sign," I blurted out.

She looked up at me, and her face wasn't gloomy at all. It was a mother's face, sweet, gentle and caring. "Thank you," she said, and I was warmed by it.

And even more surprising was the doleful woman next to her. "I was thinking the same thing," she volunteered, and a man standing next to me concurred, and before I knew it, my little section of the packed subway car was changed into—what shall I say?—Christmas joy.

The train reached Fifty-ninth Street, and the woman got up to leave. "God bless you," she fairly sang to me. But I had been blessed already.

Joy to the world, Father, joy to the world.   —*Van Varner*

TUE

15

But if we hope for what we do not see, we wait for it with patience.   —ROMANS 8:25 (RSV)

My son Geoffrey knows what he wants and has a saint's patience to work for it.

"I can wait," he said, age eight, when the bike he yearned for wasn't due at the store for six months. "I can wait," was his reply to the waiter when told at his twelfth birthday party that roast duck, his favorite dish, took an hour to prepare. "I can wait," he says now, a fifteen-year-old 3-D computer animation buff, at the news that the equipment he needs is not yet on the market. The salesmen are pushing a makeshift version, but Geoffrey is saving up for exactly the right item.

Like any kid, waiting comes hard for Geoffrey. He was disappointed to tears when the bike he yearned for wasn't in stock. He was famished at his birthday dinner. And he craves that computer part with a teenager's consuming passion. Yet despite the fierceness of his present desires, he values even more the rewards the future offers. He's already planning for a project when the computer part comes in.

"Why settle for less than the best?" he insists.

Lord, grant me the conviction that in You the best is yet to be and the patience to wait upon Your grace.
                                    —*Linda Ching Sledge*

WED

16

Thy money perish with thee, because thou hast thought that the gift of God may be purchased with money.   —ACTS 8:20

While Christmas shopping, I mused over the window display signs that marked some luxurious gifts. "For the man who has everything," one placard read. "Pamper the woman of your dreams," stated another. There were no price tags visible, so my assumption was that money was no object.

If that were the case, I wondered, and I could give my loved ones any gift in the world, what would it be? Mansions, stocks, cars, vacations, diamonds? The best things the Wise Men could conceive of were gold, frankincense and myrrh. I wondered if they fretted over their gifts for Jesus.

But the best gift is more costly, the Bible tells us. It even surpasses the widow's mite—though she gave her last coin. Christina Rossetti wrote about it in her famous poem:

> What can I give him,
> Poor as I am?
> If I were a shepherd, I would bring a lamb;
> If I were a wise man,
> I would do my part;
> Yet what I can I give him—
> Give my heart.

That's something all Christmas shoppers, including me, need to ponder.

> *Help me remember, Lord,*
> *The best of all gifts was not*
> *Festooned with bells and bows;*
> *The best gift the world has ever seen*
> *Was wrapped in swaddling clothes.*
> —*Fred Bauer*

THU
17 *Take heed that ye do not your alms before men. . . .*
—*MATTHEW 6:1*

In early June, the little town of Cave Springs, Georgia, welcomes visitors to its annual arts festival. Between a cave where pure water gushes and a free-flowing river where trout hide from barefoot fishermen, a host of artisans set up their tents in the public park.

Wandering through the festival's art display, I stopped before a painting of an old raw-board farmhouse. The house's sagging front porch was heaped with presents: bicycles, a scooter, several boxes of groceries. In the midst of it all, a small boy with a red cowboy hat perched on his head was dancing.

As I puzzled over the painting, the artist approached me. "My daddy had left us some months before," he explained softly. "Mamma didn't think we'd have a Christmas. But I was a little fellow, and I couldn't help praying and believing. When I peeped out the window on Christmas morning, there were all those presents. We never knew who left them, but the feeling of dancing across the porch in that new red hat has stayed with me. Sooner or later, I just had to paint it."

The impact of that painting just won't let me go: Someone out there performed an anonymous act of kindness on a long ago night, a good deed that lives on and reaches out from an artist's canvas.

For those of us who haven't yet accepted Jesus' invitation to give in secret without fanfare or thanks, this illustration of selfless giving poses an interesting question: Might some barren porch or hopeful heart be waiting for my touch? Has God stretched an empty canvas somewhere near, where I can quietly, anonymously, paint His love?

Father, point me toward empty porches. With only You watching, I want to leave my offering there.   —Pam Kidd

---

Herald of Healing

Thou shalt know Him when He comes,
Not by any din of drums,
Nor the vantage of His airs,
Nor by anything He wears;
Neither by His crown,
Nor by His gown,
But His presence known shall be
By the holy harmony
Which His coming makes in thee.

—*AUTHOR UNKNOWN*

FRI
18

In thee shall all families of the world be blessed.
—GENESIS 12:3

I was an only child. In addition to my parents and grandparents, I had eight aunts and eight uncles. Some were married but none had any children, so I became everyone's child. This could be good and not so good. Like the time when Mother enrolled me in piano lessons. My Aunt Helen, who loved ballet, thought dancing would be better. My mother tried to explain why piano was her choice. It didn't matter; there were arguments.

Then came the year when I was four and, wonder of wonders, they all agreed that I should have a dollhouse. But it was no ordinary house. First, Daddy and Uncle Charlie bought the wood, then drove to Uncle Ben's to get the frame cut out on a special saw. Then there were windows, doorways and a stairway to the third-floor playroom to be cut out.

Meanwhile, the ladies in my family, including my mother and both grandmothers, were busy sewing. Aunt Emma created the most beautiful yellow chiffon bassinet for the nursery. Aunt Billie, who worked for an interior decorator, got wallpaper and rug samples. The guest room was done in blue and white. If you looked closely, you realized that the end tables on either side of the bed were empty thread spools painted blue and white. The bed itself was just a block of wood covered in blue satin and white lace.

That Christmas Eve everyone gathered at my house. As Daddy unhooked the front and back of the house so I could see inside, I looked around at all the smiling faces who had come, I thought, to see this wonderful gift that Santa Claus had brought. It was years later that I learned the truth. And ever since then, not a Christmas passes that I don't recall it and thank God for a wonderful family that put themselves into a gift for me.

Dear God, I thank You for Christmas memories.
—Eleanor Sass

SAT
19

The flowers appear on the earth; the time of the singing of birds is come. . . .
—SONG OF SOLOMON 2:12

I needed a miracle. My mother's health was failing, and it had come to the point where the doctor said she should no longer live alone. She was on a "wait list" for a retirement home, but now her time for waiting was running out.

As I was chasing through the neighborhood one Saturday morning, a yard sale sign caught my eye. It featured exotic plants. *Maybe I'll find something to cheer us up.* As I browsed through a jumble of plants, the young woman running the sale held up a wilted orchid, entwined around a simple terra cotta pot.

"*This* was my Dad's pride and joy," she said sadly, "and look at it now!" The tears welled up in her eyes. "This is called the Christmas Orchid. Its white blossoms represent the purity of Christ. Dad always said if it bloomed by Christmas Day it meant special blessings for all of us. 'One more year, one more miracle!' he'd declare." Her voice went down to a whisper, "Last year was his last miracle."

"I'll buy it!" I said.

"Oh, please, I couldn't possibly sell Dad's orchid! Here, let me give it to you. I hope you can perk it up."

It took a lot of mist-spraying, and much praying, but two small shoots with tiny furled buds finally came up from the clay-entwined roots. A few days before Christmas, it burst into exquisite white bloom.

"Look, Mum, the miracle happened," I grinned as I took it to her. "Expect a blessing!"

The blessing came, a vacancy in the retirement home. We moved my mother in, and with her went her Christmas orchid.

This Christmas, open the eyes of our hearts, sweet Jesus, to see the miracles all around us.   —Fay Angus

---

SUN **THE GIFTS OF CHRISTMAS**
20 A Gift of Self
        "Give good gifts to your children. . . ."
                            —*MATTHEW 7:11 (NAS)*

Two months before Christmas, I sensed the Lord instructing me, "Don't give any gifts this year, Marion." Appalled, I wondered what my family and friends would think if I obeyed these peculiar instructions.

"What about my grandchildren, Lord? What about Katie and Jamie?"

Give them yourself: your time, your energy, your full attention . . . and one very small thing. Give this year's Christmas money to missions and to the genuinely needy people you meet.

Well before Christmas, I told my friends and family that I wouldn't be giving gifts that year. Everyone smiled and nodded, even the children. Then, a week before Christmas, I invited Jamie and Katie to spend the night with us. My husband Gene and I had cleared our calendar for twenty-four hours. Gene read the Christmas story from the Bible, and we took turns answering their questions and imagining what it was really like on that wondrous night. Then we took them to Stone Mountain to see miles of Christmas lights and stopped for dinner at their favorite fast-food restaurant.

Back home, I explained that I did have a very, very small something for them. I'd hidden simple directions that led them to surprises all over the house. The girls giggled and began the Christmas scavenger hunt. Jamie could read most of the instructions to Katie. "A cat will help you," she read. Under a china cat, they found another clue on a slip of paper: "Look in the looking glass." On the mirror, Katie discovered, "Go to the manger." At the nativity scene under my giftless tree, they found another clue. Finally, they held the "small things," tiny dolls made from rags by a mountain woman. "A baby!" the girls breathed in unison.

Jamie and Katie are teenagers now, and there are four more grandchildren. But the girls still reminisce about that strange Christmas when there were no gifts under the tree.

I'm stingy with myself, Lord. Show me how to give myself away. —*Marion Bond West*

MON
21 *For he that is mighty hath done to me great things. . . .* —*LUKE 1:49*

Jenny is an unprepossessing child. Shy, awkward, a little ungainly, she seemed an unlikely choice for Mary in the church Christmas pageant. No parent was heard to complain, but then our pageant has always had its casting irregularities (including the boy who insisted on playing a camel one year).

That morning, there was the usual display of nerves and high spirits, the flashing of cameras, the last-minute tweaking of a halo, the mouthing of a well-rehearsed line. I went to my spot in the gallery to watch. The Annunciation came early. A teenaged boy wearing sneakers underneath his white robe told Mary that she would bear the Baby Jesus. Jenny, dressed in blue, walked down the center aisle and responded, "My soul doth magnify the Lord, and my spirit hath rejoiced in God my Savior" (Luke 1:46-47).

Jenny's voice was strong and confident, filling the church. Her diction was crystal clear. To my amazement and to everyone else's, she went on, "For he hath regarded the low estate of his handmaiden. . . ." She was going to recite all ten verses of Luke's song of Mary (1:46-55). We sat on the edge of our pews. Before our eyes, Jenny was transformed from a nine-year-old wallflower to a brave, commanding soul.

Never missing a beat, she made her way through the entire speech. When she was finished, the congregation burst into spontaneous applause. Better than any preacher, Jenny had given us the message of that moment. God could take a young peasant girl and make her the mother of His Son. God could transform a life into something awe-inspiring.

Take my life, Lord, and let it be changed by You.

—Rick Hamlin

| TUE | *And the angel said to them, "Be not afraid; for behold, I bring you good news of a great joy which will come to all the people. . . ."* |
| **22** | *—LUKE 2:10 (RSV)* |

Weak and depressed from a monthlong bout with strep throat and respiratory flu, I struggled to prepare for Christmas. After the children and I baked cookies, my husband Alex took them up to bed. I longed to follow them and collapse in bed, but I sank into a chair and stared at the kitchen floor. *It must be swept,* I thought, *or flour, sugar and sprinkles will be tracked all over the house.* I begged God for the strength to finish this task.

When I walked outside to shake out the rug, I nearly gasped at the black sky sparkling with stars. Watching the dazzling sky, I thought of the shepherds, perhaps also out under such a sky tending their sheep. Little did they suspect that their sky—and their lives—would soon be ablaze with joy.

I wondered if I'd ever feel strong again. Yet my troubles seemed trivial compared to my friend Pat, awash with grief after two funerals this week for her dear brother and uncle. And my friend Rosemary, whose teenage daughter Ann ran away.

Looking up at the starry sky, I whispered a prayer for them . . . and sensed a message from the shepherds and angels: Be faithful to your daily work; persevere in prayer. The Messiah will come to you, to give you the help and strength you need.

Inside, I finished sweeping the floor, still coughing and needing my bed, but comforted . . . for my Savior was with me, in illness or weakness, in turmoil or grief.

Lord, help me to remember in my times of watching and waiting, the dark skies of my life will again be filled with joy.
—Mary Brown

<hr/>

WED

23 *Open my eyes that I may see wonderful things. . . .*
—PSALM 119:18 (NIV)

It was Christmastime and my office-mate Roger had one request on his gift list that he'd lost all hope of finding: an old-time aluminum Christmas tree like the one his fiancée Paula had adored as a girl growing up in the fifties. Knowing how I haunt flea markets and junk shops, Roger asked for my help. I searched everywhere and called everyone I knew who might know of one for sale. My leads led me nowhere.

Then on Christmas Eve, a friend and fellow nostalgia buff telephoned to wish me a Merry Christmas. "Sorry I couldn't find you one of those old silver trees," he remarked. "I've put out at least fifty feelers, but they're scarce as hen's teeth this year."

In the background, I heard his sister holler, "Someone wants one of those dreadful silver Christmas trees? I have one in the attic just taking up space." I was off to her house like a horse charging out of the gate at the Kentucky Derby.

That evening when Paula came through the door, the house was dark except for the glowing wheel of lights. When Paula heard the sound of the grinding motor, she threw down her purse and ran toward the tree like a five-year-old.

Roger and I love to recount that story whenever we need a shot of Christmas spirit at work. It never fails to put us in an "all things are possible" frame of mind, despite the pressures of the workaday world. But even more than that, it's a wonderful year-round reminder that life is a continual Christmas. For God has placed what we need all around us, though sometimes hidden in the most ordinary places.

Thank You, loving Father, for opening my eyes to Your wonderful gifts.
                                                                    —*Roberta Messner*

THU	THE GIFTS OF CHRISTMAS
24	A Gift of Healing
	And they were filled with fear. —*LUKE 2:9 (RSV)*

I was seven years old the Christmas Eve of 1943. Our family doctor had come on a house call, and he and my widowed mother were talking quietly over by the window. I pretended to examine the carefully wrapped gifts under the tree while I listened to their hushed conversation. "I want you in the hospital tonight," Doc told my mother. "I suspect double pneumonia."

"I won't go, not on Christmas Eve, Doc." Mother was adamant.

It seemed so strange to be afraid on the most wonderful of all nights. I tried to fight the fear: *Maybe I'll get a bike this year and. . . . Who cares what I get if Mama is. . . ? Maybe I'll get the black patent-leather shoes. . . . What difference will that make if Mother is. . . ?*

Doc, defeated, gave me a quick hug, and I managed to give him a smile. He left, looking way too serious for Christmas Eve. Mother lay down on the sofa. Never in my life had I seen her resting. The marvelous aroma of the tall cedar tree had lost its magic. I decided not to speak about my terrible fear.

In bed, I curled up into a ball and tried hard to feel the Christmas Eve excitement once again. But the fear had blocked it out entirely. *What if Mother. . . ? Dear God, please don't let my mother die. Please make her well. Please!*

At the first hint of light, I crept into the living room. I didn't look under the tree; I looked at my mother. She sat by the fireplace in her familiar green robe, as she always did on Christmas morning, sipping hot chocolate. The fire made happy, popping sounds and filled the small room with a glorious amber glow. Even before I saw the bicycle, my heart felt Christmas again.

The shepherds trembled with fear on that first Christmas Eve, Father. With them, let me exchange my fear for faith.
—*Marion Bond West*

FRI

25

THE GIFTS OF CHRISTMAS
A Gift of Jesus
And I pray that Christ will be more and more at home in your hearts. . . . —*EPHESIANS 3:17 (TLB)*

When I was quite young, my mother and I lived with three other families in a long, brown-shingled apartment house with green awnings. That Christmas we watched with fascination as I.V. Hulme, who lived in one of the apartments, erected a huge nativity scene in the front yard. Even though it was cold enough to see my breath, I stayed outside and watched all the activity—hammering, measuring, sawing. The manger was flat like a billboard and the figures were two-dimensional cutouts. But it looked magnificent to me. The story of Christmas—Baby Jesus—had come to *my* front yard.

At night the scene was illuminated by hidden lights, and the pointed star high above looked absolutely real. During the day, I'd go up close to the scene. Somehow, I felt like an actual part of it, as though I, too, had come to worship the Christ Child. "Hi, Baby Jesus," I'd say, "I'm glad You're in my front yard this Christmas." On Christmas morning, I bundled myself up and ran outside to see Him even before I'd opened my presents. I gave Him a kiss and whispered, "Happy birthday, Jesus!" I longed to "rescue" the Baby and take Him inside where it was warm.

I had no idea it was He Who'd come to rescue me.

This Christmas Day and every day, I thank You, Lord, for coming into our world—and into my heart.
—*Marion Bond West*

SAT

26

[Love] is not arrogant or rude. . . .
—*I CORINTHIANS 13:5 (RSV)*

I was sixteen years old and he, I was certain, was the most arrogant man in the world. He was music director of a large New York City church, used to working with professionals. He'd arrived to conduct the Christmas concert in our small town's biggest church, including choirs from all the local churches, the high school orchestra and my dance class.

We'd rehearsed our separate segments for weeks and believed that we were ready. He quickly set us straight. Nothing we did was satisfactory. I was grateful not to be one of the singers. His ear could detect a voice a quarter-tone off; his baton would rap on the music stand, then point straight at the offender.

There were two more sessions with him before the night of the concerts, as he rapped and drilled us into shape. At the dress rehearsal the morning of the service, he was more critical than ever. The risers for the choirs were too high, the costumes for the dance too long. "If he's this hard to please now," I worried to my mother as she shortened the condemned skirt, "what will he be like tonight?"

I soon found out. As we assembled in the church basement, the director led us in a prayer. "Father, we've all worked hard. Accept now our offering to You." The critic, the demanding taskmaster, had vanished; in his place, a man humbly bringing his gift to the stable. Things went wrong, as they always do. The bassoon player had an abscessed tooth and couldn't play. A baby shrieked all the way through "Silent Night." But the man presided with the serene demeanor of one who knows that God, not he, is the true Director.

God of love, give me the joy of working hard, the peace of leaving the results to You. —Elizabeth Sherrill

---

SUN

27

And Jesus said to him, "The foxes have holes, and the birds of the air have nests; but the Son of Man has nowhere to lay His head." —MATTHEW 8:20 (NAS)

Like many Americans, I've been a tumbleweed most of my life, blown from place to place by the prevailing winds. As a son of missionaries, I moved frequently around the world. As a pastor, I've served churches in five different states. Now in middle age, I sometimes just want to go home.

But where is home? My mother has lived in Monroe, Georgia, only a few short years. Her house holds no memories for me; I don't know her neighbors; the town is not part of my personal history. Yet when I yearn for home, I think of my mother.

As I enter Mom's house, I smell a familiar aroma. She's cooking dinner: always the roast beef, carrots, potatoes, gravy and biscuits of my youth. Every Sunday after church our family shared this meal.

Walking through unfamiliar rooms, I spot furniture and knick-knacks from the past. There are the crystal glasses that my grandfather gave my mother on her wedding day. The lamps by the couch are antiques from the Philippines, where my parents were missionaries. Mother's bedroom furniture figures in my earliest memories as a three-year-old crawling into the large mahogany bed early on Christmas morning, urging my parents to get up and open presents. I touch my father's dresser and open the top drawer, expecting the contents to look the same as they did thirty years ago.

I guess none of us can ever go home again—not really, not on this earth. But good memories can help to heal our displaced souls. Even when home bears no street address.

Father, help me to feel at home with You today.

—Scott Walker

MON   *I heard the voice of the Lord, saying, Whom shall I*
28 *send, and who will go for us? Then said I, Here am*
     I; send me.   *—ISAIAH 6:8*

Last winter, just after those disastrous tornadoes had swirled through Ohio, Pennsylvania and Ontario, Canada, a woman on television said something that affected me deeply. She was one of the survivors in a little, hard-hit Pennsylvania town. The camera showed her surrounded by men in large, black, flat-rimmed hats clearing debris, hauling lumber, rebuilding wrecked homes. These men were members of the Amish sect. They had come *en masse*, by buggy and by bus, to help these people—strangers to them—in distress. Their presence was not surprising, for with the Amish, helping others is a tradition, a way of life.

"When the Amish came," the woman on television said, "it was as though God had reached down with His own helping hand."

His own helping hand, I mused to myself, and for a moment as I watched one of the Amish taking a strong grip on a hammer, it seemed to me that I was seeing God's hand at work. Then I looked at my own hand, and I saw it in a way I had never seen it before. Have you ever thought, just as I did then, of your hand as God's helping hand?

Lord, give me the strength to work, and the wisdom to work for You.   *—Ruth Stafford Peale*

29   *The whole earth is full of his glory.*   *—ISAIAH 6:3*

"How do you like living in an Empty Nest?" an acquaintance asked recently as we found ourselves standing next to each other in a buffet line at a potluck dinner.

I've gotten that question often this year, probably because many people know that I used to dread the thought of living in an Empty Nest. But now that my husband Lynn and I have reached the end of our first year in this new season of life, I have a different perspective.

"The empty nest is a bad name for a good place," I told her, as we spooned our way through a variety of salads.

She looked a bit surprised, so I started to explain, just as we reached the chicken casseroles and lasagnas. "The empty nest sounds like a bad place because the word *empty* implies there is nothing left in a home after the children move out. It sounds like a place where parents wander aimlessly through quiet rooms, mourning their *full* pasts and *empty* futures.

"Now I do admit that after we took Kendall, our youngest, off to college, I faced a period of transition when I grieved the passing of a precious era. But slowly, Lynn and I began to discover the good parts of this simpler new chapter of life."

"Like what?" she asked.

"Like the freedom to eat only baked potatoes for dinner at eight P.M. Or work all afternoon on a project, without worrying about taking care of others. Or best of all, the joy of rekindling our relationship, often neglected by the demanding distractions of children. In the last year, we've gone on more bike rides and walks, rented more movies, and spent more time sharing our thoughts with each other. We've grown to depend on each other in a whole new way.

"The empty nest is full of potential," I concluded, just as we reached the yummy desserts . . . which seemed entirely appropriate.

Thank You, Lord, that each season of life has its fullness.
                    —Carol Kuykendall

WED

30 *O magnify the Lord with me, and let us exalt His name together.* —PSALM 34:3

At the end of every year, I take down my calendar and review what I've written on it during the past twelve months. As I remember the year's events, I praise God for all the ways He has shown himself to me in good times and bad.

This past year, I took a Bible study class on the names and titles of God in Scripture. As God's people came to know Him better through their experiences, they found new ways to describe and praise Him. As I leaf through my calendar, I begin to use a few.

As the marked-up old calendar reminds me of family member's surgeries, I pray, "Thank You, OUR HELP, for sustaining us and for recovery." As I read of doctors' appointments when an odd symptom put fear in our hearts, I pray, "Thank You, PRINCE OF PEACE" (Isaiah 9:6) for removing fear. I read of weddings and babies and reunions and say, "Thank You, LIGHT OF LIFE" (John 8:12). And the funerals: "Thank You, GOD OF ALL COMFORT (II Corinthians 1:3). For meetings and projects completed, wonderful vacations taken, "Thank You, OUR GUIDE" (Psalm 48:14). In every joy and sadness and blank spot in the past year, my GOOD SHEPHERD (John 10:11) has been there, loving me.

Like the believers of old, we can give God "praise names," too. So, as I hang up the blank new calendar marking the unknown, I say, "Thank You, FATHER OF THE NEW YEAR."

Lord, please fill each of the days that our calendars mark with Your presence and love. —Marjorie Parker

THU

31 *I will instruct thee and teach thee in the way which thou shalt go. . . .* —PSALM 32:8

For at least a year, I've been asking God one question: *How can I best serve in my remaining years?* No answer seemed to come. Then one night during the listening part of my evening prayer time, I settled into the silence of simply being present with God in love.

Sitting in my prayer chair in the darkened bedroom, I gazed out the window. Softly falling snowflakes glittered briefly in a shaft of moonlight and then disappeared, as others moved into the light. *How brief their glow,* I thought. Since I was looking out an upstairs window, I couldn't see the collective effect of the snow-blanket forming on my lawn below.

Though I heard no voice, these words formed in my mind: *You will be given only one step at a time. When you sense a leading, test it by asking: Does this action have* heart? *If so, trust it. Follow it, though you may not see its purpose. If you are faithful in this, you will be given the next step.*

Well, that certainly wasn't the answer I expected! I wanted something more specific. I wanted to be shown the whole path. Nevertheless, I've been following the leadings, which have included such diverse things as spending time in the art museum, praying alone in an empty church at mid-week, calling a friend I haven't seen in years, taking a walk through the cemetery, telling my grandson Zack the story of his great-great-grandfather's life. I have no idea how these all relate or where they may lead, but like snowflakes glistening in the moonlight, each one has stirred my heart in a different way.

At this time of fresh beginnings, I'd like to suggest a different way to start the new year. Instead of making resolutions and setting long-term goals with planned destinations, let's try to:

- Listen for God's leadings.

- Ask of each one: Does this action have *heart?*

- If so, follow it—it comes from God.

- Wait and listen for the next step.

I can't promise a treasure at the end of the trail, but I know the cumulative effect will be something beautiful. I trust this because I know the God Who guides the listening heart.

As the year unfolds, Lord, I will trust the loving Mystery that You are, with each step I take. —Marilyn Morgan Helleberg

My Healing Journey

1 _____

2 _____

3 _____

4 _____

5 _____

6 _____

7 _____

8 _____

9 _____

10 _____

11 _____

12 _____

13 _____

14 _____

15 _____

16 _____

17 _____

18 _____

19 _____

20 _____

21 _____

22 _____

23 _____

24 _____

25 _____

26 _____

27 _____

28 _____

29 _____

30 _____

31 _____

Fellowship Corner

WHO'S WHO IN DAILY GUIDEPOSTS

Welcome to our Fellowship Corner, where you can catch up on old friends and meet the newest members of our Daily Gudeposts *family. We've asked our fifty-three contributors to tell us how "God's Healing Touch" has been at work in their lives during this past year. They've got some surprises for you, so come on in and enjoy the conversation!*

 "One of our dreams has been to cruise through the Panama Canal," writes FAY ANGUS of Sierra Madre, California. "This is the year my husband and I did it. An adventure that dramatically enlarged both our world and our hearts. The lush vegetation of the rain forests and touring such fascinating places as Costa Rica were awesome, but my favorite times were the days we spent at sea. While John took in various shipboard activities, I spent hours alone on the small deck adjoining our cabin. Here, the memory of my father rode the waves with me. With wind-whipped spray washing my face of tears and whitecaps churning up a stormy sea, the separation of the years fell away. Then came the healing of God's love, as from the defining line of the horizon that brought heaven down to earth, and I cast my cares and many painful memories onto the waters and saw them swallowed up by the whirlpools of the deep."

 "It's been a year of changes," says *Daily Guideposts* editor ANDREW ATTAWAY. "John Joseph is already crawling through our apartment at warp speed, clearing off any surface he can reach and happily emptying bookcases. His big sister Elizabeth's personality keeps growing along with her vocabulary. At 2 ½, she's devoted to animals, from the lowly mudskipper to the mighty elephant. And a newly enlarged family has meant

a larger apartment—in northern Manhattan, where we're lucky to have Rick Hamlin as a neighbor. At work, there's been an exciting new project, *The Guideposts Prayer Companion,* to encourage and support our Guideposts family." But not all changes have been easy. "Julia's asthma attack was a trial for all of us, but through the help of so many friends at Guideposts, we felt God's healing touch at work in and around us."

"John Joseph arrived five days late," writes JULIA ATTAWAY of New York City, "and he is a big, happy baby who adds sunshine to our lives—at all hours of the night!" Adapting to having a second child was the first of several changes the Attaways faced during the year. Three weeks after moving to a new neighborhood, Julia suffered an asthma attack that left her hospitalized for five days. "It was a traumatic event for all of us, especially the children, who had never been without Mommy before. One of the things that came out of that wrenching separation was a better understanding of how healing is a process of remembering, of bringing things back to their rightful order. When we remember Christ's presence in our lives, we can be healed even if we can't be cured."

KAREN BARBER says, "There were times this past year when I stopped and wondered, *How on earth did I get here?* It seems as if everything about our lives changed. My husband Gordon took a new job, and we were off on our tenth move, this time to Alpharetta, Georgia. That meant new schools for Chris, 16, and John, 6, riding around in the minivan with one eye on the road and one eye on the local map, meeting new neighbors, and finding a new church. Our oldest son Jeff began his freshman year at Duke University. And on top of all of this, my first book *Ready, Set . . . Wait* was published (Baker Book House). When I find myself feeling like a stranger in my new life, I seek God's healing touch as Jesus declares, 'Courage. It is I' (Matthew 14:27, GNB). I remind myself that no matter where I am or what new thing I'm doing, Jesus is, as always, right there with me."

"My husband Leo and I are parents of four and grandparents of six," says ALMA BARKMAN of Winnipeg, Manitoba, Canada. "A highlight of the year was driving to Alaska and Yukon in our van, then taking the ferry down to the Marine Highway to Vancouver Island. Shortly after our trip, I was made acutely aware of God's healing touch when cloudy cataract tissue was removed from my right eye and an artificial lens inserted. During the procedure, I marveled at how God uses people as instruments of healing. Pain of any kind tends to blur my perspective, but I now try to ask myself, 'In the eyes of the Great Physician, am I the patient or the doctor?' I find that switching the focus from self to service changes my whole outlook."

In the fall of 1996, FRED BAUER and his wife Shirley (now a retired school librarian) of Princeton, New Jersey, bought a house on the Gulf of Mexico, in Englewood, Florida, where they hope to spend more and more time golfing, swimming, fishing, reading, volunteering (Meals on Wheels and a dog shelter, so far), and hosting their four children, their mates and grandchildren. Once in a *Daily Guideposts* devotional (Fred's been on board from the beginning of the book), he told about a woman who opined, "Florida sunsets aren't as beautiful as they once were." But Fred, looking out his front door, demurs. On a scale of one (cloudy) to ten (heavenly), he's seeing more golden nines and tens than ever before. "Could be my stronger glasses," he ventures, "but more likely it's clearer faith-vision." Speaking of faith, Fred ran into a little faith-testing health problem a year ago that brought new awareness of God's healing touch, amazing grace and measureless love. Not to mention His magnificently painted sunsets.

"Keith and I celebrated our 19th anniversary this year," says first-time *Daily Guideposts* contributor RHODA BLECKER of Los Angeles, California. "And my 'family,' the community of Benedictine nuns with whom I am affiliated as a Jew—after more than fifteen years of waiting—dedicated and began praying in their exquisite new chapel. And this year I was privileged to have been a sort of unconscious instrument of God's healing, when I heard from many people who received strong messages of healing from my novel *Commencement* (Ballantine Books; written as Roby James). From the nurse-practitioner who insisted the members of her recovery group read it, to the young sufferer from chronic illness who told me she kept it by her bed, to the woman who sent it to a friend in an incest survivors group in northern California, all have gifted me with evidence of their healing, and filled me with gratitude, which itself heals."

"Our kids keep growing, our lives keep going," says GINA BRIDGEMAN of Scottsdale, Arizona. Three-year-old Maria started preschool, and says her favorites are coloring and singing. Ross, 8, a third-grader, had a busy year of firsts: a Cub Scout camp-out; a piano competition in Tucson; and a desert horseback ride. Gina's husband Paul won an award for one of his Grand Canyon University theater scene designs, and also appeared as Charlemagne in the school's production of *Pippin*. Gina continued giving speeches and leading play shops for the Fellowship of Merry Christians, and attended her 20th high school reunion. "Remembering old times brings to mind when I most feel God's healing touch," Gina says. "It's in the forgiveness of old wounds, angry words and painful slights. Healing begins when I forgive, which happens only because God forgives me every day."

For MARY BROWN of Lansing, Michigan, the thrill of last year was visiting South Africa where her husband Alex gave nuclear physics seminars. "Our 4-year-old son Mark loved seeing the baboons and monkeys, and 9-year-old Elizabeth delighted in finding shells and rocks (even gemstones)." Mary and Alex witnessed God's healing power at work there. "Our hostess Rina told us about a powerful Reconciliation Weekend she had attended. A group of people from different racial and economic backgrounds began asking for and giving forgiveness for ways they had mistreated each other in the past. Then they honestly shared their personal needs and pledged ongoing prayer for one another. I was reminded again to open my life and relationships to God's healing by using those powerful tools of forgiveness, honest sharing and praying for others."

For MARY LOU CARNEY and her family, this year brought a mixed bouquet of sadness and joy. Mary Lou's mother died after a stroke last spring. "She was my best friend," Mary Lou says, "and my biggest cheerleader." On the happy side, daughter Amy Jo and her husband moved from Dayton, Ohio, to Chesterton, Indiana, where they bought a condo. "Only 1.8 miles from us," Mary Lou laughs. Brett continues to work with his father in the family excavation business. Gary (whose health is fine after his bout with heart disease) helped Brett build a three-unit apartment building of his own. Brett lives in the lower apartment where he has plenty of room for his most prized possession: his pool table. Mary Lou continues to edit *Guideposts for Kids,* which reaches half a million children bimonthly. "God has been my continual balm as I wade through the grief of Mother's passing. His love and availability 'unbreak' my heart daily."

"Barbara and I have been keenly aware of God's healing presence during the past year," says KENNETH CHAFIN of Louisville, Kentucky, "as we have experienced life in its ups and downs. Joy as our children gathered a host of longtime friends to celebrate my 70th birthday, comfort in the prayers of others as I buried a younger brother the week before Christmas, and amazement as I lay in surgery and followed on the monitor as the cardiologist opened a totally blocked artery. This year we plan to look at houses in Houston, Texas, with the sobering awareness that even as we try to move closer to our children, their interests and opportunities may move any or all of them someplace else. Wherever we end up living, I plan to spend a little more time growing flowers and to get reacquainted with my fly rod."

These past months have been full of transition and change for MARY JANE CLARK of Durango, Colorado, and her husband Harry. Among their six kids, there were three graduations and two weddings. The youngest went off to college, a daughter is studying in England, and a son and his wife moved to Africa to live and work for a time. Several recent experiences of God's healing touch have been "up close and personal." Harry's mom recovered from a serious stroke, then Harry had successful surgery for prostate cancer, followed by minor surgery for skin cancer. "At the same time we have several friends who are fighting losing battles with cancer, and we can't help asking, *Why?* We have no satisfying answers to that question, but we do know that in the midst of our pain and struggles, God is there."

It's been a wondrous year for MARK COLLINS of Pittsburgh, Pennsylvania. In 1996, the book he co-edited on Fred Rogers, *Mister Rogers' Neighborhood: Children, Television, and Fred Rogers,* was published by the University of Pittsburgh Press. Last November, his third daughter Grace joined her sisters Faith and Hope in the Collins clan. But, he reports, the new additions—both personal and professional—came at a price. "The lyrics to old rock songs keep going through my head, especially a line from Jackson Browne: 'I don't know where that road turned into the one I'm on.' Here I sit, on the eve of my 39th year, wondering where the time has gone, wondering what it all means. I'm not sure what the answer is, but right now I think I'll have a beer."

"My husband Bob and I feel we acquired some new hands and feet this past year," writes DRUE DUKE of Sheffield, Alabama. "They all belong to friends who rushed to us, exemplifying God's healing touch. In June, when Bob fell and crushed a vertebra in his back, a neighbor responded to my call for help and stayed with us until the ambulance arrived. During Bob's 'down time,' friends sent cards and flowers and ran errands for us, and when our air conditioner and dryer broke, men from our church came to replace the parts. The youth of the church assumed complete care of our yard for the entire summer. Then in November, when I had a heart attack, one man stayed overnight with Bob so he would not be alone while I was hospitalized. The day I was released, two ladies arrived at our house with a hot dinner and told us others would follow until I felt stronger. Their love was our assurance of God's using them to bring His healing touch to us."

The rigorous curriculum at the California Institute of Technology in Pasadena, where KJERSTIN EASTON is a sophomore, doesn't leave much time for rest and relaxation. But the beauty of the campus and the support of the close-knit Caltech community are always an encouraging reminder of God's love when times are tough and there's no time to visit her family. "And I felt God's own healing touch this year," writes Kjerstin. "During midterms I came down with a terrible ear infection, and sometimes it seemed I would never get all my work done. But it did get better, and with help from friends and faculty, I caught up. The most amazing thing about it, though, is the healing of a hearing loss I had dealt with since childhood. The doctors were surprised, but I knew God was watching out for me."

ERIC FELLMAN of Pawling, New York, has felt God's healing touch often in his life. "When I was 21, I was severely injured in an accident and not expected to live. My mother and my wife organized people to pray, and God allowed me to live. During recovery it was unclear whether my right hand and arm would ever work properly, and again God allowed a complete healing. As I have gone along in life, I have met many wonderful people who did not receive 'healing' in this fashion. Their loved one died, or their cancer did not go away. This troubled me until a wise minister explained, 'Everyone who asks God for healing is healed. It is just that with some the healing does not include a physical cure.' Since that time I have watched in wonder more at those who are healed without a cure. The grace and goodness of their lives are so much more than my own, I feel embarrassed that God expended such energy curing me. It causes me to live each day in gratitude and inspires me to do my best to be a healing agent in the lives of others."

On a November night, just before this past Thanksgiving, in Savannah, Georgia, word came that ARTHUR GORDON's 16-year-old granddaughter had been in a terrible car crash, suffering brain damage among other injuries. Doctors were not sure that she could live. "Our daughter Leigh, the girl's mother, remembers vividly one episode from that night of misery and despair. Among the trained nurses in the room with the victim was an African American woman with a religious medal around her neck. 'The Blessed Virgin can help you,' she said softly to Leigh. 'The Lord Jesus will never deny His mother anything.' She put her arms around Leigh and rocked her gently to and fro, repeating over and over, 'He will never deny His mother anything.' At the heart of prayer is a mystery that none of us can fully understand. All we know is that today this child is walking again, her memory is returning, and she is able to attend school three times a week. So there is gratitude in our hearts, and the words of the nurse keep echoing in our minds: 'He will never deny His mother anything.' "

OSCAR GREENE of West Medford, Massachusetts, and his wife Ruby made their first extended visit to their beloved Maine in three years. Ruby enjoyed Kennebunk Beach while Oscar lectured at the State of Maine Writers' Conference at Ocean Park. Oscar's duties at Grace Episcopal Church increased when he was asked to chair the ushers, to reinstate the Sunday Adult Coffee Hour and to contribute to the church newsletter while continuing to convene the Monday evening Bible study. Oscar felt "God's healing touch" came one day after his May 28 birthday, when he was asked to deliver the eulogy at the funeral of his friend and former landlord. "This helped me to thank Warren publicly for sharing his home when our need was desperate. This comforted his family, and it comforted me."

"Last year," says EDWARD GRINNAN, "my mother-in-law Wilma Cruise of Creston, Iowa, suffered a terrible stroke. We thought we had lost her, but her healing was nothing short of remarkable." She is confined to a wheelchair and a nursing home now. Recently, Julee and Edward, who live in New York City, "kidnapped" Wilma and whisked her off to Arizona for a winter vacation. "As soon as she was awake after the stroke, Julee was on the phone talking to her every day. The less we treated her like an invalid, the more progress she made. We kept giving her things to look forward to—visits, trips, presents." But the greatest healing Edward saw was in the people around his mother-in-law. "As time passed and God worked, everyone got better."

"The one thing I'm proudest of this past year," says RICK HAMLIN, "is the junior baseball league I started for kids in our neighborhood. The reason this is such an accomplishment is that I know nothing about baseball. But last year when I discovered that there wasn't a good baseball option for many kids in our upper Manhattan neighborhood, I started making telephone calls, lots of them. And after asking a lot of questions, I came up with an idea and got lots of help from plenty of other parents so that on the weekend after Easter we had seventy kids out on a ball field next to the Hudson River. For two months kids played, parents cheered and coaches strategized. By season's end, I knew a little bit more about baseball and a lot more about how much you can do with good advice and prayer and friends' help."

MADGE HARRAH of Albuquerque, New Mexico, has had a busy year, teaching creative writing classes, speaking at writers' conferences and promoting her latest historical novel *My Brother, My Enemy* (Simon & Schuster). Madge also edits her church's annual Advent book of daily devotions, *Light in the Darkness*, written by members of the congregation. In addition, she coordinates the prayer chain for her church, responding to prayer requests for healing, comfort and support, which come from people both inside and outside the church. "I've seen God's healing love effect amazing changes in people's lives," she says. "Prayer is one of God's great gifts, and it's available to us all."

"My absence from the *Daily Guideposts* family these past few years has left a void," says SCOTT HARRISON of Mechanicsburg, Pennsylvania. "But it was necessary when I laid aside my scalpel to begin a career as CEO of an international orthopedic company. It soaked up every spare second. After too many days (and nights) trudging through airports, we merged with a similar company and I again have time to write. That period was also marked by the death of our daughter Ann as she was doing volunteer service among the mountain people in northern Thailand. So after years of relying on God's healing touch for success in my surgery, I was now His patient, dependent completely on His care.

And as He did so many times for my patients, He patiently brought about healing so that I can again pick up my scalpel, now in Kenya, East Africa, where we are building a hospital for crippled children. And as the message of Christ is shared, we are seeing crooked legs—and lives—being healed."

This has been a less active, more contemplative year for MARILYN MORGAN HELLEBERG of Kearney, Nebraska. In addition to enjoying her children and grandchildren, she has spent time deepening friendships and reflecting on her life. In the fall, she attended a twelve-day retreat in Arizona, which included three days of juice-only fasting, silence and prayer. "It changed my relationship with God, as well as with food!" She also spent the month of February at her mountain cabin, writing and "just soaking up the beauty of the softly falling snow, the strength and solidity of the mountains, and the grace of the sky-reaching evergreens, some of them planted by my grandfather when I was a child. Truly, God's healing touch was everywhere I looked! And as always, it was good to get home to my family and friends, and to take up, once again, the more active part of my soul's journey."

"Isn't it amazing how God often reaches out to us through perfect strangers?" comments PHYLLIS HOBE of East Greenville, Pennsylvania. "I was standing in line at a department store when I noticed a woman staring at my hands. My fingers had been afflicted with arthritis for years, and usually I hid my hands. 'Don't they hurt you?' she asked. 'Yes,' I said, a bit annoyed. Years ago I had consulted doctors, but found I was allergic to the pain relievers they prescribed. Lately, the pain had been getting worse, and my hands were losing their strength. 'I used to be like you,' the woman said. Then she held out her hands, which looked normal. She told me about a group of doctors in Philadelphia (only forty miles away) who specialize in treating hands. Now, after arthritic joints have been replaced and months of therapy, my hands work beautifully. And no pain. Some might say it was coincidence that brought me and that woman together. I know better."

"This has been a year of near tragedy and triumph," writes MARJORIE HOLMES of Manassas, Virginia, "beginning with the news that Melanie, my youngest, had cancer. But thanks to wonderful doctors, thousands of prayers, a terrific husband and two sons to live for, plus her own shining faith, she is not only healed but dancing again! This is the greatest blessing of my life. Beside that, all else pales. But another healing joy was the publication of my book *Still By Your Side—How I Know a Great Love Never Dies* (Crossroad), about the remarkable messages the Lord let me receive from George after his death and how I have dealt with grief. Each chapter opens with a prayer, and it is comforting so many people. All four of my children and their families were with me for Christmas. All healthy and happy, thank God. What mother could ask for more?"

"I am now an official senior citizen," writes MARY RUTH HOWES of Jersey City, New Jersey. "A fact that, along with my retirement, sometimes fills me with amazement. At the same time I am enjoying my more leisurely mornings, now that I don't have to rush to get buses and trains into New York City. I haven't stopped working, however, but keep so busy with editing and reviewing jobs that I've sometimes asked myself, 'When do I really retire?' Between freelance jobs, church affairs and work on the house, I don't have much time to twiddle my thumbs. And I thank God for His healing power extended to me throughout my life, especially when at age 6 I had typhoid fever in a small town in China, and then at 12 was operated on for appendicitis by a Japanese doctor in occupied Shanghai."

"In my second year as a financial consultant in Nashville, Tennessee," says BROCK KIDD, "I still look forward to each new day in this business, where nothing is ever humdrum. Late last year, renovations to the apartment building where I lived forced a move. It was a hassle and a big disappointment, but I ended up renting a house with two college buddies. I'll never forget driving up to the new place after work one night. Tired and a little lonely, I turned the corner and discovered that my sister Keri had come by and filled the trees in the front yard with tiny Christmas lights. In a way, that's the story of my career, so far. Occasionally, someone hangs up on me, other people back out of their commitments. But then a bright face appears at my office door, or some client calls expressing his or her appreciation for something I've done for them. It's as though God knows just when to drop by and string up a few lights to boost my spirits, heal my disappointments and remind me just how good life really is."

"In many ways, this has been a year of remarkable healing," says PAM KIDD of Brentwood, Tennessee. "Of course, the best healings are those star-studded kind, like the one we learned about through an E-mail while we were halfway around the world in Beijing, China. 'Just had to let you know the good news,' wrote our church-family member Lynn McCalla. 'The doctor says Larry Taylor's cancer has disappeared!' But, I guess it's the everyday healings that touch our lives the most. When David, Brock, Keri and I were blessed with the chance to visit our friends in China, I found a personal healing of many of the prejudices I had previously held. The goodness of the Chinese people taught me that my way wasn't the only right way." Back home, Pam is venturing out toward a greater faith, willing herself to keep believing in what's good, to keep thinking about what's lovely and to replace negative inclinations with positive acts. "I'm not really great at this faith thing, but with each small victory comes a small healing."

"Terry and I have just 'walked the aisle' as father and mother of the bride," writes CAROL KNAPP of Big Lake, Alaska. " 'What a perfect day it was,' to quote Tamara, who married Rich Holschen on January 3. I can't believe how fast I dropped out of the high school scene once my last one graduated. I am doing some private tutoring—give me a short story to analyze over memorizing the periodic table any day! When you've loved mothering like I have, the prospect of empty rooms—and four offspring flung far and wide in diverse parts of the country—is a potential emotional cave-in. God healed my hurt before it began with His assurance of 'a plan and a place, covered by His grace' for each of my children. Instead of feeling emptiness, I am spilling over with pride and pleasure at the confident approach with which they are embracing life!"

"When it comes to seeing God's healing touch in my life, I think I'm farsighted," says CAROL KUY-KENDALL of Boulder, Colorado. "I see it better from a distance, such as when I look back over my shoulder at those times when I felt most fragile and wounded. Maybe that's because God's healing process works slowly from the inside out as I learn to trust His promises . . . in the midst of worries about a child's health, in reaching a place of forgiveness in a relationship or self-acceptance in the midst of self-doubt. I see God's healing most clearly when I've passed beyond it. This is the theme of my new book, *A Mother's Footprints of Faith* (Zondervan), a collection of personal stories. My husband Lynn and I are thankful to have our three grown children living in places that we like to visit. Derek is in Colorado Springs, but planning a move to Portland, Oregon. Lindsay is in Phoenix, Arizona, and Kendall is going to college in Santa Barbara, California. We haven't had a wedding yet, but we appear to be teetering on the brink of those plans. We've been told to 'stand by,' which has become our job description for parenting in this stage of life."

This past year held many challenges for ROBERTA MESSNER of Sweet Run, West Virginia. Her book *Increasing Patient Satisfaction: A Guide for Nurses* (Springer Publishing Company), co-authored with a nurse colleague, was released. Patients' perceptions of their health-care experiences have long been of interest to Roberta. "As both a consumer and provider of health care, I've noticed it's not enough to give high quality care," she explains. "It's equally important that patients and their loved ones know we really care about them as people." This year, Roberta once again found herself on the receiving side of the bed rail as she underwent more surgery to remove tumor growth around her eye. "I've been blessed with caregivers who far exceed my expectations," she says, "and that's such a comfort with the many changes facing health care today. But the greatest comfort of all is the unchanging presence of the Great Physician. His healing touch reaches the innermost places where technology and caring human hands can't go."

KEITH MILLER of Austin, Texas, writes, "I am excited about the theme 'God's Healing Touch,' because this past year my wife Andrea and I finished a book, *The Secret Life of the Soul* (Broadman & Holman). This book represents God's healing touches in my life for the past fifty years, and how these touches have changed my whole vision concerning what God can do to transform our lives and relationships. In a way, I am more excited about this book than any I've written. I'm doing much less traveling for speaking than I have the past few years, and I hope to finish a novel I've been working on. Andrea and I get 'grandkid fever' more than ever these days and look forward to more time with the folks we love. Although life is not trouble-free, most of my prayers lately are 'Thank You, God!' and 'I love you!' I am praying that all the readers of *Daily Guideposts, 1998* will have a blessed year of learning and loving."

The "Linda" pen pal club that was mentioned in LINDA NEUKRUG's February 26 devotional for last year is going strong. "I never realized just how many Lindas there are until so many started writing me to say they wanted Linda pals! My husband Paul's grandmother passed away this year. Her family and friends gathered in England to remember the 102-year-old woman, and celebrated her life while mourning her death. This year, I gave blood for the first time—I was surprised at how easy it was, and am now urging everyone I know to do it, too! And God's healing touch worked in this Linda's life on lightening my times of depression. What helped lessen it? Prayer, being kinder to myself, learning to take in compliments and talking about problems. In short, bringing it out into the light rather than considering it a shameful secret to be hidden."

This year finds MARJORIE PARKER and husband Joe, of Wichita Falls, Texas, celebrating their 25th wedding anniversary and facing some bittersweet changes. Daughter Joanna graduates from high school, where she's won honors both scholastically and as a basketball player, and will leave home to enter Texas Tech University. Daughter Sarah—also an honor student—excitedly faces the challenge of a new life as a high-school freshman. Marjorie continues her freelance writing from home and mentors a third-grade student. Last year, when Marjorie lost her 104-year-old grandmother, an uncle and her father, she marveled at God's healing touch in the kindness and support of family, church and friends. "I'll never again underestimate the value of a visit or a comforting message from a friend during a time of loss. God's healing touch continues to amaze me."

"I am at the office every day," says RUTH STAFFORD PEALE of Pawling, New York, "except when speaking engagements take me all over the country. In spite of all this, I find time to be involved in the lives and careers of my three children, eight grandchildren and five great-grandchildren. It is exciting to stay close to a large growing family scattered all over the country. A grandson is teaching in Wyoming, two granddaughters are specialists in program development in Boston, Massachusetts, one is a teacher in San Francisco, California, another is a newspaper reporter in Cincinnati, Ohio. A gifted librarian turned full-time mother lives in New Hampshire, and a professional business consultant has his office in New York City. A deep spiritual presence has permeated all our activity and life this year. God has directed our path in many ways. The growth and influence of Guideposts depends on the loyalty and help of all our subscribers. We thank God every day."

BILL PEEL of Nashville, Tennessee, is making his first appearance in *Daily Guideposts,* along with his wife Kathy. They have three sons, John, Joel and James—"the Peel dream team," writes Bill. "If I had to choose my favorite spot in the world, it would be beside a murmuring stream just outside of Crested Butte, Colorado. In the quiet shadows of overhanging evergreens, behind big, scattered rocks, lurks one of God's most intelligent creatures, the rainbow trout. More times than not, these wily river residents manage to elude my best efforts. No matter how much money I spend on the most exotic new fly or how much time I spend mastering a new technique, I'm usually outsmarted. I've found that the best objective in fly fishing is just to be there. The quietest times in my life seem to be when it's just me, the fish and the river. And it's not surprising that it seems to be a lot easier to hear God's whisper in that place."

This is the first *Daily Guideposts* appearance for KATHY PEEL. Kathy is a writer and speaker on the subject of family management. She lives in Nashville, Tennessee, with her husband Bill and their three sons John, Joel and James. "I'm learning that life is a lot like my learning how to use in-line skates as opposed to the four-wooden-wheel roller skates of my childhood. Now that I've grown up, the pace is faster and the equipment is sleeker. I'm taking the curves at breakneck speed, many times feeling out of control and not knowing how to stop. I fall, crash, skin my knees and emotions regularly. It's time I practiced learning to brake slowly in life, look for some natural plateaus to slow me down, learn some simple techniques, so I can enjoy gliding along, actually experiencing the daily scenery and company of those I love. Sure, I hit some bumps and take some falls, but with God's help, I'm equipped and prepared to get up and go on. Yes, this year I've learned that in-line skating and life can both become an exhilarating ride."

"With the four boys gone from the nest," says ROBERTA ROGERS, "last year was the one where I began to flap my wings. Opportunities gave my husband Bill and me some wonderful travels from our White Plains, Maryland, home—as far west as Denver, Colorado (son Tom), and Santa Fe, New Mexico; as far south as the Gulf Coast; as far north as West Hartford, Connecticut (my mother Kathryn), and Cape Cod, Massachusetts (son Pete). God's loving touch restored some old friendships and added some very special new ones. Bill's mother Marian turned 90, and flew to be with us and all four boys at Christmas. John began to build toward a dream; David won honors at college. But for me, the dearest of God's healing touches was in wakeful nights where I learned of His *Abba*-hood (fatherhood) in real and wonderful ways. At 55, I am learning to be a child!"

ELEANOR SASS returns to *Daily Guideposts* after what she calls "a three-year sabbatical." And on April 1, 1996, Ellie retired from her job as associate editor at *Guideposts* magazine. "Since I'd been employed steadily for forty years (thirty-two of them at Guideposts), I thought it was a nice round number to go out on." Ellie *loves* her retirement. So does her dog Wally. They take long walks around their Manhattan neighborhood and have recently begun visiting a Brooklyn nursing home where Wally entertains the residents by demonstrating his therapy-dog talents. "It is here where I see God's healing touch," Ellie says. "Patients who mostly sit in wheelchairs staring blankly into space suddenly smile and begin talking about their long-ago experiences with their own beloved pets. It's heartwarming to listen to them."

In 1997, President Pelfrey named DANIEL SCHANTZ as one of six distinguished alumni of Central Christian College in Moberly, Missouri, where Dan is teaching in his thirtieth year. Wife Sharon went to work as a Title One reading aide at East Park Elementary School, and her mother Ruth Dale is coping better with the loss of her husband Edsil. Dan and Sharon became grandparents for the second time when Silas Tennyson was born to older daughter Teresa and her husband Dan Williams of Kansas City. Younger daughter Natalie is planning to home-school 5-year-old Hannah, and her husband Matt received a promotion to nursing supervisor. They live in New Franklin, Missouri. What began as a spell of unusual fatigue sent Dan through extensive medical tests for a suspected pituitary problem. "It's wonderful to be myself again," he says, "but at times I felt the doctoring was worse than the disease. Sometimes the Great Physician has to hurt in order to heal."

"This year, my husband Ernie and I vacationed in Cape Cod," writes SUSAN SCHEFFLEIN who lives in Putnam Valley, New York. "Away from our hectic schedules, we sat on the beach and contemplated the waves. In the sun and silence, we opened ourselves to the serenity of God's healing touch." *Why do we allow ourselves to get so stressed when God's peace is always available?* "Lately, when I wake in the middle of the night and think of all I have to do, I start praying for others. I feel God's soothing touch and soon fall back to sleep knowing everything will be fine."

"This has been the busiest year of my life," says PENNEY SCHWAB of Copeland, Kansas. "Then again, I say that every year." Four grandsons make holidays lively for Penney and her husband Don. Her responsibilities as executive director of United Methodist Mexican-American Ministries have grown as the agency has added new health education programs to complement medical, social and spiritual services. "God's healing touch came through the Scriptures, particularly Isaiah 40:31, reminding me to 'wait on the Lord to renew my strength.' It came as I looked back in the journal I've kept for many years and saw written evidence of God's presence. And it came with special joy as I listened to Ryan read, played ball with David, watched Mark's fascination with purple balloons and kept Caleb for the first time overnight."

In 1997, ELIZABETH (Tib) SHERRILL and her husband John celebrated fifty years of marriage, writing and traveling in Europe as in their first years together. "Not quite as it was," says Tib, who when not traveling in Europe resides in Chappaqua, New York. "In 1947, we had two bicycles, two pads of yellow paper and a supply of pencils. Last year to do the same work we carried a computer, a printer, an adapter, a box of computer paper—and needed a car to carry it all." Working on the theme of healing, she says, made her newly aware of the miracle of healing they've witnessed just in their own family. "Cancer, stroke, heart attack—and those are just a few of the physical ones."

When JOHN SHERRILL's 10-year-old grandson Jeffrey began asking questions about his Army service during World War II, John was surprised at the strong emotions aroused. "I was a foot soldier in Italy," John says, "and I kept those memories to myself for decades. I saw devastation and death, and I locked it all inside to fester. As often as my wife Tib and I were in Italy together, I avoided returning to certain areas. So when we were there last year, I took her to all the battle sites I could find and told her everything I could remember. Surprisingly, it was a healing experience. The negative memories began to fade, and positive ones—especially recollections of American and Italian friends—became fresh again."

LINDA CHING SLEDGE's sabbatical leave from teaching provided the occasion for the Sledges to play host to their far-flung clan. They traveled from their home in Pleasantville, New York, to Hawaii, where son Geoff celebrated his 16th birthday at a huge Chinese-style feast. Fall ushered in California in-laws who enjoyed the foliage and an insider's tour of *Reader's Digest,* where husband Gary works as assistant managing editor. Thanksgiving proved a raucous, joyous affair as Oregon- and Hawaii-born nephews and nieces descended from their East Coast colleges to eat and sing and play. Best of all were intimate winter Sundays in Manhattan sharing restaurant meals with son Tim, now living and working as a financial analyst in the city. Linda returned to her students energized, and saw everywhere the miraculous mending of broken lives through the simple, courageous act of opening a book.

"As we moved from our beloved home in South Salem, New York, to Nashville, Tennessee," writes SHARI SMYTH, "I have felt God's healing touch like a hand on my shoulder both comforting me in my loss and coaxing me to embrace the new. And I have seen God's healing touch in my daughter Sanna's continued recovery from drug and alcohol addiction and her return to her faith . . . no less a miracle than if she'd been brought back from the dead. It has been a year of rediscovering the rock-solid truth that no matter how far we travel, God is there. And no matter how deep we sink, God is there. We cannot escape His healing, settling presence."

"Oh, to have had a stroke and been an employee of Guideposts!" states VAN VARNER of New York City. "It was no surprise to find that my friends here were caring ones, and unusually so. Suppose you had to spend a lot of time in the dictionary (how to spell 'recommend,' two c's or two m's—you knew the answer once), or you had to try desperately (it's spelled with an e after the p) to say what you wanted in a meeting—and the meeting waited . . . and no one made you feel self-conscious. It was no surprise that everyone made me feel loved, just as they did before my stroke, because love runs through the organization like a never-ending stream. Though Guideposts is far, far larger now, and Grace and Len LeSourd and the good doctor are dead, what they gave is alive, and everyone, including you readers, can feel it. Perhaps I am using that love selfishly, in the hopes that I can provide a little reference to the past, but my friends here, and elsewhere, do not let on. Oh, to have had a stroke and been an employee of Guideposts is something wonderful."

SCOTT WALKER of Waco, Texas, writes, "The two words for the last year within our household are *blessed* and *busy*. I like relating to people and find preaching to be a stimulating challenge. I also enjoy teaching seminary students at Baylor University. I was able to publish a new book this year, *Glimpses of God* (Augsburg), and am trying to finish another. My wife Beth is working with international students at Baylor. She has a sense of passion for this task and is very good at it. Drew, 14, is very involved in tennis and is in tournaments almost every weekend. Luke, 11, loves basketball and is a baseball card fanatic. And Jodi, 8, has decided that she wants to be a writer and is composing her first stories at her new rolltop desk. Perhaps the greatest challenge is to live well the days that God has given to us. To squeeze every ounce of opportunity from each day, but to also relax and enjoy the journey. It's a good life. And God is such a wonderful God!"

DOLPHUS WEARY of Mendenhall, Mississippi, continues to travel around the country, speaking in churches as well as to groups that want to minister holistically to the disadvantaged community. "God has given me a special message of healing called 'Building Bridges of Reconciliation.' There is a lot of healing taking place in the South as well as in other areas in the country." Dolphus serves on the Board of Mission Mississippi, which is about healing across racial and denominational lines throughout the state. He completed his Doctor of Ministry degree at Reformed Theological Seminary in Jackson. This year, he and Rosie will celebrate twenty-eight years of marriage. Danita is in her second year of medical school in Memphis, Tennessee; Reggie is a senior at Tougaloo College in Jackson, Mississippi; 10-year-old Ryan is a fifth-grader at Genesis One Christian School.

"I am beginning to feel as if I really belong to the Guideposts family," says BRIGITTE WEEKS of New York City, "as I contribute to this, my third edition of *Daily Guideposts*. In quiet ways, this book has changed my life as sweaters for refugee children, knitted by readers, arrive in the mail—more than two hundred to date—and as I hear from others who have shared the experiences of watching children become adults. This year my youngest son left home, meaning all three of my children are grown and working—two of them in the world of books, which both surprises and pleases me. I miss them, but there are different rewards watching them encounter the working world and shared laughter as they complain about the high costs of living. Showing up for a family dinner, home-cooked by Dad, is now a treat rather than a chore!"

"God's healing touch continues to enable my 88-year-old mother to take her stand against cancer," says MARION BOND WEST of Watkinsville, Georgia. "She's doing remarkably well. Well enough to go back to her home in Elberton for a day's visit. She insisted on driving her cherished 1960 white Chevy (with 47,000 miles) around her neighborhood and waving to surprised friends. We were overjoyed that God's healing touch extended to our beloved Red Dog. When she was hit by a car and one of her back legs was shattered, she required two complicated surgeries and external pins. We brought her inside with us for six months while the healing took place. She's as good as new! Even though Gene retired from the ministry this year, God continues to place people in our path who need His healing touch. We like to share with them Psalm 147:3 (RSV): 'He heals the brokenhearted, and binds up their wounds.' "

BRENDA WILBEE of Bellingham, Washington, is glad to have survived the year gone by. "I'm looking forward to a year with considerably less 'drama.' Both my boys totaled their cars on the freeway. One kid set the record: He'd owned the car twenty minutes! Unlike his mother (or brother), he did *not* lose his shirt. In fact, he cleared his losses and came out $1,100 ahead.

My disasters have always been disasters, but Blake? I'm going to have to keep an eye on that boy, and take lessons. In the meantime, I write, draw and garden. For those of you waiting for more Sweetbriar books, you can quit asking—check your bookstores."

"As I write this," says ISABEL WOLSELEY of Syracuse, New York, "it has been nearly a year since I lost my precious mother. Because she lived to the age of nearly 98, I guess I assumed she'd always be there to discuss things with. Yet I'm still saying to myself, 'I must show Mom this photo of the grand-kids.' Or, I want to tell her, 'Guess who came to visit me today!' But while remembering our warm times together and the high moral values she passed on to me and my family, healing is coming even though her life has been severed from mine."

Authors, Titles and Subjects Index

A Note from the Editors

This original Guideposts book was created by the book division of the company that publishes *Guideposts*, a monthly magazine filled with true stories of people's adventures in faith.

If you have found enjoyment in *Daily Guideposts, 1998*, and would like to order additional copies for yourself or as gifts, the cost is $13.95 for either the regular print or the Large Print edition. Orders should be sent to Guideposts, 39 Seminary Hill Road, Carmel, New York 10512.

We also think you'll find monthly enjoyment—and inspiration—in the exciting and faith-filled stories that appear in our magazine. *Guideposts* is not sold on the newsstand. It's available by subscription only. And subscribing is easy. All you have to do is write to Guideposts, 39 Seminary Hill Road, Carmel, New York 10512. When you subscribe, each month you can count on receiving exciting new evidence of God's presence, His guidance and His limitless love for all of us.

Guideposts is also available on the Internet by accessing our homepage on the World Wide Web at http://www.guideposts.org. Send prayer requests to our Monday morning Prayer Fellowship. Read stories from recent issues of our magazines, *Guideposts, Angels on Earth, Guideposts for Kids* and *Positive Living*, and follow our popular book of daily devotionals, *Daily Guideposts*. Excerpts from some of our best-selling books are also available.